LONDON: A SOCIAL AND CULTURAL HISTORY, 1550-1750

Between 1550 and 1750, London became the greatest city in Europe and one of the most vibrant economic and cultural centers in the world. This book is a history of London during this crucial period of its rise to worldwide prominence, during which it dominated the economic, political, social, and cultural life of the British Isles as never before nor since. *London: A Social and Cultural History, 1550-1750* incorporates the best recent work in urban history, accounts by contemporary Londoners and tourists, and fictional works featuring the city to trace London's rise and explore its role as a harbinger of modernity as well as how its citizens coped with those achievements. It covers the full range of life in London, from the splendid galleries of Whitehall to the damp and sooty alleyways of the East End. Along the way, readers will brave the dangers of plague and fire, witness the spectacles of the Lord Mayor's Pageant and the hangings at Tyburn, and take refreshment in the city's pleasure gardens, coffeehouses, and taverns.

Robert O. Bucholz is Professor of History at Loyola University in Chicago. He is the coauthor (with Newton Key) of *Early-Modern England 1485-1714: A Narrative History* (2nd ed., 2009) and *Sources and Debates in English History 1485-1714* (2nd ed., 2009) and the coeditor (with Carol Levin) of *Queens and Power in Medieval and Early Modern England* (2009).

Joseph P. Ward is Associate Professor and Chair of the Department of History at the University of Mississippi. He is the author of *Metropolitan Communities: Trade Guilds, Identity, and Change in Early Modern London* (1997) and is the editor or coeditor of several other scholarly books.

$\mathscr{L}$ONDON

A Social and Cultural History,
1550–1750

Robert O. Bucholz
Loyola University

Joseph P. Ward
University of Mississippi

CAMBRIDGE
UNIVERSITY PRESS

CAMBRIDGE UNIVERSITY PRESS
Cambridge, New York, Melbourne, Madrid, Cape Town,
Singapore, São Paulo, Delhi, Mexico City

Cambridge University Press
32 Avenue of the Americas, New York, NY 10013-2473, USA

www.cambridge.org
Information on this title: www.cambridge.org/9780521896528

First published 2012

Printed in the United States of America

A catalog record for this publication is available from the British Library.

Library of Congress Cataloging in Publication Data

Bucholz, R. O., 1958–
London : a social and cultural history, 1550–1750 / Robert Bucholz, Joseph Ward.
   p.   cm.
Includes bibliographical references (p.) and index.
ISBN 978-0-521-89652-8 (hardback)
1. London (England) – Social conditions.   2. London (England) – Social life and
customs.   3. London (England) – Economic conditions.   4. London (England) –
Civilization.   I. Ward, Joseph.   II. Title.
HN398.L7B83   2013
942.1–dc23   2011050687

ISBN 978-0-521-89652-8 Hardback

To our students

Contents

List of Illustrations and Maps

Illustrations and maps follow page xvi.

Illustrations

Maps

List of Abbreviations and Conventions

DC: *The Daily Courant*, 34 vols. (1702–35).
ED: *The Diary of John Evelyn*, ed. E. S. De Beer, 5 vols. (Oxford, 1955).
LE: *The London Encyclopaedia*, ed. B. Weinreb, C. Hibbert, J. Keay, and J. Keay, 3rd ed. (2010).
LG: *The London Gazette* (1665+).
NDNB: *The New Oxford Dictionary of National Biography*, ed. C. Matthew, B. Harrison, and L. Goldman (2004).
PD: *The Diary of Samuel Pepys*, ed. R. Latham and W. Matthews, 11 vols. (Berkeley, 1970–83).
TNA: The National Archives (formerly Public Record Office), Kew.

NB: Here, *City* and *City of London* refer to the area governed by the lord mayor and Court of Aldermen, mostly but not entirely within the ancient walls. The uncapitalized *city* and *metropolis* refer to greater London, including the City, Westminster, unincorporated Southwark, and the coterminous parishes beyond the walls.

Where known, the birth and death dates of persons named in the text are given in parentheses after their names. Unless otherwise noted, the dates given after the names of rulers (including popes) are their regnal years.

Spelling in quotations is in the original form except where changes are required for the sake of clarity.

Acknowledgments

This book originated from a suggestion by Bob Bucholz's undergraduate supervisor, Daniel Baugh, in the fall of 1986, that he might want to prepare a seminar course on early modern London to add to his teaching portfolio. First offered at Cornell in the spring of 1988, the course migrated with Bob to Loyola, Chicago, when he assumed his present position there. In the meantime, Joe Ward had begun his studies in the economic and social role of the London livery companies with Paul Seaver at Stanford. Beatrice Rehl from Cambridge University Press then suggested turning the fruits of that teaching and scholarship into a book. This being a work of synthesis, the authors are utterly beholden to the work of many fine scholars of London, whose names appear all too briefly in the notes. They would particularly like to acknowledge their debt to two magisterial works, Stephen Inwood's *History of London* and *The London Encyclopaedia* compiled by Ben Weinreb and Christopher Hibbert, revised by Julia and John Keay, trusted companions in our trek through the metropolis, whose influence on the final product will be obvious. We owe another great debt to our home institutions, Loyola University, Chicago, and the University of Mississippi, for purchasing indispensable databases like the Burney Collection of Seventeenth- and Eighteenth-Century English Newspapers, Early English Books Online, Eighteenth-Century Collections Online, and The Making of the Modern World; providing funding necessary to support the purchase of rights for images; and in Bob's case, granting a semester's leave from teaching.

Perhaps above all, this work has benefited incalculably from the input of our students, both graduate and especially undergraduate in Bob's "History 319: London Life and Culture" class over the past 25 years. Bob and Joe would also particularly like to acknowledge with thanks Bob's faithful London host and walking companion, Michael Cook, as well as Regina Buccola, Rob Butler, Caryn Chaden, Patricia Clemente, Kerry Cochrane, David Dennis, Andrew Donnelly, Mary Donnelly, John Donoghue, James Dunn, Tracy Foxworth, Timothy Gilfoyle, Joel Gillaspie, Thomas Greene, Jo Hays, Elizabeth Hermick, Stephen Jeffries, Christopher Johns, Scott Johnson, Theodore Karamanski, Newton Key, Brian Lavelle, Carole Levin, Michael Leyden, Arthur Lurigio, Gerard McDonald, Leanna McLaughlin, Eileen McMahon, Krystina Mendoza, Shana Meyer, Marcy Millar, Oliver Miller, Carol Peebles, Jeannette Pierce, Julian Putkowski, Thomas Ridgedell, Kyle Roberts, Sir John and Lady Frances Sainty, Antonia Savarese, Claire Schen, David Starkey, Alan Turner, Victoria Uecker, Albert Vogt, Steve Wallman, the late Patrick Woodland, and above all, Laurie Bucholz and Sue Grayzel for criticism, correction, help, and encouragement.

Illustrations

1.1. C. J. Visscher (1587–1652), panoramic view of London from the south bank, 1616, London Metropolitan Archives.

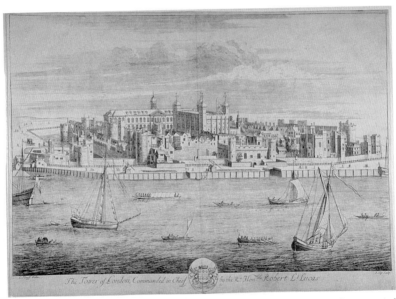

1.2. Leonard Knyff (1650–1722), south view of the Tower of London, engraving executed c. 1700, London Metropolitan Archives.

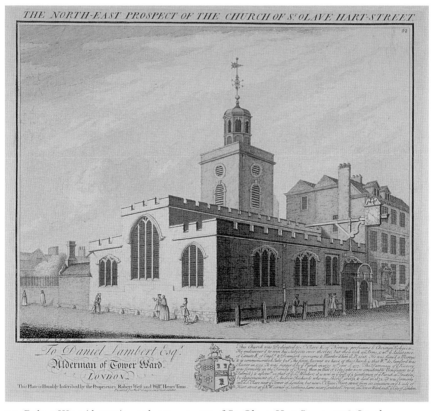

1.3. Robert West (d. 1770), northeast prospect of St. Olave, Hart Street, 1736, London Metropolitan Archives.

1.4. John Thomas Smith (1766–1833), The Old House, Grub Street, London, 1791, Bridgeman Art Library.

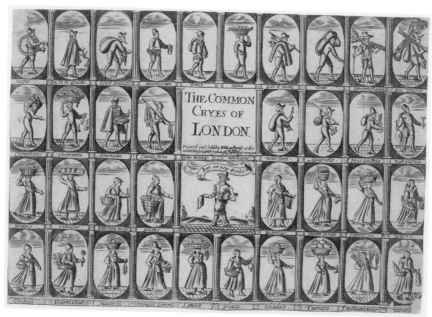

1.5. British School (c. 1660), The Common Cryes of London, British Museum.

1.6. Wenceslaus Hollar (1607–1677), interior view of the Royal Exchange, c. 1660, London Metropolitan Archives.

1.7. William Herbert (1772–1851) and Robert Wilkinson (fl. 1785–1825), Procession of Marie d'Medici along Cheapside, 1638, 1809, Bridgeman Art Library.

Prospect of GUILD—HALL.   VÛE DE L. HÔTEL DE VILLE À LONDRES.

1.8. Anon., front view of the Guildhall, etching c. 1700, London Metropolitan Archives.

1.9. Wenceslaus Hollar (1607–1677), south elevation of St. Paul's Cathedral, etching executed 1818, London Metropolitan Archives.

ORIENTALIS PARTIS ECCL: CATH: S: PAVLI PROSPECTVS INTERIOR

1.10. Wenceslaus Hollar (1607–1677), interior view of St. Paul's Cathedral's east end, c. 1656, London Metropolitan Archives.

1.11. Anon., view of Covent Garden from the south, engraving executed c. 1720, London Metropolitan Archives.

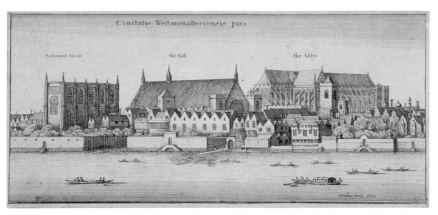

1.12. Wenceslaus Hollar (1607–1677), view of the Palace of Westminster and Westminster Abbey, 1647, London Metropolitan Archives.

2.1. L. P. Boitard (fl. 1733–1767), "The Imports of Great Britain from France," etching executed in 1757, London Metropolitan Archives.

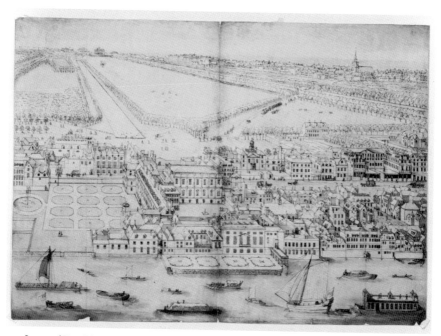

3.1. Leonard Knyff (1650–1722), A Bird's Eye View of Whitehall Palace, c. 1695, Bridgeman Art Library.

3.2. Attr. to Hendrick Danckerts (c. 1625–1680), Whitehall Palace and St. James's Park, Bridgeman Art Library.

COMME MESSIEVRS DV CONSEIL PRIVE VIENNENT SALVER LA
REYNE DANS SA CHAMBRE

3.3. Marie d'Medici's drawing room, from M. (Jean-Puget) de La Serre (c. 1600–1665),
Histoire de l'entrée de la reyne mère du roy tres Chrestien, dans la Grande-Brétaigne (1639),
HOLLIS 009628756, Houghton Library, Harvard University.

3.4. After Lucas de Heere (1534–1584), Lord Mayor, Aldermen and liverymen, Bridgeman Art Library.

4.1. C. J. Visscher (1587–1652), the Globe Theatre, detail from an engraving, 1616, Bridgeman Art Library.

4.2. English School (seventeenth century), the Swan Theatre, Southwark, Bridgeman Art Library.

INSIDE OF THE DUKES THEATRE
in Lincoln's Inn Fields.
as it appeared in the reign of King Charles II.

Rabel sculp.

*This view represents the stage of the above Theatre, and its very elegant frontispiece, during the perform-
ance of a scene from Elkanah Settle's Empress of Morocco. The Theatre itself was deserted twelve
years after its foundation, for the one in Dorset Gardens; being found too small and incommodious
for the company that visited it. Part of it was discovered by the late fire in Bear Yard. Its size
must have been extremely small, compared with our present Theatres.*

4.3. English School (nineteenth century), interior of the Duke's Theatre in Lincoln's Inn
Fields during the reign of King Charles II, 1809, Bridgeman Art Library.

The Daily Courant.

Wednesday, March 11. 1702.

From the Harlem Courant, Dated March 18. N. S.

Naples, Feb. 22.

ON Wednesday laft, our New Viceroy, the Duke of Efcalona, arriv'd here with a Squadron of the Galleys of Sicily. He made his Entrance dreft in a French habit; and to give us the greater Hopes of the King's coming hither, went to Lodge in one of the little Palaces, leaving the Royal one for his Majefty. The Marquis of Grigni is alfo arriv'd here with a Regiment of French.

Rome, Feb. 25. In a Military Congregation of State that was held here, it was Refolv'd to draw a Line from Afcoli to the Borders of the Ecclefiaftical State, thereby to hinder the Incurfions of the Tranfalpine Troops. Orders are fent to Civita Vecchia to fit out the Galleys, and to ftrengthen the Garrifon of that Place. Signior Cafali is made Governor of Perugia. The Marquis del Vafto, and the Prince de Caferta continue ftill in the Imperial Embaffador's Palace; where his Excellency has a Guard of 50 Men every Night in Arms. The King of Portugal has defir'd the Arch-Bifhoprick of Lisbon, vacant by the Death of Cardinal Soufa, for the Infante his fecond Son, who is about 11 Years old.

Vienna, Mar. 4. Orders are fent to the 4 Regiments of Foot, the 2 of Cuiraffiers, and to that of Dragoons, which are broke up from Hungary, and are on their way to Italy, and which confift of about 14 or 15000 Men, to haften their March thither with all Expedition. The 6 new Regiments of Huffars that are now raifing, are in fo great a forwardnefs, that they will be compleat, and in a Condition to march by the middle of May. Prince Lewis of Baden has written to Court, to excufe himfelf from coming thither, his Prefence being fo very neceffary, and fo much defir'd on the Upper-Rhine.

Francfort, Mar. 12. The Marquifs d' Uxelles is come to Strasburg, and is to draw together a Body of fome Regiments of Horfe and Foot from the Garrifons of Alface; but will not leffen thofe of Strasburg and Landau, which are already very weak. On the other hand, the Troops of His Imperial Majefty, and his Allies, are going to form a Body near Germefhein in the Palatinate, of which Place, as well as of the Lines at Spires, Prince Lewis of Baden is expected to take a View, in three or four days. The Englifh and Dutch Minifters, the Count of Frife, and the Baron Vander Meer, and likewife the Imperial Envoy Count Lowenftein, are gone to Nordlingen, and it is hop'd that in a fhort time we fhall hear from thence of fome favourable Refolutions for the Security of the Empire.

Liege, Mar. 14. The French have taken the Cannon de Longie, who was Secretary to the Dean de Mean, out of our Caftle, where he has been for fome time a Prifoner; and have deliver'd him to the Provoft of Maubeuge, who has carry'd him from hence, but we do not know whither.

Paris, Mar. 13. Our Letters from Italy fay, That moft of our Reinforcements were Landed there; that the Imperial and Ecclefiaftical Troops feem to live very peaceably with one another in the Country of Parma, and that the Duke of Vendome, as he was vifiting feveral Pofts, was within 100 Paces of falling into the Hands of the Germans. The Duke of Chartres, the Prince of Conti, and feveral other Princes of the Blood, are to make the Campaign in

Flanders under the Duke of Burgundy; and the Duke of Maine is to Command upon the Rhine.

From the Amfterdam Courant, Dated Mar. 18.

Rome, Feb. 25. We are taking here all poffible Precautions for the Security of the Ecclefiaftical State in this prefent Conjuncture, and have defir'd to raife 3000 Men in the Cantons of Switzerland. The Pope has appointed the Duke of Berwick to be his Lieutenant-General, and he is to Command 6000 Men on the Frontiers of Naples: He has alfo fettled upon him a Penfion of 6000 Crowns a year during Life.

From the Paris Gazette, Dated Mar. 18. 1702.

Naples, Febr. 17. 600 French Soldiers are arrived here, and are expected to be follow'd by 3400 more. A Courier that came hither on the 14th. has brought Letters by which we are affur'd that the King of Spain defigns to be here towards the end of March; and accordingly Orders are given to make the neceffary Preparations againft his Arrival. The two Troops of Horfe that were Commanded into the Abruzzo are pofted at Pefcara with a Body of Spanifh Foot, and others in the Fort of Montorio.

Paris, March. 18. We have Advice from Toulon of the 5th inftant, that the Wind having long ftood favourable, 22000 Men were already fail'd for Italy, that 2500 more were Embarking, and that by the 15th it was hoped they might all get thither. The Count d' Eftrees arriv'd there on the Third inftant, and fet all hands at work to fit out the Squadron of 9 Men of War and fome Fregats, that are appointed to carry the King of Spain to Naples. His Catholick Majefty will go on Board the Thunderer, of 110 Guns.

We have Advice by an Exprefs from Rome of the 18th of February, That notwithftanding the preffing Inftances of the Imperial Embaffadour, the Pope had Condemn'd the Marquis del Vafto to lofe his Head and his Eftate to be confifcated, for not appearing to Anfwer the Charge againft him of Publickly Scandalizing Cardinal Janfon.

ADVERTISEMENT.

IT will be found from the Foreign Prints, which from time to time, as Occafion offers, will be mention'd in this Paper, that the Author has taken Care to be duly furnifh'd with all that comes from Abroad in any Language. And for an Affurance that he will not, under Pretence of having Private Intelligence, impofe any Additions of feign'd Circumftances to an Action, but give his Extracts fairly and Impartially; at the beginning of each Article he will quote the Foreign Paper from whence 'tis taken, that the Publick, feeing from what Country a piece of News comes with the Allowance of that Government, may be better able to Judge of the Credibility and Fairnefs of the Relation: Nor will he take upon him to give any Comments or Conjectures of his own, but will relate only Matter of Fact; fuppofing other People to have Senfe enough to make Reflections for themfelves.

This Courant (as the Title fhews) will be Publifh'd Daily: being defign'd to give all the Material News as foon as every Poft arrives: and is confin'd to half the Compafs, to fave the Publick at leaft half the Impertinences, of ordinary News-Papers.

LONDON. Sold by E. Mallet, next Door to the King's-Arms Tavern at Fleet-Bridge.

5.1. *The Daily Courant*, March 11, 1702, The Image Works.

5.2. John Chessell Buckler (1793–1894), view of the Tabard Inn on Borough High Street, Southwark, 1827, London Metropolitan Archives.

5.3. William Hogarth (1697–1764), "Beer Street," 1751, London Metropolitan Archives.

5.4. William Hogarth (1697–1764), "Gin Lane," 1751, London Metropolitan Archives.

5.5. British School (c. 1650–c. 1750), interior of a London Coffeehouse, British Museum.

A View of Vaux Hall Gardens, shewing the Grand Walk at the entrance of the Garden & the Orchestra with the Musick Playing. Vûe des Jardins de Vaux Hall, ou l'on voit la Grand Allée à l'Entrée du Jardin et l'Orchestre avec les Musiciens exécutant une Symphonie.

5.6. Samuel Wale (1721–1786), view of Vauxhall Gardens, etching executed c. 1751, London Metropolitan Archives.

5.7. William Hogarth (1697–1764), Innocence Betrayed, plate I of "A Harlot's Progress," 1732, London Metropolitan Archives.

6.1. William Hogarth (1697–1764), The Industrious 'Prentice Out of his Time, plate VI from "Industry and Idleness," 1747, Bridgeman Art Library.

6.2. Nathaniel Parr (1723–1751), Admission of Children to the Foundling Hospital, 1749, Bridgeman Art Library.

6.3. Thomas Rowlandson (1756–1827), Trial in Progress at the Old Bailey, 1809, Bridgeman Art Library.

6.4. William Hogarth (1697–1764), The Idle 'Prentice Executed at Tyburn, plate XI of "Industry and Idleness," 1747, London Metropolitan Archives.

7.1. L. P. Boitard (fl. 1733–1767), "The Sailor's revenge . . . ," etching executed 1749, London Metropolitan Archives.

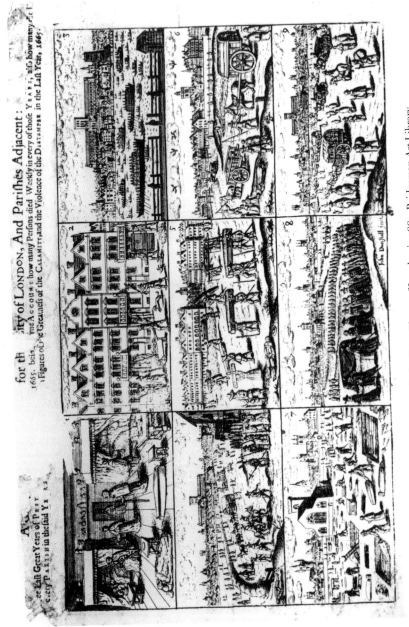

8.1. John Dunstall (d. 1693), the Great Plague of London in 1665, Bridgeman Art Library.

8.2. Great Fire of London, Dutch School (seventeenth century), Bridgeman Art Library.

8.3. Wenceslaus Hollar (1607–1677), map of the City of London after the Great Fire, 1666, London Metropolitan Archives.

Le monument érigé en memoire du grand incendie de Londres.

8.4. Anon., view of Monument's west side, etching c. 1700, London Metropolitan Archives.

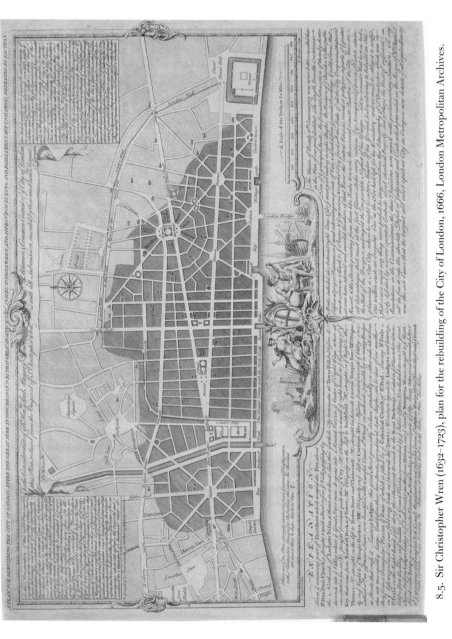

8.5. Sir Christopher Wren (1632–1723), plan for the rebuilding of the City of London, 1666, London Metropolitan Archives.

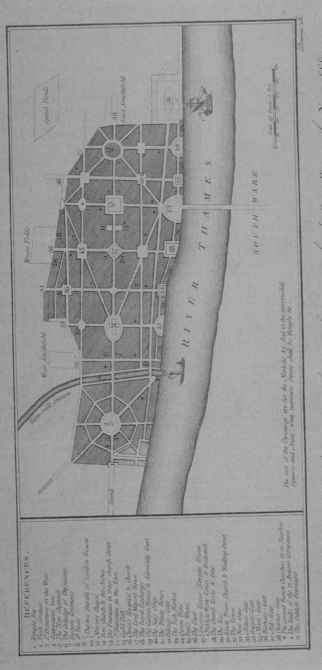

REFERENCES.

1 Temple Bar
2 Fleet Conduit
3 St Dunstans in the West
4 Sergeants Inn
5 The New Channel
6 The Colledge of Physicians
7 Doctors Commons
8 St Pauls
9 The two Sheriffs of London Houses
10 Mercers Chapel
11 Bow Church & the Arches
12 The Fountaine in Grace=Church Street
13 Conduit
14 3 Fountaines in the East
15 Guild Hall
16 Gresham Hospital & Church
17 The Lord Mayors House
18 The Royal Exchange
19 The Custom House & Admiralty Court
20 The Navy Office
21 The Pump House
22 Billings=Gate
23 The Fish Market
24 Queen Hithe
25 Pauls Wharf
26 The Fleete
27 Sessions House, Newgate Prison
+ Bridewell Work House & Bridewell
28 The Church Yards & Inns
29 Black Fryers Church & Wedding Street
30 The Tower
31 New=Gate
32 Alders=Gate
33 Cripple=Gate
34 Moor=Gate
35 Bishops=Gate
36 Old=Gate
37 Dowlers=Inne
38 The several Parish Churches so in Number
+ The several Parish Churches so in Number
✚ The Halls of the 12 Ancient Companies
◦ The Publick Fountaines

*The rest of the Openings are for the Markets &c And in the piecemeal
Squares and Streets what narrower Streets shall be thought fit.*

Sir JOHN EVELYN's PLAN *for* Rebuilding *the* CITY *of* LONDON, *after the* Great Fire *on the* Year 1666.

London, Published as the Act directs, by Alex.ʳ Hogg at the Kings Arms N.º16 Paternoster Row.

Scale of Paces & Feet

8.6. John Evelyn (1620–1706), plan for the rebuilding of the City of London, 1666, London Metropolitan Archives.

8.7. Frederick Nash (1782–1856), interior view of St. James's Piccadilly, 1806, London Metropolitan Archives.

8.8. Canaletto (1697–1768), St. Paul's Cathedral, 1754, Bridgeman Art Library.

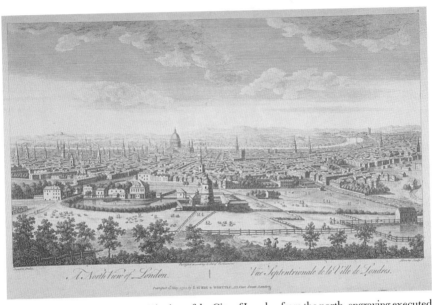

c.1. Canaletto (1697–1768), view of the City of London from the north, engraving executed 1794, London Metropolitan Archives.

c.2. John Bethell, two houses in Queen Anne's Gate, Westminster, early eighteenth century (photo), Bridgeman Art Library.

c.3. T. Rowlandson (1756–1827) and A. C. Pugin (1769–1832), Bank of England, Great Hall, 1809, Bridgeman Art Library.

c.4. William Hogarth (1697–1764), The Rake in Bedlam, plate VII from "A Rake's Progress," 1763, Bridgeman Art Library.

c.5. Anon., interior view of the choir of St. Paul's Cathedral, etching executed c. 1750, London Metropolitan Archives.

c.6. Anon., view of Temple Bar, etching executed c. 1700, London Metropolitan Archives.

c.7. Johannes Kip (1653–1721), panoramic view of London from Buckingham Palace, 1720, London Metropolitan Archives.

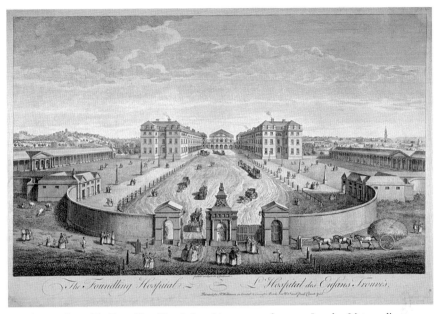

c.8. Anon., view of the Foundling Hospital, etching executed c. 1750, London Metropolitan Archives.

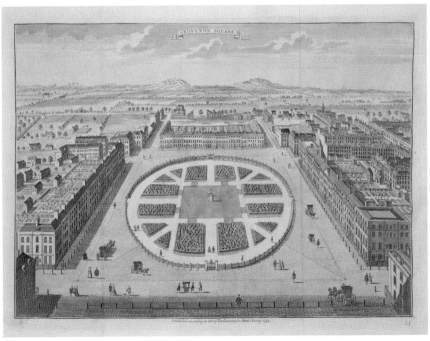

c.9. English School (eighteenth century), Grosvenor Square, 1754, Bridgeman Art Library.

c.10. Thomas Bowles (1690–1767), view of St. James's Palace and Pall Mall, 1753, London Metropolitan Archives.

c.11. Marco Ricci (1676–1730), view of the Mall and St. James's Park, c. 1710, Bridgeman
Art Library.

c.12. Canaletto (1697–1768), Ranelagh Gardens, the interior of the Rotunda, c. 1751, Bridgeman Art Library.

c.13. Canaletto (1697–1768), London seen through an arch of Westminster Bridge, 1746–1747, Bridgeman Art Library.

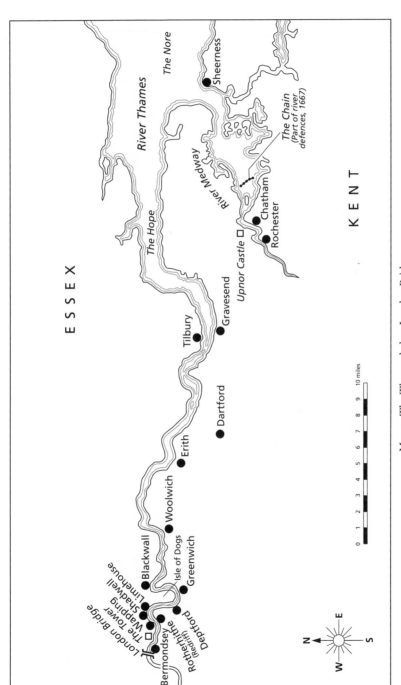

Map 1. The Thames below London Bridge.

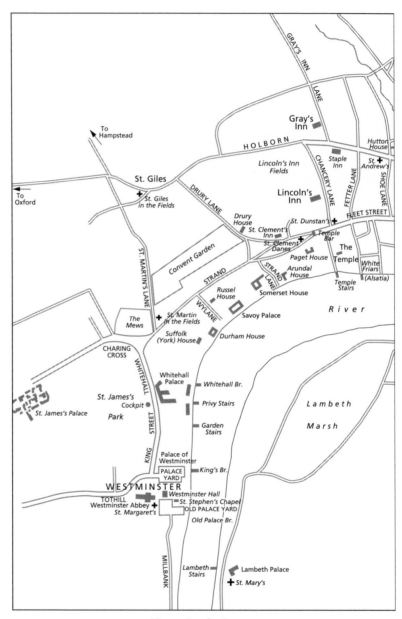

Map 2. London in 1550.

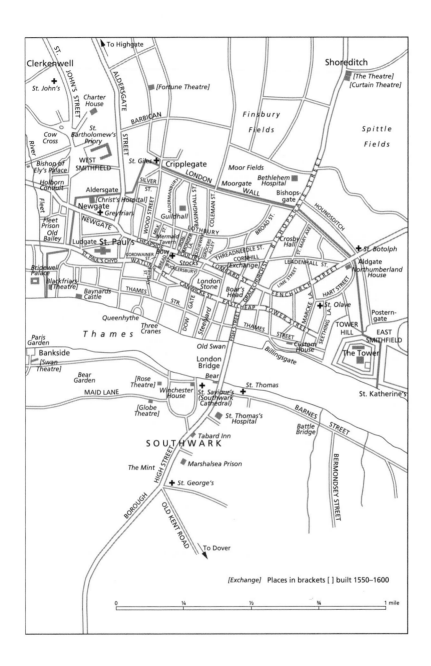

Clerkenwell

St. John's

ST. JOHN'S STREET

To Highgate

Charter House

ALDERSGATE STREET

[Fortune Theatre]

Shoreditch

[The Theatre]
[Curtain Theatre]

Cow Cross

River

Bishop of Ely's Palace

Holborn Conduit

Fleet

St. Bartholomew's Priory

BARBICAN

WEST SMITHFIELD

St. Giles

Cripplegate

Finsbury Fields

Spittle Fields

Aldersgate

SILVER ST.

[Christ's Hospital]

LONDON

Moor Fields

Newgate

Greyfriars

ALDERMANBURY

WOOD STREET

BASINGHALL ST.

COLEMAN ST.

Moorgate

WALL

Bethlehem Hospital

Bishops-gate

Guildhall

BISHOPSGATE STREET

HOUNDSDITCH

Fleet Prison

NEWGATE

MILK ST.

Old Bailey

Ludgate

St. Paul's

CHEAPSIDE

Mermaid Tavern

POULTRY

St. Botolph

Northumberland House

Bridewell Palace

Blackfriars [Theatre]

Baynards Castle

ST. PAUL'S CHYD

CORDWAINER ST.

WATLING

BOW ST.

BREAD ST.

FRIDAY ST.

Stocks

GRESHAM ST.

LOTHBURY

GRACER'S ALLEY

THREADNEEDLE ST.

[Exchange]

CORNHILL

Crosby Hall

ST. MARY AXE

LEADENHALL ST.

Aldgate

THAMES

London Stone

CANNING ST.

Boar's Head

LOMBARD ST.

GRACECHURCH ST.

LIME STREET

FENCHURCH STREET

HART STREET

St. Olave

MARCKE LANE

SEETHING LANE

Posterngate

Queenhythe

Three Cranes

DOW GATE

Steelyard

EASTCHEAP

THAMES

TOWER STREET

STREET

TOWER HILL

EAST SMITHFIELD

Thames

Paris Garden

Bankside

[Swan Theatre]

Old Swan

London Bridge

THAMES

Billingsgate

Custom House

Old Swan

Bear

Bear Garden

[Rose Theatre]

MAID LANE

Winchester House

St. Saviour's (Southwark Cathedral)

Bear

St. Thomas

BARNES STREET

St. Katherine's

The Tower

[Globe Theatre]

St. Thomas's Hospital

Battle Bridge

Tabard Inn

SOUTHWARK

HIGH STREET

The Mint

Marshalsea Prison

St. George's

BOROUGH

OLD KENT ROAD

BERMONDSEY STREET

To Dover

[Exchange]   Places in brackets [ ] built 1550–1600

0   ¼   ½   ¾   1 mile

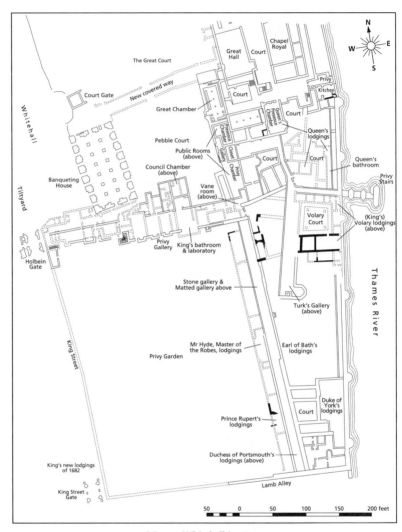

Map 3. Whitehall in 1670.

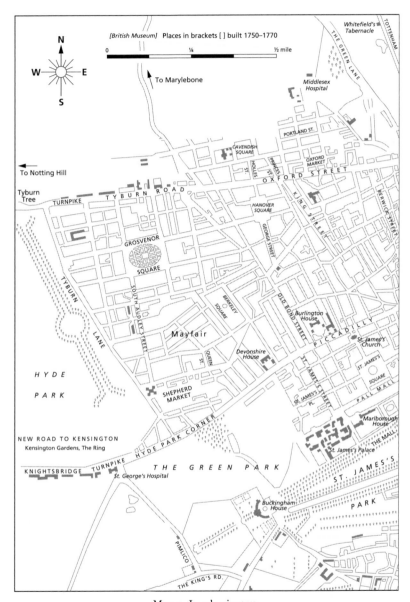

[British Museum] Places in brackets [ ] built 1750–1770

0   ¼   ½ mile

N
W — E
S

To Marylebone

To Notting Hill

Whitefield's
Tabernacle

THE GREEN LANE

TOTTENHAM

Middlesex
Hospital

PORTLAND ST.

CAVENDISH
SQUARE

OXFORD
MARKET

HOLLES ST.

PRINCES ST.

OXFORD   STREET

KING   STREET

BERWICK   STREET

Tyburn
Tree

TURNPIKE   TYBURN   ROAD

HANOVER
SQUARE

GEORGE STREET

GROSVENOR

SQUARE

TYBURN

LANE

SOUTH AUDLEY STREET

Mayfair

BERKELEY

SQUARE

QUEEN   ST.

HYDE

PARK

SHEPHERD
MARKET

Devonshire
House

Burlington
House

PICCADILLY

St. James's
Church

OLD BOND STREET

ST. JAMES'S STREET

ST. JAMES'S
SQUARE

PALL   MALL

SI. JAMES'S
PL.

Marlborough
House

NEW ROAD TO KENSINGTON
Kensington Gardens, The Ring

KNIGHTSBRIDGE   TURNPIKE   HYDE PARK CORNER

St. George's Hospital

THE   GREEN   PARK

St. James's Palace

THE MALL

ST. JAMES'S

PARK

Buckingham
House

PIMLICO

THE KING'S RD.

Map 4. London in 1750.

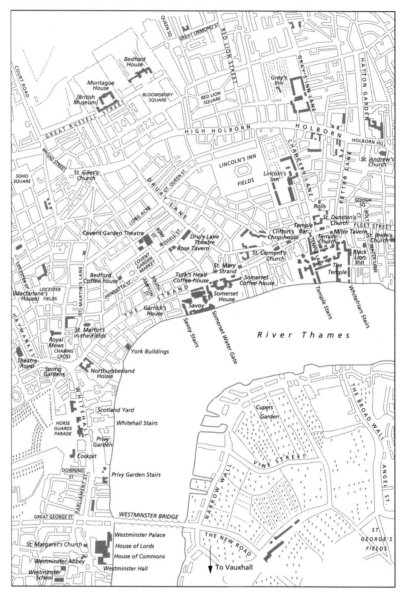

Map 4 (*cont.*)

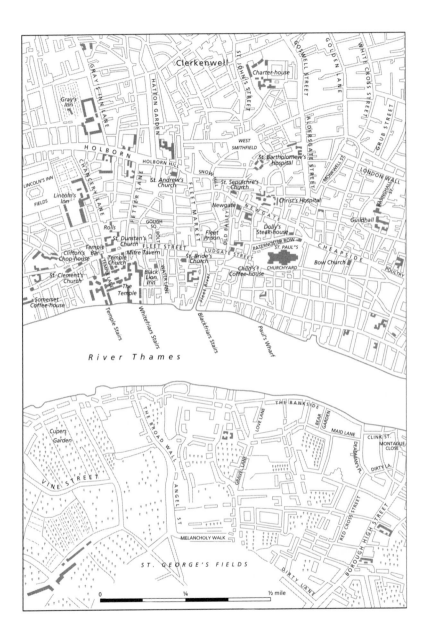

Clerkenwell

Charter-house

GRAY'S INN LANE

Gray's
Inn

ST. JOHN'S STREET

GOSWELL STREET

GOLDEN LANE

WHITE CROSS STREET

HATTON GARDEN

WEST
SMITHFIELD

St. Bartholomew's
Hospital

ALDERSGATE STREET

GRUB STREET

HOLBORN

CHANCERY LANE

LINCOLN'S INN
FIELDS

Lincoln's
Inn

HOLBORN HILL

St. Andrew's
Church

SNOW

St. Sepulchre's
Church

Christ's Hospital

MONKWELL ST.

LONDON WALL

BASINGHALL ST.

FETTER LANE

FLEET STREET

FLEET MARKET

Newgate

NEWGATE

Guildhall

Rolls

GOUGH
SQ.

BOLT CT.

OLD BAILEY

St. Dunstan's
Church

Fleet
Prison

Dolly's
Steak-house

Temple
Bar

Clifton's
Chop-house

Mitre Tavern

Temple
Church

LUDGATE STREET

PATERNOSTER ROW

ST. PAUL'S

CHEAPSIDE

POULTRY

St. Clement's
Church

TEMPLE LANE

Black
Lion
Inn

WATER LANE

St. Bride's
Church

Child's
Coffee-house

CHURCHYARD

Bow Church

The
Temple

Somerset
Coffee-house

Temple Stairs

Whitefriars Stairs

Fleet River

Blackfriars Stairs

Paul's Wharf

River Thames

THE BROAD WALL

THE BANKSIDE

Cupers
Garden

LOVE LANE

BEAR
GARDEN

MAID LANE

CLINK ST.

MONTAGUE
CLOSE

VINE STREET

GRAVEL LANE

DEADMAN'S PL.

DIRTY LA.

ANGEL ST.

RED CROSS STREET

BOROUGH HIGH STREET

MELANCHOLY WALK

ST. GEORGE'S FIELDS

DIRTY LANE

0   ¼   ½ mile

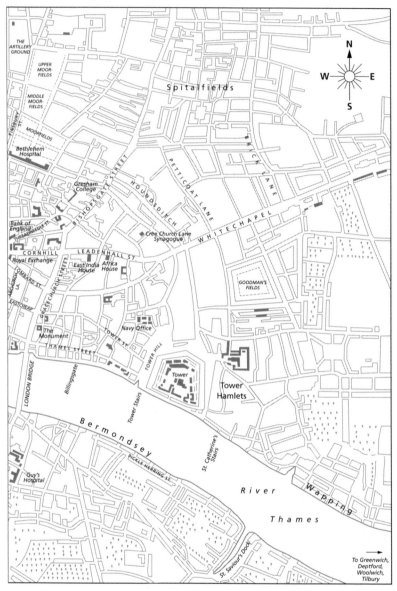

Map 4 (*cont.*)

$\mathscr{I}$NTRODUCTION: London's Importance

$\mathscr{B}$etween 1550 and 1750, London became Europe's largest city, a world-bestriding economic and cultural center, and the crucible for many of the hallmarks of modern life. This book presents London's history during the period when it rose to global prominence and came to dominate the economic, political, social, and cultural life of the British Isles as never before, nor, it will be argued, since. *London: A Social and Cultural History, 1550–1750* synthesizes recent work in urban history, testimony by contemporary Londoners and tourists, and fictional works in which the city plays a part to trace London's rise, its role as a harbinger of modernity, and the ways in which its inhabitants coped with those achievements. One of those inhabitants, Samuel Johnson (1709–1784), famously said "there is in London all that life can afford." Indeed, to evoke the full range of Londoners' experience, it is necessary to traverse the whole of the metropolis, from the splendid galleries of Whitehall and St. James's to the damp and sooty alleys and courts of the City outparishes, along the way braving the dangers of plague and fire; witnessing the spectacles of the lord mayor's pageant and the hangings at Tyburn; and taking refreshment in the city's pleasure gardens, coffeehouses, and taverns. Having spent some years making this trek ourselves, the authors trust confidently that, at its end, readers will find themselves, to echo Johnson again, no more tired of London than they are tired of life.

LONDON'S IMPORTANCE

In 1550, as this book opens London was already the most prominent city in England, containing its principal harbor; its largest concentration of population, wealth, and culture; and its capital, in suburban Westminster.

But England, sitting on the periphery of Europe, the military equivalent of Denmark, the economic inferior of Flanders, was not a terribly important country. In fact, it could be argued that London's greatest significance in 1550 was as the funnel through which the ideas and products of other, more powerful European states passed into England. Two centuries later, much had changed. London was still the seat of government and greatest city in England, but England was now the dominant country in the British Isles, a leading player in Europe, and the proprietor of a worldwide empire. Indeed, by the end of the Seven Years' War in 1763, the Union Jack flew from Canada to India, and from Gibralter to Tahiti. London was not only the capital of that empire, but the continent's greatest port, its financial and banking center, and its largest city, inhabited by about 675,000 people. That population had long ago overflowed London's ancient walls. Although many Londoners still lived in the heart of the old City, even more had expanded the metropolis to the west, populating the West End and Westminster, south across the river to Southwark and beyond, and northward to the suburbs of Marylebone, Hoxton, and Islington. Suburban growth and better roads and coaches meant that prosperous Londoners could now have the best of city and country life by commuting, working in London but living in Surrey or Hertfordshire.

Indeed, one of the problems for the historian of early modern London is that it is sometimes difficult to figure out where it ended. Given its commercial reach across the English Channel to Antwerp, Amsterdam, Hamburg, Lisbon, and the Mediterranean, and the tentacles of trade and government London came to extend across the Atlantic, Pacific, and Indian Oceans, one could argue that it never really did end. By 1750 London had surpassed Amsterdam as Europe's financial and banking hub and become the great entrepôt for Europe's most desirable products: sugar and tobacco from the Americas; fabrics, spices, and tea from the Indies. It was a cornucopia of culture anchored by a vibrant commercial theater and concert life and a thriving and relatively free press, to which would soon be added great public institutions like the British Museum and the Royal Academy of Arts. This economic and cultural synergy generated immense real estate and entertainment opportunities, and helped catapult Britain to the front rank of nations. But much of London's commercial wealth depended on the expropriation of foreign lands and the transatlantic sale and exploitation of Africans slaves, the last bitter episode in the greatest forced migration in history. At home, London's voracious prodigality produced massive problems and anxieties: like Los Angeles or Singapore today, London in 1750 was a shock city of palaces and slums, concert halls and gin joints, churches and brothels, possibility and fear.

Clearly, London's growth was neither easy nor inevitable. During the period covered by this book, Londoners endured the usual urban problems of overcrowding and disease, crime and poverty, isolation and alienation. Moreover, they endured two changes of royal dynasty, two revolutions, one successful restoration and one that nearly succeeded; incessant constitutional crises; frequent plots and counterplots; repeated wars and insurrections, some of which (in 1554, 1601, 1642–1643, 1648–49, 1658–1661, 1667, and 1688) were waged in or near London's streets; repeated deadly visitations of plague and an array of other diseases; innumerable fires culminating in the Great Conflagration of 1666; high taxes; repeated reputed crime waves; the Gin Craze of the 1730s; and the world's first major stock market crash, the South Sea Bubble of 1720. Individual Londoners died at alarming rates, yet London itself could not be stopped. It was replenished, rebuilt, and flourished. Londoners rose to ancient challenges like poverty, disease, and crime with proto-modern solutions like the London Foundling Hospital, possibly the world's first incorporated charity, and the Bow-Street Runners, a primitive municipal police force. It was in London that many of the hallmarks of modernity got their start, received their perfection, or were popularized for the Anglophone world, including constitutional monarchy, participatory democracy, modern government finance, an effective civil service, a relatively free press, the first commercial music concerts, the first viable commercial theater since ancient times, novels, newspapers, clubs, insurance, decent street lighting, three-piece suits for men, and on and on. With the possible exception of Amsterdam, no other city on the planet did more to catalyze modernity.

LONDON'S UNIQUENESS

As should be obvious, London was very different from the small towns and villages its immigrants came from and was therefore not typical of the experience of most Englishmen and women, either in 1550 or 1750.[1] During the early modern period, most people did not live in cities: perhaps only 10% of the English population in 1550, a little over 20% in 1750. Most who did so lived in relatively small cathedral cities, county seats, and market towns like Salisbury, Hampshire; Dorchester, Dorset; or Richmond, Yorkshire. Compared with London, these towns were not really very urban at all: a thousand or so people living in just a few streets huddled around a cathedral or market square only a few yards from open fields. The largest cities beyond the capital were Bristol, a western seaport on the River Severn; Norwich, a cloth town in East Anglia; and York, the most important city in the north. All were important regional centers, virtual provincial capitals, but even their populations stood between 8,000 and 12,000 in 1550 – barely one-tenth the size of London. Indeed, by the end of our period, some outlying London parishes would be larger.

Throughout our period, most English men and women lived in rural villages of as many as 500 or as few as 50 inhabitants. In the rugged north and west of England, the settlements tended to be even smaller, consistent with the sheep-farming and forest economies that prevailed there. Even in the more fertile and populous manors of the southeast, where arable farming was practiced, villagers had to pitch in to survive a bad harvest or a harsh winter. Isolated, small, and poor, dominated by the local landlord and clergy, with no choice of religious denomination, these communities tended to be hierarchical and close. The sort of freedom, privacy, and personal space that we moderns expect was unheard of. Rather, people occupied small, flimsy wattle-and-daub or wood-frame thatched houses, packed closely together to keep out cold winter winds. That meant that every member of your family lived his or her life close to each other; every neighbor knew your business, your parents, and therefore your social rank. That would have important implications for your mental and social outlook, or what historians call *mentalité*.

The Church was the early modern institution that attempted most consciously to shape *mentalité*. Physically, the village church was usually its most prominent, and often its only stone, building. It was officially the religious center of the village, because only the state Church, an uneasy mix of Protestant and Catholic practice in 1550, was tolerated before the 1640s. This was where Sunday services were held, holidays (Holy Days) celebrated, and all the important rites of human passage solemnized: birth (baptism), marriage (matrimony), and death (funeral and burial services). The weekly sermon was also the major source of news in the village. Given the importance of religious belief and practice to early modern life, it should come as no surprise that the church was also the social center of the village, its churchyard the site of holiday feasting and church-ales, Sunday and holiday sports, wedding receptions and wakes.

Perhaps the Church's most important function in early modern life was to bolster a concept of order based on a strict, God-ordained hierarchy. When sixteenth-century men and women thought about the universe, they assumed that it had been created by God, and that He had arranged it according to a master plan. Physically, they still tended to think of the Ptolemaic universe, with the Earth at the center and the moon, sun, planets, and stars orbiting around it. When considering the inhabitants of that universe, they liked metaphors, such as that of the body politic: the state was like a human body, with the king as the head, the aristocracy as the arms and shoulders, and the tenant farmers and poor as the legs and feet. Other popular metaphors for the English polity included a tree, a ship, a building, and even the strings on a lute. Perhaps the most comprehensive and powerful such metaphor, however, was what later historians have called the Great Chain of Being. In this scheme, God had arranged the universe's creatures in a hierarchy, from top to bottom, as follows: God (who dwelled everywhere); angels (who traversed the heavens, between God and man); man (who dwelled on the Earth); animals (Earth); plants (Earth); and stones (Earth). At the core of the Earth, farthest from God, were the damned souls in hell. Each rank was further subdivided, with those at the top given their supremacy by God: thus medieval theologians had divided angels into nine ranks, beginning with those closest to God, the seraphim. Similarly, the animal hierarchy was headed by the lion, king of the beasts; plants by the mighty oak; and stones by the regal diamond.

So also with Man: the king was at the top of the human chain, the fount of honor, God's personal representative on Earth. He was followed by the titled nobility (dukes, marquesses, earls, viscounts, and barons), a tiny elite of about 60 families in 1550 that nevertheless owned 5% to 10% of the land. The male head of each noble family sat by right in the House of Lords. The gentry came next, consisting of about 10,000 to 15,000 knights, esquires, and plain gentlemen in 1550. The most prominent sat in the House of Commons, after having been nominated for election by their peers. Thanks to the recent decision of Henry VIII to confiscate and sell monastic estates (1536–1548), this group now owned perhaps one half of the land in England. Land was power in early modern England, and so, despite amounting to less than 1% of the population, this newly expanded gentry joined with the nobility to form England's ruling elite. Moreover, because of their extensive holdings, worked by armies of servants and tenants, they themselves need never do manual labor. Indeed, the ability to *not* work was one of the criteria for gentility in early modern England and formed the most important dividing line between the people who mattered and those who did not. (This would play oddly in London: see later discussion.) Below this level, the yeomanry were substantial farmers who might do manual labor themselves but employed additional laborers to do the really heavy work on the farm. Husbandmen were small farmers, probably renters from a bigger landowner, who could afford only a handful of servants. Cottagers rented a cottage with no farm attached and were constantly on the edge of subsistence. Laborers had no home of their own; they lived and worked on someone else's farm. During the winter months or in old age, when work was hard to come by or beyond them, they might shade off into the poor, who might or might not have a permanent residence but could not make ends meet.

Each of these ranks was made up of families whose members were themselves ordered by gender and age as follows: father, mother, male children (in birth order), and female children (in birth order). Fathers, like kings, were thought to have been given their authority within the household – their kingdoms – by God. Their wives were considered by the law to be *femes coverts*: they could own no property and make no contracts without their husbands' permission. A substantial householder – say a yeoman farmer in the country or a merchant or tradesman in town – governed not only his wife and children but also live-in servants and possibly apprentices.

Perhaps the aspect of the chain of being most alien to us moderns is that it was not a ladder: because it was God's plan, because everyone was placed in his or her rank by the Supreme Being, because all authority came from Him, it was a grave sin to attack the chain, to disobey your superiors, or even, in theory, to try to rise to another rank. Thus, English society in 1550 valued order, not opportunity; conformity, not originality; community, not individuality. English people were terrified of disorder and chaos, because if hierarchy and order were the hallmarks of God, surely their opposites were those of Satan. Still, when we consider that the top three ranks of the human chain represented less than 1% of the population of England, yet owned perhaps 70% of the land and nearly 100% of the power, we might well ask why the other 99.5% put up with all this? One reason is that the harshest potential effects of inequality were mitigated by two related beliefs: paternalism and deference. Paternalism was the belief, also taught from the pulpit and embodied in royal proclamations and parliamentary statutes, that people placed at the top of the chain had a responsibility to look after those below them. Kings and aristocrats were enjoined to watch paternally, as did God the Father for whom they deputized, over their flocks by providing military protection in time of war, justice in royal and manorial courts, jobs and economic assistance in hard times, and hospitality at holidays. The mayor, aldermen, and livery companies of London also believed in paternalism, but their ability to fulfill its dictates was increasingly compromised by the sheer magnitude of London and its problems. In return, people in the lower ranks of the chain were supposed to provide deference, that is, allegiance, obedience, and respect. They did this by attending church on Sunday; paying their taxes and tithes; keeping the king's law and Church or canon law; and by showing both obedience and respect to their landlords, masters (employers), and fathers.

So, in theory, every single creature in God's universe had a master and could be placed precisely in this hierarchy. Generations of royal proclamations and Sunday sermons reinforced this idea and taught everyone what was expected of them. Throughout the Middle Ages, however, repeated baronial and popular rebellions, most recently the Wars of the Roses, had threatened order and hierarchy (see later discussion). Moreover, in 1550 and for many years thereafter, religious reformation and economic change posed an even greater threat to the certainties of the chain. But perhaps the greatest challenge to traditional notions of hierarchy in 1550 came from London.

In theory, the ancient walled City of London, defined by its royal charter, was every bit as hierarchical as the rest of the country, administered by a lord mayor and the aldermen of its 26 wards, the masters of its 80 or so livery companies, and the vestries of its 111 assorted parishes. The City's freemen, journeymen, apprentices, and (in the first two cases) their wives and children were supposed to live out their deference and inferiority daily by following the orders of their masters, paying dues to their livery companies, dressing modestly and sitting in church according to their respective ranks, bowing, curtseying, tipping their caps, and "giving the wall," that is, stepping into the street (which doubled as an open sewer) when meeting a social superior out of doors. In practice, however, London was more than just the chartered and walled City. This wider, metropolitan London was arguably the place in England where the Great Chain of Being was most consistently under attack and least likely to work. First, there was its sheer size: London had long ago expanded beyond its walls and was throughout the period growing out of all proportion to the rest of England. At the beginning of this book, greater London's population of about 120,000 was ten times larger than its nearest provincial rivals. Over the course of the next two centuries it would grow fivefold, to about 675,000, whereas the population of England and Wales would only double, from about 3 million to nearly 6 million souls in 1750. London grew by in-migration, draining the countryside of people to the tune of 6,000 a year in the late sixteenth century and perhaps 8,000 a year by the early eighteenth. No wonder that in 1616 James I complained, "With time England will onely be London, and the whole countrey left waste."[2]

To further complicate matters, London had its own chain, in fact many intersecting chains, that were hard to place within the overall scheme of king, nobles, and gentry. There was the City of London's government, headed by the lord mayor, the chamberlain, recorder, sheriffs, and other great officers, the Court of Aldermen, Common Council, and Common Hall, and assorted lesser officers, shading off into the wards and parishes (see Chapter 3). Nearly all these luminaries were members of the London livery companies, themselves ranked (twelve great companies and about seventy lesser companies), divided into liverymen, householders, journeymen, and apprentices (see Chapter 2). They were followed by everybody else. On the one hand, these hierarchies, based on wealth and achievement, gave London some sense of order and coherence. On the other, they did not fit neatly into the main chain, which was essentially rural and based on birth, nor even sometimes with each other. Where did the lord mayor of London, almost always a wealthy merchant, fit in the Great Chain of Being? Did he rank with a gentleman? He was usually lower born, yet often wealthier and more powerful, a veritable merchant-prince worth over £50,000 by the mid-eighteenth century, more than all but the greatest aristocrats. What of a rich merchant generally? A prosperous attorney? A struggling tailor? The Great Chain of Being said nothing about them, partly because the source of their status did not fit its principles. They worked for a living, yet the chain said that those closest to God did no work. They were successful because of their labor, their skills, their credentials, and their wealth, but the chain ranked people according to birth.

Indeed, although most of the popular metaphors for the English polity rested on the principle that one's personal status was assigned by God at birth and remained frozen over time, London was famous for its social mobility, its inhabitants growing rich or poor, rising or falling in status, very quickly. That was the very point of one of the most famous nursery rhymes taught to generations of English children: the story of Dick Whittington. According to a legend dating to the early seventeenth century, Whittington was a poor scullion from the country working for a wealthy London merchant. Discouraged by his prospects, he decided to return home with his cat, but on his way out of the city, at Highgate Hill, he heard the bells of St. Mary-le-Bow (Bow Bells) calling to him:

> *Turn again, Whittington,*
> *Once Mayor of London!*
> *Turn again, Whittington,*
> *Twice Mayor of London!*
> *Turn again, Whittington,*
> *Thrice Mayor of London!*

So Whittington turned back and reapplied himself to his apprenticeship. There are different versions of the tale from this point; nearly all involve his faithful cat, who was so good a mouser that he won Whittington a fortune, enabling the erstwhile kitchen boy to marry his master's daughter, become a prosperous trader himself, and, eventually, lord mayor three times.

In fact, there really was a Dick Whittington (c. 1350–1423), and he really did become lord mayor three times. At his death he left several important charitable bequests, some of the fruits of which are still aiding Londoners today, including Guildhall Library. But when historians researched the roots of the tale, they found that he was not a scullion at all, but the third son of Sir William Whittington (d. 1358), owner of extensive estates in the west of England. Thus, his real story illustrates not so much how a poor boy could make good in London, but how the rich tended to get richer and how its mayors and aldermen were drawn from prosperous families. Still, what matters here is not the reality, but that English children grew up being told that there was endless opportunity in London if only they worked hard and persisted. London's most famous myth could only play havoc with the notion that God placed people in immutable ranks.

Perhaps even more threatening to the Great Chain of Being, London's sheer size made it a place where newcomers could lose or reinvent themselves. In the village, everyone knew everyone else. In fact, social stability depended on people knowing each other, knowing who your father and mother were. Your rank and status were enforced by your fellow villagers: to put on airs was an unforgivable social sin. But in the human ebb and flow of London it was much harder to tell who was who, or who belonged to whom. It is true that London had its own hierarchies; social rank was reinforced, especially in the first century of our period, by special clothing (liverymen and vestrymen wore gowns; poor pensioners wore badges). Guilds, parishes, and neighborhoods provided community and could be nearly as close-knit, even claustrophobic, as the village, but they could not possibly absorb, sort, and assimilate easily or quickly those 6,000 to 8,000 newcomers arriving every year. Put another way, if you found village life stifling, one way to escape from your place in the rural chain was by going to the city.

This might have been especially true for women. Contemporaries noted, often ruefully, that in London more than anywhere else in the kingdom, women had opportunities to work and play beyond the domestic sphere usually accorded them in the countryside. In London was the court, where aristocratic women like Anne Boleyn (c. 1500–1536) in the sixteenth century or Sarah Churchill, Duchess of Marlborough (1660–1744) in the eighteenth achieved position and power undreamed of elsewhere. Below this level, there were female apprentices and inn, tavern, shop, and bawdy-house keepers. Upper class women paid each other visits and went shopping in the Royal or New Exchanges (see Chapters 1 and 2), while their maids and kitchen staff roamed the entire city on errands – delivering messages; buying bread, meat, and milk; fetching water – all unchaperoned. Women were active in the law courts as plaintiffs, witnesses, and defendants, and some even tried to evade the limitations of being *femes coverts* by forming informal financial networks. It should be obvious that the economic and social fluidity of London threatened to make nonsense of the Great Chain of Being.

Early modern London gave birth to a burgeoning public sphere of stage plays, street musicians, taverns, and (later) coffeehouses, brothels, and pleasure gardens, not to mention the busiest printing presses in the nation. None of this was good for the chain, if only because so many of these institutions paid little respect to birth rank and involved dissimulation or faking identity. Actors pretended to be other people; broadside sellers and balladeers sold truth, lies, and rumors about celebrities without distinction; authors wrote under pen names or anonymously (see Chapters 4 and 5). Foreign trade and exploration brought contact with other cultures, which might embrace different principles of hierarchy, whereas the luxury goods so traded enabled Londoners of middling and lower rank to ape and even impersonate their betters (see Chapter 2). Indeed, the migration of people and goods from across the British Isles, Europe, and the ocean helps to explain why early modern London was home to more religious and cultural diversity than other parts of England and Wales (see Chapters 2 and 4). London's wealth and size also made it prone to crime and riot (see Chapters 6 and 7), traditional threats to those in authority. Finally, as we shall see in the next section, despite its reliance on a royal charter for its authority, the City government could be remarkably independent of the Crown that everyone else was supposed to obey (see Chapters 3 and 7).

For all these reasons, London was a place, to some extent even in 1550 and certainly by 1750, in which many of the rules of the Great Chain of Being either did not apply or were honored more in the breach than in practice. Put another way, early modern London was trying out institutions and attitudes that cannot help but strike us as modern, including constitutional monarchy, relative social fluidity, and the first tentative steps toward freedom of movement, assembly, speech, religion, and economic opportunity, as well as greater opportunities for women. Before proceeding further it might be worth asking: how did this obviously unusual place become that way?

LONDON'S HISTORY TO 1550

Medieval Londoners, displaying a genius for self-promotion that their descendants inherited, made up an ancient pedigree for their city. They claimed that, long before the incarnation of Christ, and in some chronicles, even before the foundation of Rome, one King Brut or Brutus, a descendant of Aeneas and a refugee from the Trojan Wars, founded London. According to this story, London was originally called *Trinovant*, or "new Troy." (In fact, there actually was a Celtic tribe called the Trinovantes when the Romans arrived, but they did not live in cities.) According to one medieval chronicler, not only was London older than Rome, but it "possesses the liberties, rights, and customs of that ancient city Troy."[3] Londoners were always jockeying for position, in this case probably against medieval royal governments: if London's rights and privileges predated kings, then kings could not take them away. But the association with Troy was also a warning of London's vulnerability: like that city, it could fall. Unfortunately, this foundation story is nonsense, yet another London myth. For London's origins, we are better off relying on the hard data of archaeology rather than the fancies of medieval chroniclers.

In fact, London was a Roman invention. It was the Romans who established its commercial, political, military, and religious importance, as well as many of its lasting landmarks (e.g., the bridge and wall). Although *London* is a Celtic word, possibly meaning (appropriately) "wild" or "bold," there is no evidence of any large settlement at this location before the Romans got there. In year 43 of the Common Era, the Emperor Claudius (41–54 CE), returning to the scene of one of Julius Caesar's (lived 100–44 BCE) triumphs, dispatched an invasion force of about 40,000 troops under Aulus Plautius (fl. 24-48) that easily defeated a local tribe, the Catuvellauni, and established a base camp at Westminster. Within seven years, the Roman Governor, Ostorius Scapula (d. 52), had established a permanent trading post called *Londinium* on the north bank of the Thames at its highest point, what is today Cornhill.

Despite its marshy ground, the site probably attracted the Romans because it resembled that of Rome itself. London straddles the Thames as Rome straddles the Tiber, at an elevated point just where the river is still deep enough to form a harbor for big ships traveling east to west, yet narrow enough to be bridgeable, allowing transit north and south. The high ground made Londinium defensible, like Rome. The combination of an east–west river and a north–south bridge made both cities crossroads for immigration and trade. Eventually, Londinium would become the junction for six major roads into the interior. The river connected the interior with the English Channel, the North Sea, and the rest of imperial Europe. The first Roman bridge connecting Londinium on the north bank with the much smaller settlement of Southwark on the south bank was probably built by 60 (see Map 2); successive structures on this spot would provide London's only bridge until 1750. In 60, Londinium already stretched from Cornhill to the river, had a thriving market, and was the largest Roman settlement in Britain. Erecting a large timber quay by 80, the Romans thus established London's first important role: it was a harbor, crossroads, and commercial *entrepôt*. Archaeological evidence shows that Londinium was fully integrated into the imperial trading system, consuming olive oil from Africa and Iberia; Rhenish wine and Mediterranean pottery; Italian lamps, tableware, and sculpture; and grain from the local countryside.

In 60 CE, Londinium was sacked and burned, and 70,000 of its inhabitants were massacred in the revolt of the Iceni. After the revolt was suppressed, the Romans rebuilt the city with a forum, temples, and basilicas, baths, an amphitheater, and, to prevent a repetition of recent history, a makeshift wall and a fort with 1,500 soldiers near modern Cripplegate. By 200 the wall had been renovated to be 18 feet high and 6 to 9 feet thick, punctuated by a series of gates and ringed by a ditch 6 feet deep (see Map 2). Besides the bridge, this wall would become London's most prominent landmark. It set London's boundaries for the next 1,500 years and was still used as a defensive barrier right up to the Civil Wars of the 1640s. This, plus London's location along the major east–west artery into the country, established London's military importance: whoever controlled London controlled access to the fertile Thames valley.

Londinium was also the site of the governor's riverside palace, making it the capital of Roman Britain and the essential contact point for imperial policy. Londinium's internal government consisted of two senior and two junior magistrates assisted by a town council comprising 100 Romano-Celtic property owners elected annually by free-born male citizens. Nearly from the beginning, therefore, London was run by a wealthy elite, but with democratic elements. As the Roman Empire became a Christian empire in the second, third, and fourth centuries, Londinium's temples were converted into churches and confirmed a fourth role for the city: it was a religious center. Londinium got its first Christian bishop by 314. Finally, the streets of Londinium were interconnected with Roman Britain by Roman roads, laid out so straight and built so well that many form the basis of modern roads into the countryside today. Thus, Oxford Street and Watling Street, built on top of the old Roman roadbeds, connect to the west and east, respectively by the A40 and A5. Roman Ermine Street began what used to be called the Great North Road, now the A10, which ran from Bishopsgate all the way to Yorkshire. Those roads were crucial to all four of Roman Londinium's functions: trade (obviously), governmental and religious communication from the capital to the countryside, and the movement of troops.

Those troops were necessary because from the third century on, Roman Britain, like the rest of the Roman Empire, was under siege by marauding tribes, first Picts and Scots from the north and then, from the fourth century, Angles, Saxons, and Jutes from the continent. This could help to explain why Londinium's population began to decline in this period. After the Empire pulled the garrison in 410, the city lost much of its reason for being: Southwark was abandoned, coinage fell out of use, and, without military protection, commerce, government, and religion began to collapse. There is almost no evidence of urban habitation within the walls between 450 and 600, although archaeology has uncovered an Anglo-Saxon settlement along the river to the west. Historians and archaeologists still debate whether Londinium was abandoned entirely or merely shrank to a shadow of its former self. Most suspect that its population dwindled to perhaps a few thousand, smaller than Wimborne Minster, England, or Hendersonville, North Carolina, today.

It took centuries for London to recover its importance, beginning with religion. In 597, Pope Gregory I (590–604) sent St. Augustine (d. 604) to Britain to begin a revival of Christianity by converting the Anglo-Saxons. One of his famous successes was Aethelberht, King of the Saxons of Kent (c. 590–616). To demonstrate his faith, Aethelberht established London's first cathedral, built of wood and dedicated to St. Paul, beginning about 604. There has been a St. Paul's Cathedral in the metropolis ever since. By the eighth century, London was once again a Christian city, kings and commoners making so many bequests and endowments to redeem their souls from Purgatory that the Church ended up owning much of the city's land and building stock. By 1200 some 126 churches had been built within the walls, their spires lending a verticality to the previously horizontal (i.e., river, bridge, wall) profile of the city. In addition, endowed Church hospitals and schools provided most of what we would today call social services.

Between 600 and 800, "Lundenwic," as the Anglo-Saxons called their settlement, began to be a great port again, "a market-place for many peoples who come by land and by sea," according to the English monk Bede (674–735).[4] Gold coins reappeared by 640. A national, even international, trading system developed in which raw materials like tin (from the west of "Angle-land" or England) and wool were shipped out to the north and Europe, whereas finished goods like wine and metal tools were imported in. Admittedly, this amounts to a colonial trading economy: early medieval England and its largest city were sideshows to the emergence of new states in Europe. As some tribes began to consolidate their holdings, a series of regional kingdoms emerged in East Anglia, Essex, Kent, Mercia, Northumbria, Sussex, and Wessex in what later historians called the *heptarchy*. The kings of Essex in the southeast, subservient to those of Kent, found Lundenwic a convenient administrative and military center. In Kentish law, London merchants had to register their transactions with the king's reeve in a great hall: the first step toward renewed taxation. The Anglo-Saxons also developed the "folk-moot," an open air court of all citizens that met on high ground east of St. Paul's, by the eleventh century three times a year, to maintain order. Gradually, London began to reestablish its religious, commercial, and governmental significance.

The fact that London also bordered Mercia and Wessex made it a central location, but this did not make it a great capital. Between 600 and 900, the dominant Anglo-Saxon kingdom was not based in the southeast: Northumbria was the most powerful monarchy in the seventh century,

Mercia in the eighth. During the ninth century, the kings of Wessex, based in the southwest up the Thames valley from London, became the dominant power among the Anglo-Saxons. Establishing their capital at Winchester, the Wessex line, most notably King Alfred (871–899), sought to unite all of Angle-land into a semblance of what we today know as England. They faced two obstacles to this goal, however, one internal, one external. The internal obstacle was London itself: the metropolis had an independent streak and resisted incorporation into a Wessex empire, preferring at first to remain something of an independent city-state. The external obstacle was far greater, because just as the Wessex monarchs began to try to consolidate their gains, England faced a series of invasions by the Vikings.

Based in Scandinavia, between 790 and 1100 the Vikings became a menace to all Europe, riding their swift longboats down European rivers and across the North Sea and beyond to attack any human settlement – city or monastery, camp or village – that promised plunder. Naturally, an increasingly prosperous Anglo-Saxon London was a tempting prize. In 842 the monks who kept the *Anglo-Saxon Chronicle* recorded "a great slaughter in London." In 851 London was taken by storm and held off and on by Viking kings until 886. Evidence of Viking occupation can be found today in a few London place names: the church of St. Clement Danes and five different St. Olafs. The Vikings also might have originated the *husting*, an assembly or court to handle debt, land, and trade that met weekly.

In the long run, the Viking raids were good for both the Wessex kings and their largest city. They forced those kings to develop institutions (e.g., a militia, the *fyrd*; a regular tax called the *Danegeld* and the infrastructure to collect it) that proved indispensable as they pushed the Vikings back and solidified their rule in England. London's wealth, both taxable and lendable, was crucial to the war effort. In 886 Alfred "liberated" London from the Vikings and was for the first time acknowledged as king of the English. Thus began the tradition that any would-be ruler of England had to hold London. At the same time, London's inhabitants, who had been forced back into the old walled city, acknowledged that they needed the protection of powerful kings. So, for the first time since Roman rule, London was integrated into a larger governmental entity. Alfred and his successors strengthened the city's fortifications, laid out a grid street pattern, and established quays at Queenhithe, Billingsgate, and Dowgate. It was also under the Wessex kings that the city was divided into wards, each headed by an alderman. Although the capital remained at Winchester, London became ever more important to the running of the country. Indeed, so long as Viking invasions continued in the tenth and eleventh centuries, as London went so did England: if London resisted successfully, as it did in 994, 1009, and 1013, the invasion failed. If London capitulated, as it did to Swein in 1014, so did the country. In fact, Londoners turned this to their advantage, eventually claiming a right to name the king of England.

Toward the end of the Anglo-Saxon period, the Wessex dynasty began to give London more of the function of a capital. Beginning in 1045, Edward the Confessor (1042–1066) founded a magnificent abbey to the west of the city at Thorn Ey (Thorney Island). There had been a religious shrine there since the seventh century, when according to legend, St. Peter had appeared and promised the inhabitants good fishing. In the late tenth century St. Dunstan (d. 988) founded a Benedictine monastery. So the famously pious Edward was building on existing foundations when he began construction of Westminster Abbey and a royal palace for his own use to go with it. Westminster was not technically part of the City of London; it was a seigneurial manor nominally run by the abbot of St. Peter's, that is, Westminster Abbey, but was really under royal control. Westminster would remain legally separate from the rest of London proper until the nineteenth century. It would also increasingly become the center of national government, as well as the site of the coronations and most of the burials of Edward's successors. By the time of Edward's death in 1066, greater London was once again the most prosperous port in England, a religious center, and shared with Winchester many of the functions of government. As that year would show, London was also still the military key to the country at large.

It is generally accepted that, following the death of the childless Edward the Confessor on January 5, 1066, William the Conqueror (lived 1027–1087) earned his nickname, won the English crown, and established the Norman line of kings by slaying the Anglo-Saxon Harold II (1066) and defeating his forces at the Battle of Hastings, Sussex on October 14. As it turned out, however, killing the previous king and defeating his army was not enough: the Conqueror needed London. There the surviving Anglo-Saxon leaders had rallied to another claimant, Edgar the Aetheling (c. 1052–1125). William spent the remainder of the autumn securing Kent before marching on the city. Halted at the southern end of London Bridge, needing to convince the city's leaders and the Anglo-Saxon ruling class that he meant business, he burned Southwark and much of the surrounding countryside in retaliation. The bishops, earls, and citizens of London got the message and submitted to the Conqueror. Once again, London spoke for the nation: William I (1066–1087) was crowned in Westminster Abbey on Christmas Day 1066.

The Norman kings naturally made London – or, specifically, West-minster – their capital because of its great wealth and ease of access to Europe. Recall that William and his descendants were still Dukes of Normandy. Peripatetic like all medieval kings, they maintained extensive holdings in France, which they considered to be every bit as much a part of their realm as, say, Kent or Devonshire. London's location on the Thames made it a convenient place from which to come and go between the two halves of their empire. The Norman kings also introduced a new, Norman-French–speaking ruling class who displaced the old Anglo-Saxon elite in office, titles, lands, and wealth. Naturally, William did not trust his Anglo-Saxon subjects, so he started building castles. The most famous of these he established on the southeast corner of London's wall on the north bank of the Thames: the Tower of London. Originally consisting of just the four-turreted keep, or White Tower, this imposing fortress could rake the entrance to the port of London with long-bow, later cross-bow, and later still, gunfire. Its strategic location enabled it to safeguard the city from outside invaders – or to keep watch on its inhabitants. Over the course of the next millennium the Tower would serve as a fortress, a royal palace, and a notorious prison for the most prominent accused rebels and traitors. Perhaps its greatest impact was psychological: it was for some time one of the tallest structures in London. When viewed from the south bank, it formed one of two "bookends" – along with the Westminster complex to the west – framing St. Paul's Cathedral in the middle. If the other two called on Londoners to fear God, the Tower taught them to dread His lieutenant, the king. Just in case, William the Conqueror built another famous castle upriver at Windsor, just twenty miles away.

Anyone possessing a nodding acquaintance with the political history of medieval England knows that William's successors needed those castles, because the period from 1066 to 1550 was one of intermittent conflict between the king and his barons, punctuated by odd periods of stability. Throughout, London's strategic location, wealth, and prestige made it a key player in those conflicts. Precisely because London could tip the balance in favor of an incumbent king or a traitorous usurper, both sides sought to woo it, which put London in an enviable position – if it were not sacked. Generally, when the king was strong and successful,[5] City authorities were only too happy to lend him money and support, providing huge tax revenues, loans, and troops. (Early in medieval history those loans were provided by Jewish bankers, but after their expulsion in 1290, Italian bankers took over the business.) But when the king was weak, and his rule subject to question by powerful barons,[6] London asserted its independence, sometimes refusing to grant money and men unless the king made concessions; sometimes refusing help outright; or even opening its gates to traitors. It did so to the rebels against King John in 1215, to Simon de Montfort, Earl of Leicester (c. 1208–1265) in 1263, to Wat Tyler (d. 1381) in 1381, Jack Cade (d. 1450) in 1450, and Edward, Duke of York (1442–1483) in 1461. But it turned on the pretender Matilda (1102–1167) in 1141 and shut London Bridge to Wyatt's rebels in 1554 (see below and Chapter 7). As this implies, London could be fickle: York became King of England (1461–1483), but Tyler was killed by the lord mayor of London. When Cade was defeated, his head was mounted on London Bridge to overlook the very passage through which he had ridden in triumph.

Often, to win municipal support, medieval kings granted powerful concessions, usually by means of a charter under the Great Seal of England, spelling out that London was a municipality with certain privileges and powers. For example, Henry I (1100–1135) or possibly his nephew, Stephen (1135–1154), granted London a charter limiting its total tax burden to £300 and establishing the right to elect a sheriff to act as a go-between with the king and collect taxes, to hold its own courts, to trade free of certain taxes and tolls, and to avoid paying Danegeld or billeting troops. It worked. When Stephen was challenged by his cousin Matilda for the throne of England in 1141, Londoners marched out of the City gates and welcomed his approaching army. They then attacked Matilda at her pre-coronation feast. The coronation was thwarted, and Stephen won back his throne.

An even better example of the pattern is provided by the reign of that famously bad medieval king (at least in the eyes of subsequent generations), John (lived 1167–1216). John served as regent for his brother, Richard the Lionhearted (1189–1199), when he was away on Crusade. In 1191, John marched on London and used his power as regent to recognize it as a self-governing commune under a mayor in return for recognition of his right to succeed. After Richard's death in 1199, John did succeed (1199–1216) but was forced into a series of military campaigns in France to secure his authority. This meant high taxes and City loans. Once again, John greased the wheels by granting a new charter expanding London's rights, in particular granting its aldermen the power to elect their mayor annually in 1215. Later, Londoners would emphasize their independence by referring to him as a lord mayor, but John's wars disrupted trade, increased taxes, and worst of all, proved unsuccessful. Having offended his nobles, the Church, towns, and virtually every other group that mattered in England, he returned defeated and discredited in 1214. Early the next year, despite his attempts to win London over, a group of dissidents within the City opened its gates to the rebels. That crucial act provided the base from which to exact the Magna Carta from the king in June 1215 at Runnemede Meadow, just a few miles outside of town. Magna Carta, or the Great Charter, guaranteed the rights to consultation and due process of the barons, the Church, towns, royal wards, persons accused of crimes, property holders, and many other groups. It represents one of the earliest attempts in postclassical Western history to limit the power of rulers and is often regarded as the foundation for later assertions of right by the English people. London's support was the crucial piece; once again, as the City went, so went the nation.

Subsequent kings tried to revoke the privileges granted by John. Henry III (1216–1272) set aside the aldermen's choice for mayor ten times between 1239 and 1257 and favored French merchants over English ones. London responded by refusing to grant him taxes in 1255 and supporting a usurper, Simon de Montfort, from 1263 to 1265. Perhaps the nadir of medieval Crown–City relations was reached when, in 1263, Queen Eleanor (c. 1223–1291) tried to escape to Windsor by river but was cannonaded with refuse from London Bridge. In December the City gates were opened to Montfort's army. In 1265, Henry won back control after defeating Montfort at the Battle of Evesham. He retaliated by dispossessing sixty leading Londoners, suspending the privileges of the City for two years, imposing heavy fines on its citizens, and granting Eleanor the revenues of the merchants on London Bridge. Londoners would long remember the consequences of choosing the wrong side.

Henry III's son Edward I (1272–1307) also remembered. He strengthened the Tower, adding the outer wall. He broke the ruling oligarchy of families who had dominated London to this point, opening aldermens' positions to members of prominent trades such as fishmongers, coopers, and skinners. He favored alien merchants and Italian bankers who could lend him money for his many military campaigns without challenging his authority. In 1275, Edward introduced the first regular customs duties on exports of wool and leather – soon to be the most valuable taxes in the royal portfolio. He also established wool markets – staples – at Dordrecht, Brabant, Malines, and Antwerp that benefited London merchants immensely. St. Omer followed in 1313, Calais in 1363. He even ruled the City directly from 1284 to 1297 but was eventually forced to relent. London's privileges were reconfirmed in the next reign by the weak Edward II (1307–1327). The new charter of 1319 decreed that only members of trade guilds (known as "livery companies" because of the ceremonial robes that their leading members wore) could trade in London. After Edward seemed to renege, Roger Mortimer (1287–1330) rebelled in 1326, seized the Tower, freed its prisoners, gave the keys to the citizens of London, and used the London mob to intimidate Parliament to demand the king's removal, which happened in 1327.

In short, because London played such a decisive role in the success or failure of rebellion, a king had far more to lose than did the City. When he kept Londoners' loyalty, he kept his crown. For example, during the Peasants' Revolt of 1381, a mob of countrymen and London craftsmen stormed and plundered Lambeth, Savoy Palace, and the Temple Church; freed the prisoners in the Marshalsea, Fleet, and Newgate Prisons; and beheaded lawyers, Flemish merchants, tax collectors, and the Archbishop of Canterbury. But the lord mayor of London, William Walworth (d. ?1386), stood by Richard II (1377–1399), raised the City militia, and at a parley with the rebel leader, Wat Tyler, dragged Tyler from his horse and stabbed him to death, effectively ending the rebellion. In 1399, Londoners, offended by another royal attack on City privileges, turned on Richard and supported his deposition by Henry Bolingbroke, Duke of Lancaster (lived 1367–1413; reigned as Henry IV 1399–1413).

During the Wars of the Roses (1455–1485), London tended to support whichever regime (Lancastrian or Yorkist) was in power. But in 1461, Londoners closed their gates to Queen Margaret of Anjou (1430–1482), the ruthless leader of the Lancastrians, after their recent victory at Wakefield, and opened them to the Duke of York, who, by their acclamation, became King Edward IV. Once again, London could claim to have picked a king. A quarter century later, in the late summer of 1485, after the Yorkist Richard III (1483–1485) lost his crown in battle on Bosworth Field, the City fathers welcomed the victor, Henry Tudor, Earl of Richmond (1457–1509), now Henry VII (1485–1509), at Shoreditch with trumpets, poems, and a gift of 1,000 marks. Both moves proved shrewd, because Edward IV and Henry VII turned out to be strong, practical, and efficient monarchs whose respective peace policies meant lower taxes, safer loans, and healthier trade. Indeed, both Edward IV and Henry VII consulted with London merchants and government officials on fiscal matters and worked out favorable commercial agreements with continental powers. If the City's love affair with the Yorkists proved fleeting, that with the Tudors lasted to the end of the line.

Rebellion and riot were not the only challenges facing medieval Londoners and their rulers. Medieval sources complain of the usual urban problems of street violence, poverty, crime, prostitution, "the immoderate drinking of fools and the frequent fires."[7] Built mostly of wood, London suffered devastating fires in 1077, 1087, 1092, 1100, 1133, 1136, and 1212, when spectators crowding onto London Bridge to watch a conflagration in Southwark became victims themselves after the bridge caught fire. Some 3,000 are said to have died. London's food supply was generally reliable, but during the European famine of 1315–1317 Londoners were forced to eat their dogs. Undoubtedly the greatest disaster to befall medieval London was the Black Death, almost certainly some form of plague, spread along trade routes, which killed perhaps 15,000 people in a total metropolitan population of 45,000 from 1348 to 1349. Worse, the plague returned in 1361/62, 1368/69, and repeatedly thereafter until 1665 (see Chapter 8). Ironically, the resultant labor shortage yielded high wages and low prices for those who survived. Still, these catastrophes and the economic dislocation they brought did nothing to stabilize the political situation.

LONDON IN ENGLAND'S HISTORY 1550–1750

Things would not get any easier for London or the English people during the period of time covered by this book. Given London's obvious centrality to the national histories of England and the British Isles, and the importance of those wider histories for that of London, it should come as no surprise that they figure prominently in the following pages. Unfortunately, the history of Britain from 1550 to 1750 is far too complex to summarize in just a few pages, and we recommend perusal of one of the many book-length studies on the subject.[8] The following section is intended to identify, briefly, some of the larger national themes with which the history of early modern London intersects. (Readers already familiar with these themes might wish to move on to the next section.)

In 1550, England was ruled by the boy king Edward VI (1547–1553), the heir for whom Henry VIII (1509–1547) had jettisoned his first wife and his allegiance to Rome. The larger-than-life figure of Henry VIII still loomed over Whitehall, Westminster, and the kingdom, because in seeking his divorce; having Parliament make him Supreme Head of the Church; driving the Pope out of England; making war on France, Scotland, and Ireland; spending money that he did not have to do so; offending the remaining Catholic powers (the Holy Roman Empire and Spain); and forcing his people to choose between their loyalty to him and that to their faith, Henry left for his successors a raft of unresolved issues. As a result, for the next 200 years the English would debate the questions of sovereignty (i.e., the relative power of the king and Parliament), religion (Catholic vs. Protestant), foreign policy (England vs. France, Spain, Scotland, and Ireland, but also how far England should commit to foreign entanglements generally), finance (how to pay for the Crown and its wars), and local control (center vs. locality, court vs. City, capital vs. the rest of the British Isles and eventually the colonies).

The religious issue was probably the most fraught. Henry's reformation affected London in particular immediately and dramatically. First, the nature of worship changed (see Chapter 4). Henry himself vacillated between mandating reform and traditional, if nonpapal, Catholic liturgy in a series of injunctions and articles. His son's regime embraced Protestantism wholeheartedly, repealing the heresy laws, encouraging the eradication of elaborate church decoration, abolishing saints' days and Lenten traditions, continuing his father's dissolution and confiscation of Church lands, and requiring attendance at Sunday services in English according to the new *Book of Common Prayer* by Acts of Uniformity in 1549 (2 & 3 Edw. VI, c. 1) and 1552 (5 & 6 Edw. VI, c. 1). These measures were for the most part welcomed by Londoners, many of whom had, even before the Reformation, embraced reformist heresies, like Lollardy. Protestantism took root in London because it was a port and therefore among the first places that Protestant books and travelers alighted. Perhaps also because Protestantism emphasized literacy and individual interpretation of Scripture, which appealed to a city full of literate merchants, many Londoners embraced reform. Moreover, Protestant aristocrats benefited from the opening up of the London land market (see Chapters 1 and 4). But others stayed loyal to the Old Faith. The result was a parish-by-parish struggle over liturgy and practice mediated but never really controlled by the Bishop of London, a royal appointee who, in the words of one incumbent, "is always to be pitied."[9]

Because Henry's children were raised in divergent faith traditions and the first two had short reigns, late sixteenth-century England was buffeted between Lutheran Protestantism under Edward; a reversion to Catholicism under Mary I (1553–1558); then a compromise Church of England under Elizabeth I (1558–1603). Mary enforced the return to Rome by burning 237 men and 52 women at the stake, many of them adolescents, most of humble background, who refused to conform. The decision to burn about fifty of them at Smithfield, London's meat market, might sound strange to us, but markets, being large, open-air public places, were traditional venues for exemplary punishment in front of many witnesses. Because London had embraced Protestantism at a higher rate than the rest of the country, Mary wanted to make a point by striking at the heart of heresy. Had she lived longer or her marriage to Philip II (1556–1598) of Spain produced an heir, England might have stayed Catholic and the Protestant martyrs largely forgotten, in the same way that the popular imagination has forgotten the hundreds of Catholics executed by her successor, Elizabeth. Instead, Mary I died childless in 1558, was succeeded by her Protestant sister, and branded in the popular imagination as "Bloody Mary." It is perhaps little wonder that, at her death and Elizabeth's accession on November 17, 1558, the bells rang in London.

Between 1559 and 1563, Parliament named Elizabeth I chief Governor of the Church of England, mandated a Protestant theology and an English-language liturgy, but retained a Catholic-style episcopal hierarchy and much traditional Catholic ritual. Most Englishmen and women accepted the compromise settlement, but reform-minded Protestants, many of them London merchants and tradesmen, would never abide by the "mingle-mangle" of Protestant theology and Catholic practice. Seeking to "purify" the English Church of its Catholic vestiges, they would be excoriated by opponents as "Puritans" and intermittently persecuted for the next century by the Crown and Church establishment. Still, most Puritans stayed within the Church of England before 1642, hoping to complete its reformation. They dominated many City parishes, most notably St. Antholin Budge Row, St. Saviour Southwark, and St. Stephen Coleman Street. Where they could not get the vicar whom they wanted, they endowed lectureships for Puritan preachers.

On the opposite side of the religious spectrum, die-hard Catholics, encouraged by the papacy, the Catholic powers, and from the 1580s, a clandestine Jesuit missionary movement, shunned Church of England services. They came to be seen as a potential "fifth column" by the Crown, their Protestant neighbors, and the Catholic powers. Some did engage in plots against the state, most infamously the Guy Fawkes Gunpowder Plot to blow up the royal family at the state opening of Parliament in 1605. This discredited the loyalty of the rest and led to a series of harsh laws levying heavy fines against Catholic "recusants" for missing Church of England services, and making it treason to be a Catholic priest in England. This legislation eventually drove the Old Faith underground. These tensions, plus London merchants' aggressive moves to break into Spanish trade with the New World, led to war with Spain from 1585 to 1604 and a thwarted invasion attempt by the Spanish Armada in 1588. The Spanish also tried to destabilize Ireland, nominally ruled from London but still Catholic and often rebellious, to use it as a staging ground for another such invasion.

In 1603, the Virgin Queen Elizabeth, last of the Tudor line, died. This brought the Stuarts, already kings of Scotland, to the English throne in the persons of James I (reigned in England 1603–1625) and Charles I (1625–1649). Their high notion of the royal prerogative, spendthrift ways, High Church anti-Puritanism, and peace policy with the Catholic powers alienated many of their English and Scottish subjects. This was especially true in London, where Puritan merchants, tradesmen, apprentices, and servants, encouraged by Puritan preachers and pamphleteers, came to believe that the Stuarts were engaging in a popish absolutist plot to subvert the English constitution in church and state (see Chapter 7). The eventual result was a series of Civil Wars (1637–1660) in which London was the decisive source of manpower and wealth on the anti-Royalist or Parliamentary side. After the defeat and execution of Charles I in 1649, England tried a republic ruled by Parliament, the Commonwealth (1649–1653); then a Protectorate under Oliver Cromwell (1653–1658). The Commonwealth in particular frightened the landed ruling elite by experimenting with a free press and religious toleration. Its dissolution by the army and replacement by General Cromwell in 1653 marked a more authoritarian solution to England's troubles. For a few years the Protector gave England efficient government, a Puritan social policy, and an aggressive Protestant foreign policy that pleased London merchants with successful trade wars against the Spanish and the Dutch. But these came at the cost of high taxes, oppressive surveillance by a military state (the Major Generals), and a draconian policy toward the Catholic majority in Ireland. Following Cromwell's death in 1658, a period of instability ensued, culminating in

1660 when London crowds demanded the Restoration of the Stuarts in the person of Charles II (1660–1685). Immediately following the Restoration, a High Church religious settlement was imposed that drove Puritans from public life in revenge for their disloyalty during the Civil Wars. No longer in a position to "purify" a church from which they had been expelled, they would henceforth be known as Dissenters.

Charles II was a wily and charismatic figure, capable of disguising his attractions to absolutism, Catholicism, and Louis XIV's (1643–1715) France with wit and charm. Unfortunately, his inability to father a legitimate heir meant that he would be succeeded by his far less charming brother, James, Duke of York (1633–1701), from 1672 a professed Roman Catholic. Between 1678 and 1681 a group of antiabsolutist, anti-Catholic, and anti-French (or pro-Parliament, pro-Dissenter, and pro-Dutch) politicians in Parliament, known as the Whigs, formed England's first modern political party. In what came to be known as the *Exclusion Crisis*, they argued that Parliament had both the right and the duty to bar Catholics from the throne. They also favored freedom of conscience for Dissenters. In response, a second party, the Tories, defended the hereditary succession, strong monarchy, the religious monopoly of the Church of England, and the Stuarts' pro-French foreign policy. Both parties relied heavily on propaganda from London printing presses and support from London mobs (see Chapter 7), but in the end Charles refused to countenance disinheriting his brother. At his death in 1685, James became King James II (1685–1688) and almost immediately began to alarm his subjects by advocating toleration for Catholics. In 1688, at the invitation of several prominent peers, William of Orange (1650–1702), James's son-in-law by his daughter Mary (1662–1694) and the Protestant Stadholder of the Netherlands, invaded, ostensibly to protect the rights of the Church of England. James fled to France, and Parliament asked William (1689–1702) and Mary (1689–1694) to assume the Crown in what came to be known as the Glorious Revolution of 1688/89 (see Chapter 7).

The Glorious Revolution solved most of the issues first raised by Henry VIII. First, England would remain High Church Protestant but tolerate Puritan Dissenters. Second, it would be a constitutional monarchy: the king remained powerful, but his financial and diplomatic situation now dictated that he would have to call Parliament annually and choose ministers backed by a majority of its members. Indeed, when push came to shove over matters like filling the throne, Parliament was now sovereign, diverting the succession away from James's Catholic heirs toward the

Protestant Hanoverian family by the Act of Settlement of 1701 (12 & 13 Will. III, c. 2). Because Louis XIV supported a Jacobite restoration and Catholic emancipation, the Revolution would solve the foreign policy question by precipitating two wars with France: the Nine Years' War (1688–1697) and the War of the Spanish Succession (1702–1713). Because Louis was the wealthiest ruler of his time, Parliament, working closely with London's financial community, had to solve the Crown's financial problems with innovative financial strategies and practices (the Financial Revolution), tapping England's growing commercial wealth to raise the money to defeat him (see Chapter 2). In the end, London's financial might combined with the generalship of John Churchill, Duke of Marlborough (1650–1722) brought Louis to a final settlement in 1713 by the Treaty of Utrecht. At Utrecht, the Sun King promised to recognize the Protestant Succession (i.e., that Parliament could choose the Protestant George, Elector of Hanover [1660–1727] over the Catholic "Pretender" Prince James [1688–1766], son of James II), and England won important colonies and trading posts at Gibralter, the eastern coast of Canada, and in the Caribbean, as well as the right to supply slaves to the Spanish colonies of the New World (the *Assiento*). These gains extended the empire ruled from Westminster, laid the foundations for English commercial prosperity, and cemented London's domination of European commerce for a generation. The British victory also helped to perpetuate the misery of the Catholic Irish (who had supported the Jacobites in the first war) and the atrocity of the slave trade.

In the meantime, when the last Stuart, Queen Anne (1702–1714), died in 1714, she was duly succeeded by Parliament's nominee, George of Hanover, who became George I (1714–1727). He and his son George II (1727–1760) presided over a relatively stable era of high politics in which one minister, Sir Robert Walpole (1676–1745; prime minister 1720–1742), and one party, the Whigs, controlled the state and its vast fields of patronage. Walpole stayed in power for more than two decades because he had the support of the king and the Church of England, maintained popular polices such as peace and low taxes, and used that patronage to buy support in Parliament and in the countryside. He fell in 1742, in part because he mishandled the War of the Austrian Succession (1740–1748). This war saw one last, failed attempt at a Jacobite restoration, "the '45," led by James II's grandson, Bonnie Prince Charlie (1720–1788). In this and the subsequent Seven Years' War (1756–1763), England's constitutional settlement and way of life were less at stake than the balance of power in Europe and the control of North American and Indian trade. These wars would conclude by the Treaty of Paris (1763), in a resounding British victory and London's dominance of those trades.

By the end of the period covered by this book, the questions left over from the Tudors had largely been settled. New questions, about government reform, the political power of the increasingly wealthy middle class, the relationship of government to the economy, how and whether England should hang on to its American colonies, the morality of the slave trade, the best treatment of the poor, the role of popular and print culture, and others, would come to the fore in the later eighteenth century, and again they would be debated and often settled in London. But those are issues for another book.

London's Historiography

London has always been a subject of fascination. In recent years, a number of especially fine books on its history have appeared: Peter Ackroyd, *London: the Biography* (2003); Roy Porter, *London: a Social History* (1994); John Russell, *London* (1997); and above all in size and achievement, Stephen Inwood, *A History of London* (1998). But these books take the long *durée*. Early modern London has of late been left to studies that are much narrower in chronology and scope, like Peter Earle, *A City Full of People: Men and Women of London 1650–1750* (1994) and Maureen Waller, *1700: Scenes from London Life* (2000), both of which concentrate on the early years of the eighteenth century. Older studies are perhaps more successful at integrating London's demographic, economic, political, and social history with its rich store of anecdote across a longer period, notably M. D. George, *London Life in the Eighteenth Century* (1925; reprinted 1984); Dorothy Marshal, *Dr. Johnson's London* (1968); and George Rudé, *Hanoverian London 1714–1808* (1971). The most recent of these books was published more than 40 years ago, however. Since then there has been an explosion of fine work on London, in articles, specialized monographic studies, and collections of scholarly essays (see Bibliography).

As with the history of Britain generally, much of the scholarly work on early modern London rarely crosses the mid-seventeenth century divide. This has produced two very different historiographies. For the last half-century, social and political historians of early modern London to 1660 have been exercised by the question "Was it stable?" Taking their cue from contemporaries' complaints about their city, in particular the regretful nostalgia of John Stow's (1524/25–1605) *Survey of London* (1598, expanded 1603), some historians have emphasized the challenges posed by sixteenth-century religious change and early seventeenth-century political crisis; the antagonism between Puritan reformers and both elite and popular culture; London's unprecedented physical and demographic growth; the absence of a municipal government with jurisdiction over the whole; the burdens placed on local institutions as the city ballooned; and the alleged breakdown in the kind of human interaction and neighborly assistance that we associate with the village community. Certainly, early modern Londoners did feel themselves overwhelmed at times by disease, crime, dirt, noise, bad air, and above all, people – foreign and domestic, vagrants, con men, big-bellied women, scolds, and orphans. This has led some scholars to portray a London that was always on the point of careening out of control, with apprentice ready to rise against master, native against foreigner, vagrant against householder, and subject against king. For the endless stream of migrants to London, it could be an especially cold and unwelcoming place. In this view, for most Londoners generally, life in the overcrowded and dirty city was nothing short of an urban Hobbesian state of nature, "nasty, poor, brutish and short."

Other historians paint a different London. They point out that the streets of London did not erupt in revolution prior to 1642 and that there were plenty of institutions to link Londoners together and help them get through life. They would emphasize that even in times of crisis – for example, the food shortages of the 1590s – Londoners rioted, but on a limited scale, mostly seeking to reinvigorate rather than overturn civic customs and institutions. The governors of London knew that they had to keep basic services, like the food supply, in operation, and for the most part they succeeded. They also maintained a loose network of hospitals and collected and distributed the Poor Rates – which really did provide crucial assistance to many of the most needy. Admittedly, the authorities sometimes used social policy as a hammer against behaviors and groups that they did not like, but these historians would also point out that the widespread participation of citizen and noncitizen, men and even women, in the city's official life implied a strong degree of consent for such policies. In a national context, Tudor and early Stuart London was largely loyal to the Crown until the 1640s, and even in rebellion it might be said to have followed archipelago-wide trends as much as it set them. In any case, not all Londoners broke with the king during the Civil Wars and Revolution of the seventeenth century, and even those who did continued to obey their lord mayor and aldermen, to serve their parishes, to trade, and to look after their poor. There were many reasons for this fundamental stability: members of the City elite were nearly all of the same religious tendencies (godly Protestants of varying sorts); early modern London was not riven by factions *à la* Renaissance Florence; the membership of competing organizations (e.g., trading companies, livery companies) tended to overlap; many of their officers had risen from humbler ranks, and they made some attempt to attend to the concerns of householders, journeymen, and apprentices. In short, paternalism was not dead yet in early modern London. One might recall further that London's size and economic vitality allowed for new opportunities, second starts, and the kind of social mobility that, when upward, can do much to reconcile people to their lot.

It is perhaps ironic that historians of the period after 1660, when London really did betray signs of instability – more growth, greater economic and social polarization, an increase in political and religious tensions, more fear about crime, more riots, higher death rates – have more or less lost interest in the question of whether London was internally stable. Rather, although providing plenty of examples of conflict and disturbance, scholars of the long eighteenth century seem to view London's demographic and economic expansion as a sign of fundamental stability. They are more interested in the city's general prosperity and impact on national trends in politics, society, and culture than they are in signs of collapse. All agree that London's financial and commercial success had a profound effect on the economy of Britain and the world. They also emphasize the rise of a new kind of elite urban culture – polite, refined, and cosmopolitan. At the same time, even as older democratic institutions like the wardmote declined, ordinary Londoners nevertheless came to have a stronger voice in the government of the nation and metropolis through voting, crowd action, and their participation in an increasingly public sphere of discourse through the print culture that was read and debated in coffeehouses and clubs. Despite the onslaught of plague, fire, and war, after the Restoration London authors often wrote optimistically about their city, culminating in the celebration that is John Strype's *Survey* (1720; expanded 1754). Perhaps in part because intellectuals like John Graunt (1620–1674) and Sir William Petty (1623–1687) were beginning to grapple with London's actual numbers, the many maps and guidebooks that sprang up after the turn of the eighteenth century display a growing confidence in the place, increasing pride in its greatness, and even boosterism. Thus Robert Seymour's

A *Survey of the Cities of London and Westminster, Borough of Southwark, and Parts Adjacent* (1734) begins:

> London is the Metropolis of Great Britain, the Seat of her Monarchs, the largest in Extent, the fairest built, the most populous, and best inhabited City in Europe, or, perhaps, in the whole World; nor yields it to any in the Advantages of Trade and Commerce.[10]

Even when an eighteenth-century author like Daniel Defoe (?1660–1731) called London a "monster," the allegation was often couched amid words of grudging admiration.

Admittedly, not every historian celebrates the energy, size, and wealth of eighteenth-century London. Historians of poverty, crime, and riot take a more jaded view. Marxists in particular see a city of exploiters and exploited, gripped by steady, if low-level, class conflict, ready to come apart not perhaps in citywide revolution, but in personal rebellions of violence against proprietors and property. This brings us to a related debate about London's diversity. Contemporary writers stressed not only London's growth, but its increasing lack of unity and coherence. Early in the eighteenth century, Joseph Addison (1672–1719) argued in the *Spectator* that London was

> . . . an Aggregate of various Nations distinguished from each other by their respective Customs, Manners, and Interests . . . the Inhabitants of St. James's . . . are a distinct people from those of Cheapside, who are likewise removed from those of the Temple on the one side, and those of Smithfield on the other, by several Climates and Degrees in their way of thinking and conversing together.[11]

A half-century later, James Boswell (1740–1795) agreed but divided the city by vocation and avocation, not geography:

> I have often amused myself with thinking how different a place London is to different people. They, whose narrow minds are contracted to the consideration of some one particular pursuit, view it only through that medium. A politician thinks of it merely as the seat of government in its different departments; a grazier, as a vast market for cattle; a mercantile man, as a place where a prodigious deal of business is done upon 'Change; a dramatick enthusiast, as the grand scene of theatrical entertainments; a man of pleasure, as an assemblage of taverns, and the great emporium for ladies of easy virtue.

This raises the question of whether the title of this book is based on a false assumption. Perhaps there were no Londoners at all but, rather, Cheapsiders, Templers, East Enders, West Enders, Thames-sidemen, courtiers, Parliament men, merchants, servants, men and women of pleasure, pickpockets, shop-lifts, coal heavers, milk maids, etc., etc. But as with the contemporary term *Puritan*, people in early modern England might have had trouble defining the place, but they knew London when they saw it. We are reassured that Boswell concludes his dissection of London's diversity by reasserting the metropolis as a category of analysis: "But the intellectual man is struck with it, as comprehending the whole of human life in all its variety, the contemplation of which is inexhaustible."[12] Reassured, and as we embark on our attempt to master what London cabbies call "the Knowledge," humbled.

THEMES AND ARGUMENTS

The book's dates demarcate its themes. In 1550, London was just emerging from the first stage of the Reformation. The Tudor state was mature and beginning to fund exploration and charter trading companies. Above all, late-medieval London was on the cusp of the demographic expansion that would transform it by several orders of magnitude into the great economic and cultural engine of early modern England. By 1750, that engine had rebuilt the metropolis into an imperial capital, an international *entrepôt*, a cornucopia of culture, and a vast melting pot of humanity. London would continue to be all those things into the present day. By 1750, however, it faced economic competition from the Atlantic ports of Great Britain and cultural and social competition from Edinburgh and several provincial capitals, all of which took the metropolis as a model. Although London remained dominant, many of its attractions were no longer exclusive.

Between those two dates, we argue for two principal themes: (1) how the sleepy port and court town of a second-rate power on the fringes of Europe became an imperial capital, a world city, and a harbinger of modernity; and (2) how at least 6,000 to 8,000 immigrants a year came to London, acclimated themselves to it, built it into a great metropolis, and became Londoners. Along the way, they developed institutions and habits of mind that we tend to find familiar and congenial: personal liberty, equality, democracy, and their hallmarks economic and religious freedom, freedom of assembly and a free press; cosmopolitanism;

secularism; pragmatism and even a measure of feminism; social fluidity based on merit and wealth; a value for practicality, rational proof, and scientific knowledge over the dictates of tradition and religious dogma; and a critical attitude toward authority. Admittedly, in 1550 these hallmarks of modern life barely existed in London if at all, but by 1750 they had all been tried and many were fully established, if not unchallenged, as the norm in the great conurbation on the Thames. In particular, in a society that privileged hierarchy and inequality, the trend of London was toward equality, because its inhabitants old and new had relatively expansive opportunities to fashion themselves as they willed, and they were more likely to be judged there on their merits than anywhere else in Britain. In short, London was the freest place in the archipelago, if not the continent.

These themes would seem to fit comfortably within a larger Whiggish narrative of the expansion and development of the modern British constitutional, military, and commercial state, but there was nothing inevitable about London's, let alone Britain's, increasing prominence, power, wealth, or modernity, nor were the opportunities and benefits of growth distributed evenly in metropolitan society. This book thus complicates the picture of progress by addressing the demographic, economic, and cultural consequences of the rise of modern London, which many contemporaries and some historians saw as parasitical. Admittedly, by addressing the hopes, fears, surprises, and experiences of London's people, by recording how they faced and overcame the crises of disease, fire, crime, poverty, and war, it will be impossible to avoid entirely some celebration of that combination of proud humility, recalcitrant loyalty, and spirited resilience known to all the world as the Londoner.

1. London in 1550

*O*ur contemplation of London must begin, as London began, at the river.[1] The River Thames is a slow-moving and rather murky body of water, flowing west to east, about a quarter to an eighth of a mile wide as it passes through the city. To this day, the sinewy thread of the Thames is London's most notable topographical feature, the curving line around which the metropolis orientates itself. As we have seen, this was not by chance. The Romans founded London in imitation of their own great capital city, so that, like Rome, London sits on its river at exactly the spot where it narrows enough to bridge (see Map 1). That confluence of west–east river and south–north bridge made London both a military choke point and an economic funnel long before our arrival sometime in 1550.

THE APPROACH FROM THE WEST AND NORTH

But in 1550, the river is not how most new Londoners come to town. Although it is possible to get there by boat, it is much more likely that we would arrive by land – on horseback if a gentleman or a wealthy merchant or their wives, on foot or on the back of a cart if a poor migrant looking for work – along dusty roads from all points of the compass. Perhaps the most spectacular land approach to London is the way Dick Whittington might have come from Gloucestershire, from the north and west, down the Great North Road through Hertfordshire to Finchley, down Hampstead Heath and Highgate Hill (both a hill and the road down it, although the latter was not laid out until 1386, a generation after Whittington's boyhood trek), to Islington, through the wall at Aldersgate into Aldersgate Street (see Map 2). If taking this route, we would naturally pause at the top of Highgate Hill, for this spot affords us our first glimpse of the great city. Looking south and slightly east, the first sight of England's capital would be astonishing to anyone from a tiny village. First, we spy the horizontal spectacle of the river, a silver-green snake undulating from horizon west to horizon east, dividing the city in two. On closer inspection, we realize that most of the city lies on our side of the river. Looking up across it to the smaller community of Southwark on the opposite or south bank, we see that the two are connected by London Bridge. The keen-eyed observer will make out houses and shops on the bridge and ships and barges in the river, reminding us that this is the commercial crossroads of the nation.

Lowering our gaze to the more crowded northern bank, we see that London's skyline is dominated by one great feature, bracketed by two smaller ones. The city's central vertical profile is dwarfed by the astonishing height of the spire of St. Paul's Cathedral, more than 460 feet tall, the highest in England. In 1550 that spire had not long to greet us, because it would be struck by lightning and burn within a dozen years, leaving a far stubbier cathedral profile. If we imagine our arrival on a sunny day, however, the light glints off the steeple as if it were a sword point. Surrounding it, we begin to perceive the towers and spires of more than a hundred medieval churches, all crammed against each other in the square mile within the walls that forms London's heart. Looking along the river on either side of this conglomeration, in 1550 we can clearly see where London begins and ends: to our left, the assemblage of houses and shops drops off past the Tower of London, the city's eastern "bookend." Farther left beyond this, where today the East End bustles, we see open fields where Londoners grow food, raise cattle, and delight themselves with strolling or archery. Moving our gaze left to right, we see again the square mile of the walled city, and then to the west, a few large buildings outside it; beyond that a narrow road along the river lined with noble palaces called the Strand; and finally, as the river curves south away from us, on the southwestern horizon to our extreme right, the impressive but isolated complex of buildings forming London's western "bookend" at Westminster: the Abbey, minus the as yet unbuilt towers that modern visitors know; Westminster Hall, low and long; and Westminster Palace, narrow and vertical.

Above all of this we might notice a hazy cloud of smoke from London's many wood fires. That cloud will become thicker and darker over the next two centuries as the metropolis expands and turns to coal for heat. The cloud, like the river, drifts east, because both the prevailing winds and the current flow that way. This will be crucial for the city's development: because wind and water thus carry London's smoke and sewage eastward, its wealthiest residents will gravitate west, upwind and upstream. That is why the West End will always be the smart end of town. That is also one reason why, from its very beginnings over the next century, the East End will be considered poor and relatively undesirable.

THE APPROACH FROM THE EAST AND SOUTH

To get a closer look at the city in 1550, we might take a different approach, from the east or south, through the borough of Southwark. Southwark consists of five manors (i.e., Paris Garden, the Clink, the Guildable Manor, the King's Manor, and the Great Liberty Manor). The first two of these are very poor, filled with people who make their living on the river or from human weakness, and fall under the jurisdiction of the county of Surrey. The more prosperous last three manors have just been purchased by the City of London in 1550, adding almost one-half again to the size of the lord mayor's jurisdiction and forming a foothold on the south bank of the Thames, London's 26th ward, Bridge Ward Without. Before this, Southwark lay largely outside of City control, which might help to explain why, over the next half-century, it became the home to several underground religious communities, both Anabaptist and Catholic, or why long before that it was the venue for a variety of popular recreations, where Londoners went for a good – or slightly illicit – time.

From the east or south we approach Southwark by the Old Kent Road, an ancient track built over the old Roman highway of Watling Street, terminating in Borough High Street. Because this is the main entry point to London from Surrey or Kent, the High Street is "a place of great receipt of people and trade,"[2] full of inns and hostelries where we can get a bed, a meal, or a drink. The most famous are the Tabard and the Bear at Bridge Foot. Both have been around since the fourteenth century and are recognized local landmarks. The Tabard is renowned as the starting point for Chaucer's fictional Canterbury pilgrims; although fallen on hard times by 1550, it would be remodeled at the end of the sixteenth century, playing up the literary connection. We will visit the Bear momentarily. Southwark is busy with road and river business, but it is not very big in 1550: we are only a few paces from the Thames. This confirms what we observed at Highgate: that London did not develop equally, like Budapest, on both sides of the river. As its name implies, Southwark was regarded as an appendage: founded in Roman times, its name literally means "south work," that is, a complex to the south of the main event.

The greatest landmark in Southwark is Southwark Cathedral. There has been a cathedral on this site since the seventh century, and a monastery since the ninth century, dedicated to St. Mary Overie. The current Gothic building was started about 1220 to replace a previous structure destroyed by fire. Just a few years before our visit, in 1539, Henry VIII had dissolved the monastery, confiscated the church, and reorganized it as St. Saviour's parish church. During the next century the church fabric will decay, but in 1550 the tower of St. Saviour's offers one of the greatest views in England: even more spectacular than the long-range one from Highgate Hill, it would be engraved in panoramas of London by Claes Visscher (1587–1652) in 1616 (see Illustration 1.1), and Wenceslaus Hollar (1607–1677) in 1647. These would portray many of the same principal features we see in 1550, with the exception of St. Paul's truncated spire and new building filling in many of the once open fields beyond London's ancient wall. Climbing to the top and looking north, we see what we saw from Highgate but up close and from the other (southern) side: across the river, the north bank is all steeples and towers; below us, the south lies relatively undeveloped and flat. Downriver to our right, we see the curve of the Thames around the Isle of Dogs, and in it ships of many sizes from great merchantmen to the small barges that Londoners hail as taxicabs. As trade grew in the mid-sixteenth century, so did the shipping infrastructure downriver to the east – docks and shipyards, carpenters' and sailmakers' shops, alehouses and brothels increasingly line the banks to our right, engulfing villages like Bermondsey and Rotherhithe on the south bank; Wapping, Shadwell, Limehouse, and Blackwall on the north. These riverside settlements will also be the preferred location for messy, smelly, but necessary industries like brewing, brickmaking, and tanning. Shifting our gaze upriver right to left, we see the battlements of the Tower of London commanding the Thames. Then, directly before us, the City within the walls, a mere square mile filled with spires and turrets, dominated by St. Paul's. Slightly to the left are the noble and bishops' palaces that we saw earlier from Highgate. Finally, on our left as the river curves south, Westminster Abbey, Palace, and Hall. Just before them, right on the river and therefore not noticed from Highgate, we see a low-lying complex of buildings: Whitehall Palace, the seat of the royal court, confiscated by Henry VIII from Cardinal Wolsey in 1529.

Continuing to face west (upriver) but lowering our gaze to the south bank on which St. Saviour's stands, we spy a smaller palace on the southwestern horizon. Lambeth Palace is the London residence of the Archbishop of Canterbury. It still stands in the twenty-first century, the last of the bishops' palaces along the Thames. Following the bank back around the curve and further lowering our gaze to the western foreground, in 1550 we see before us about 100 acres of swampy riverbank, Paris Garden. Originally Church land, it was confiscated by Henry VIII and eventually awarded to the bailiff of Southwark, William Baseley (fl. 1542). He turned it into an outdoor bowling alley/gambling den. Over the next two centuries, Paris Garden would evolve into London's first pleasure garden, a sort of amusement park for grown-ups, where thick foliage covered all sorts of nocturnal activities.

Lowering our gaze still further, we see more former Church land turned to profane use, a manor recently run by the Bishop of Winchester called "the Clink." Its main street, running parallel to the river, Bankside, has been lined with brothels since Roman times – the notorious Bankside stews. During the Middle Ages they were owned and regulated by the reverend bishop, whose own riverside palace sits conveniently nearby; indeed, south bank prostitutes were called "Winchester geese." Because the idea was to contain vice in one place outside the City walls and use the wages of sin for the charitable work of the Church, the good bishop drew up rules and limited opening hours. Among those charitable works was St. Thomas's Hospital, just off of Borough High Street, partly endowed by Dick Whittington and well known for treating poor people, including the Winchester geese. Thus, Henry VIII's reformist minister Thomas Cromwell (c. 1485–1540) referred to it as "the bawdy hospital of St. Thomas in Southwark."[3] Just south of the stews was the Clink Prison: misbehaving customers could be put "in the Clink." The arrangement worked well until Henry VIII closed the stews in 1546, a few years before our visit. Londoners found their services indispensable, and they would reopen by 1600; indeed, the city's most famous early seventeenth-century brothel, the Holland's Leaguer, would be located here.

Because it was former Church land, the Clink formed a "liberty." A liberty usually began as part of an ecclesiastical estate (in this case, that of the Bishop of Winchester), where civil law did not apply. Even after dissolution and confiscation by the Crown, a liberty's privileges remained untouchable by civil authorities, except as the sovereign allowed. There were twenty-four such sanctuaries complicating government and law enforcement in Tudor London, four of them in Southwark. To give another example, nearby, a half-mile to the south of Bankside, is Suffolk Place, where Henry VIII established a royal mint. The mint would be torn down in 1557, but the site remained a liberty associated with sanctuary for debtors into the eighteenth century. In fact, the Crown did appoint constables, and from 1608, Justices of the Peace (JPs) to address criminal matters in several liberties on the north bank, but even there the City still had trouble enforcing civil statutes and collecting taxes.

Just to the south of the stews is another dubious landmark of south bank frivolity, the Bankside Bear Garden. From at least 1546, when Henry VIII himself paid a visit, bears and other wild animals were tormented by dogs for the sport of jaded Londoners. Two generations later, the Bear Garden would be joined by London's first outdoor theaters: the Rose (1587), the Swan (actually in Paris Garden, 1596), and the Globe (1598). This further reinforced the reputation of the south bank as a center for culture of which the authorities did not approve: plays were not always respectful of authority, diverted apprentices and journeymen from their trades, and brought together large crowds that might thereby spread disease or sedition. On play days, the theaters would raise flags, easily seen from across the river. At this signal, Londoners of all descriptions, from nobles to tradesmen and apprentices – the notorious "groundlings," who paid only a penny to see a play – would abandon their work or other pleasures, cross London Bridge, or take barges landing at Paris Garden stairs. After the play one could have a drink in Paris Garden itself. Although the pleasure garden and the theaters would be closed by Parliament in 1642, some form of pleasure garden, most famously the New Spring Garden established at Vauxhall in 1660, would continue to exist on this side of the river until 1859. In other words, throughout our period, if you wanted a slightly racy time, you headed for the south bank.

RIVER, BRIDGE, AND DOCKS

In most other respects it was the east–west axis, not the north–south, which has meant the most to Londoners. Because the commercial London stage does not yet exist in 1550, and because our interest is scholarly, we must cross the river and explore the northern bank. The obvious way to do that might seem to be to take London Bridge, the only land route across the river until 1750, stretching north from just below our gaze at Southwark Cathedral. The stone structure before us dates back to 1176, a replacement for earlier models previously burned. It consists of nineteen arches, a drawbridge, and a gate on the Southwark side. Those arches create treacherous rapids and two pools in the river, the Upper Pool above London Bridge to the west, the Lower Pool below it to the east. Because the drawbridge has not worked properly all this century, the heart of the port of London is that second, Lower Pool. This is where most of the big ships moor and unload their cargoes into barges and wherries for transport to the docks on the north bank. In 1599, half a century after our visit, Thomas Platter (1574–1628) "beheld one large galley next the other the whole city's length from St. Katherine's suburb [just east of the Tower] to the bridge, some hundred vessels in all, nor did I ever behold such large ships in one port in all my life."[4] Writing in 1586, William Camden (1551–1623) was more poetic: "A man would say, that seeth the shipping there, that it is, as it were, a very wood of trees disbranched to make glades and let in light, so shaded it is with masts and sails."[5]

Because even in the Middle Ages real estate in London was at a premium, by 1550 the bridge is almost completely covered with houses and shops. In 1550, another medieval custom renders the span gruesome: beginning in 1305, the severed heads of traitors were mounted on pikes at the battlements of the Southwark Gate to warn anyone entering London of the rigor of royal justice. In 1535, the heads of Sir Thomas More (1478–1535) and John, Cardinal Fisher (c. 1469–1535), executed for opposing Henry VIII's break from Rome, could be seen here; five years later, with justice that was poetic if nothing else, that of their nemesis Thomas Cromwell, Earl of Essex. The heads do not seem to have deterred many; London Bridge is a perennial traffic jam. Partly to avoid this traffic and partly to sample a method of travel more characteristic of London, we hail a barge instead. In 1550, both the north and south banks have numerous stairs and watergates leading down to the river. The greatest inhabitants of London – the king, the lord mayor, assorted bishops and nobles – own magnificent, elaborately decorated barges to transport them along the water. Witnessing the king's barge, banners flying, trumpets playing while he proceeds upriver to Hampton Court or downriver to Greenwich is one of the free entertainments to be had just by living in London. But being poor scholars we must hire.

Fortunately, every public watergate along the riverbank is lined with watermen advertising their trade in time-honored London fashion, by calling out "Oars! Oars!" – the early modern equivalent of a taxi rank. We book passage at a convenient set of steps behind the Bear at Bridge Foot, right at the Southwark end of London Bridge. Embarking, we try to avoid the thick mud as we step into the boat, settle in, and proceed in a stately fashion across the river, threading our way among the big ships, the 2,000 wherries counted by William Harrison (1535–1593) in 1577, and the swans, which are all personal property of the king: to injure one is a felony. As we pass under a canopy of bowsprits and stern galleries, it is fascinating to hear the languages and accents of traders from France, Germany, the Low Countries, Sweden, Denmark, and assorted coastal regions of the British Isles. But if the Thames is an aural delight, the sights and smells that accost us along the river are not so pleasant. It will not be until the nineteenth century that London constructs a modern underground sewer system. In the meantime, the runoff from London's garbage and nightsoil emptied into London's streets is carried by frequent rain into gullies and small streams like the Fleet River down to the Thames. As noted earlier, it flows east, as the Thames does. Poor Wapping! Poor Greenwich!

Thus, we are happy to reach the north bank. We dock just east of the Tower at St. Katherine's Stairs. Being poor scholars, we set out, like most Londoners, on foot. The prosperous mostly ride, and the streets are full of workmen's carts and work animals, and the sights, sounds, and smells they leave behind. There are as yet few private litters but no cabs or carriages. The coach would be introduced only in 1564; the hackney carriage by 1605, and the first cabstand in the Strand in 1634. By that time there would be 6,000 hackney coaches jamming the streets of London, and we could travel – slowly – from Temple Bar to Westminster for 12 pence. But in 1550 we have little choice but to walk down streets made foul with human and animal refuse. Heading west along Thames Street and looking left, we encounter the series of wharves that make London the greatest port in the British Isles. Of these, by far the most important is Billingsgate, where, according to John Stow, are unloaded "fish, both fresh and salt, shell fishes, salt, Orenges, Onions, and other fruits and rootes, wheate, Rie, and graine of diuers sorts for seruice of the Citie, and the parts of this Realme adioyning."[6] It would become more narrowly associated with fish and foul language in the seventeenth century. Beyond the bridge lies the Steelyard, where the Hanseatic merchants from North Germany live apart, governing themselves, issuing their own currency, avoiding contact with Londoners, and importing furs, timber, linen, iron, and fish. Their privileges and standoffishness were resented by English merchants, and within the year Edward VI will revoke them, although the Hansa would not be formally expelled until 1598. Because the Customs duties collected from trade are the mainstay of the royal revenue, it is important for the government to regulate the docks, in particular, to know which ship is docking where, and so seventeen legal docks will be established in 1559 between the Bridge and the Tower. Sitting just north of them on Thames Street is the Custom House, where the duty is collected. The medieval structure will burn down in 1559, again in 1666, and partially in 1714, but it will always be rebuilt on this same prime real estate.

Here, like the royal Customs officials, we can watch the commerce of England at work, as raw wool is loaded onto barges and lighters for ferrying out to the big ships, and fish, wine, timber, and finished cloth are unloaded from them. We also hear the hammering and sawing of carpenters and shipwrights mingled with the music of Cockney speech, see the stitching of sailmakers, and observe the whole panoply of maritime activity associated with any port. London's trade has been growing since a series of treaties made with continental powers in the late fifteenth century, in particular the Magnus Intercursus of 1496, which gave its merchants trading rights in Antwerp. As we have seen, London's maritime industry and docks grew with it, creeping east along the river to Wapping, Shadwell, Rotherhithe, and beyond. These communities would not penetrate inland until the end of the century, however, and so in 1550 St. Katherine's represents the eastern border of London's built-up area. Beyond it, market gardens grow food, and cattle graze where Whitechapel, Stepney, Hackney, Poplar, and Bethnal Green will soon stand. In 1605, John Stow remembered how, in his boyhood, East End lanes

> ... had on both sides fayre hedgerowes of Elme trees, with Bridges and easie stiles to passe ouer into the pleasant fieldes, very commodi-ous for Citizens therein to walke, shoote, and otherwise to recreate and refresh their dulled spirites in the sweete and wholesome ayre, which is nowe within few yeares made a continuall building throughout, of Garden houses, and small Cottages: and the fields on either side be turned into Garden plottes, teynter yardes, Bowling Allyes, and such like.... [7]

From the docks, we double back to St. Katherine's Street and ascend it to St. Katherine's Hospital. The hospital was founded by Queen Matilda (1103–1152), consort of Stephen in the twelfth century, to house the poor. In 1442, a new charter designated St. Katherine's a royal peculiar, responsible to only its own master and the lord chancellor of England. The hospital was dissolved at the Reformation, but the land remains a liberty, like the

Clink and the Mint, and despite having two JPs and two constables, it is more or less outside of civic jurisdiction. The embryonic East End is an arrival point for immigrants and is already one of the poorest and least desirable districts of London, "pestered with small tenements and homely cottages" according to Stow,[8] but it is also among the most colorful and industrious parts of mid-Tudor London.

TOWER AND WALL

Many of St. Katherine's inhabitants work at the Tower of London, and so like them we head west, navigating our way up Tower Hill through an area known as Tower Hamlets. From this commanding position, the Tower dominates this part of London visually and also aurally, when its guns thunder out on royal birthdays and other special occasions (see Illustration 1.2). It has grown significantly since William the Conqueror first erected the great keep with its four towers. By 1550, the Tower has many more buildings surrounded by a moat and a wall 18 feet high and 15 feet thick at its base. Here the king keeps his armory and a menagerie of wild animals first established in the thirteenth century and opened to the public by Queen Elizabeth. Under James I, the menagerie would grow to include eleven lions, two leopards, two mountain cats, three eagles, two owls, and a jackal.

Traditionally, English monarchs spent the nights before their coronation at the Tower; indeed, by 1550, this is nearly the only time that members of the royal family use it as a residence – at least voluntarily. Nevertheless, the Tower retains tremendous symbolic importance, indicating the king's relationship to London and so London's importance to the kingdom. Thus, in 1553, when Mary I rode a tide of Tudor loyalism to the crown over Lady Jane Grey (1537–1554), the first place that she visited on entering the city was the Tower. There, in what was surely a staged event, she freed several prominent Catholics imprisoned under her brother, including the Duke of Norfolk (1473–1554) and Bishop Stephen Gardiner (c. 1495–1555). Within a few weeks, their places would be taken by "Queen" Jane, her advisor the Duke of Northumberland (1504–1553), and, in March 1554, Princess Elizabeth, confined on suspicion of complicity in Wyatt's Rebellion (see Chapter 7). Indeed, the prisoner list under the Tudors and Stuarts was a veritable who's who: Queens Anne Boleyn and Catherine Howard (c. 1524–1542), charged with adultery; assorted Dukes of Norfolk and Somerset and Earls of Essex, charged mostly with treason; Archbishop Cranmer (1489–1556) for heresy; Cardinal Fisher, Sir Thomas More, and Archbishop Laud (1573–1645) for treason; and Sir Walter Raleigh (1554–1618) in 1592 after his seduction of Elizabeth Throckmorton (1565–c. 1647) and again in 1603 for trying to place Arabella Stuart (1575–1615) on the throne. Raleigh practically set up house in the upper floors of the Bloody Tower with his wife and son: he established a laboratory for experiments, wrote his *History of the World*, and was visited by Henry, Prince of Wales (1594–1612), before finally being executed in 1618. In general, royal executions took place before a small number of witnesses within the walls on Tower Green, but nobles and other traitors were dispatched before large crowds on Tower Hill, just to the northwest.

Because Tower Hill is within the City's wall, we reach its highest point by walking through the Postern Gate to the north of the Tower. In 1550, the Postern was one of the eight gates that funnel people and goods through London's ancient wall. Following the wall counterclockwise, they are the Postern Gate, Aldgate, Bishopsgate, Moorgate, Cripplegate, Aldersgate, Newgate, and Ludgate. Each gives its name to the street that passes through it and the district around it. Like the gate at the southern end of London Bridge, each is routinely shut at night: Tudor London has a curfew of 8 PM in winter and 9 PM in summer. By the early seventeenth century the gates might stay open until 10 PM; they reopened at 4 AM. Each has a guardhouse that, in the case of Newgate, had evolved into a notorious prison. As with London Bridge, the heads of less fortunate malefactors could end up on pikes as a warning to those who dared disturb the peace of the City. The wall itself is about 18 feet high and 6 to 9 feet thick, with battlements: a formidable challenge to an invader – or any drunk out past curfew!

Finding no execution to watch on Tower Hill, we seek a more edifying experience. Walking a few paces down Tower Street, we turn right at Seething Lane. The name of the street, an Old English word for *chaff*, from a grain market nearby, is disappointing, but because it is close to the Tower, in the 1580s it will be home to such luminaries as Sir Francis Walsingham (c. 1532–1590), Elizabeth's secretary of state and "spymaster general," and in the 1660s to the diarist Samuel Pepys (1633–1703). At the end of the street we come upon their parish church, a tiny but charming building, St. Olave Hart Street (see Illustration 1.3). Built in 1450 near the site of a medieval battle against the Danes, it is named for King Olaf II of Norway (reigned 1015–1028), who fought on the side of the Anglo-Saxons. This is one of only a handful of medieval churches to survive the

Reformation, the Fire, and the Blitz into the twenty-first century, although German bombs forced the reconstruction of much of the interior in the 1950s. In the twentieth century Sir John Betjeman (1906–1984) would call it "a country church in the world of Seething Lane."[9] On entering in 1550, we note the pointed arches and many side chapels for multiple masses characteristic of medieval churches. The large windows filling the east and west walls let in plenty of light, and at least some of the pre-Reformation wall and ceiling painting and statuary survives: overhead, we see a galaxy of painted stars. Hoping to finish our journey before the real stars rise and London goes dark, we exit back down Marcke Lane to Tower Street.

The City

We are now within the Roman walls of the old city, or as Londoners call it, with monumental self-centeredness, "the City." This area of just 330 acres is the core of the City of London, although as we have seen, the lord mayor's jurisdiction extends beyond the walls and indeed over the Thames for a few acres in every direction. Although everything beyond that grew from this core, communities like Shoreditch to the north and east, Clerkenwell to the north, Westminster to the west, and the downriver maritime settlements noted earlier are outside of the City proper and therefore outside of the lord mayor's jurisdiction. In 1550 they are instead administered by a hodgepodge of officials of the counties of Middlesex or Surrey, among others (see Chapter 3); that is, legal and governmental London was much smaller than the metropolis that contemporaries referred to as "London."

Because the medieval city developed haphazardly, the old Roman grid street pattern has been distorted. Some larger streets do still run parallel to the river, like Tower Street-Eastcheap and Canwicke (Candlewick, later Cannon) Street; others run perpendicular to it, like Fish Street, Gracious (later Gracechurch) Street, and Bishopsgate Street. In 1550 these major thoroughfares are adorned with stately guild halls and the townhouses of wealthy nobles, but over the course of the next century most noble proprietors would flee west to be near the court and to avoid the crowding and stench of the growing city. For example, Northumberland House, Aldgate, once the London seat of the powerful Percy family, was turned into a complex of bowling alleys and gambling dens. A riverside house once owned by the Dukes of Norfolk became a brewery. Between the great streets has grown up a bewildering maze of lanes, alleys, and courtyards containing more modest dwellings. Because of the need to cram as many people within the walls as possible, houses "commonly of timber and clay with plaster . . . , are very narrow in the front towards the street, but are built five or six roofs high" overhanging the road, their tops almost touching (see Illustration 1.4).[10] Although this provides shade in summer, it also blocks out the light and fosters one of the hazards of walking the streets of London: the custom of emptying out night soil – human waste – from upper windows into the open street, so that it might be washed away by the rains. One popular explanation for the British euphemism "loo" for toilet is that it derives from the old warning "Gardyloo"; that is, "Watch out below." Another reason to watch out is that these ramshackle and crowded houses have a tendency to fall or burn down with alarming frequency.

As we move west down Tower Street, we begin to encounter mercantile London. Our first notice is not visual but aural, as we hear London's famous street cries. In the early seventeenth century, several prominent musicians like Orlando Gibbons (1583–1625) and Thomas Weelkes (?1576–1623) would set these words in motets:

> *God give you good morrow.*
> *New muscles, new lilly white muscles*
> *New fresh herrings, new thornback new*
> *Hot mutton pies hot, rosemary and*
> *Bayes, quick and gentle, . . .*
> *Buy any inke will you buy any inke, very fine writing inke*
> *Will you buy any inke*
> *Oysters, three pence a pecke at Bridewell . . .*
> *What ist ye lacke fine wrought shirts or smocks*
> *Ha ye any corns on your feet or toes*
> *Good gratious people for the lords sake pitty the poore*
> *Women, we lie cold and comfortless, night and day on the cold. . . .*

Although the criers were generally mobile (see Illustration 1.5), shopkeepers and manufacturers in particular trades tended to congregate in the same part of town: silkweavers in Spitalfields, gunsmiths near the Tower, and booksellers in St. Paul's churchyard. Because the London livery companies set prices and wages (see Chapter 2), there was no real competition and no reason to set up shop in an underserved area.[11] Thus, as we walk west down Eastcheap – the old English word "ceap" or "chepe" means a market – we encounter rows of butchers. This is London's traditional meat market, although by 1550 the main market has moved farther west to Smithfield. After a morning of scholarly perambulations, we might stop for refreshment along this street at the Boar's Head Tavern, to be immortalized half a century hence as the hangout of Falstaff and his band in Shakespeare's *Henry IV* plays. From here we might carry on west onto Canwicke Street, or head south, back down to the river to the market on New Fish Street, the commercial associations of each of which should be obvious.

Having no need of fish or candles, we instead turn northward at the corner of Gracious Street and Eastcheap and head up Cornhill to reach three consecutive streets to our left, forming a wedge that meets at the Poultry: Lombard Street, then Cornhill (the street), and finally Threadneedle Street. This is the commercial heart of London and when twenty-first-century Londoners refer to "the City," this is its epicenter. The sixteenth-century associations of Cornhill and Threadneedle streets are easily told: "corn" means grain in Tudor English, and this is where the grain factors meet. Threadneedle Street is the home of the Merchant Taylors' and Needlemakers' Companies. But in 1550 the most interesting of these streets is Lombard, because this has been London's banking center ever since moneylenders from Northern Italy, the Lombards, settled here in the Middle Ages. In 1550 we can watch the bankers at work just as easily as carpenters and butchers, for the traditional method is to transact business in the open air while walking along the street. This perhaps worked fine in Italy, but London's weather is more formidable. This explains why, at Christmas 1565, the City would give warning to forty-five householders living on Cornhill, mostly clothworkers and drapers, to move. A consortium led by Sir Thomas Gresham (c. 1518–1579), a wealthy and public-spirited mercer, had purchased the site between Cornhill and Threadneedle to build the Royal Exchange (see Illustration 1.6). The Royal Exchange was a collonaded piazza with shops above, modeled on the Bourse at Antwerp, that operated both as a mercantile exchange and a shopping center housing milliners, apothecaries, booksellers, and goldsmiths. Gresham's venture was so successful that a New Exchange would be built in the seventeenth century along the Strand. Both were popular gathering places, not unlike shopping malls today, where men and women could meet, window shop, and purchase the exotic luxury goods arriving from the continent, Asia, and the Americas in ever increasing amounts from the early seventeenth century on (see Chapter 2).

Descending Cornhill, we see that all three streets meet at the Poultry, once London's poultry market, which in 1550 is a place where many merchants live. This street is also the site of the Poultry Compter on our right, the oldest of three lord mayor's prisons. A little farther west we come to a cross street called Ole Juree, Old Jewry, or, by the eighteenth century, Old Jury. The second name is the most accurate, for this was the site of the Jewish ghetto from at least the twelfth century until their expulsion by Edward I in 1290. The area remained a haven for religious dissenters: a little farther north is Coleman Street, which harbored evangelical heretics before the Reformation and Puritan and Dissenting meetings thereafter.

At the end of the Poultry we find the Great Conduit, where Londoners can take water piped in from springs in rural Paddington. The water flows by gravitational force through wooden pipes to this and to other free public standpipes located in prominent locations such as the City gates. London place names like Sadler's Wells still remind us of this source of water. The Great Conduit marks the beginning of London's chief shopping street in 1550, Cheapside (see Illustration 1.7). Cheapside, the widest and most impressive thoroughfare in central London, is usually on the route of royal and civic processions. It is lined with magnificent shops, some four stories high. Its south side between Bread and Fryday Streets is known as Goldsmith's Row, where a German visitor in 1600 saw "all sorts of gold and silver vessels exposed to sale; as well as ancient and modern medals, in such quantities as must surprise a man the first time he sees and considers them."[12] By the early seventeenth century, however, some of the more prestigious trades began to move west, to the Strand, to follow aristocratic money. This led John Chamberlaine (1553–1628) to complain in 1622 "to see booksellers, stocking men, haberdashers, point-makers, and other meane trades crept into Goldsmithes Rowe, that was wont to be the bewtie and glorie of Cheapeside."[13]

Each of these shops is marked with a sign, either carved in stone into the facade of the building or, increasingly, of wood hanging perpendicular to it, combining some iconic symbol – the sun, a dolphin, a mermaid – with a depiction of the object sold. Written description was less important at a time when perhaps one half the men in London and nearly all women were illiterate. These shops were really workshops with a few samples; there was no stock, and goods were made to order. Their proprietors and their servants lived above the shop. As we pass, we might spy the lady of the household or an idle apprentice standing in the doorway, the former keeping watch over her neighbors, the latter looking for an excuse to join his fellows for some fun. They did not have to go far, because Cheapside is lined with famous taverns: the Bull Head, the Eagle, the Goat, the Mitre, the Nag's Head, and the Star. It was at the Bull Head that Sam Pepys would have "the best venison pasty that ever I eat of in my life"[14] more than a century after our visit.

Cheapside is the backbone to which are connected many other streets, named for the trades carried on in them: off to our right Grocer's Alley, Ironmonger Lane, and the dairymen of Milk Street; to our left grocers and mercers in Soper's Lane, bakers in Bread Street, more fishmongers in Fryday Street (probably referring to the Catholic tradition of eating fish on that day), and shoemakers in Cordwainer Street. Clearly you could get all of life's necessities on and about Cheapside, although you would have to walk farther than in a modern supermarket. Nearly all of these occupational groups have their own livery company (see Chapter 2), with its own hall nearby, usually an impressive Gothic building that adds variety and splendor to the shops and houses. Here, each company's leadership deliberates over membership and sets rules for trade while the whole membership might come together for an annual feast.

In fact, if we turn right up Ironmonger Lane and proceed to Basinghall Street, we encounter a good number of distinguished livery halls on our right – the Weavers', the Coopers', the Girdlers,' and the Masons' – filled with commemorative plate and statuary, decorated with images celebrating their loyalty to the Crown and respective crafts, mostly paid for by bequests from deceased members. Most of these halls would be torn down by nineteenth-century developers. To our left is an even more imposing building, London's city hall, the Guildhall (see Illustration 1.8). The Guildhall was built in 1411 and would survive the Fire in 1666 and a bomb hit in 1940 to remain the official headquarters of City government into the twenty-first century. This is the seat of the lord mayor, where the Court of Aldermen and Common Council, the legislative branches of London government, meet (see Chapter 3). One of the largest halls in England, it is often the site of state trials: Anne Askew (c. 1521–1546) for heresy in 1546; the Earl of Surrey (1516/17–1547) and Lady Jane Grey for treason in 1547 and 1553, respectively; and Archbishop Cranmer for heresy, later in 1553.

Having been disappointed of viewing these exciting events by just a few years, we head back to Cheapside. To our left is old St. Mary-le-Bow, a church whose bell tower, rebuilt in 1521, rang out the curfew in central London. According to tradition, to be a true Cockney, one must be born within the sound of Bow Bells. Because Cheapside is such a wide public space, it was often a site for exemplary punishment, both at a fountain at the western end called the Standard, and at a pillory sometimes used when a tradesman sold shoddy goods. Cheapside also sports the famous – or infamous – Cheapside Cross, one of numerous such crosses, decorated with the pope, the Virgin, and the Apostles, erected in 1290 by Edward I at the spots where the coffin of his deceased Queen Eleanor (1241–1290) rested on its sad procession from the place of her death in Wales. In 1550, during the first flush of the Reformation, this papist totem was frequently attacked by Protestant preachers, but it would survive until 1643.

At the west end of Cheapside we pass the Little Conduit, before being confronted by the magnificent bulk of St. Paul's Cathedral, subsequently known as Old St. Paul's after it burned down in 1666 (see Illustration 1.9). This is easily the greatest Church in England and, as we recall from seeing it from afar, the most prominent building in London. Indeed, at 585 feet long it is also the largest building in the City and, with Westminster Abbey, one of two great national churches in the metropolis. Here, both Henry V and Elizabeth I attended thanksgiving services for the victories at Agincourt and over the Spanish Armada in 1415 and 1588, respectively. In 1471, during the Wars of the Roses, the corpse of Henry VI (reigned 1422–1461) was exhibited in St. Paul's to show that he was really dead. In 1501, Prince Arthur (1486–1502) and Katherine of Aragon (1485–1536) were married here.

St. Paul's is a great *local* institution as well. Adjacent to the building is St. Paul's Churchyard, site of two famous organs of information in early modern London. First, the churchyard is crammed with bookstalls owned by the great printers and stationers on Fleet Street and patronized by literate Londoners like Samuel Pepys in the seventeenth century. Second, in the northeast corner of the churchyard is Paul's Cross, a freestanding pulpit that Thomas Carlyle (1795–1881) called "the Times Newspaper of the Middle Ages." Here, kings are proclaimed, papal bulls read (until 1534), and royal marriages, military victories, and excommunications announced. This is also where, in Catholic times, Luther's works and Tyndale's translation of the Bible were publicly burned. Above all, from this pulpit are delivered some of the most notable sermons in London, to crowds in the open air. Among the speakers over the years were such influential and charismatic preachers as Hugh Latimer (c. 1485–1555), Miles Coverdale (1488–1569), Stephen Gardiner, John Donne (1572–1631), and

William Laud. Afraid of the power of this pulpit, Parliament would order it destroyed in 1643.

The cathedral itself had begun to go into eclipse long before, however, as a result of the Reformation. Most of the land owned by the dean and chapter was confiscated, leading to a fall in revenue, which led in turn to an inability to maintain the building's fabric. Moreover, much of Paul's statuary and stained glass was removed as idolatrous, its high altar replaced with a communion table, and the nave itself, known as Paul's Walk (see Illustration 1.10), became a "common thoroughfare between Carter Lane and Paternoster Row for people with vessels of ale and beer, baskets of bread, fish, flesh and fruit, men leading mules, horses and other beasts."[15] On weekdays, lawyers, government officials, and even tradesmen set up shop in the aisles. Servants hang about a certain pillar looking for employment: this is where Falstaff first hires Bardolf.[16] Only the choir and the crypt (known as St. Faith's Chapel) remain for services. The rest of the cathedral has become another bourse, where business deals are struck, professionals consulted, produce and horses sold across tombs, and the baptismal font commandeered as a counter. In 1561 Bishop James Pilkington (1520–1576) would ascribe the lightning strike that burned down the spire to God's wrath at how His cathedral was being misused: "The south side for Popery and Usury; the north for Simony; and the horsefair in the middle for all kinds of bargains, meetings, brawlings, murders, conspiracies; and the font for ordinary payments of money."[17] Offensive as this might be to religious sensibilities then and now, it should be remembered that if St. Paul's is a great national church, it is also in some ways London's parish church, if that can be said of a city with more than 110 individual parishes. As in the early modern village church, St. Paul's is much more than a place of worship; it is also a social and cultural center for the local community.

By the early seventeenth century, the decaying fabric of St. Paul's had become a national scandal. In 1638, Charles I, encouraged by Archbishop Laud, commissioned Inigo Jones (1573–1652) to do something about the cathedral. He renovated much of the interior and designed a new, if somewhat incongruous, classical portico for the West Front. Restoration continued slowly until the Civil Wars, during which parliamentarian troops used the building as a barracks and Jones's portico was given over to petty tradesmen and beggars. These groups inflicted further damage to the cathedral, and the roof fell in. In 1657, James Howell (?1594–1666) described the ruinous structure as looking "like the hulk of a great weather beaten Ship, that had crossed the Line eight times . . . and lies rotting upon the Carine."[18] Old St. Paul's was in terminal decline when, in 1663, the dean and chapter asked Christopher Wren (1632–1723) to survey the building. The resulting plan was accepted six days before the Great Fire of 1666, which rendered it superfluous. Some idea of Old St. Paul's' continuing importance to its "parishioners" might be derived from the fact that during the Fire, many brought their belongings to store in the crypt, thinking the stone cathedral impregnable. Its loss would be the terrible climax of the conflagration, and a great psychological blow to all Londoners (see Chapter 8).

As we head west, down Ludgate Hill to the Ludgate itself, we pause to gaze northward at legal London. One gate north, at Newgate, is London's criminal court, the Old Bailey, and its most notorious jail, Newgate Prison. In 1550, the Old Bailey is not yet old, having just been built in 1539. Three stories tall and made of brick, it looks more solid than intimidating, but it is here that most of London's felonies are tried; the prison is conveniently located next door. Traditionally, City gates had holding cells for malefactors arrested as they tried to enter, and so the evolution into a prison by the twelfth century was natural. During the period covered by this book, prisons were temporary detention centers for those awaiting trial or the execution of a sentence. That is, no one was sentenced to Newgate for a term of months or years; rather, they waited here to be tried, and if found guilty, to die. The one exception was debtors, who, if they could not escape to a liberty like the Mint, might find themselves arrested, placed in Newgate, and forever incarcerated because there was no way to work off their debt while in prison. This was a hellish fate, for Newgate was already in a dilapidated state by the end of the sixteenth century: poorly ventilated, overcrowded, and subject to a malady called "gaol fever" (typhus), which often carried the prisoners off before the hangman did.

FLEET STREET AND THE STRAND

Turning sadly away, we pass through Ludgate, farther down Ludgate Hill, onto Fleet Street, the principal artery of an area west of the wall but still under the lord mayor's jurisdiction called Farringdon Ward Without. Almost immediately our noses are accosted by an awful stench. Fleet Street is named for the River Fleet, a tributary of the Thames that flows from Hampstead south, through Camden Town, crossing Holborn and Fleet Street before it empties into the larger waterway. During Roman times, the Fleet was a defensive barrier; in the Middle Ages, cutlers, butchers, and tanners used it to dispose of animal carcasses and by-products of metallurgy and leatherworking. Because the river cut right through the City, it also served as a convenient open sewer. People complained about the stench as early as the thirteenth century, and it had to be cleaned out in 1502 and would be so again in 1606. By the mid-seventeenth century it was more of a ditch than a river.

Looking to our right as we cross over Fleet Bridge, we note Fleet Prison on the east bank of the ditch, famous for debtors and state prisoners. Looking left, we see the gates of an abandoned palace, Bridewell, whose history provides an index of how this part of London was changing. The area is named for a holy well dedicated to St. Bride. It came to royal attention after 1512 when the king's palace upriver at Westminster suffered a serious fire. As the old medieval pile was unsuitable to begin with, and the Tower not much better, Henry VIII needed a new, modern London residence, and so he built Bridewell Palace out of brick on the banks of the Fleet River between 1515 and 1520. In 1522, he entertained the Holy Roman Emperor, Charles V (1519–1556), here while on a state visit, and it was in Bridewell that the first consultations with the papal legate took place over the King's Great Matter (his desire to divorce Katherine of Aragon) in 1528. Whether it was the intransigency of the pope or the aromas of the Fleet that left a bad odor, once Henry VIII acquired Whitehall in 1529 he lost interest in Bridewell. In the 1530s the insalubrious palace was rented to the French ambassador. Finally, in 1553 Edward VI would give it to the City to house vagrants and orphans and to punish those guilty of misdemeanors. Contemporary London had a vagrant problem: Tudor economic policies, rapid inflation, and the dismantling of much of the Catholic charitable infrastructure drove many poor migrants to a city stripped of social services (see Chapters 2 and 7). Bridewell was designed as a workhouse and hospital for those unable to work (the "impotent" or "deserving" poor) and as a short-term prison for those thought unwilling to do so ("sturdy beggars"), minor offenders, lewd women, and vagrants, who were publicly whipped once a week. The idea was that the impotent poor would partially pay for their support and avoid sin-inviting idleness by spinning hemp and splitting stones, whereas the criminal poor would be inspired to reform themselves. Although the experiment always had mixed results (see Chapter 6), other such workhouses appeared in London, at Clerkenwell and Westminster, and in the country at large. All were named "bridewells" in tribute to the original, and when that original burned down in the Great Fire, it was rebuilt.

Making a note to avoid incarceration in this social experiment, we head farther west along Fleet Street holding our noses – and our purses. Throughout our period, from the Middle Ages to the eighteenth century, Fleet Street was a popular staging area for apprentice riots and other youthful gangs who might accost an unsuspecting tourist: "the street-boys and apprentices collect together in immense crowds and strike to the right and left unmercifully without regard to person; and because they are the strongest, one is obliged to put up with the insult as well as the injury."[19] This reminds us that London's streets were contested territory where the innocent pedestrian had to negotiate horses, carts, mud, pickpockets, drunks, brawls, beggars, barrels being rolled into taverns, porters bearing heavy loads, craftsmen working at their benches, criers and urchins hawking everything from broadsides to brooms, and housewives standing arms akimbo in their doorsteps judging – and sometimes insulting – all who dared to enter their neighborhood. To our left is the dissolved Whitefriars Monastery, which would evolve by the end of the century into another liberty, Alsatia, a notorious "combat zone" infested by London's criminal underworld.

Arguably far more edifying is the fact that, since the establishment of a press here in 1500 "at the sign of the Sun" by Wynkyn de Worde (d. 1534), Fleet Street has been a publishing center. We can try to get our scholarly works published at the printing house of John Byddell (fl. 1531–1544), who moved into de Worde's house after his death. In 1553, Richard Tottell (c. 1528–1593) would found his law bookshop at "The Hand and Star" and remain open for business there for the next 41 years. Not only was he granted a patent to print Common Law books, but he was also a great literary publisher, bringing out More's *Dialogue of Comfort* (1553) and Tottell's *Miscellany* (1557), which contains some of the earliest sonnets in English by Thomas Wyatt (?1503–1542) and Henry Howard, Earl of Surrey (?1517–1547). The printing connection continues into the twenty-first century; the words *Fleet Street* have long been shorthand in England for the gentlemen (and now women) of the press.

The prominence of legal booksellers along Fleet Street is no accident, because we are only steps away from London's four great law schools: the Middle Temple and Inner Temple along Fleet Street; Lincoln's Inn to the north at the end of Chancery Lane; and Gray's Inn still farther north across Holborn on the lane named for it. Along with the nearby Old Bailey, Newgate, Fleet, and Bridewell Prisons, these four institutions, dating back to at least the fifteenth century, form the heart of London's legal district. Although early modern London does not have a university, the four Inns of Court provide something of the same atmosphere. Since the Middle Ages they have trained barristers and housed their offices. Typically, students attended for seven or eight years, receiving instruction in the law from practicing barristers. They were also taught dancing, music, and history to prepare them to move among gentlemen – yet another way in which London afforded social mobility. As a result, the Christmas revels at the Inns of Court were famous, lasting from All Saints' Day (November 1) to Candlemas (February 2), and sometimes attended by royalty. The Middle and Inner Temple before us are named for the Knights Templar who once owned this property. In 1550, as today, the two temples consist of lawyers' chambers, but each also has a hall and chapel. The magnificent Middle Temple Hall, completed in 1573, will be the site of the premier of Shakespeare's (1564–1616) *Twelfth Night* in 1601. The Elizabethan associations are especially strong, since Sir Walter Raleigh, Sir Francis Drake (1540–1596) and Sir John Hawkins (1532–1595) spent time here. Perhaps they enjoyed ambling down to the gardens by the river. The Middle Temple Gardens are the fictional setting for the scene in the *Henry VI* plays in which the Dukes of York and Somerset pluck a white rose and a red rose, respectively, to signal their enmity and so the start of the Wars of the Roses. Not wanting to start a war or be tossed out by the porters, we merely admire the flowers and the magnificent view. Turning south, we see Paris Garden across the river. Turning southeast, we see Southwark Cathedral and London Bridge. Finally, looking east from whence we came, the great city rises before us, capped by the ramshackle magnificence of St. Paul's; but we are headed west.

Walking back up to Fleet Street through the Middle Temple gatehouse, we turn left, back onto the road, and immediately cross under yet another arched gate, Temple Bar, which lets us into the Strand. Temple Bar was built in 1351 and, par for the course, has a prison attached to it. It represents the outermost reaches of the legal City of London. It is a tribute to the long-standing independence of the City that, beginning with Elizabeth's procession to celebrate the Armada victory at St. Paul's in 1588, even the sovereign must ask permission to cross this line when traveling east. On state occasions the royal party stops here to ask entry of the lord mayor, who always grants it and submits the City sword as a mark of loyalty. The sword is then returned to him so that he may carry it before the sovereign in procession. Because we are moving west and are far less threatening than a Tudor monarch, we proceed without incident, if not necessarily without trouble: Temple Bar was a choke point for London traffic until its removal in the nineteenth century.

The Strand might be the principal surface artery connecting the City and Westminster, but it started life in the Middle Ages as a riverside bridle path. As recently as 1532 it was still "full of pits and sloughs, very perilous and noisome [stinking]."[20] In that year it was ordered to be paved. Still, given the horse and cart traffic and contemporary sanitary customs, even in 1550 we may find ourselves splattered with mud – or worse. Looking up from our stained hose, to our left we see a series of stately riverside palaces stretching all the way down to Westminster: the Outer Temple, Paget (later Leicester or Essex) House, Arundel House, Somerset House, Savoy Palace, Russell (later Bedford) House, Durham House, Suffolk (later York) House, and finally the former York Place, now Whitehall Palace. Named for the bishoprics from which they were confiscated, or the peers to which they were awarded, each was at one time or another the metropolitan headquarters of a powerful clerical or noble clientage faction, and so most figure in subsequent chapters.

If we look right, we see rows of shops: in 1500, Andrea Trevisan (1458–1534) counted fifty-two goldsmiths' shops along the Strand, "rich and full of silver vessels, great and small."[21] These craftsmen had followed the elite, who wanted to be nearer the court, west, but if we look just beyond them to the north, the buildings of the city trail off and we see open land. On the future site of Trafalgar Square stands the Royal Mews, or stables. To the north between Ludgate and the Mews lie Lincoln's Inn Fields and Convent (later Covent) Garden, both as yet undeveloped. St. Martin's and St. Giles's "really were 'in the Fields'" as Stephen Inwood puts it.[22] Foxes were hunted where are now Tottenham Court Road and Oxford Street, and the district known today as Soho, famous for nightlife, was named after a hunting call. In short, in 1550 the area we think of as the West End was essentially rural. As late as May Day 1663, Pepys could write of riding "with some trouble through the fields and then Holborne &c. toward Hide parke."[23]

Between 1550 and 1750, the West End would all be filled in, moving the center of London's gravity beyond the walls, to the west. That process began partly thanks to the Dissolution of the Monasteries. Between 1536 and 1547 Henry VIII and Edward VI pushed through Parliament a series of laws dissolving all Church-run monasteries, hospitals, schools, and chantries (small chapels endowed to pray for the souls of the dead). Several Catholic bishops fell afoul of the regime (Cardinals Fisher and Wolsey [c. 1470–1530], for example) and their land was confiscated as well. The Crown thus commandeered twenty-three major religious houses in London. The result was a revolution in metropolitan land ownership: perhaps two-thirds of London had been owned by Church foundations. Suddenly, the Crown acquired vast amounts of real estate as well as monastic buildings and bishops' palaces, the greatest of which, Wolsey's York Place, became Henry's Whitehall Palace. The idea behind the confiscation was that the former Church lands would endow the monarchy and save it from Henry's debts. But Henry, needing quick cash in the mid-1540s to pay for a series of wars with France and Scotland, kept only a fraction; he or his son sold or gave away the rest. This would lead to a massive rebuilding over the next century. To take one of the most spectacular examples, Edward Seymour, Duke of Somerset (c. 1500–1552), brother of Henry's third queen, Jane Seymour (1508–1537), and Edward VI's uncle, received two bishops' palaces, an inn of Chancery and a church along the Strand, which he knocked down to build a magnificent riverside palace called Somerset House. Less spectacularly, Blackfriars became a famous indoor theater; part of the grounds of St. Claire Minories became a bowling alley.

Another beneficiary of the dissolution was John Russell, first Earl of Bedford (c. 1485–1555), rewarded for putting down the Catholic "Prayer Book" Rebellion in 1549. The resulting Russell estate in London is vast, encompassing much of the area west of the wall, including the former "Convent Garden" once owned by the monks of Westminster Abbey. Because London grew in the opposite direction from the prevailing winds and river current, this western land was prime for development. Moreover, the rise of the London social season between 1590 and 1620 meant that the elite wanted to live in the West End, or "the town," as they called it, because it was closer to the court at Westminster and Whitehall and well away from the noise and stench of the City. As early as 1600 there was a small colony of aristocratic houses just north of the Strand in St. Martin's Lane, and soon after another in Drury Lane, developed by the Earls of Salisbury (1563–1612) and Clare (1564–1637), respectively. In 1627, Francis Russell, fourth Earl of Bedford (1587–1641) commissioned Inigo Jones to design an even grander tract of houses "fitt for the habitacions of Gentlemen and men of ability" at "Covent Garden," just north of the Strand. Jones was heavily influenced by Italian Palladian architecture and the need to provide accommodation that was airy yet secure from the street. The result was London's first square, with three sides of tall terraced houses, completed on the west side by St. Paul Covent Garden parish church (not to be confused with St. Paul's Cathedral) in a matching neoclassical design, fronted by impressive columns (see Illustration 1.11). The security of this arrangement derived from the facts that (1) ingress and egress to the square could be controlled at narrow checkpoints; and (2) only families of the best quality could afford the high rents of £150. Some of this exclusivity would be traded for convenience around 1650, when a market was added in the center of the square.

Covent Garden set trends in several ways. First, it was London's first major housing development. Later, in the seventeenth and eighteenth centuries, when it began to decline as a fashionable address, the Russells, the Cavendishes, the Grosvenors, and other great aristocratic families would finance similar developments to the north and west on land granted by or leased from the Crown at very long leases on favorable terms. Second, they would copy the Covent Garden plan by developing their properties as squares. As a result, the West End of London would look far different from the tumbledown City: by 1750 it would be a network of neat symmetrical squares, surrounding regular gardens and lawns (see Conclusion). But all that lay in the future in 1550. For now, Londoners were free to roam and enjoy the fields beyond the Strand.

WHITEHALL AND WESTMINSTER

Our business being somewhat more serious, we continue down the Strand to Charing Cross. The area was originally a separate village in the Middle Ages known as Charing, which means "to turn" in Old English, presumably because the river turns south here. From this point, the north bank becomes the west bank, and the south bank, the east. One of the city's busiest corners, a place for royal proclamations and site of a pillory, it was said in the early seventeenth century that if you wanted to know the news in London, all you had to do was go to Charing Cross. The cross for which the corner is named is the last erected by Edward I in 1290 to commemorate his deceased queen. Like the cross at Cheapside, it was frequently a target of Protestant reformers, and would be pulled down by Parliament in 1647. Following the river, we turn onto Whitehall (street) and get a good elevated view of Westminster and the complex of buildings that form the heart of

English government. Walking toward them, we encounter, mostly on our left but also straddling the street to our right, a rambling hodgepodge of halls, towers, gates, and galleries that compose His Majesty's Palace of Whitehall. Whitehall Palace sits on the site of the original York Place, the ancient palace of the Archbishop of York, located conveniently across the river from that of his fellow Archbishop (of Canterbury), Lambeth Palace. The most famous recent incumbent, Thomas, Cardinal Wolsey, had used the immense wealth he received from multiple bishoprics and government offices to expand York Place into a palace surpassing the splendors of the king's London houses at Bridewell and Westminster. This was a mistake, because Wolsey worked for the covetous Henry VIII. At Wolsey's fall in 1529, Henry confiscated the palace, renamed it Whitehall, and expanded it across the street that took its name, adding Holbein Gate, a cockpit, tennis courts, and a tiltyard for tournaments.

The result before us is, like Henry himself, exuberant but undisciplined, an assemblage of impressive structures that seem to have little to do with each other and follow no plan apart from the curve of the river. In the seventeenth century, the rise of neoclassical architecture would render Whitehall unfashionable, and there would be periodic plans under the Stuarts to start again and create something more regular and dignified, like the Louvre in Paris. But the Stuarts were chronically short of money, and could do little but add to the existing structure. Jones did build a magnificent neoclassical Banqueting House along the street for James I, its ceiling painted by Rubens, to act as a Presence Chamber for ambassadorial receptions and theatrical productions. Charles I would fill the palace with magnificent art. Ironically, he was executed from a scaffold built just outside the Banqueting House in 1649. The revolutionary regimes sold off much of the artwork that Charles had bought, but from 1653 Cromwell used Whitehall as his seat as lord protector. At the Restoration there was an attempt to buy back many of Charles I's treasures, and both Charles II and James II launched extensive renovations. (We visit Charles II's Whitehall in Chapter 3.) The latter would build an opulent Catholic Chapel that scandalized his Protestant subjects. After the Revolution of 1688/89, although Whitehall remained the official residence of the British court, William and Mary avoided it, not least because the combination of all those West End chimneys spewing soot and its damp location down by the Thames were hard on William's asthma. So he was not unduly upset when a Dutch laundress accidentally burned the palace down in 1698 by placing some washing too near an open fire. There were repeated plans to rebuild Whitehall, but by this time English kings were utterly beholden to Parliament, which had other matters to fund. Only Jones's magnificent Banqueting House survives today.

Following the burning of Whitehall in 1698, the English court moved its official residence across St. James's Park to the northwest (on our right), to St. James's Palace. St. James's Palace was originally built as a hunting lodge for Henry VIII, and the open countryside between the two palaces was frequently used for hunting and hawking by his descendants. If we stroll into these open fields, we might very well encounter the royal retinue, thus reminding us first of how wild and untamed the future West End is, and second of how the monarchy provides, then as now, endless free spectacle to the residents of greater London. Even in 1550 St. James's is a modest palace, and subsequent generations would find it far too dumpy to be the official residence of the court, yet so it remains today. In fact, because the court remained firmly ensconced in the West End, the area to the north of St. James's would fill up with fashionable houses in the seventeenth and eighteenth centuries.

Turning away from St. James's Park, we continue down Whitehall and its extension as King Street to the heart of the capital, the complex of buildings laid out in the Middle Ages as Westminster (see Illustration 1.12). Originally governed by the dean and chapter, in 1585 Westminster would be divided into twelve wards and placed under the jurisdiction of a Court of Burgesses. The burgesses acted very much like the City's aldermen or a bench of JPs. They were selected by the dean or a secular high steward, who was in turn a royal nominee: the Crown was careful to maintain control in its own backyard.

The religious and emotional heart of the Westminster complex is Westminster Abbey. As we have seen, there has been a religious foundation here since Anglo-Saxon times. According to legend, the church was built in the seventh century by King Sæberht of Essex (d. 616/617) on a site then known as Thorney Island. St. Dunstan established a Benedictine Abbey in the tenth century, on which Edward the Confessor grafted his own expanded foundation between 1042 and 1066. From 1245 to 1272, Henry III, who was, like Edward, a self-consciously pious monarch, pulled down the Norman-style cruciform Edwardian building and erected the present high Gothic masterpiece, although the twin towers known to modern visitors would not be built until the eighteenth century.

If St. Paul's is London's parish church, then Westminster Abbey is the nation's, and so we enter with due reverence. After our eyes adjust to the dark, we look up to note the very high nave, the tallest in England, at 103 feet. Soon, we are greeted by one of the many canons (priests) of the Abbey, who offers to be our guide: this is a way for the church and its clergy to support themselves. If he knows his history – no certain thing given the state of the English clergy in the turbulent mid-Tudor years – he informs us that every English king who received a coronation since Harold II has been crowned here. At the end of the nave we see Edward the Confessor's ancient coronation chair, beneath which sits the Stone of Scone, on which Scottish kings were traditionally crowned until it was commandeered by Edward I in 1279. It would not be returned until 1996. English kings have also been buried here since Edward the Confessor died just eight days after his Abbey was consecrated. At the end of the nave, we come to the apse, with several chapels radiating from it, many of them endowed by dead kings and queens. Of these, the most magnificent is the one that Henry VII built in perpendicular style between 1503 and 1512 at a cost of about £14,000. The Henry VII Chapel will house the bones of most of his Tudor, Stuart, and early Hanoverian descendants under elaborate fan vaulting.

In 1550, it is not yet the case that great statesmen are buried at Westminster Abbey, but Poet's Corner is already established in the south transept in fact if not in name, because Geoffrey Chaucer (c. 1340–1400) lies here. Within a century, so will Edmund Spenser (?1552–1599) and Ben Jonson (1572–1637). At the funeral of the former, it is said that his fellow poets threw manuscript works into the grave after him. When Jonson asked to be buried in the Abbey, he quite modestly requested that "two feet by two feet will do for all I want," and so he was buried standing up.[24] The poet's connection may have something to do with the fact that England's first great printer, William Caxton (c. 1415/24–1492), had his shop near this spot, at the sign of the Red Pale, close to the south door adjoining the Chapter House, from 1476 to his death in 1492. The shop was then taken over by the aforementioned Wynken de Worde, who moved it to Fleet Street in 1500, but booksellers continued to frequent the porch of the Abbey. Like St. Paul's, Westminster Abbey is not an inconvenient place to do business and even to sell one's wares.

The Abbey was dissolved as a monastic foundation under Henry VIII, restored under Mary, and then dissolved again under Elizabeth: here, too, Westminster Abbey reflects the history of the nation. During the Civil Wars, the New Model Army used the church as a barracks and stable, thus demonstrating their disdain for High Church sensibilities. According to one account, they

> broke down the [communion] rails before the Table and burnt them in the very place in the heat of July but wretchedly profaned the very Table itself by setting about it with their tobacco and all before them.[25]

Perhaps somewhat presumptuously given this behavior, Lord Protector Cromwell, his son-in-law Henry Ireton (1611–1651), and the chief justice at Charles I's trial, John Bradshaw (1602–1659), were all buried in the Abbey after their deaths. They were exhumed in 1660 by a Restoration regime bent on retribution. Famously, their corpses were hanged, drawn, and quartered, and their heads placed on stakes outside of Westminster Hall. Cromwell's would remain in place until it blew down circa 1688. Eventually, it would be donated to his alma mater, Sidney Sussex College, Cambridge – arguably the strangest alumni gift in history.

Westminster Hall was built in 1097 by William II (1087–1100) as an extension of Edward the Confessor's palace. At 240 feet long and 92 feet high, it is the largest hall in England, although William Rufus, as he was also called, thought it a "mere bedchamber." We are more easily impressed by its sheer size and hammer-beam roof. Unfortunately, the effect is compromised somewhat on any given day in 1550 because the hall is divided into the various law courts that meet here: King's Bench, Chancery, Exchequer, and Common Pleas. The hall also contains shops and stalls to entice or refresh those pleading a case or waiting for a verdict. On court days it is thronged with litigants and spectators, especially when the weather is bad, because it is a good place to get in out of the rain: another indoor public square and proto-shopping mall in early modern London. Naturally, it was also a favorite hangout for nippers (cutpurses), foisters (pickpockets), and queans (prostitutes). The hall assumes its full magnificence when the law courts are cleared for a great state trial, as occurred here in 1535 for Sir Thomas More and Cardinal Fisher, in 1536 for Anne Boleyn, in 1552 for the Duke of Somerset, in 1606 for Guy Fawkes (1570–1606) and the other Gunpowder Plot conspirators, in 1641 for the Earl of Strafford (1593–1641), and most spectacularly of all, in January 1649 for the trial of King Charles I. More happily, the king's coronation banquet traditionally takes place here. Despite being limited to the best people, early modern household accounts reveal plenty of complaints about stolen cutlery and rowdy behavior on these occasions.

Perhaps the dramatic highlight of the evening was when, again according to tradition, the hereditary champion of England, a member of the Dymock family in full armor, rode into the hall to issue a challenge to anyone questioning the new monarch's right to the throne. To the encouragement of everyone's digestion, the challenge was never returned, and the new sovereign celebrated by drinking to the champion's health from a gold cup.

Among the many guests at a coronation banquet would be peers and members of Parliament. In 1550, they perform their legislative work in Westminster Palace. The palace was built by Edward the Confessor as his principal London residence and served as the official seat of the English court until damaged by fire in 1512. As we have seen, Henry VIII abandoned it, first for Bridewell and then permanently for Whitehall. What to do with a half-burned royal palace on prime real estate? Give it to Parliament. The House of Lords met in the White Chamber. It was the undercroft to this part of the building that Guy Fawkes and his fellow Catholic conspirators rented and filled with barrels of gunpowder in the hope of blowing up the king and political elite at the state opening of Parliament on November 5, 1605. The search that uncovered Fawkes and the gunpowder is reenacted before every state opening. The House of Commons met in St. Stephen's Chapel after it was secularized in 1547. This space was too small for the full membership, leading to a hothouse atmosphere in which members crowded together, shoulder to shoulder, on the former choir benches. The speaker's chair, and a table for the mace and books, were placed close to where the old altar was, which might explain the modern custom of bowing to the speaker on entry. The antechamber served as a lobby for counting votes. As this suggests, the arrangement was entirely ad hoc; moreover, the building was in constant disrepair. It should be recalled, however, that in the sixteenth century Parliament was not so much a regular institution of government as an occasional, brief, and (from the monarch's point of view) often regrettable occurrence, usually called and dismissed as quickly as possible. Thus, Westminster Palace must have seemed perfectly adequate in 1550 for these meetings. It was only after the Glorious Revolution of 1688/89, when parliamentary sessions became annual events lasting most of the London season from autumn to spring, that the building's flaws began to pinch. Despite numerous patches and renovations, it continued to serve until it burned down in 1834.

Because this is the seat of court and capital, the area is full of lodging houses for members of Parliament, courtiers, and, prior to the Reformation, pilgrims to the Abbey. Shopkeepers pursuing luxury trades (e.g., gold, cloth) like these customers, but even though their shops might be located outside of the City proper, they are still subject to the regulations of the livery companies, whose royal charters typically give them influence across the metropolis. Finally, because the rich congregate here, so do the poor, resulting in more crime and begging than we might expect. The Abbey and its precincts were longstanding sanctuaries for debtors and criminals, hence the names of several nearby streets: Broad Sanctuary, Little Sanctuary, and Thieving Lane. As in Fleet Street, we hold onto our purses.

Although we have walked but three miles, the variety and bustle of London in 1550 are such that it has been an exhausting day. Having seen official, governmental, and religious London, we might double back into the fields of St. James's Park to refresh ourselves or we might head down to the river by Whitehall or Westminster Stairs to contemplate all that we have seen. Because of the bend at Westminster, if we crane our heads in a semicircle from right to left, looking south, then east, and finally north, we see it all: the south bank, starting with Lambeth Palace just across the river from us to our right, then moving left, the trees of Paris Garden and Southwark Cathedral. Directly in front of us, but at a distance, London Bridge, piled high with precarious houses and shops. To its immediate left, at the top of our leftward vision, the City itself, crammed into the walls, the steeples of its churches gathered around St. Paul's like hordes of children about their mother. Turning more to our left, on the north bank, we see a row of stately palaces, culminating in Whitehall and the Westminster complex from which we have just come. The scene makes little noise, just the occasional call of the bargeman, the bells of the city churches striking the hour, or perhaps an occasional vote by acclamation from Westminster Palace. Yet in all the whir and hum of that great conurbation something remarkable is happening. Its inhabitants scurry about – coming and going, working and playing, eating, drinking, writing, reading, praying, ordering, begging, nipping, making court and making shift, living, dying, and all the while ever becoming Londoners.

$\mathscr{2}$. The Socioeconomic Base

THE DEMOGRAPHIC REALITY

$\mathscr{T}$he most important fact about early modern London, the one about which contemporaries and historians are universally agreed, is that it was growing – from about 120,000 souls in 1550 to 675,000 in 1750 – and growing faster than England as a whole. Why did London's population grow faster than the rest of the country's? London's demographic expansion could not have been caused by the reproduction of its own population, because early modern London's death rate was higher than its birth rate: out of every 1,000 Londoners, 35 would be born each year, but 40 would die.[1] The reasons for London's deadly demographic profile should be obvious from our tour of the city in 1550: the population density in London's core was 100 persons per acre in 1550, rising to about 200 by the time of the Great Fire in 1666. Many of these people were housed in ramshackle, multistoried, timber-frame-and-plaster constructions crammed into narrow alleys and small courtyards, with the corollaries of overcrowding, disease, crime, fire, and structural collapse. In the 1660s, the French Ambassador wrote, "People fill the cellars." The authorities associated overcrowding with poverty and disease, specifically plague, as a royal proclamation noted in 1580:

> . . . yet where there are such great multitudes of people brought to inhabit in small rooms, whereof a great part are seen very poor, yea, such as must live of begging or by worse means, and they heaped up together, and in a sort smothered with many families of children and servants in one house or small tenement, it must needs follow (if any plague or popular sickness should by God's permission enter amongst those multitudes) that the same would not only spread itself and invade

the whole city and confines . . . but would be also dispersed through all other parts of the realm, to the manifest danger of the whole body thereof. . . . [2]

Indeed, between 1563 and 1665, London experienced six major outbreaks of plague, each of which killed between 3% and 20% of its population (see Chapter 8). Less spectacularly, London's overcrowding and location along a sometimes foul river bred all sorts of other diseases that could kill one just as swiftly, for example, diphtheria, dysentery, influenza, measles, scarlet fever, smallpox, sweating sickness, tuberculosis, typhoid fever, typhus, and whooping cough. The Gin Craze of the 1730s and 1740s made those decades especially deadly. But much of London's morbidity can be explained by high rates of infant mortality: according to the Bills of Mortality, 40% of the deaths in London between 1700 and 1750 were children under 2 years of age. In some parts of early modern London, fewer then 60% of the children made it to age 15. Disease apart, for the first half of our period, London had an imbalance of female to male inhabitants of 113 to 100, made worse by the requirement that apprentices remain unmarried. When people forbidden to marry nevertheless produced a child, they might be tempted to abandon or kill it. Finally, as any urban dweller will tell you, cities are physically dangerous places: unexpected deaths from accidents in the streets, on building sites, and in the river (most people did not know how to swim) were common in early modern London. No wonder that, between 1550 and 1750, Londoners were dying faster than they were being born.

Yet London grew throughout our period, by about 2,750 souls per year during its second century. Because London was not reproducing itself, it must have been attracting and absorbing a constant stream of immigrants to reach that figure: about 6,000 a year to 1650 and perhaps 8,000 a year to 1750. England might never have been "onely London" as James I feared, but it held about 7% of the English population by 1650 and 11% by 1750. In effect, London was soaking up vast numbers of English men and women, as well as Scots, Irish, and others from abroad, attracting them with the opportunity to rise but often killing them once they got there. Migrants flocked to London for many reasons. The wealthy came to attend the court or Parliament, to be served by London's leading professionals, to be entertained, to shop, or simply because they found country life boring. As we have seen, before the Reformation, lordly bishops built enormous palaces along the Strand to be where the action was. After the confiscations of the mid-sixteenth century, many of these palaces were awarded to great courtiers, who renovated or rebuilt them. In the seventeenth century, however, aristocrats began to retain fewer servants, spent more time at court, and sought comfort and privacy, rendering such large establishments outmoded. Instead, the greatest peers built splendid London townhouses, smaller versions of their country houses, often designed and decorated by famous artists. Robert Sidney, Earl of Leicester (1595–1677) erected Leicester House in the 1630s in what is now Leicester Square; Richard Boyle, Earl of Burlington (1612–1698) completed Burlington House in the 1660s on Piccadilly; and Ralph Montagu, later Duke of Montagu (1638–1709), built Montagu House in Bloomsbury in the 1670s, then rebuilt it after a fire in the 1680s. All three played an important role in the political and cultural history of the nation, the first as a meeting place for opposition politicians in the late seventeenth and eighteenth centuries; the second as the eventual headquarters of the Royal Academy and the Royal Society; and the third as the first home of the British Museum.

Below this level, a Tudor Member of Parliament up for a session might rent rooms at an inn, a tavern, or above a shop. Increasingly after 1600 even lesser nobles and gentlemen began to rent more splendid lodgings on short leases or purchase long-term leases of smart townhouses in fashionable areas near the court, like Lincoln's Inn Fields or Covent Garden. Even rented lodgings might be substantial: in 1621 Francis Clifford, Earl of Cumberland (1559–1641) paid £16 a month for a house in St. Martin's parish with a great chamber, five lodging chambers, two garrets, a kitchen, and two cellars. The early Stuarts objected to their landed aristocracy abandoning their responsibilities in the country, but despite periodic proclamations urging them to go back to their country estates, demand outgrew supply, leading to the expansion and filling in of the West End as the century wore on.

Members of the elite began to speak of a London "season," from autumn to spring, when the court was in town, the law courts in session, the theater in full swing, and the city full of the "best" people. As in previous periods, some men attended Parliament (in theory, over the course of the period, between 70 and 160 peers in the House of Lords and from about 380 to nearly 560 gentlemen in the House of Commons) when it was in session (annually from 1689), and some held high office. They and their families frequented the court, the theater, the pleasure garden, and from 1656, the opera; from 1672, public concerts; from 1711, masked balls (see Chapter 4). Aristocratic men could relax at taverns, and, from the mid-seventeenth century, coffeehouses and private clubs (see Chapter 5). Aristocratic women took coaches to visit other aristocratic women, laying the groundwork for an English salon culture. These people deserted London in the hot, unhealthy summers, however, leading Horace Walpole (1717–1797) to complain of August in 1760 "there is not a coach to be seen . . . just as it always is at this season."[3] Still, by 1700, London had become so congenial that many landowners migrated back to their great estates only to keep Christmas and to avoid the city's summer heat.

Thus, the Stuart and early Hanoverian aristocracy was increasingly "amphibious" between the country and the capital and at home in both. This shuttling between country and city became easier in the seventeenth century with the development of better roads, coaches with springs, and more reliable postal services, including a London penny post at the end of the century. From the mid-1650s there were regular stage services between London inns and Exeter to the west, Chester to the northwest, and York and Newcastle to the north: Oxford was just 13 hours away and Bath 2 days by "flying coach." All of these developments – along with the exodus of the nobility from the City for the more open spaces of the West End, the concomitant evolution of the great noble townhouse, and the slightly less ostentatious accommodation to be found in London squares, the establishment of the London season, and the ever-expanding trade in luxury goods – made possible a new kind of aristocratic life, that of an urban gentry that increasingly spent most of its time in the metropolis.

What about those who could not afford sleek coaches and smart townhouses? Most everyone else came to London for economic opportunity. The younger sons of gentlemen, as well as the male offspring of yeomen, merchants, and professionals, often sought education in the law and social graces at the Inns of Court or took up valuable apprenticeships in London's leading merchant or banking houses. Below this level, people were attracted by the greatest concentration of jobs in northern Europe. London was Britain's primary fabricator of ships, tools, furniture, mathematical instruments, clocks, clothing, shoes, books, paper, and other items. Above all, in 1550 perhaps one-third of London's adult male workforce had something to do with the manufacture of textiles, including spinners, weavers, fullers, brushers, shearers, dyers, and packers. Circa 1700 there were 10,000 looms in Spitalfields, and the East London silk industry employed 40,000 to 50,000 workers. In the eighteenth century, Clerkenwell watchmakers turned out thousands of gold and silver timepieces, although the most notable craftsmen of the age, Thomas Tompion (1639–1713) and Daniel Quare (1648/49–1724), were based in Fleet Street and Exchange Alley, respectively. Thomas Chippendale (1718–1779) of St. Martin's Lane and Huguenot and Dutch craftsmen supplied an endless demand for chairs, tables, and beds. Skilled workers in all of these industries were attracted by wages that were higher in London than anywhere else in England, by about one-third. Admittedly, in the sixteenth century especially, prices were often higher still, leading to a decline in real wages in London between 1500 and the 1580s of 40%. The 1590s, gripped by war and a series of bad harvests, saw a further, if temporary, plunge of 20%.

Still, agricultural laborers from around the British Isles came hoping for any opportunity at all. During the first century covered by this book in particular, the state of the national economy practically drove these people from the countryside. Between 1500 and 1650 the population of England and Wales more than doubled, from about 2.3 to over 5.2 million souls. Unfortunately, neither agriculture nor cloth making, the two most important industries in England, were flexible enough to employ this expanding population. In fact, the cloth industry was depressed for much of the period, because the European market was both flooded with English wool and disrupted by the Wars of Religion. Moreover, the pressure of this growing population on a limited supply of food, land, and housing drove prices and rents up. One can see why many English people thought that there was no future in their town or village: as late as 1685, Sir John Reresby (1634–1689) complained in Parliament of "our tenants all coming hither, finding by experience that they could live here better in a cellar or a garret than they could . . . in the country on a farm of £30 rent."[4] So they took to the roads and came to London to do manual labor in manufacturing or construction or London's vast service industry or domestic service. Contemporaries worried about London's disproportionate growth, that it was, in the words of John Graunt, "perhaps a Head too big for the Body,"[5] draining the countryside of human capital. But one wonders what would have happened to the English economy and social structure if there had not been a London to absorb what was, in economic terms, excess population.

London also drew people from beyond England's borders. By the late sixteenth century, 4% to 5% of London's population were aliens, including Scots, Irish, Welsh, French, Dutch, and a handful of Jews and Africans, many of them living "under the radar" in the liberties. Scots, Irish, and

Welsh came to London for the same reasons as English migrants. So did continental cloth workers. Dutch, Flemish, and French Protestants (the latter called *Huguenots*) were also fleeing religious persecution. By 1593 there were already 631 French families in London. That number would expand over the next century to perhaps 25,000 people, thanks to Cardinal Richelieu's (1585–1642) crackdown of the 1620s, and again after Louis XIV revoked the toleration of Protestants enshrined in the Edict of Nantes in 1685. Many Huguenot dyers and weavers settled near Soho or in the weaving community at Spitalfields, where they helped the English silk industry and other consumer crafts like stocking knitting and ribbon making get off the ground. Others were innovative gunsmiths, watchmakers, and glassmakers, some of whom were embraced by native guildsmen eager to take advantage of their technical expertise. Still others came as artists and entertainers: the painters Hans Holbein the Younger (1497–1543), Marcus Gheeraerts the Younger (1561/62–1636), Peter Paul Rubens (1577–1640), Anthony Van Dyck (1599–1641), Wenceslaus Hollar, Peter Lely (1618–1680), Antonio Verrio (c. 1639–1707), Godfrey Kneller (1646–1723), Leonard Knyff (1650–1722), and Canaletto (1687–1768); the musicians Alfonso Ferrabosco (1543–1588), James Paisible (c. 1656–1721), and George Frideric Handel (1685–1759); and the sculptor John Michael Rysbrack (1694–1770) are only the most famous in a very long list. The impresario Johann Jakob Heidegger (1666–1749) summed up their experience: "I was born a Swiss, and came to England without a farthing, where I have found means to gain £5000 a-year, and to spend it. Now I defy the ablest Englishman to go to Switzerland and either to gain that income or spend it there."[6] Their innovation and entrepreneurialism were good for the economy, and many producers and consumers welcomed both, but small craftsmen, journeymen, and apprentices sometimes resented the competition, leading to occasional anti-immigrant riots (see Chapter 7).

Although officially expelled from England in 1290, there had always been a small, secret Jewish community in London. From the 1650s, when the Cromwellian government eased restrictions, Spanish *moranos* and Dutch *sephardim* sought asylum in England. At the Restoration, London merchants, fearing the competition, petitioned Charles II to expel the Jews again, but he refused in 1664, by which time there were almost a hundred Jewish households in London. Instead of converting, they established a synagogue at Creechurch Lane in the City and a cemetery at Mile End. They soon became crucial to London's financial life as goldsmiths and jewelers. After 1700, *Ashkenazi* Jews from Germany and Poland began to arrive, and by 1750 there were about 8,000 Jews living in London, mostly settled in poorer suburbs like Whitechapel, Mile End, or Petticoat Lane.

Other Europeans and Africans came as merchants, although, as the slave trade grew, increasing numbers of black people, both slave and free, came from the American colonies. The first black slave arrived in London in 1555. Elizabeth I's attempts to expel them in 1596 and 1601 failed. Instead, many upper-class families thought it stylish to keep a well-dressed slave and bestow on him a classical name (e.g., Pompey, Cato). Samuel Pepys employed a black cook named Doll and actually sold a boy in 1680. There was great debate over whether a slave was emancipated once he reached English shores because there was no statutory basis for the practice there. In 1772, Lord Chief Justice Mansfield (1705–1793) took a step toward abolition by deciding in effect that slave contracts were invalid in England absent such a statute. Most free blacks found work as sailors or servants. By the 1760s it was said that some 20,000 blacks lived in London, but Stephen Inwood thinks the real figure closer to 5,000. In any case, London drew from a trans-Channel and transoceanic population. To quote Peter Linebaugh, "Outcasts, runaways, mariners, castaways, the disinherited and the dispossessed found in it a place of refuge, of news and an arena for the struggle of life and death."[7] A place of bondage for some, London offered opportunity and a fresh start for most, while exposing its native inhabitants to a wider cultural and racial mix than any other place in England.

BECOMING A LONDONER

The experience of coming to London must have been overwhelming, particularly for newcomers from the countryside. From the moment of your first glimpse of the metropolis, whether from Highgate Hill, Bankside, or the river itself, this place was like no other in your experience. For starters it was so vast that not even the most experienced coachman or porter could know all of its streets, not least because they were not signposted nor houses numbered until the 1760s. In 1606 Thomas Dekker (c. 1572–1632) gave some idea of what it must have been like to walk those streets for the first time:

> In every street, carts and coaches make such a thundering as if the
> world ran upon wheels: at every corner, men, women, and children

meet in such shoals, that posts are set up of purpose to strengthen the houses, lest with jostling one another they should shoulder them down. Besides, hammers are beating in one place, tubs hooping in another, pots clinking in a third, water tankards running at tilt in a fourth.[8]

Never before had you been jostled by so many people "as it were in a throng, wanting elbow roome."[9] Never before would you have breathed air so foul, between the odors of thousands of work animals and "such a cloud of sea-coale, as if there be a . . . volcano on a foggy day."[10] Never before would you have heard so many different accents, seen so many styles of dress, coveted so many products, or been exposed to such a variety of customs and religious practices.

Take religion, ostensibly a focus of unity and promoter of conformity. In 1550 everyone in England was nominally a member of the Church of England, and there were in London about 120 parishes of which to be a part. After the Reformation, there was sometimes violent disagreement about what that Church should believe and how it should worship. In the village, these matters were determined by the landlord and the parson, often following directions from the Crown. But in London itself there were churches to suit every taste, from Catholic or crypto-Catholic cells at court or in Montague Close across the river in Southwark, to reformist (soon to be called Puritan) communities throughout, especially in Cripplegate and Coleman Street Wards in the City. By the early eighteenth century, perhaps 100,000 Londoners, 20% of the city's inhabitants, were Dissenters from the national Church, worshipping in 80 meeting houses spread throughout the metropolis. There were fourteen Huguenot churches in Westminster alone. Nowhere else would you encounter so many Baptists, Quakers, Presbyterians, Congregationalists, Jews, Muslims, and Catholics, some pursuing their faith in secret. In 1738 John Wesley (1703–1791) had his conversion experience in a meeting house in Aldersgate Street and soon began to lay the foundations for Methodism by visiting prisoners at Newgate and preaching to the crowds at Tyburn. Those crowds of course included Yorkshiremen and Kentishmen, Scotsmen and Irishmen, Frenchmen and Dutchmen, Africans and Americans.

One possible result of all this variety and sensory overload might be initial feelings of bewilderment, loneliness, alienation, perhaps even what modern sociologists call *anomie*. Thus John Harrower, newly arrived from the Shetland Islands on January 18, 1774: "This day I got to London and was like a blind man without a guide, not knowing where to go, being freindless [sic]." Similarly, an inmate of the Clerkenwell bridewell petitioned for release in 1722, although "I have not one friend to do any thing for me."[11] As a newcomer to London you would soon learn that your accent, customs, and habits were uncommon, even odd, and counted for little among such a sea of humanity. In contrast to the close-knit life that you had left in the village, you would encounter scores of people with whom you might not, could not, form long-term relationships: whereas there were many established families at the middling level, below that too many people died or moved on to other jobs or other parts of town for that kind of stability. Your relationships would therefore be far more casual than in the village. There, everybody knew your rank, position, job, and family, and those were for life. In London, nobody need know you; nothing need be for life. If you found a better job, you moved on. If a friend moved away or died, you had no time to mourn and plenty of possible replacements. In early modern London, no one was indispensable; no one's loss left a gaping hole in the fabric of society.

Some historians have posited that the experience of coming to London tended to privilege or produce a new kind of person: rational in his or her economic decision making, open minded about new ideas, flexible in coping with the ups and downs of a new, more capitalist economy – in short, a Londoner. On the one hand, the Londoner had to adjust to the possibility of losing her position on Tuesday and finding a new one on Wednesday. On the other hand, the city's great size and social fluidity meant that the Londoner, whether new or old, male or female, could always start afresh; Moll Flanders in Daniel Defoe's novel of the same name is always reinventing herself. If her situation does not work out, she simply moves to another part of town, assumes a new identity, and begins again. We will explore this notion further, as well as the economic implications of London's growth in general, later in this chapter and indeed throughout this book. For now, it is important to establish the psychological and social dimensions of the process of adjustment that all immigrant Londoners faced. As indicated above, that experience must have been exciting, full of possibility, especially for women who roamed freely across the capital unchaperoned, whether young ladies paying visits or servant girls running errands. But London could also be frightening, dislocating, and perplexing. According to the old medieval maxim, "City air makes one free," but it also divorced newcomers from family and community. No wonder that Elizabethan writers complained that self-interest and the city's flexible economy were destroying traditional fixed relationships, or that a century later the Scots tourist Robert Kirk opined, "The city is a great vast wilderness."[12]

Still, it is important not to overstate this. In its own way, London was just as hierarchical and interconnected as the village, with its lord mayor drawn from the Court of Aldermen, themselves drawn from a few elite, interrelated mercantile families; the Common Council, representative of the citizenry but filled with guild, ward, and parish leaders (see Chapter 3); the guilds themselves, which divided their ranks into wardens and assistants, liverymen, householders, journeymen, and apprentices, who were themselves divided from alien and stranger tradesmen; the wards and parishes, the former run by the alderman and his deputy, the latter by vestries dominated by the longest resident and most substantial citizens. At the bottom came many subordinate offices – constable, scavenger, and so forth – that could be filled by residents of modest means, with the potential to give them a sense of responsibility to and identification with their parish. Admittedly, the prosperous increasingly chose to pay a fine rather than serve. Just as in the village, this hierarchy was spelled out for all to see by the order in which people sat in the parish church's pews on Sunday, the most prominent families toward the front. Just as in the village, JPs, churchwardens, constables, and housewives knew their neighborhoods and worked with fellow parishioners to identify and root out vagrants, idlers, adulterers, fornicators, bastard bearers, slanderers, scolds, sabbath breakers, blasphemers, and drunks. Working in their favor was the fact that inner-city parishes were small, averaging less than 4 acres and 137 households or 300 people apiece in the 1630s. Most guilds consisted of a few hundred colleagues. Finally, just as the village had an elaborate calendar based on the agricultural and liturgical seasons to give a temporal rhythm to the year, so City and parish had their annual round of feasts and processions, the most important of which celebrated the installation of a new lord mayor every October 29 (see Chapters 3 and 5).

In short, there was much to belong to in London, many close-knit institutions, groups, titles, and responsibilities to give one a sense of status, identity, and community. To judge from the evidence of wills and court documents, prosperous Londoners, at least, identified strongly with their companies, parishes, and neighborhoods. Even "humble" London was in many ways a confederation of little parish and neighborhood communities, where the values of neighborliness, watchfulness, and involvement in one another's business were very strong, for good or ill. We have just noted that the churchwarden, the constable, and the respectable matron at the doorstep or the standpipe looked out for the shiftless, the inebriated, the sexually incontinent, and those too sleepy or too contrary to attend church services. This might lead to being presented to the JP, the wardmote, or an ecclesiastical court, but it might also lead to help. The widowed, the orphaned, and the destitute could appeal, often successfully, to community and neighborhood values for assistance, often in the form of lodging or "outdoor relief" on the Poor Law (see Chapter 6). Even business had a neighborly aspect. Money was scarce, and so local shops relied on their own credit with suppliers for stock and gave it to customers they knew for goods, creating webs of trust stretching across the city and down into the neighborhood. Neighbors loaned each other money, kept each other company during lyings-in, and prepared the bodies of their dead for burial. Londoners assembled to cheer the lord mayor and aldermen as they processed down Cheapside at the former's installation, yet they also defied City ordinances to attend the funerals of plague victims. In between there were company, parish, and neighborhood feasts and evenings at the local tavern or alehouse. In fact, the streets themselves were meeting places where work and sociability took place.

How did a newcomer become a neighbor? Working against cohesion and neighborliness was the fact that so many Londoners were new to town and therefore largely unknown in the parish on arrival. Many started off in the big parishes beyond the City walls like St. Margaret Westminster or St. Mary Overie, which might extend to over 100 acres and populations of more than 3,000 in the 1550s. By 1650 St. Botolph Aldgate to the northeast numbered more than 10,000 souls; St. Giles Cripplegate, St. Martin-in-the-Fields, and St. Dunstan Stepney, to the north, west, and east, respectively, contained 25,000 to 30,000 apiece. No wonder that legal scholars have found less evidence of neighborly cohesiveness, fewer people who knew their neighbors well as the period wore on and London grew. Once in London, the employment opportunities for immigrants depended on gender, the circumstances of their parents, and prior training. The preferred option for a young man whose family had the money was to purchase a place with a master tradesman as his apprentice. If he were older and skilled already, he might hire himself out as a journeyman.

In any case, apprentices, journeymen, and servants began the process of socialization as Londoners by joining their master's household. The household was a Great Chain of Being in microcosm, the master/husband/father (and, usually, guild member) at the head supervising the moral and economic discipline of his family. The two were related because, typically in early modern cities, a merchant or tradesman lived with his family plus a journeyman, two apprentices, and at least a couple of servants above his shop. The ground floor would be devoted to the manufacture of shoes, barrels, candles – whatever his trade – with finished goods displayed in a showroom, a window, or on a foldable counter known as a *bulk*, a stall, or stall board on the street frontage of the house. These would be few, as most goods were made on spec; that is, they were ordered to be made up to the specifications of the purchaser. Below the master in the household hierarchy came the wife/mother, who supervised housekeeping and cooking and often helped in the shop, followed by children, journeymen, apprentices, and servants, all with a role to play in the family's economic well-being. Hours were long: the Common Council regulations of 1538 decreed that journeymen work 6 AM to 6 PM in winter, and two additional hours in summer, with long breaks for breakfast, dinner (lunch), and in the afternoon. In the eighteenth century, shops with finished goods stayed open from 7 AM or 8 AM until 8, 9, or even 10 PM. In addition to cooking and helping out in the shop, women fought a constant battle against London's soot, scrubbing the house from top to bottom two or three times a week. But in an age before the assembly line, the pace of work was probably relaxed, enlivened with good-natured banter and raillery.

For those without the means to an apprenticeship or the training to be a journeyman, there was service. A great noble or gentleman might have a dozen or more servants – butlers and valets, secretaries and chaplains, housekeepers and maids, cooks, footmen, and grooms – even in rented lodgings. In an age when there were few labor-saving devices – no washing machines or vacuum cleaners – families of any means employed a servant or two: in 1695, 57% of households in a two-parish sample had at least one. For most respectable service, one needed experience and at least a verbal recommendation. Failing that, one might try to build on a connection with relatives or fellow villagers who had gone before and succeeded in establishing themselves in the metropolis. Thus did Edmund Halsey (fl. 1696-1729) come to London in the later seventeenth century with only 4 shillings and sixpence in his pocket, and a family connection to the Anchor Brewery in Southwark. Hired as a "broomstick clerk" and general dogsbody, he married the master's daughter and rose to become owner and a Member of Parliament (MP). Innkeepers and publicans provided word-of-mouth connections, but this begs the question of how one secured their good opinion if one could not afford to patronize them. By 1689, the first professional employment agency, or Servant's Registry, was operating in the Strand, "where masters of all sorts and servants and apprentices, and nurses of all kinds will find in a short time what they desire, as also hunters, stewards, butlers, chamber-maids of rooms, milkmaids, lacqueys."[13] Men with few skills and no money for an apprenticeship might head for the nearest street corner to hire themselves out for construction work or to that column in the nave of St. Paul's that served as a common meeting point for would-be domestic servants and masters.

If a young girl came from a good family, she might arrive in the capital with a reference to be a nanny or a schoolteacher; or if her parents could afford it, she might apprentice herself to a seamstress. Ordinary young women were most likely to enter menial domestic service: in Peter Earle's study of 1,004 late seventeenth- and early eighteenth-century working women, 64% of those 24 or younger followed this line of work, but only 30% of those aged 25 to 34, with a much smaller proportion of older women. Domestic service was a young single woman's game, played prior to marriage. Such work paid only between £2 and £6 a year in the period from 1650 to 1750, plus room and board. This was comparable to what many parishes gave out in poor relief; although not quite a living wage, it might be supplemented by tips or perquisites like access to leftover food and selling the master's old clothes at rag fairs. Servants moved about quite often, rarely staying for more than a year, and so there were always plenty of new openings. A young girl from the country might very well be taken up by a family looking for a maid or a seamstress, as was the case with the fictional Moll Flanders before coming to London. As Moll found out, as a member of the household she depended entirely on the whim of her master. One of the stereotypical London stories is that of a young maid new to city ways who becomes her master's lover, only to be discarded at the first signs of pregnancy.

Possibly even less lucky was the girl who became a barmaid or worked for an innkeeper. Least lucky of all, the young girl, fresh off a cart from the country, who became a hawker of goods in the streets or fell in with a "mother midnight" – a madam – who offered the devil's bargain of a place to stay and food to eat in return for becoming one of her girls in the stews of Southwark or Smithfield or, after 1700, the area around Covent Garden (see Chapter 5). James Boswell records an encounter with a prostitute in 1763 who fits the profile: "She who submitted to my lusty embraces was a young Shropshire girl, only seventeen, very well-looked, her name

Elizabeth Parker. Poor being, she has had a sad time of it!"[14] Such a life was hard and often cut short, either by venereal disease or by the all-to-easy progress from prostitution to theft to Tyburn tree. But even brothels and homosexual "molly houses" provided some kind of community, and one can well understand how a frightened and lonely young girl or boy might take up a mother midnight's offer.

Indeed, there was a slight chance that that young girl might, if she survived and played her hand shrewdly, end up a madam herself in one of the more substantial businesses open to female management. All together 5% to 10% of London businesses were run by women, most commonly in the food and drinks trades, textile shops and pawnshops, but the account books for the rebuilding of London's churches after the Fire of 1666 include payments to Ann Brooks, smith; Sarah Freeman, plumber; and the widow Pearce, painter. Because so many middle-aged London merchants and tradesmen married young women, London always had lots of widows. Some 10% to 20% of London households were headed by widows, and guild custom allowed them to operate as independent businesswomen. Older women without property took odd jobs cleaning, doing the laundry, mending clothes, nursing the sick, and acting as midwives.

THE LIVERY COMPANIES

If each member of the family found his or her place as part of the household chain, then each household found its place in London as part of the city's chain and, at the beginning of the period, more particularly in its relationship to a guild. The fundamental fact of economic life in London from 1550 to 1650, if less so thereafter, is that it was organized around guilds, or as Londoners preferred to call them, livery companies. A *livery company* was an organization of tradesmen granted a royal charter to regulate prices, wages, and quality of workmanship, as well as provide some level of economic security for members within the City of London. Only those who were "free" of a guild or freemen, that is, introductory members who paid a quarterly fee called *quarterage*, could trade within the City's limits. Full company members were called liverymen: traditionally, each trade had its own distinctive uniform or livery. The guild distributed charity to sick or unemployed members, widows, and orphans, and the wealthier companies maintained endowments that supported hospitals, almshouses, and schools. The companies also regulated citizenship and therefore voting rights: only freemen could vote for aldermen, common councilmen, and a host of subordinate offices, whereas only liverymen had the right to vote for the lord mayor, sheriffs, and the City's four MPs. In return for these privileges, the companies traditionally provided the Crown with loans and troops, and the City with social and economic stability.

In a sense, the livery companies were the City's response to the Great Chain of Being. Beginning around the twelfth century, they grew out of the medieval Church's hostility to certain aspects of capitalism, in particular, the potential for sharp practice and social mobility. In fact, some companies began as religious fraternities and each had its own church, often named after its patron saint: saddlers at St. Martin-le-Grand, skinners at St. John Walbrook, painters at St. Giles Cripplegate, brewers at All Hallows, London Wall. This was convenient, because practitioners in particular trades tended to live and work in specific parts of town. At the beginning of the fourteenth century, companies won the right to regulate the freedom to trade in London. Thereafter they sought to moderate the harshest aspects of capitalism by setting standard prices for goods sold, a standard wage for workers, and a standard of quality, detailing materials and how they were to be used in manufacture, to all of which members had to adhere. In fact, the Crown typically empowered companies, through their royal charters, to inspect the quality of work in their trades up to three miles beyond the City's border. The idea was to ensure sufficient profit for members without letting anyone grow too rich or poor; a sufficient wage for workers to avoid movements of labor from employer to employer; and reasonable quality and price for consumers. The charitable foundations noted previously were intended to provide security for members' families if a master became ill or died. Finally, livery companies fostered community amid the potentially faceless anonymity of the town, with feasts frequently held in the company hall, and before the Reformation, annual processions on the patron saint's day.

Most cities had one guild for all trades, but in 1550, London, with its diverse economy, had about eighty. Not all livery companies were equal, however; wholesalers and retailers who only sold products tended to be wealthier than the craftsmen who made them, and they endowed their companies accordingly. Consequently, a hierarchy developed, headed by the twelve great companies (in order): the Mercers, the Grocers, the Drapers, the Fishmongers, the Goldsmiths, the Skinners, the Merchant Taylors, the Haberdashers, the Salters, the Ironmongers, the Vintners, and the Clothmakers. Companies also varied in size: the

Merchant Taylors had 2,500 members, the Plumbers 58. Perhaps the most obvious manifestation of a company's status was its guild hall. Most were built in the fourteenth or fifteenth century; some were converted Church properties. Here, sitting among images and bequests of past members, the company's governing Court of Assistants met for deliberations, its liverymen for elections, and the membership as a whole for feasts in which the community of, say, grocers or ironmongers could be reaffirmed. In fact, the larger companies tended to be more hierarchical and less convivial: divided into liverymen, yeomen freemen (householders and journeymen), and apprentices, only the liverymen attended the annual election feast of a great company; journeymen had their own quarterly drinking. Thus the guild offered some of the community but also some of the structure and hierarchy to be found in a medieval village. Clearly, livery companies were no enemies to the Great Chain of Being.

So, the first question for many on arrival in London was: how did you become free of, that is, join, the guild? You could inherit the freedom or buy it, but by far the most common course was to rise by the traditional route, starting as an apprentice. For a set tuition, a master agreed to take in an adolescent, teach him the "mysteries" of the trade, and feed, clothe, and house him as a member of his household, with a higher status than a servant. According to legend, apprentices started young, at age 14, but recent research, on the Carpenters' Company in particular, indicates that few began service before age 17 and that the average age at beginning was $19\frac{1}{2}$. Although seven years was the traditional term, some apprenticed for as many as a dozen. Apprentices were forbidden to marry, which, combined with a gender ratio of 113 men to 100 women prior to 1650, further tended to depress London's birth rate. (That ratio would gradually be reversed by 1700.) The vast majority of apprentices were male, but throughout the period some young women apprenticed, usually as seamstresses or textile workers. Typically, apprenticeships were paid for by one's parents, the premiums ranging circa 1700 anywhere from £10 to £40 to a cooper or a milliner to £200 to £500 to a great merchant. Thus, they tended to be most available to those from already moderately prosperous backgrounds.

In fact, most trades hardly required seven years of training; most apprentice time was spent learning to read and write. (In the late sixteenth century, 82% of London apprentices could sign their own names – admittedly a crude measure of rudimentary literacy.) Apprentices therefore tended to be young men with time on their hands. The idle apprentice was well known to have the capacity to get into trouble, drinking, partying, rioting, or absconding with his master's goods or money. With roughly 30,000 apprentices in London in 1600, they potentially represented a considerable force for disorder (see Chapter 7). If contemporary literature and art is full of lazy and dishonest apprentices (most notably, William Hogarth's [1697–1764] print series, *Industry and Idleness* of 1747), it also portrays more than a few oppressive, cruel masters. Fortunately, neither party in the agreement lacked redress: both could complain to their company's Court of Assistants, whose records are full of such disagreements. Still, these represent only a fraction of the number of master–apprentice relationships, and so one cannot argue for their typicality. In any case, many apprentices – some 60% in the first half of the period – never completed their terms of service. Some died. Others fled, perhaps overcome by feelings of homesickness or resentment toward a strict master.

Those who did complete their apprenticeships joined the lowest rank of freemen and became journeymen. At this point, the graduating apprentice was presented to the guild and "called to the freedom," swearing an oath before its wardens and paying a fee of up to 3 shillings 4 pence. Thereafter, to maintain their freeman status and right to trade, they would, like all virtuous London tradesmen, pay quarterage, usually 8 pence a quarter (or 2 shillings 8 pence a year). A freeman was also responsible for paying rates (taxes), serving in local office, and hanging a lantern on his dwelling on moonless nights. A few days after admission to the freedom, the new journeyman was taken to the Guildhall to be made a citizen, which gave him the right to vote for all sorts of minor offices. A very few women, mostly widows and single daughters of deceased guildsmen, were allowed the freedom to carry on the dead man's trade, but almost none was granted citizenship.

Most journeymen had no desire to spend their most productive years living and working under another man's roof; the majority sought to amass enough capital, at least £100 in seventeenth-century London (£500 to £10,000 for a goldsmith or a brewer), to open their own shops and become householders in their own right. Here, their former master could be crucial: a favored former apprentice could become his heir, possibly, like Dick Whittington, marry his daughter, and in time take over his business. The prospective householder still had to pay a stiff entry fine to the company, and in some companies create a "proof-" or "master-piece" that would demonstrate that he knew fully the mysteries of his craft. Three-quarters of journeymen were able to do so and become householders. But if one wanted full membership, including entrée to high company office (i.e., assistant, master, warden), the right to vote for the lord mayor, sheriffs, and MPs, as well as access to the schools, hospitals, and other charitable schemes promoted by the guild, one had to go further and become a liveryman. So, after a few years and after paying another fee, the applicant would be voted on by his prospective fellow members. At this level, the result was by no means a foregone conclusion: only 25% of householders became liverymen. Precisely because the livery company operated a monopoly over a limited "pie" and distributed benefits so freely within the membership, it was crucial to keep the membership small. On the one hand, there is evidence that entry fines grew stiffer and standards of workmanship stricter as time went on, especially in big companies (i.e., the Merchant Taylors, the Drapers). On the other hand, London's mortality rate was high and places opened up rapidly, especially to those who had married a master's daughter. For those who wanted no part of any of this, or could not afford to establish themselves as householders, the alternative was to set up shop beyond the City's borders, out of easy reach of the guilds but with little access to City markets, or to simply remain a journeyman in perpetual subordination in a master's shop.

Londoners who worked in suburban areas outside of the lord mayor's jurisdiction were not required to join livery companies, although their work might still come under their scrutiny. London's population grew fastest in these areas, eventually outstripping the City: in 1560 only one-fifth of Londoners lived beyond the City limits; by 1640 more than one-half of the population did so. As a result, the relative place of the companies in London's economy diminished over time: the Grocers and Fishmongers gave up searches for illicit trade circa 1700, the Vintners in 1708, the Distillers in 1723. The last conviction in Middlesex for trading without having served a seven-year apprenticeship was in 1677, although isolated prosecutions took place until 1707. Finally, on November 22, 1750, London's Common Council decreed that, if the demands of freemen grew "unreasonable," employers could hire non-freemen, thus making trade "free" in the City of London. Even so, the leading companies still retained vast amounts of property in London and the provinces that underpinned their charitable endowments. That made them continual players in London's real estate market, and the resultant wealth ensured that the schools, hospitals, and charities that they ran would continue to flourish into the twenty-first century. Moreover, metropolitan government remained entwined with the guilds, not least because membership still determined citizenship and voting rights. That meant in turn that it was still desirable for ambitious newcomers to join a company. As social and political institutions the livery companies therefore remained important throughout the period covered in this book, even if their economic roles had been transformed.

THE TRADING COMPANIES

In 1550, the movers and shakers of London were not only members of livery companies; they also belonged to trading companies. Like a guild, a trading company was a union of merchants whose goal was to secure and preserve a monopoly on trade. It was different from a guild in that, first, it was generally concerned only with foreign trade; and, second, only with the retail and not the manufacture of goods. For example, the Merchant Adventurers, the first great trading company in England, was an organization of merchants mainly selling cloth to Europe. Third, as this implies, the great trading companies, although based in London, were national in membership and international in scope: the Merchant Adventurers' official headquarters was Antwerp. Other companies, like the East India or Massachusetts Bay, focused not on particular commodities but trade with particular overseas markets. Fourth, unlike the guilds, great trading companies were not especially associated with the Church, nor did they take much responsibility for the well-being of their members. In this alone, they represent a move away from community and toward modern free-market capitalism. As with the guilds, however, their monopolistic privileges were enshrined in royal charters enforced in law. In return for their special status they were among the Crown's most generous lenders, growing increasingly important during Elizabeth's war with Spain. In this, they represent the very antithesis of free-market capitalism.

The Company of Merchant Adventurers was founded in 1407. It was patterned after the highly successful Hanseatic League of Northern Germany, which established trading privileges in London in 1267. As late as the fifteenth century, much of London's overseas trade was funneled through resident foreign merchants: Germans, Flemings, Italians, and small numbers of Jews, Portuguese, and even Icelanders, often encouraged by the Crown as a counterweight to the wealth and power of native merchants. The Merchant Adventurers were founded to reverse this. Although some trading companies would eventually become joint stock companies, most, including the Merchant Adventurers, were not investment opportunities. Rather, the Adventurers were more of a trade association or lobbying group led by fifty rich London overseas merchants who banded together for physical, economic, and political protection. The first they secured by combining to send out fleets rather than single ships; the second and third by generous loans to the Crown and effective lobbying of Parliament against all rivals foreign and domestic. In 1485 they secured an act forbidding the import of wine in foreign vessels; in 1489, similar restrictions on clothing dye. As a result, between 1500 and 1600, the Merchant Adventurers came to dominate London's foreign trade, which in turn composed about two-thirds to three-quarters of England's total overseas trade. The bulk of that commerce (90%) consisted of textiles, mostly raw wool shipped to Antwerp for finishing into wool cloth and then sale to the European market. After 1550, as English cloth manufacturers grew more skillful, increasing amounts of cloth were finished in England before shipping to Antwerp. This meant that the Fullers' and Clothworkers' companies wanted in on the trade. But their political clout was no match for the Merchant Adventurers: in 1564, Parliament decreed that only Merchant Adventurers could ship cloth to Europe.

As this implies, the Merchant Adventurers were, for a time in the late sixteenth century, a fabulously wealthy and powerful group. Although they were generally liverymen as well, they tended to be much more prosperous than most who wore the gown. In the sixteenth century, they lived like minor princes, usually in the center of the City in large multistory, multichimneyed houses, their rooms decorated with molded plaster ceilings, expensive tapestries, and ornate carved furniture, their presses loaded with gold and silver plate, and their closets bulging with expensive gowns lined with velvet and fur. No government could afford to offend them, not least because the late Tudors and early Stuarts, always short of cash, depended on the loans they made. In 1552 they persuaded Parliament to revoke the privileges of the Hanseatic merchants in London; in 1598 they got their German competitors expelled altogether.

During the first half-century covered by this book, Merchant Adventurers dominated London's politics as well as its trade. For example, just about every lord mayor and most aldermen who sat between 1550 and 1580 were Merchant Adventurers. But their power began to wane as the wool trade declined and other trades and trading companies rose to take their place. Beginning around 1550 wool began to experience a century of stagnation or slow growth, punctuated by dramatic slumps in 1551–52, 1562–64, 1571–73, 1586–87, 1603, 1607–11, 1614–16, 1621–26, 1629–30,

1641–42, and the 1650s. One reason for the leveling off of wool exports was that the Antwerp staple, England's principal market for wool in the Low Countries, was in the eye of a political, religious, and military storm during the second half of the sixteenth century. Shipments to Antwerp were disrupted by the Wars of Religion, the Dutch revolt against Spanish rule from 1566 to 1609, England's war against Spain from 1585 to 1604, and the Thirty Years' War, 1618 to 1648. Even during relatively quiet periods, Antwerp might be closed to English trade by its Spanish governors. The Merchant Adventurers tried to find other staples, but none was as convenient to them or their customers as Antwerp. In any case, wool prices began to fall at the end of the sixteenth century because the European market was flooded with the stuff. English manufacturers responded with new, lighter, cheaper forms of wool cloth known as the "new draperies." These were moderately successful, leading to some good years at the beginning of the seventeenth century, but the overall foreign demand for wool continued to lessen and its price to fall. During bad years, merchant incomes stagnated, cloth workers lost their jobs, and farm families went without valuable supplementary income from shearing, carding, spinning, and weaving. After 1640, wool remained England's biggest export, but as a shadow of its former self.

Fortunately, at precisely this moment, English demand for imports from the East – spices, fabrics, dyes, medicines from the Levant or India, even through Russia – took off. Unfortunately, England's commercial crisis occurred in the midst of a worldwide competition for trade and colonies circa 1600 on the part of the great European powers, including Portugal, Spain, France, and the Netherlands. In short, the English would have to fight for this trade: the privateering campaigns of Hawkins and Drake were early examples of this. Simultaneously, the Crown, worried about unemployment, desperate to save the wool industry but also intrigued by the possibility of vast wealth from overseas commerce such as rival monarchs were accruing, began to explore more systematic options. The result, often greased by well-bribed courtiers or vast loans to the Crown, was a series of royal charters to new companies beginning with the Muscovy Company in 1555 and continuing with the Spanish Company (1577), the Eastland Company (to trade with the Baltic, 1579), the Turkey (later the Levant) Company (1581), the Senegal Adventurers (1588, eventually the Royal Africa Company), the East India Company (1600), the Virginia Company (1606), the Massachusetts Bay Company (1629), and the Hudson's Bay Company (1670). This spurred exploration, privateering, the import luxury trade, and the rise of a new City merchant elite, who began to take over the mayoralty, court of aldermen, and the collection of Customs for the Crown. By 1603, only one-third of the Court of Aldermen were Merchant Adventurers; others were drawn from these companies. By 1640/41, sixteen of the twenty-nine aldermen serving in those years were Levant or East India Company directors. Finally, in 1689, the Merchant Adventurers lost their monopoly on cloth exports.

In most cases, the new companies had no intention of finding new markets for wool. Rather, their goal was to take advantage of increasing Spanish and Portuguese weakness to tap into home demand for lucrative commodities like silks, cotton, calico, indigo and other dyes, fruits, spices, and later tea in the case of the Levant and East India Companies, and timber and naval stores by the Eastland Company. The Virginia Company aimed at North American colonization and gold mining but eventually specialized in tobacco. That tobacco and, later, cotton and West Indian sugar were increasingly harvested by Africans sold into slavery in the New World by the Royal Africa Company. The Massachusetts Bay Company specialized in colonization and animal pelts. By the middle of the seventeenth century, imports were far more significant than exports, and London was the capital of a nascent trans-Atlantic British Empire that included the East Coast of what is now the United States and sugar and tobacco-growing islands in the Caribbean like Jamaica and Barbados, as well as an extensive trading network that extended to Asia.

The greatest of the trading companies was the East India, headquartered in Leadenhall Street, Cornhill. This organization was founded on a new and different principle from the others. Whereas most of the other companies were merely unions of merchants, the East India, along with the Muscovy Company, was one of the first joint-stock companies in England; that is, it was an investment opportunity for anyone who could afford the stiff stock price of £50 per share. Thus, rather than mount an expedition oneself under the auspices of the Merchant Adventurers or the Eastland Company, one shared the risk by investing in a company that took care of arranging voyages, and early in the seventeenth century, arming ships and raising armies to combat the Dutch and French East India Companies. Joint-stock companies had the merit of opening up foreign trade to nonmercantile investors: courtiers, urban professionals, and landowners who would not have considered investing in a particular risky voyage might put their money in something as substantial as the East India Company. That, in turn, tied all these groups together in a London-centered web of investment that did much to further enrich the elite and middle classes. Similarly, several trans-Atlantic colonies, the West Indies in particular, were developed by consortia of Puritan-leaning aristocrats, upstart merchants, and planters, partly to provide a safe refuge from Laudian persecution (see Introduction and Chapter 7). This could have had only a corrosive effect on class prejudice: it is more difficult to look down on a man when he is your business partner. The increasingly close relationship thus forged among the government, the landed aristocracy, and the London merchant community during the second century of this book, much of it worked out not at Whitehall or the Royal Exchange but in the more public sphere of taverns and coffeehouses on Cornhill, would be unknown in many European countries. In the eighteenth century, Voltaire would see it as the explanation for England's greater wealth and military success vis-a-vis France.

The great trading companies might have opened up the enterprise of foreign trade to a wider investment pool than the Merchant Adventurers, but they were still government-sanctioned monopolies. Before 1640 foreign trade remained unfree, channeled by the Crown for its own purposes and toward its own friends. Often, monopolies to sell particular products (and therefore take a hefty cut of their profits) were granted to favored courtiers, infringing on the rights of the guilds. Even those monopolies were always under threat, because a new group of merchants or courtiers fronting for merchant partners might offer the sovereign an even more tempting deal (e.g., a loan, a lump sum, or a cut of the profits). The resultant decision might or might not be good for trade overall. On the one hand, the Stuarts' encouragement of luxury trades like native silk production often did increase quality and demand. On the other hand, court favoritism could have disastrous consequences. For example, in 1614 a London alderman and Eastland Company member with court connections named William Cokayne (1559/60–1626) bribed several prominent courtiers to secure the right to establish a dyeing industry in England. His object was to bypass both the Merchant Adventurers and the Flemish cloth finishers; to interest the king, he projected an additional £40,000 in Customs revenues. To facilitate the scheme, the government suppressed the export of unfinished cloth, shutting down numerous smaller operations, and thus throwing many cloth workers out of their jobs. Worse, the undercapitalized Cokayne project collapsed by 1617, and with it much of the English cloth industry. Ominously, guildsmen complained of their freedom being traversed and of being sold into bondage.

THE COMMERCIAL REVOLUTION

After the Civil Wars, the Commonwealth and restored Stuart governments laid important foundations for London's commercial growth through legislation and conquest. By the mid-seventeenth century, the Dutch had replaced the Spanish as England's greatest commercial rivals, both in the Far East and the American colonies. From this point, Parliament tried to protect not monopolies of privileged English traders from other English traders, but all English traders from the Dutch and other foreign competitors. For example, it passed a series of Navigation Acts in 1650/51, 1660 (12 Chas. II, c. 18), and 1663 (15 Chas. II, c. 7), which taken together forbade foreign powers from trading directly with England's overseas possessions and required all such trade to be carried in English merchant ships with crews that were at least 75% English. Imports to England from other countries had to come in English ships, or ships from the originating country – thus freezing out the Dutch carrying trade. From 1660 all tobacco, sugar, ginger, cotton, and indigo shipped to or from English plantations in America, Africa, or Asia had to go through an English port. These products, especially sugar, were in very high demand and therefore the most lucrative on the Atlantic. Three times, from 1652 to 1654, 1664 to 1667, and 1672 to 1674, the English and Dutch went to war, partly because of this legislation. Despite England's losing the second and third of these wars, the Navigation Acts stayed on the books, enforced by a Royal Navy that was expanding in size and competence.

The effect on London's trade and shipping industry was tremendous. First, English shipbuilding prospered, not least along the Thames east of the Tower in places like Wapping, Rotherhithe, and Deptford. In 1572, the total English merchant marine amounted to perhaps 50,000 tons; by 1629 it came to 115,000; by 1702 it numbered 323,000, almost one-half of which was London owned. Second, the acquisition of Bermuda in 1612, Barbados in 1627, and Jamaica in 1655 made possible the expansion of the lucrative sugar and slave trades, while that of New York in 1664 drove the Dutch from North America. Meanwhile, the period from 1650 to 1730 saw a boom in the size of the American colonial population (including the British West Indies, and from 1713 Newfoundland, but excluding slaves) from 55,000 to 538,000. That population would supply about one-half of Britain's transatlantic imports and absorb almost one-quarter of its exports.

In general, the merchants trading with the American colonies came from different backgrounds from the more established members of the old trading companies: while the company merchants tended to be from well-known mercantile families, Royalists and later Tories, the colonial merchants were relative social upstarts, often Puritan, parliamentarian during the Civil Wars, and Whigs afterward. These "interlopers" had long urged an end to the privileges of the great trading companies, demanding in effect free trade for Englishmen. With the weakening of the Crown after the Civil Wars, they began to achieve their goal. In 1673 they broke the monopoly of the Eastland Company to Scandinavia. As we have seen, in 1689 the Merchant Adventurers finally lost their trading privileges. In 1698 a New East India Company, started by Whig merchants, challenged the old East India Company, long run by Tories. (They would merge in 1709.) After 1689, the Levant, Russia, and Royal Africa companies also went into decline, although the Hudson's Bay Company retained its monopoly on furs until 1763. As a result, the opportunities for merchants in overseas trade became less exclusive, and less restrictive.

Overall, the evolution of the livery companies; the rise, then fall of the trading companies; the creation of joint stock companies; the expansion of the British merchant marine; the exploration of new markets; the driving of the Dutch from North America; the continued rise of the "new draperies"; and the expansion of credit facilities with the stock market boom and Financial Revolution (see later discussion) contributed to an unprecedented expansion in trade. Between 1660 and 1700 London's volume of trade more than doubled. After that date things slowed because of the rise of rival Western ports like Glasgow and Liverpool and the disruption of commerce caused by French privateers in the Nine Years' and Spanish Succession wars from 1689 to 1713 (see Introduction). But thanks to the trade provisions of the Treaty of Utrecht (1713), the eventual harvest from those wars was a bumper crop for trade. The acquisition of Gibralter, Nova Scotia, St. Kitts, and the *Assiento* slaving contract to the Spanish New World expanded British trade in the Mediterranean, Canada, Italy, Spain, and the Spanish colonies. In 1750, with the end of the War of the Austrian Succession, London was poised for another period of growth.

The result was so profound that historians have called it the Commercial Revolution. Overall, British overseas trade expanded in total annual gross value from £5.5 million in 1640, to £7.9 million in 1663–69, to £14.5 million by 1722–24. Britain's most important trade was no longer the export of wool, but the importation of sugar from the West Indies and its re-export, along with colonial produce and Asian goods (i.e., cottons, silks, spices, and indigo from India, and by the 1720s, tea from China) to Europe. Sugar was the prize commodity of the eighteenth century. Demand rose steadily, from 26.2 million pounds a year in the late 1660s, to 42.5 million by the early 1700s, to 92.6 million pounds by the late 1720s. By the early eighteenth century, sugarcane, as well as tobacco and later cotton, was mostly harvested by African slaves rather than indentured servants. It was during the late seventeenth century that the notorious "triangular trade" with Africa and North America hit its stride, the deals worked out at Africa House, the Jamaica Coffee House, or Lloyd's Coffee House, all on Cornhill. Although London would lose its dominance of the sugar, cotton, tobacco, and slave trades to Western ports like Bristol and Liverpool after 1750, it remained an important embarkation point, a source of credit (e.g., Barclays, the Bank of England), as well as the principal port through which slave-harvested tobacco and sugar were shipped for re-export to Europe. In short, during the last hundred years of our period and beyond, much of London's prosperity was erected on the backs of captive and exploited Africans and at the expense of Native Americans driven slowly from what had once been their land.

That prosperity and the atrocities that made it possible were fueled by insatiable demand. As England's population growth slowed down and the labor market shrank after 1660, wages rose, providing more disposable income for ordinary men and women. At the same time, large landowners, professionals, merchants, and monied men (see discussion later) were doing well enough to want luxury items. To meet this demand, the markets and stalls of London overflowed with madeira and port wine from Portugal; figs, raisins, and oranges from Spain; silks and olive oil from Italy; sugar, tobacco, furs, and salt fish from America; coffee from the Middle East; and the goods of India and China noted previously. The continent wanted these things too. Thanks to the Navigation Acts, all of this trade flowed to Britain and the continent through British ports, most often London: from 1722 to 1724, the metropolis handled over 80% of England's imports, 67% of its exports, and 87% of its re-exports (see Illustration 2.1). Some contemporaries bewailed London's commercial dominance. Even that lifelong Londoner and quintessential optimist Daniel Defoe blamed the metropolis for the decline of provincial ports like Ipswich, Suffolk:

> But the neighbourhood of London, which sucks the vitals of trade in this island to itself, is the chief reason of any decay of business in this place; . . . many good seaports and large towns, tho' farther off than Ipswich, and as well fitted for commerce, are yet swallow'd up

by the immense indraft of trade to the City of London; and more decay'd beyond all comparison than Ipswich is supposed to be; as Southampton, Weymouth, Dartmouth, and several others.... [15]

Other writers were more celebratory. Joseph Addison caught the sense of London as a marketplace for the world's goods, as well as a meeting place for the world's peoples, in *The Spectator* of May 19, 1711:

THERE is no Place in the Town which I so much love to frequent as the *Royal-Exchange*. It gives me a secret Satisfaction, and in some measure, gratifies my Vanity, as I am an *Englishman*, to see so rich an Assembly of Countrymen and Foreigners consulting together upon the private Business of Mankind, and making this Metropolis a kind of *Emporium* for the whole Earth. I must confess I look upon High-Change to be a great Council, in which all considerable Nations have their Representatives.... I am infinitely delighted in mixing with these several Ministers of Commerce, as they are distinguished by their different Walks and different Languages: Sometimes I am justled among a Body of *Armenians*; Sometimes I am lost in a Crowd of *Jews*; and sometimes make one in a Groupe of *Dutchmen*. I am a *Dane, Swede,* or *Frenchman* at different times; or rather fancy my self like the old Philosopher, who upon being asked what Countryman he was, replied, That he was a Citizen of the World.

London had become the great crossroads of the world's trade, and the London merchant a cosmopolitan figure. Londoners – indeed, Britons generally – now had access to all of the world's commodities:

Our Ships are laden with the Harvest of every Climate: Our Tables are stored with Spices, and Oils, and Wines: Our Rooms are filled with Pyramids of *China*, and adorned with the Workmanship of *Japan*: Our Morning's Draught comes to us from the remotest Corners of the Earth: We repair our Bodies by the Drugs of *America*, and repose ourselves under *Indian* Canopies. My Friend [the merchant] Sir ANDREW [Freeport] calls the Vineyards of *France* our Gardens; the Spice-Islands our Hot-beds; the *Persians* our Silk-Weavers, and the *Chinese* our Potters. Nature indeed furnishes us with the bare Necessaries of Life, but Traffick gives us greater Variety of what is Useful, and at the same time supplies us with every thing that is Convenient and Ornamental.[16]

The new culture of shopping created, in part, by the Exchanges, had social as well as economic implications: men and women with money and time went to the "Change" not only to patronize the numerous goldsmiths', jewelers', haberdashers', linen drapers', perfumers', stationers', and map, print, and booksellers' shops, but also to simply walk about, to see and be seen, in one of the few unfettered venues for the social interaction of the sexes in all of Britain. Presumably, they gave no more thought to how these goods got there than Addison had done.

THE FINANCIAL REVOLUTION

The capital thus generated made London merchants rich: a few, like the financier Sir John Banks (1627–1699) or the German immigrant Peter Vansittart (fl. 1650–1695), were worth over six figures, although fortunes of £5,000 to £15,000 were more common. The capital from trade did more, however: it precipitated another revolution. After all, what do you do with all of that money? Traditionally, a great nobleman would spend it on conspicuous consumption – a townhouse, a coach, another estate – whereas a successful merchant would plow it back into trade. If you could not make up your mind, prior to 1700 you could leave it with a goldsmith. Goldsmiths were used to securing valuables in strong vaults because of the nature of their stock, and they had to preserve spotless reputations to do business. From the mid-seventeenth century on, they began to operate like proto-banks, taking deposits, making loans, paying or receiving interest, and backing up Exchequer tallies and bills of exchange. In this they were assisted by scriveners who drew up legal documents, arranged mortgages, and so forth. London goldsmiths also had close ties to the Crown, to which they were important lenders. It is a sign of London's growing wealth that, beginning in the 1570s, Queen Elizabeth forsook the Antwerp money market for loans by consortia of City businessmen. Between 1650 and 1750 men like Sir Thomas Viner (1588–1665) and his step-nephew, Sir Robert Viner (1631–88), or Sir Francis Child (1641/42–1713) established banking dynasties. Some, like the younger Viner, were ruined by the Stop of the Exchequer in 1672, when Charles II suspended payments of his debts (see later discussion). But several of the survivors evolved into full-fledged banks, a few of which – Child and Co. in Fleet Street, Coutts and Co. in the Strand – still operate. By the 1720s, there were twenty-five such banks in London receiving deposits, paying out interest, issuing notes of exchange, and making loans. Because the legal rate of interest was 6%

before 1714 and 5% thereafter, money was relatively cheap, loans readily available, and new ventures easy to start.

Although your money was safe at Viner's or Child's, it could not grow very fast. More lucrative were investments in joint-stock companies. As we have seen, these had been around since the late sixteenth century. As government-backed trading monopolies became extinct at the end the seventeenth century, there was an explosion of new companies: 11 in 1689, 93 by 1695. These companies sold stock in products and ventures as diverse as glass bottles, convex lights, lute strings, sword blades, gunpowder, mines, and fisheries. As the variety of this list implies, there was no government regulation of the new stock market, nor were professional standards very high. In 1696 the first stock market crash led to a statute limiting the number of brokers or "jobbers" to 100 and expelling them from the Royal Exchange. Between that date and the establishment of a formal London stock market in 1773, jobbers traded stocks in the informal surroundings of London coffeehouses: domestic investors met at Jonathan's or Garraway's in Exchange Alley, Cornmarket, near the Royal Exchange. Overseas merchants, shipowners, and sea captains convened nearby at Lloyd's, on the corner of Lombard Street and Abchurch Lane. Edward Lloyd (c. 1648–1713) kept a ready supply of all of the London papers so that his customers could stay abreast of the shipping news. Not only did they pool information, but they also made deals with each other and with specialist marine underwriters to insure voyages, which in turn encouraged greater risk taking. By 1750, Lloyd's coffeehouse was on its way to becoming the world's greatest marine insurer. We will address coffeehouses in greater detail in Chapter 5, but here it is important to note that their relative lack of tradition and low entry fee (a penny), combined with the availability of London newspapers, made them attractive watering holes for the respectable gentleman and the on-the-go merchant. Patrons drank strong coffee, read the news, shared gossip, and exchanged opinions, cash, and credit across class lines.

At the same time, this wide-open atmosphere and the lack of government regulation meant that there was nothing to prevent a charlatan from selling stock in a company that did not exist or had no real prospect of producing a profit. It was not for nothing that Johnson's *Dictionary* (1755) defines a *stock-jobber* as "a low wretch who makes money by buying and selling shares in funds." Many investors did not understand that the value of stock was symbolic of the fluctuating market value of actual *products* being sold. Most saw only that the stock market tended to rise. In fact, the market was very volatile. Of the ninety-three joint-stock companies in existence in 1695, only twenty-one were still around in 1717. The ground was laid for an even greater stock market crash, the South Sea Bubble of 1720.

The South Sea Company was a Tory response to the East India Company and the Bank of England (see discussion later). It had been created in 1711 to trade with the Spanish colonies of the New World, a concession that the government hoped to secure in the peace negotiations ending the War of the Spanish Succession. In 1718, a Whig government led by James, Earl Stanhope (1673–1721) and Charles Spencer, Earl of Sunderland (1675–1722) allowed the South Sea Company to take over three-fifths of the national debt in return for interest payments and certain trading privileges. As with the Cockayne scheme a century earlier, the deal was greased with bribes and kickbacks. Once it was announced, there was a run on South Sea stock, which rose in value by nearly 1,000% in the summer of 1720. When it became clear that the company was not making a profit (having engaged in almost no actual South Sea trade), the stock price collapsed, ruining many investors and discrediting the government. The Stanhope-Sunderland administration fell, and the new Chancellor of the Exchequer, Robert Walpole, persuaded the Bank of England and the East India Company to assume much of the loss, thus saving the government's finances and making his career. Surprisingly, neither the South Sea Bubble nor the low reputation of stock-jobbers did much to dissuade people from investing in stocks. The reason is simple: here more than in any other branch of London's economy, a small investment could yield a big profit in very little time. One company to salvage a Spanish treasure galleon yielded profits of 10,000% to its investors, but whole fortunes could be lost just as fast.

Was there no more stable form of investment? Today, that role would be played by government bonds. But in the seventeenth century the credit of the government was anything but good. Stuart monarchs, chronically short of cash, were frequently borrowers (from the City itself and individual wealthy aldermen and merchants) but dilatory repayers, often ruining middling merchants who had been so rash as to lend to them. The Corporation and City merchants loaned money not so much for the possibility of a great return as a quid pro quo for those lucrative trading privileges enjoyed by the great trading companies. But, as we have seen, those privileges were being rescinded in the later seventeenth century. Moreover, the government's credit hit a new low in 1672, when in the midst of his preparations for the Third Anglo-Dutch war, Charles II suspended payment on his debts. The Stop of the Exchequer was not technically a bankruptcy, because the government promised to pay up eventually. But it never lived up to that promise, and the failure to pay over the course of many years ruined several prominent goldsmith bankers and merchants like Viner. Why should anyone lend money to the government ever again?

After the Glorious Revolution of 1688/89, the Crown's need for money was acute, because it was fighting a continental war against the wealthiest and most powerful monarch in Christendom, Louis XIV. To win the war, William's government needed lots of ready cash – quicker and more abundant cash than could be raised by taxes. The king's chancellor of the exchequer, Charles Montagu, later Lord Halifax (1661–1715), saw an alternative source of income in the wealth flowing into the country from the Commercial Revolution. The Customs and Excise (a sales tax), directly dependent on the volume of trade, were already the most profitable taxes in the Crown's portfolio. The Parliaments of the 1690s raised Customs rates as high as 25% and extended the Excise to all sorts of new products, including leather, coal, malt (important for brewing), salt, spices, tea, coffee, and wine. Such taxes took a long time to collect, however, and raising the rates further might stifle the Commercial Revolution. Much better to persuade big and middling merchants and investors in trading ventures to loan ready money to the Crown voluntarily, but this was a tough proposition after the Stop of the Exchequer.

In 1693, Parliament authorized the government to solicit a loan of £1 million on the security of a fund fed by the Land, Excise, and other taxes. This marks the establishment of the nations's funded National Debt. For the first time, interest on the debt was to be paid out of a specific "pot." This made such loans more attractive, because their repayment seemed much more secure. Montagu went further by proposing that in future the government make no promise to pay back the *principal* of such loans by any particular date; instead they would remain outstanding for the course of the war, if not longer. The government did promise to pay lenders interest as high as 14%, out of the fund described earlier, for life while the principal was outstanding. This meant that if England won the war and the lender lived, he and his family could make their investment many times over. This was so attractive that, as time went on, the government found that it could lower the interest paid and still find takers. Later, the Crown also offered lenders self-liquidating annuities for several lives or for

99 years and sold tickets to public lotteries. They also charged corporate bodies like the East India Company, and in the next reign, the South Sea Company, vast sums in return for the privilege of being allowed to exist.

The greatest example of this fund-raising strategy, and Montagu's crowning inspiration, was the charter for the Bank of England, established in 1694 at the instigation of a Scottish merchant, William Patterson (1658–1719). In return for an immediate loan to the Crown of £1.2 million, the Bank was allowed to sell stock in itself, receive deposits, make loans, and even print notes against the security of its loan to the Crown. Subscribers received 8% interest out of an annual fund of £100,000 generated by taxes. Its directors were among the most prominent monied men in the City. The connection to the London business community was underscored by the Bank's location, not in Westminster but in the City. It opened in 1694 in Mercers' Hall, Ironmonger Lane, then moved to Grocers' Hall, Princes Street, before finally establishing itself at its current location, on Cornhill at Threadneedle Street in 1734. In future years, "the old Lady of Threadneedle Street" would be the Crown's largest single lender, its principal banker, and the manager of the funded national debt that Montagu had initiated under William III.

The fiscal expedients described previously, which the historian P.G.M. Dickson identified as the *Financial Revolution*, had a profound influence on London and on the nation. First, in the short term, they enabled the Crown to raise fabulous sums of money very quickly. This funding enabled it to recruit and supply the great continental armies and maintain the vast fleets necessary to stop Louis XIV in 1697 and vanquish him in 1713 (see Introduction). Not only was the Sun King's great dream of a Franco-Spanish Empire dashed, but Protestantism in Britain and Europe, a British Empire in the New World, and parliamentary sovereignty in England all were secured. As Defoe would later recognize, it was "not the longest sword, but the longest purse that conquers."[17]

In the long term, the wealth produced by the Financial Revolution would ensure Britain's growing military domination of Europe in the eighteenth century, and the world in the century after that. Throughout this period, the British government would have at its disposal enormous armies and navies and the expanding bureaucracy necessary to oversee and supply them. For example, it has been estimated that the central administration comprised some 4,000 officials in 1688. By the 1720s it came to more than 12,000, most of them based in London (see Chapter 3).

That infrastructure would make possible victory in subsequent wars, in particular the Seven Years' War (1756–1763), which would bring more lucrative colonies: the remainder of Canada; all of the American territories to the Mississippi including Florida; Grenada, Dominica, Tobago, and St. Vincent in the West Indies; Senegal in Africa; and the removal of French East India Company troops from India. All of this would add to Britain's – and so London's – wealth from overseas trade.

The long-term socioeconomic significance of the Financial Revolution was that it made investors, usually Whig financiers and government contractors who supplied the war, very wealthy very fast. In fact, it seemed to create a new class of men. As the Tory MP Henry St. John (1678–1751) wrote in 1709: "A new interest has been created . . . & a sort of property wch was not known twenty years ago is now encreased to almost equal to the *terra firma* of our island."[18] Contemporaries called this new group "moneyed men," for they made their wealth not from the land (hence St. John's allusion) or even from the sale of goods, but from the exploitation of credit. Moreover, they played so important a role in government finance that they often advised the Crown on fiscal matters. In London, they came to dominate the mayoralty and Court of Aldermen: by the mid-eighteenth century perhaps a quarter of the latter were either bank or company directors. They thus acquired influence not only on fiscal policy but also on foreign, domestic, and metropolitan policy as well. Because the National Debt would never truly be paid off and the British government was now committed to service that debt for the foreseeable future, it would continue to need these men.

The rise of this new interest worried conservative contemporaries, Tory landowners in particular. In 1710 Jonathan Swift (1667–1745) expressed these sentiments in his periodical *The Examiner*, No. 13. Just as a modern observer might begin with the cars driven by the newly successful, Swift calls attention to the horses and carriages lining London's streets:

> Let any man observe the equipages in this town, he shall find the greater number of those who make a figure, to be a species of men quite different from any that were ever known before the Revolution; consisting either of generals or colonels, or of those, whose whole fortunes lie in funds and stocks; so that power, which according to the old maxim was used to follow land, is now gone over to money; and the country gentleman is in the condition of a young heir, out of

whose estate a scrivener [lawyer] receives half the rents for interest, and has a mortgage on the whole. . . .

In some ways this is simply a more specific version of the old fears about London's growth. Where before London's entertainment and employment opportunities were draining the country of people, now its financial power was draining it of capital while corroding the Great Chain of Being by creating new wealth. The wars, the Financial Revolution, and the government bureaucracy invented to fight them threatened to undo the traditional hierarchy based on birth and land, and concentrate financial and social power in London. Landowners in the countryside grew poor because they were paying the Land Tax, while London-based military men (who made huge profits from subcontracts for uniforms, weaponry, and food), government officials (whose jobs depended on the war), government contractors (who supplied food, uniforms, and weaponry), and "moneyed men" (who invested in government loans, funds, and lotteries) all became wealthy. Anyone could rise. It was no recommendation to the Rev. Dr. Swift that many of these upstarts were Dissenting Whigs, nor did it bode well that the average English man or woman found the new financial instruments complicated if not impenetrable: "through the contrivance and cunning of stock-jobbers [brokers], there has been brought in such a complication of knavery and cozenage, such a mystery of iniquity, and such an unintelligible jargon of terms to involve it in, as were never known in any other age or country in the world."[19] Even worse, in Swift's eyes, was the deliberate contracting of massive debt, to be paid off who knew when? Thus, at the deepest level, Swift's anxieties about London updated those of James I. Both feared a city on the make, growing, buccaneering, and cozening the nation.

The City and its new wealth had their defenders, however. Possibly in response to Swift, Joseph Addison visited the Bank of England twice in 1711, once in reality, the second time in a dream in *The Spectator*, No. 3:

> Methoughts I returned to the Great Hall, where I had been the Morning before; but to my Surprize, instead of the Company that I left there, I saw towards the Upper-end of the Hall a beautiful Virgin seated on a Throne of Gold. Her name (as they told me) was *Public Credit*. The Walls, instead of being adorned with Pictures and Maps, were hung with many Acts of Parliament written in Golden Letters. At the Upper end of the Hall was the *Magna Charta*, with the *Act of Uniformity* on the right hand and the *Act of Toleration* on the left. At the Lower

end of the Hall was the *Act of Settlement*, which was placed full in the
Eye of the Virgin that sat upon the Throne. Both the Sides of the Hall
were covered with such Acts of Parliament as had been made for the
Establishment of Publick Funds.[20]

For Addison, the Financial Revolution was the glue that bound together
England's prosperity and England's liberties as secured in the Revolution
Settlement of 1688/89. At the center of the Revolution Settlement was
the revolutionary government's credit. That credit, based on reputation
and threatened by war, was a virtual weathervane of the state of public
affairs.

In the end, the debt never really came due, and the government's
finances never collapsed. The new financiers did not destroy landed
wealth any more than the merchants had done: in fact the two were often
combined in one person or by marriage between landed and monied
families. For a few Londoners, the wealth from the Commercial and
Financial Revolutions led to immense fortunes, often rivaling the very
wealthiest peers. Peter Earle's survey of the eighteenth-century London
mercantile classes reveals personal estates of £50,000 and £100,000, and
at least three individuals – Peter Delmé (d. 1728), Samson Gideon (1699–
1762), and Sir Gilbert Heathcote (1652–1733) – worth between £250,000
and £500,000 at death. All moved amphibiously between the worlds of
commerce and high finance. A few bought estates in neighboring counties:
Essex, Kent, Surrey, and Hertfordshire. Others bought houses in Tooting
or Clapham and commuted. In so doing, they set the pattern for a new
kind of privileged life, urban and urbane.

THE INDUSTRIAL REVOLUTION?

London's social and economic development – its population growth, its
Commercial and Financial Revolutions, the mass consumerism and money
frenzy that seemed to grip Londoners – had repercussions far beyond the
metropolis. First, London had to be fed. Just as it could not reproduce
itself, neither could it produce the grain or the meat that it consumed
daily. (Admittedly, milk came from London cows, and native fruits and
vegetables from local orchards and market gardens.) That meant that
farms and market gardens all across England, but especially in the Home
Counties, Kent, East Anglia, and the Thames Valley, had to become more
efficient and productive. That, in turn, implied increasingly specialized

agriculture: grain from Kent or Essex, dairy products from Suffolk or Essex, poultry from Norfolk or Suffolk, and cattle from Wales or the Midlands. Naturally, this grain and meat had to be transported to London – cattle on the hoof, grain by barge. That implied better roads and canals; indeed, the early eighteenth century would be a great age of canal building. London's appetite also required bigger, more reliable wagons and carts, and carrying services and mails to enable business to be transacted from a distance. The metropolis also had to be heated. Much of the growth of the Durham coalfields can be attributed to London's demand for "seacoal," that is, coal mined in the north and transported along the east coast by water. The metropolis sucked in one-sixth of the coal mined in Britain. The pressure to keep up led to new technologies, like the application of Newcomen's steam engine (1705) to drain the mines. The need for seacoal also encouraged the shipping industry. The fact that a Newcastle collier or a Yorkshire farmer had to be paid for his product at a distance also implied more flexible instruments of credit. Bills of exchange and promissory notes developed to facilitate long-distance transactions.

We have already noted the demand for luxury goods in London. As early as the beginning of the Stuart period, there was a thriving trade in musical instruments and watches, art and books, silks and other fine fabrics, exotic food and drink, mostly funneled through the two Exchanges and the shops on Cheapside and the Strand. From 1600 on, shopping at these proto-malls became one of the great pastimes of elite women and even some members of the middling classes. In the next century, entrepreneurs like Sir Josiah Wedgwood (1730–1795), the china baron, established London showrooms to display their wares. Although they might design exclusive patterns for great aristocrats, they would also put on display similar, cheaper models for purchase by London's growing urban gentry and professional class, as well as by visitors from the country. By 1750, thanks to the easy movement of information and people between city and country, London tastes were influencing the hinterlands more than ever.

According to the historian E. A. Wrigley, London's transformation into a great commercial and financial center, and the transformation of Britain into the supplier of its wants, helped to create the conditions that made possible the Industrial Revolution of the later eighteenth century. Of course, the cotton mills of the Industrial Revolution were constructed in the Midlands, North, and Scotland, at places like Manchester, Birmingham, and Preston. But London itself remained a great manufacturing center and its growth created a national market for food and fuel, forcing the elaboration of information, transportation, and fiscal networks and the development of new technologies and credit facilities. After about 1680, British prosperity fueled by the Commercial and Financial Revolutions and framed by a relative absence of inflation forced a rise in real wages that would last into the 1760s. This not only attracted workers to London from the countryside but also produced more disposable income with which to buy items previously considered to be luxuries. According to Defoe, in London "the poorest citizens live like the rich, the rich like the gentry, the gentry like the nobility, and the nobility strive to outshine one another."[21] The constant round of new fashions, the need of virtually everybody to ape their betters, stimulated consumption. Even London's deadly demographic situation "helped" by acting as a safety valve, taking in excess population from the countryside that might otherwise have slowed economic growth by increasing prices and depressing wages. Above all, London's psychological impact on its new immigrants, the way it acted as a solvent of traditions and parochial customs, encouraged rational economic decision making, casual work arrangements, and the possibility – for the survivors – of social mobility. These realities made possible the kind of mental adjustment necessary to bring about an Industrial Revolution.

$\mathscr{3}$. Royal and Civic London

$\mathscr{T}$he previous chapter addressed the business end of London, in particular the City and docks. In this chapter we move west to the court and government end of town before returning at its conclusion to the Guildhall and London's own administration. It might be objected that the court at Whitehall and Westminster might have been *in* London, but was not *of* London, since its most glittering inhabitants would probably have felt more at home at the courts of Versailles or Madrid than in the Royal Exchange or a City tavern. Although true, it is also true that the court was one of the major avenues to social advancement in London. Moreover, court and government were an integral part of the city's domestic economy: in the words of Daniel Defoe, "Between the Court and city, there is a constant communication of business."[1] We have already noted the involvement of London merchants and moneyed men in government finance and contracts. Below this level, scores of London tradesmen competed for the royal warrant naming them suppliers "in ordinary" to the household, and when the court left town or went into mourning (thus putting clothiers and haberdashers out of work), they did howl. Court rakes roamed the town looking for trouble, and many Londoners were amphibious between City and court: Samuel Pepys lived and worked in Seething Lane near the Tower, but he spent about a third of his year attending his superiors at, or just marveling at the sights and sounds of, Whitehall. Indeed, no visit to London was complete without a trip to court. Why?

THE COURT

In an age when monarchs still mattered, the court was the center of the world. We might be tempted to think of the court at Whitehall as the equivalent of the White House or Buckingham Palace, but it was much more than that, because the king's household was not merely the seat of England's government, but its social and cultural headquarters as well. For starters, the royal household was probably the largest single employer located in one place in the British Isles, with jobs for perhaps 2,000 people, plus the hundreds of personal servants of those who attended court. If we define the court more widely to include the offices of the central administration grouped around Whitehall, the total ranges from 12,000 to 16,000 by the end of our period. Not only politicians but writers, painters, composers, and even scientists all came to court for commissions and rewards. In the words of *The Gentleman's Mirror* (1665) " . . . as the centre of greatness and pomp, fashion and civility, honour and advancement, do all persons of ambition, luster, or any remarkable conspicuity, come, in hope to make their interest in, and their advance by it."[2] Thus, in the galleries of Elizabethan Whitehall, one might on any given day encounter great politicians and courtiers like Burghley or Leicester, Cecil or Essex, writers like Sidney or Shakespeare, or musicians like Byrd or Dowland. Nearly a century later, the Restoration court could counter with Clarendon or Danby, Newton or Wren, Dryden or Rochester, Purcell or Lely, royal mistresses like Castlemaine or Portsmouth, or the diarists who recorded their doings, Evelyn and Pepys.[3] Others flocked to court to marvel at the grandest facades and the most glorious interiors in the kingdom; to view the latest plays and the greatest art collection in the British Isles; to hear the best poetry, musicians, and preachers; to catch the hottest gossip; to chart the changes in the winds of politics; or merely to catch a glimpse of the sovereign. All of which reminds us that it was from this place that first England, then the British Isles, and finally a world-encircling British Empire were governed.

But what exactly was the court? A building? An administrative structure? A group of people? A set of attitudes? A state of mind? In early modern usage, the word *court* denoted all of these things, and so we might rephrase the question "What was the court?" with a series of where, who, and when questions. Where was the court? In its geographic sense, the court was located wherever the ruler happened to be. Because all early modern rulers were somewhat peripatetic, the court was a movable feast that might be sampled at any given time at any one of several royal palaces in or near London, hunting lodges beyond it, or when on progress, virtually anywhere in the realm. It was a *movable* feast not only because kings and queens became easily bored with the same old palace walls and gardens but also because early modern plumbing became easily overwhelmed by the waste products of hundreds of courtiers. Because any given palace could be inhabited by the whole household for only a couple of months before it grew foul and had to be cleansed, the sovereign and his entourage had to hit the road again and again.

Between 1529 and 1698 the official residence of the English court was the rambling riverside palace at Whitehall (see Illustration 3.1), conveniently located near the Parliament House at Westminster and big enough to house hundreds of courtiers and most of the offices of the central government. But Elizabeth liked to spend time upriver at Richmond or downriver at Greenwich. James I preferred the country pastimes of his hunting lodge at Theobalds, near Cheshunt, Hertfordshire. Charles II enjoyed the horse racing at Newmarket, Suffolk, and toward the end of his reign, considered abandoning unruly London altogether for the country delights of Winchester, Hampshire. William III did virtually abandon Whitehall for the cleaner air of Kensington, just across Hyde Park to the west. When Whitehall burned down in 1698, the old royal hunting lodge of St. James's became the official residence of the court, a status that it retains today. But Anne preferred Kensington and Windsor, whereas George II liked Hampton Court. Finally, when the monarch processed through the capital for a coronation entry or a thanksgiving service at St. Paul's, the court took over the streets of London itself.

Who was the court? Throughout the period, the king's closest advisors, his best friends, and his servants were courtiers, as we might expect. But important organs of what we might think of as "government," like the Privy Council and the secretaries of state, were also located at Whitehall and still considered to be part of the court. This was because most of those offices had started there, as the most practical way for the king to get things done. Put simply, in the early Middle Ages there was no clear distinction between court and government, between the monarch's household and his governmental bureaucracy. For example, during Anglo-Saxon times, the king's Treasury, or Chamber, was so called because it began life in his bedchamber, the chests of money literally stored under his bed. The king's secretariat, his Chancery, originated among the coterie of chaplains who accompanied him, because in those days the clergy was the only literate class – hence our modern association of the term *clerical* with both writing and religion. Because medieval kings were peripatetic, these offices traveled with him. But as the Middle Ages wore on and the sheer volume of Crown business necessitated a fixed place to do that business and to keep records, most went "out of court," that is, became separate, permanent offices independent of the royal household, almost always located in London.

As late as the sixteenth century, however, important functions of what we would today think of as the government were still performed by members of the royal household. For example, Henry VIII kept a stash of cash in the privy coffers, literally chests stored in his Privy Chamber, in the care of household officers like his groom of the stole. When the Tudors went to war they still relied on the Great Wardrobe, normally in charge of palace furniture, to supply horses, munitions, and so forth, and they still expected the two major household bodyguards, the gentlemen pensioners and yeomen of the guard, to accompany them on campaign. The yeomen continued to earn battle honors to the end of our period, fighting beside King George II at the battle of Dettingen in 1743. The king's sergeants at arms and messengers of the chamber were law enforcement officers, often taking accused traitors into custody. Finally, Tudor kings frequently sent personal attendants, like the gentlemen of the Privy Chamber, to carry messages and make diplomatic overtures to foreign rulers.

As the monarchy became more constitutional after the Glorious Revolution of 1688/89, a distinction arose between the monarch's personal household servants and the officers of the Crown staffing the administrative departments – the Privy Council, the Treasury and revenue offices, the two secretaries of state and foreign service, the judiciary, the military – necessary to govern the nation. Whereas the former came to be seen as mere domestics and possibly even freeloaders at the public trough, the latter would eventually evolve into political appointees beholden to Parliament and overseeing civil servants acting for the public welfare. This split was enshrined in law in 1698 when Parliament passed the first Civil List Act (9 & 10 Will. III, c. 23), earmarking £700,000 (out of a total net government revenue of perhaps £5 million) to the king "for the service of his Household and family and for other his necessary expenses and occasions."[4] In effect, this separated his personal finances (the court) from those of the Army and the Navy and began the process of separating them from those of the state. Fortuitously, in that same year, Whitehall, the only palace big enough to house both court and government together, burned down, forcing the decampment of the royal household to St. James's. Yet most government offices remained or rebuilt on the ruins of the old palace, thus physically separating the court from the government. Eventually, "Whitehall" would come to mean the government, not the royal court.

During our period, therefore, a distinction was growing between those who served the monarch in government offices (civil servants) and those who served his domestic needs at court (sworn household officers and servants). To this we might add a third group: those who merely attended his person and court out of habit or interest, as the spirit moved them, without office or portfolio (courtiers or *habitués*). Because these distinctions were relatively new and not yet always fully formalized, early modern people tended to blend them all together under the word *court*, but we shall be more precise. The first group, government officers, will be addressed under "Capital," the other two immediately below. The second group, household officers, worked in or about the palace, had fixed duties, and at least in theory, regular remuneration. Structurally, they were divided into three departments: the Household Below Stairs, the Chamber, and the Stables. The Household Below Stairs, presided over by a great officer called the lord steward and an administrative body called the Board of Green Cloth, comprised between 200 and 300 administrators, cooks, bakers, butlers, confectioners, turnbroaches, scourers, laundresses, porters, and so forth, who provided for the court's domestic needs: food and drink, tableware, linen, fuel, and so forth for the king, his family, those of his servants who lived at court, and guests. Many had a second life as London tradesmen who prized the royal warrant to supply the court with these necessities, and the profits so generated.

But, as we have seen, a court was far more than a domestic establishment. It was the epicenter of national political, social, and cultural life and the great stage on which the theater of monarchy was acted. It was in the public rooms and galleries of Whitehall and St. James's that political business, influence, and intrigue were carried on; high society and those trying to climb into it amused themselves; leading authors, scholars, artists, and musicians sought patronage and set the trends of fashion; and the sovereign staged splendid processions, feasts, and entertainments designed to remind his guests, foreign and domestic, that he was God's lieutenant on Earth. The Chamber comprised these public rooms as well as the 600 to 900 servants and artists who staffed them. Their head was the lord chamberlain, who oversaw the court's ceremonial and artistic life. He supervised scores of gentlemen, gentlemen ushers, and grooms, drawn from every part of the realm, whose job was to give their attendance in those rooms, most importantly the Guard Chamber, an antechamber staffed by the yeomen of the guard; the Presence Chamber, where, on great occasions, the king could be seen on his throne;

and the Privy Chamber, where, before 1603, he could find some privacy. The Chamber also included subdepartments of the Robes, Jewel Office, Wardrobes (supplying furniture), the clergy and gentlemen of the Chapel Royal, the royal bodyguards of the gentlemen pensioners and yeomen of the guard, medical personnel, artists, musicians, messengers, huntsmen, and so forth. From the reign of James I, the functions of the Privy Chamber were superseded by a separate Bedchamber, staffed at the top by peers of the realm (the groom of the stole and gentlemen of the Bedchamber), in the middle by gentle grooms and pages, and at the bottom by laundresses and necessary women to attend the king day and night, dress him, and maintain his bedding.

Finally, the Stables, which was presided over by the master of the Horse and comprising over 100 equerries, pages, coachmen, footmen, grooms, and supporting personnel, based at the Royal Mews near Charing Cross, operated as the royal motor pool, transporting the sovereign and his or her retinue from place to place. These officers also provided the attendance equivalent to that of the gentlemen and gentlemen ushers of the Chamber when the court was away from home.

Because many government functions were still based at or performed by the court, contemporaries continued to use the term *court* even less precisely to denote the current ministry; the body of its supporters in Parliament; the whole of the paid administration, whether in London or the localities; or even the totality of all those in the country at large who supported the monarch and his aims. When used in these wider senses, the noun *court* began to shade off into something of an adjective. Thus, historians sometimes write, not always convincingly, of a "Court Party" in Parliament, while contemporaries occasionally spoke of "court ways," or referred to a person's behavior as being very "court," "courtly," or "like a courtier." Indeed, the word *court* was until recently commonly used as a verb – as in "to court" – with similar connotations. Such references, almost always pejorative, suggest that, to the contemporary mind, the way people lived at court was the very opposite of the directness and honesty associated with the country or the City. Thus, early modern drama is full of vain and foolish courtly fops like Sir Fopling Flutter in George Etherege's (1636–1692) *The Man of Mode* (1676) or corrupt, scheming favorites like the Machiavellian title character of Ben Jonson's *Sejanus, His Fall* (1603), who are often contrasted with honest country gentlemen and sober, hard-working London merchants.

When was the court? The court was generally in town over the autumn, winter, and early spring, with possible exceptions under the Tudors for

Christmas revels elsewhere. This long time span, comprising about two-thirds of the year, became known as "the season," and it attracted the elite to London for much of the period. During the summer, especially under Elizabeth I, the court was away on progress. Later monarchs sometimes used the summer for military campaigns (William III), to travel abroad (George I and George II), or simply to live quietly, with skeletal attendance, at an outlying palace like Windsor (Queen Anne). This reminds us that the monarch set the tone of court life, from monastic to libertine.

When in town, the court was naturally one of the chief tourist attractions in London, and a magnet for anyone hoping to rise to the very top of society. On great alfresco ceremonial occasions – the monarch's coronation procession, royal entries, and thanksgiving services at St. Paul's – all London became royal space "which, for the time might worthily borrow the name of his Court Royall."[5] The Tudors were especially good at using London as a stage on which to enact the drama of their reigns: Henry VII's triumphant entry and coronation procession after taking the Crown at Bosworth Field in 1485; Henry VIII's insistence on a full coronation procession for Anne Boleyn in 1533; or Mary I's speech at the Guildhall, demanding Londoners' support during Wyatt's Rebellion in 1554 (see Chapter 7). But the master of these dramatic productions was Elizabeth Tudor. Gifted with an instinct for self-presentation, she knew "right well that in pompous ceremonies a secret of government doth much consist, for that the people are naturally both taken and held with exterior shewes." Take her coronation entry on January 14, 1559:

> . . . in the afternoon, shee passed from the Tower through the City of London to Westminster, most royally furnished, both for her persone and for her trayne. . . . The Nobility and Gentlemen were very many, and no lesse honourably furnished. The rich attire, the ornaments, the beauty of the Ladyes, did add particular graces to the solemnity, and held the eyes and hearts of men dazeled betweene contentment and admiratione.

If the aristocracy knew its supporting role, so did the citizenry:

> As shee passed through the City, nothing was omitted to doe her the highest honours, which the Citizens (who could procure good use both of purses and inventiones) were able to perfourme. It were the part of an idle orator, to describe the Pageants, the Arkes [triumphal arches], and other well devised honoures done unto her; the order, the

beauty, the majestie of this actione, the high joye of some, the silence
and reverence of other, the constant contentment of all; their untired
patience never spent, eyther with long expecting (some of them from
a good part of the night before) or with unsatiable beholding the
Ceremonies of that day.

Setting aside the chronicler's hagiographic tone, we can see that there
was a long tradition of royal London engaging with civic London in
such processional love fests. Both partners got to display themselves to
best advantage, both laid themselves out hierarchically, thus reinforcing
the prevailing worldview, and both responded to the cues of the other:
"As she passed the Companyes of the City, standing in their liveryes,
shee tooke particular knowledge of them, and graced them with many
witty formalityes of speech." This is the equivalent to the pointing and
waving that modern politicians do in parades and on reviewing stands. It
is designed to convince the person pointed at or waved to that the celebrity
knows them and cares about them personally. Elizabeth was particularly
good at this; indeed it may be argued that no subsequent English sovereign
has matched her common touch, or her ability to run with a cue:

> When any good wishes were cast forth for her vertuous and religious
> government, shee would lift up her hands towards Heaven, and desire
> the people to answer, Amen. . . . She cheerfully received not only rich
> giftes from persons of worth, but Nosegayes, Floweres, Rose-marie
> branches, and such like presents, offered unto her from very meane
> [poor] persones, . . . It is incredible how often shee caused her coach
> to staye, when any made offer to approach unto her, whither to make
> petitione, or whither to manifest their loving affectiones.[6]

The Tudors' frequent outdoor appearances allowed them to demonstrate their power (the size of the military entourage), their magnificence
(the richness of dress), their favor for London (the sheer fact of these
appearances), and their popularity (the size and enthusiasm of the crowd).
In effect, they played to London, not only intimidating it with power
(when Henry VII processed to and from the Tower accompanied by the
yeomen of the guard in their red livery) but also wooing it with flattery
(Elizabeth's procession described earlier). This reminds us that such processions retained an element of election by acclamation: on some level
Tudor monarchs sought London's approval, while Londoners reasserted
their "right" to select and instruct the monarch. Such ceremonies might

even be said to have enacted a covenant between ruler and ruled: the one to be benevolent, the other to be loyal. The participation of the ruling and clerical elite, always arranged in strict order of precedence, reaffirmed the English constitution in church and state and the Great Chain of Being. Nor need the monarch actually participate in person: executions on Tower Hill and burnings at Smithfield were equally intended to overawe the capital. Even under the Tudors, however, the results were mixed. Civic authorities liked to demonstrate their loyalty and the City's wealth by the texts of the pageants and the magnificence of the triumphal arches that they paid for, as well as by the turnout of liverymen in their splendid gowns. Ordinary Londoners could use such occasions to show their loyalty – but also their lack of it, as when they shunned Anne Boleyn at her coronation procession in 1533, when they dipped their handkerchiefs in the blood of the executed Duke of Somerset in 1552, or when they encouraged the martyrs at Smithfield a few years later. Londoners were perfectly willing to acknowledge and reaffirm the status quo, as long as they agreed with it.

Perhaps because of this, such royal occasions grew rare after the accession of the Stuarts in 1603. Neither James I nor Charles I particularly liked going out in public, although splendid exceptions were made for James's coronation procession in 1604, Charles's return from Scotland in 1641, and visiting foreign royalty like Christian IV (1588–1648) of Denmark in 1606 or Marie d'Medici (1575–1642) of France in 1639. Even then the Stuarts lacked the common touch: at his coronation entry James greeted the acclamations of his people with passive reserve. Worse, when Charles canceled his entry in 1626 because of a plague epidemic, he stuck the City with the costs of the unused arches "amid the murmurs of the people and the disgust of those who spent the money."[7] James I was the last English monarch to receive a full state funeral procession in 1625. Charles II was the last to make a coronation entry in 1661.

Nevertheless, the average Londoner or tourist still had ample opportunities to gawk at the monarch traversing between palaces, out hunting, or just taking the air in St. James's or Hyde Park. Moreover, there was no strict security cordon surrounding royal personages in the early modern period; rather, every subject had the right to petition his sovereign, and a good ruler was expected to accept such petitions patiently. Although Charles I, William III, and George I were famously reclusive, Elizabeth I, Charles II, or George II could, in theory, be approached by any passerby as they processed down the Strand or, in the latter two cases, sauntered about St. James's or Hyde Park. The parks were royal spaces, but they were also open to the public, the price of admission being a tip of the cap or a curtsy to any royal present. Thus, on January 15, 1669, Samuel Pepys writes: "I to White-Hall through the park, where I met the King and Duke of York and so walked with them."[8] Admittedly, Pepys was a government official well known to the king; ordinary Londoners would have had trouble getting past the throng of courtiers attending him as he walked, as depicted in a well-known painting by Danckerts (see Illustration 3.2). Still, the result was a security nightmare: in 1682 and 1696 there were plots to assassinate the king while he was out riding. Nor were firearms the only threat to a public monarch: in January 1678 a lunatic named Richard Harris was committed to Bedlam after throwing an orange at Charles II in St. James's Park.

In theory, the ruler was more secure within his own house. Porters at the gate, provost marshals, the yeomen of the guard, and the servants of the public rooms were repeatedly ordered to prevent the entry of unsuitable persons:

> Whereas it is Notorious, that severall idle p^{sons}, Men, Women and Children, Vagrants & Beggars doe frequent the Court, or about the Gates, and are commonly seene within the King's Pallace, and St. James's Parke, who can give noe Acc^{ot}. of themselves, nor have any just cause to be there. . . . [9]

The frequency of these orders suggests that they were not very effective, however. People instead seem to have assumed that the court was a public space, open to virtually anyone. Whitehall Palace must have been particularly difficult to police because of its irregular ground plan and its accessibility to the river and the park. Thus in May 1662, Mr. and Mrs. Pepys took a delightful stroll through the apparently misnamed Privy Garden, where they observed the "finest smocks and linen petticoats" of the king's favorite mistress, Lady Castlemaine (1640–1709), hanging out to dry.[10]

In fact, royal space was never fully public or private. Like London itself, it was always up for negotiation, and its flexibility was its great strength. Indoors, the court was most accessible on holidays and state occasions. During the Tudor period, the court celebrated great religious holidays in style, when the sovereign sponsored extensive revels at Christmas, Easter Sunday, Whitsuntide, and Allhallowtide. Queen Elizabeth commemorated her Accession Day (November 17) with an annual tournament in the tiltyard at Whitehall. Under the later Stuarts and Hanoverians, the court calendar celebrated New Year's Day, when courtiers exchanged expensive gifts of gold and silver; as well the sovereign's birth, accession, and coronation anniversaries. On these occasions the monarch rose to the sound of trumpets and kettledrums; attended chapel; heard a musical ode, usually with words by the poet laureate and set by the master of the music; and then possibly attended a play, a ball, gambling, or some other entertainment to round out the evening. Guests were expected to turn up in splendid new clothes – the original significance of the term *birthday suit* – especially tailored for the occasion. Men wore waistcoats embroidered with gold and silver thread, whereas women were expected to display all of the family jewels and any they could borrow. At Queen Anne's birthday in 1711, the Duchess of Buckingham (1681/82–1743) and Lady Poulett (d. 1748) "were scarce able to move under the load of jewels they had on."[11] Having "with much ado got up to the Loft" of the Great Hall to see the birthday ball for Queen Catherine of Braganza (1638–1705) on November 15, 1666, Sam Pepys found himself bewitched by the fashions:

> Anon the house grew full, and the candles light, and the King and Queen and all the ladies set: and it was endeed a glorious sight . . . the King in his rich vest of some rich silke and silver trimming, as the Duke of York and all the dancers were, some of cloth of silver, and others of other sorts, exceeding rich . . . all most excellently dressed in rich petticoats and gowns and Dyamonds – and pearls.

After carefully noting all the court luminaries present and the order of the dances in 1666, Pepys concludes "but upon the whole matter, the business of the dancing of itself was not extraordinary pleasing. But the clothes and sight of the persons was indeed very pleasing, and worth my coming, being never likely to see more gallantry while I live, if I should come twenty times."[12] No wonder that crowds gathered outside the palace gates on such occasions, as at the Academy Awards today, to see who was wearing what.

In fact, because there were no invitations or guest lists on such occasions, because the porters at those gates and the gentlemen ushers inside could not possibly know who was who, dress was just about the only criterion of admission. This explains how, in 1715, young Dudley Ryder (1691–1756), a student at the Inns of Court, made it past the gentlemen ushers and into the king's accession anniversary simply by being dressed in his "best clothes and laced ruffles" and pretending to be part of the train of the VIP in front of him.[13] In short, access to court was open to anyone who looked good and talked fast. As a result, the galleries of royal palaces were always crowded with suitors, spies, and idlers. On numerous occasions in the 1660s, Pepys recalls walking "up and down the House to hear news," "walked long in the galleries . . . four or five houres," "talking with this man and that."[14] As at the two Exchanges or Westminster Hall, a chance meeting could be parleyed into anything from political business to a romantic tryst: Pepys frequently encountered flirtatious ladies of dubious provenance at court.

Clearly, the court offered countless attractions to the curious on a near-daily basis. Let us imagine that we have borrowed appropriate clothing for a visit to the court of Charles II at Whitehall circa 1670.[15] Entering from Whitehall (street) by the Court or Palace Gate (see Map 3), we are confronted immediately on our right by Jones's Banqueting House. Here, under Rubens' magnificent ceiling, we might witness a splendid ambassadorial reception or the curious ceremony of touching for the King's Evil, in which sufferers from scrofula (a skin disease similar to leprosy) were stroked by the monarch and given a gold "healing" piece as a token of their "cure." If no such ceremony is on offer that day, we might walk east across the Great Court to the Great Hall, where we could have claimed a free meal until 1662, when that perk was abolished. In 1665 the king converted the hall into a theater with, according to Pepys, terrible acoustics. If we are too early for a play or a court ball, we might carry on a little farther east down a narrow passageway to the Chapel Royal, the Sunday and weekday services of which are open to all. This explains how Thomas Allen, a baker, could have had his pocket picked by James Burke, a vagrant, during a service in 1686. Respectable Londoners were attracted by the sermons, for the king commanded the services of the best preachers in England, many of them future bishops, as chaplains. Others came to hear the latest musical compositions of Matthew Locke (c. 1622–1677), Pelham Humfrey (1647/48–1674), or Henry Purcell (1659–1695) performed by the leading choral establishment in England. Still others were merely curious to gape at a royal in procession to chapel: in 1689 the Scotsman Robert Kirk was part of "a great crowd to see King and Queen."[16]

Under the Stuarts, the court included Catholic chapels across the park at St. James's Palace and also downriver at Somerset House until the period of the Glorious Revolution, and Lutheran, French, and Dutch Protestant chapels at St. James's thereafter to accommodate the religious inclinations of various consorts and other members of the royal family. Between 1686 and 1688, James II sponsored an impossibly opulent Catholic Chapel Royal, designed by Wren, within Whitehall itself just southwest of the Banqueting House. Thus, if spiritually curious, we might sample different rites; in fact, there is almost no other place in England to experience these sights, sounds, and smells. John Evelyn (1620–1706) marveled at the rich decor and elaborate ritual of the Catholic chapels, but also complained of "much crowding, little devotion."[17] Pepys was mostly interested in the music and people watching: writing of a Christmas Midnight Mass in 1667, he found here Londoners of all persuasions:

> The Queen was there and some ladies. But, Lord! What an odde thing it was for me to be in a crowd of people, here a footman, there a beggar, here a fine lady, there a zealous poor papist, and here a Protestant, two or three together, come to see the show. I was afeared of my pocket being picked very much.[18]

After attending a service in the Anglican Chapel Royal, we might exit by the south door and ascend the Queen's Staircase (one always ascends to meet the sovereign) toward a series of riverside rooms that compose the Queen's Apartments. Here, in the formal surroundings of the Queen's Presence Chamber, "persons of good fashion and good appearance" might catch the king dining in state with the queen. People loved the spectacle of the royal family dining formally at the mid-afternoon meal, the king hatted, sitting under the canopy of state, "with Musique & all the Court ceremonies," served by their Bedchamber staffs on bended knee from the royal plate. This attraction was so popular that the royal diners had to be railed off. One contemporary wrote of the crowd watching Charles II and his new bride, Catherine of Braganza, dine at Hampton Court in 1662: "The Hall was so full of people and it was so hot the sweat ran off of everybody's face." We can angle for a place behind the guardrail near the king: it was while "Standing by his Majestie at dinner in the Presence" that Evelyn got his first taste of pineapple.[19] This is also a great opportunity for political intrigue, for those crowding about the sovereign might get in a word as well as a bite. Despite its popularity, Charles II's successors largely abandoned the practice, choosing instead to eat most of their meals in a private dining room. Like the nearly contemporaneous abandonment of touching for King's Evil, this was almost certainly a public relations blunder.

Perhaps the greatest attraction when the court is in town circa 1670 is the drawing room. Drawing rooms were relatively informal gatherings

held two or three times a week during the court season, usually in the afternoon or early evening, in the Queen's Apartments. More specifically, these
"circles" or "courts," as they were also sometimes called, were generally
hosted by Queen Catherine in the less formal surroundings of her Withdrawing – or Drawing – Room. Typically, the queen sits in a chair without
canopy, indicating a slightly, but only slightly, more casual atmosphere.
Surrounding her at a distance is a semicircle of ladies and gentlemen –
hence the term "cerele" or "circle" for these gatherings (see Illustration
3.3). Great ministers, reverend bishops, and powerful nobles and their
ladies bow or curtsy to the hostess then stand respectfully, bareheaded.
No one sits in the royal presence unless given special dispensation, and
no man remains "covered," that is, with his hat on. After our period,
Fanny Burney (1752–1840) poked fun at the elaborate ceremony of such
occasions, her tongue only partly in cheek:

> In the first place, you must not Cough. If you find a cough tickling
> in your throat, you must arrest it from making any sound: if you find
> yourself choacking with forbearance, you must choak: But not cough.
>
> In the 2nd place, you must not sneeze . . . if a sneeze still insists upon
> making its way, you must oppose it by keeping your teeth grinding
> together; if the violence of the repulse breaks a blood vessel, you must
> break the blood-vessel: But not sneeze.
>
> In the 3rd place, you must not, upon any account, stir either hand or
> foot. If, by chance, a black pin runs into your Head, you must not take
> it out: If the pain is very great, you must be sure to bear it without
> wincing; if it brings the Tears into your Eyes, you must not wipe them
> off.[20]

Eventually, as the room fills, the crowd becomes more fluid as courtiers
begin their mating dance, maneuvering about the throng, bowing and
conversing with those in power, and avoiding the gaze and the bows of
those out of it. We are here to see and be seen, to ogle the famous, meet the
prominent, and if possible influence the powerful. Catherine of Braganza's
drawing rooms routinely drew more than 100 guests, including leading
politicians and foreign ambassadors, and so this is a great place just to hear
the news and see what the state of politics is. Nowhere else is the whole
government present before our very eyes.

If the queen desires, card tables are brought out or, if the weather is
nice, guests may promenade onto the terrace overlooking the river. At

some point, the king enters. Although some monarchs chose to observe drawing rooms from the safety of their own chairs, surrounded by their lords or ladies-in-waiting, Charles II likes to move about the circle, talking to a hopeful courtier here, snubbing a fallen favorite there. If, in sight of all the other courtiers, he takes us to a window or onto the terrace for a moment of private conversation, our reputation is made: aspiring courtiers will now approach *us*. Once conversation begins, everything depends on the monarch: Elizabeth I was acute and flirtatious, James I and Mary II loquacious, and Charles II witty and (usually) affable. But most royal conversationalists thereafter were dull: Queen Anne tended to ask people about their relations in the country, the roads they had taken to London, and the weather at home. George I had to be conversed with in German or French. Worse, once spoken to by the king or queen, we cannot leave the room without his or her permission; the annals of the court are full of tales of bladder tenacity and intestinal fortitude on the part of courtiers unable to secure a royal dismissal. If we do receive permission to leave, we exit backwards: one never turns one's back on the sovereign.

What if we want personal, private contact with him, to beg a favor or convey some piece of sensitive information? There is another way: we can seek a private audience in the royal Bedchamber. In every royal palace, there were two routes to the Bedchamber, one public, one private. At Whitehall, the public route was through the Privy Gallery, which runs all the way from Holbein Gate past the Council Chamber to the King's Private Apartments along an east–west axis, perpendicular to the river, to the south of the Queen's Apartments (see Map 3). The difficulty is that we might be subject to the prying eyes of the gallery keepers who stand at the Council Chamber door, not to mention courtiers sauntering through the gallery like that inveterate snoop Sam Pepys. What if we want to avoid such scrutiny? All leaders need a way for people to come to them out of public view. That is why courtiers frequently preferred to approach the king by the backstairs. Although usually omitted from modern tours and guide-books, the backstairs is arguably the most important nook or cranny in any royal palace, because here one can gain access to the sovereign secretly, out of public view. How does one do this?

Whitehall was such a maze that a courtier should have been able to avoid detection easily, but the least noticeable approach was from the water, either by the Whitehall Stairs, or even closer, the nominally exclusive Privy Stairs. The Privy Stairs connect to the north wing of a little court, open to the water, known as the Volary Lodgings. On the interior side of this wing we find a little set of backstairs. At the bottom stands a page of the bedchamber. Although paid only about £80 a year plus tips, this servant is a crucial linchpin of the court system; we are careful to slip him a shilling while inquiring if we might see the king. The page climbs the stairs to an anteroom just across from the King's Little Bedchamber. In this room, or the Cupola Room next door, is found the groom of the stole or, if he is not in waiting, a gentleman of the Bedchamber. These aristocratic officers are the king's closest attendants, and it is they who decide who is admitted to see the king. Obviously, they have immense power, like that of a modern White House Chief of Staff or Director of Oval Office Operations: they are the final gatekeepers for politicians, cronies, and mistresses. Unusually, Charles II relied on a groom of the Bedchamber who doubled as the keeper of the Closet, first Thomas Chiffinch (1600–1666), then after Chiffinch's death in 1666, his brother William (c. 1602–1691), to guard his access. One knowing observer remarked of William Chiffinch that he was "a man of so absolute authority that foreign as well as domestic ministers are to obey his commands." That authority led in turn to a reputation for facilitating the king's pleasures, which gave rise to other rather more odious titles, such as "Pimpmaster General."[21]

If our presence is approved, we finally enter the Bedchamber and have the king entirely to ourselves. This, with the royal Closet, a room in the west wing of the Volary Lodgings that serves as an office, is the most nearly private room in any royal palace. Here in the Bedchamber, the monarch was attended by courtiers at his ceremonial *levée* (rising and dressing) in the morning and *couchée* (going to bed) at night. Here or in the Closet he met cabinet ministers for daily conferences, signed papers, planned strategies, and saw people in private with whom he might not have wished to be seen in public. Unlike some sovereigns, Charles II would probably impress us with his wit and his ability to put us at ease. Ever the First Gentleman of England, he would be careful to flatter us, possibly showing off some of his scientific instruments or works of art, or if we are female, making a pass. Here, we can speak frankly. On departing, however, we might perhaps realize that the king has given away little and promised nothing substantive. On the way down the backstairs we might ask the page if anyone else has come to see the king that day: nobody knows more about the comings and goings at court than he.

Why did people do this? It should be obvious why tourists and sight-seers went to court, but why did the great and the good clamor and strive to work there? Why would a powerful nobleman be willing to sleep on a pallet bed near the king, put on his shirt at his *levée*, or stand ready to assist him as he relieved himself as a gentleman of the Bedchamber or groom of the stole? Why would a substantial gentleman with a nice estate in the country choose to stand and serve in stiff clothing in under- or overheated rooms, opening and closing doors for his betters as a gentleman usher? Why would a young woman of respectable birth be thrilled to be named a maid of honor, even though it would expose her to the aggressive attentions of scores of court rogues from the king on down? Some undoubtedly served simply because they swallowed the Great Chain of Being whole and believed that any place next to God's lieutenant was reward enough. Some did so out of family tradition: nepotism permeated the court. There were also the monetary rewards, ranging from a mere £18 per annum in salary for a porter to the Stables, to £300 for a maid of honor, £1,200 a year to the lord chamberlain or master of the horse, and as much as £6,000 to the groom of the stole. Moreover, there were immense fringe benefits to living and working at court: lodgings in a prime location, free meals for many officers, livery (a uniform) for many menial servants, and fees and *vails*, that is, small gratuities like the one we gave the page of the backstairs: a page could make, on average, an extra £120 a year that way. When the monarch was away, menial servants whose job was to keep the royal apartments secure would show them to anyone willing to pay! Speaking of security, most household officers could count on their jobs as long as the monarch lived and often beyond: careers of thirty, forty, fifty, and even sixty years were not uncommon. Finally, a favored servant or a courtier without portfolio might be graced with lands, titles, proceeds from a shipwreck, or a monopoly. No wonder so many hung about the galleries for hours, or if female, accepted invitations into the royal bed. If a maid of honor somehow managed to avoid being compromised, she almost always married well. In short, it was all a gamble: everything depended on the generosity of the monarch and the state of his finances. The 1540s saw courtiers gobble up lots of former Church lands, but Elizabeth I was notoriously cheap, James I generous, and so on. Even at a prodigal court there was no more stereotypical story than that of the young man or woman of promise, hanging about the galleries and staircases hoping to be noticed, but ending up penniless.

Finally, there was the attraction of power. Those who served the monarch most intimately were assumed to have influence with him. This was true even of cooks and grooms of the Bedchamber, but was especially true of the great officers. We have already seen that the groom of the stole and lords of the Bedchamber had the power to regulate access to the sovereign. At the same time, *their* access to him, and that of a few other great court and government officials, was almost unlimited. Some parlayed that access into a reputation for influence over patronage and even policy. The greatest became notorious favorites. The power of these favorites varied with the predilections of the monarch: Elizabeth I was careful to limit her favorite, the Earl of Leicester's (c. 1532–1588) actual power, whereas James I practically handed the government over to his, George, Duke of Buckingham (1592–1628). Most of Charles II's mistresses were thought to be similarly powerful. That is, people tended to assume that anyone in such intimate contact with the monarch was listened to with attention. As a result, royal favorites and mistresses were almost always hated in the country at large, because in an age when God's lieutenant could do no wrong, the only way to explain a royal mistake was to blame bad advice. Worse, that advice was thought likely to be bad, because courtiers were assumed to give advice only to benefit themselves; that is, they were assumed to be enriching themselves at the nation's expense, corrupting the constitution by secret influence – the very opposite of the honest London merchant who enriched it. These suspicions were not necessarily accurate: recent biographies of Leicester, Buckingham, William's favorite, the Earl of Portland (1649–1709), and Anne's, the Duchess of Marlborough, have all portrayed their advice as well meant and intended for the good of the nation or, in Portland's case especially, that of Europe as a whole. Nevertheless, the great courtiers did empower and enrich themselves and their followers along the way. Nor have the mistresses of Charles II, so far, received such rehabilitation. In any case, it was inevitable that the sovereign would have friends and that he would listen to and reward them. That went along with the territory of having a personal monarchy. It was only gradually, during the seventeenth and eighteenth centuries, that a notion developed that government should not only be funded separately from the royal household but also that its servants owed a loyalty to the public as well as their master.

CAPITAL

Although household expenses and salaries were paid out of the Civil List by 1750, so were the salaries of the great officers of state (Treasury, secretaries of state, and so forth), the judges, diplomatic corps, and secret service. In short, the distinction between sovereign and state, public and private, still was not fully worked out even as the period of this book closes. Put another way, if most of the central administration of Britain had gone out of court, it had not gone very far. All government officers were still considered royal servants, and in an age before electronic communication, it made sense for most of their offices to be headquartered at the court, near the sovereign. It was thus from the court in London that royal orders were sent into the localities to be carried out by armies of tax assessors, sheriffs, JPs, assize judges, Customs, and in the second half of our period, Excise officials. The Whitehall-Westminster complex was the junction box where all the wires met. Eventually, the word *Whitehall* would mean not a palace on the Thames but the government itself.

For example, the Privy Council and Cabinet (consisting of, at least, the lord treasurer, two secretaries of state, lord chancellor or lord keeper, lord president of the council, and lord privy seal), the brains of the operation, met at court. The larger Privy Council gathered at Whitehall, St. James's, and other palaces in a specially designated Council Chamber. This was usually physically close to the King's Private Apartments: at Whitehall, it was just down the Privy Gallery from the Volary Lodgings. A small Cabinet council might meet anywhere, often at the Cockpit in Whitehall, but sometimes even in the royal Bedchamber.

The Treasury, Privy Seal, Signet, and Admiralty were at Whitehall; after the palace burned down in 1698, much of what remained was taken over by government offices. Of these, the most important was the Treasury, which, from the mid-seventeenth century on, began to coordinate not only the finances but also increasingly the activities of the other offices. The Treasury began as the personal staff of the lord treasurer, an ancient office that also presided over the Exchequer, the actual repository of the king's money. Occasionally during the early modern period, and permanently from 1715, the Treasury was put into commission and run by a Treasury Board of five or so important statesmen, headed by the first lord of the Treasury. Beginning with the appointment of Robert Walpole on April 4, 1721, the first lord has usually been regarded as the king's prime minister, the effective head of the Cabinet and government, leader of the majority party in Parliament and responsible for articulating and coordinating royal policy. In 1732, in recognition of his service to the nation, George II awarded Walpole a series of properties on the grounds of the burned-down Whitehall Palace, including what was left of the old Cockpit lodgings and the house at No. 10 Downing Street, just off Whitehall (street). Walpole accepted on the condition that the house become a perquisite of office for the first lord, but it was only later in the eighteenth century that it became customary for the first lord–prime minister to live at this famous address.

The chancellor of the Exchequer acted as second in command to the first lord and was assisted by a secretary and a small army of clerks. During the seventeenth century, they worked in their offices at Whitehall directly under the Council Chamber and Privy Gallery, and opening onto the Privy Garden (see Map 3). When Walpole took possession of the Cockpit lodgings at Whitehall, however, he commissioned William Kent (c. 1686–1748) to link them with No. 10 to form a new Treasury Office. The Treasury moved into its new offices in 1735; Walpole's study would eventually become the Cabinet Room from which policy has been decided ever since. There is a certain symbolic appropriateness to the fact that, just as England evolved from a near-absolute monarchy to a constitutional one, so the site where Henry VIII and Elizabeth I had held court became the home of a prime minister, constitutionally appointed as a result of the popular vote of what was then the widest franchise in Europe. Here the prime minister lived and worked as a servant not only of the Crown but of the people as well, the Cabinet Room where decisions were made adjacent to *his* lodgings, not the king's. In this way as in others noted previously, London set a course for modernity as yet largely unknown in the other Western capitals.

The subordinate offices of the central government were concentrated nearby. We noted in Chapter 1 how the royal courts of King's Bench, Chancery, Exchequer, and Common Pleas met at Westminster Hall, technically part of the old palace of Westminster that also housed Parliament. Other offices were spread throughout the metropolis: the Ordnance at the Tower, the Navy Office just west of it in Seething Lane, and the Custom House down by the docks. These offices employed thousands of Londoners; thousands more benefited from government contracts with metropolitan shipbuilders, victualers, and printers. Thanks to the wars of the second half of our period and the resultant acquisition of a worldwide empire, those numbers were growing: there were about 1,500 central government officials in Henry VII's reign, 4,000 by James II's, 12,000 to 16,000 by Anne's, most of them based in London. After 1689 in particular, old departments like the Ordinance, Admiralty, Navy Office, Post Office, Customs, and Excise added clerks and spent more money. New departments were established, such as the Office of Trade and Plantations to administer Britain's growing colonial acquisitions, and new revenue-collecting departments (a Glass Office, Salt Office, Stamp Office, and

Leather Offices) to guarantee a steady revenue. As a result, the central government of England was a growing cash cow for London.

Some historians think that it was in these offices during our period that a new form of government service developed. Prior to 1640, most government officials were chosen on the basis of political or family connection or purchase. Many positions created in the Middle Ages had become sinecures involving little or no work. Below the level of the great officers, they were often poorly paid, their salaries having been set decades, if not centuries, previously. When the government was short of cash, that pay was often in arrears, sometimes for years at a time. This forced them to charge fees, which shaded easily into bribery, of anyone doing business with their offices. The Customs collection was so inefficient that early Stuart governments farmed it out, contracting with wealthy London merchants who paid the Crown a set amount for the right to collect the duties for whatever profit they could make. Few officials were ever removed for incompetence or corruption; rather they tended to regard their jobs as freeholds, that is, their property, which explains why they often took its papers with them if they left office. All of this also explains why English government was expensive yet ineffective at essential functions like war, revenue collection, and law enforcement.

Beginning under the parliamentary regime of the 1640s, continuing under Cromwell, and accelerating after the Revolution of 1688/89, England's many wars forced its government not only to expand but also to become more efficient. For example, Excise officers were given professional training and maintained a high standard. Although many top officials remained political appointees, changing when a Whig or Tory government fell, their immediate subordinates, like Treasury Secretary William Lowndes (1652–1724), Secretary of the Army William Blathwayt (1650–1717), or Secretary of the Admiralty Samuel Pepys were career officers who pursued reform. Admittedly, they were transitional figures in this process. For example, Pepys was appointed through nepotism and was perfectly willing to take a bribe in money or sexual favors; nevertheless, he worked long hours to economize and professionalize the Navy. Standards rose and many of the offices noted above developed an ethos of what would later come to be called "civil service." Put simply, they came to see government office as service to the Crown or the nation, not to themselves, their immediate superiors, or even the person of the sovereign. In this too, late seventeenth- and eighteenth-century London anticipated modern practice.

CIVIC GOVERNMENT

What about the government of London itself? Even more than the national administration, it was a patchwork. The City of London, with its lord mayor and Court of Aldermen sitting in the Guildhall, was an ancient and reasonably well-run establishment, but as noted previously, it did not govern the entire metropolis. Westminster, portions of Southwark, and the northern and eastern suburbs were run by ad hoc combinations of JPs, other royal appointees, and parish vestries. Apart from the occasional royal proclamation or parliamentary statute, greater London would not have a unified central authority with jurisdiction over the whole until the late nineteenth century. In the meantime, the prestige of the City's government was such that kings, privy councillors, and suburban justices ignored it to their peril; indeed, the first two often sought to control it. So, we begin at the Guildhall.

Like the nation itself, the City of London did not have a formal constitution. Its structure of government had been forged in the constitutional struggles of the fourteenth and fifteenth centuries, meaning that the disputes of the sixteenth, seventeenth, and eighteenth centuries took place within recognized boundaries. The Corporation worked closely with the Crown and the Privy Council, sometimes petitioning the latter for assistance, sometimes being ordered by the latter to address some problem, and always acting as a major lender (£120,000 between 1575 and 1598). As in the national government, authority in the City was concentrated at the top, in the hands of the lord mayor and the 25 other aldermen who formed the Court of Aldermen (see Illustration 3.4). The lord mayor served for one year, elected on September 29 by his fellow aldermen from two nominees proposed by the liverymen in Common Hall (see later discussion). From about 1560 they generally chose the most senior alderman who had not yet served. To assist the lord mayor in his executive functions, London had two sheriffs (elected annually by Common Hall on June 24), a chamberlain (treasurer), a recorder (chief legal officer), a town clerk, and from the late Tudor period, a remembrancer and a chronologer, whose jobs were to keep records of City ceremonies, rights, and privileges, and to ensure that these be maintained.

The most important of those ceremonies was the annual lord mayor's show on October 29. This tradition began in 1215, when King John specified that the new mayor present himself at court for his approval and to swear allegiance. By the fifteenth century the procession featured

minstrels and, later, devils and green men. In 1452 the lord mayor first went
to Westminster by water; his successors embarked at the Three Cranes
in Vintry Ward in the magnificent lord mayor's barge, escorted up the
Thames by the livery company barges and assorted smaller water craft.
After swearing an oath of allegiance at the Exchequer in Westminster Hall,
he returned, landing at Baynard's Castle for the main procession, paid for
by his livery company, up through Paul's Churchyard and Cheapside.
During our period, the lord mayor's pageant became even more elaborate,
taking up some of the slack after the Tudors banned the Midsummer
Watch processions (see Chapter 5) and the Stuarts withdrew from the
London crowd. Street processions featured movable triumphal arches
with religious, classical, historical, and mythological themes and pageant
texts written by City poets like Thomas Dekker and John Taylor (1578–
1653), known as "the Water Poet" because he was also a Thames bargeman. At times of Court/City tension, these texts might assert London's
loyalty or defend its ancient privileges. Often, the themes played off of
some aspect of the new mayor's lineage or reputation: that for John Leman
(1544–1632) in 1616 featured a lemon tree; Sir William Cokayne's procession in 1619 included a giant artificial cock crowing and flapping its
wings. The crowd could get boisterous, tossing dead cats and dogs and
breaking windows. In 1711 Lord Mayor Sir Gilbert Heathcote was thrown
from his horse by a collision with a drunken flower girl; ever since, the
new mayor has ridden more safely in an elaborate coach. The procession
was followed by a great feast at the Guildhall attended by the officers
of all the companies and sometimes the sovereign and members of the
royal family. The day concluded with a torchlight procession to accompany the new lord mayor back to his house. Occasional traffic accidents
apart, the whole thing must have been great fun to watch. On a deeper
level, the lord mayor's show represented another way in which Londoners
were drawn to identify with their city. It was the culmination of a ritual
year that saw the mayor and aldermen process from Guildhall to St. Paul's
on All Saints' (November 1), Christmas Day, New Year's Day, Epiphany
(January 6), Candlemas (February 21), Easter, Ascension, Pentecost, and
Corpus Christi (these last three forty, fifty, and sixty days after Easter,
respectively).

Aldermen were elected for life by their wards, with strong input from
the lord mayor, from among the wealthiest businessmen in London. As
we have seen, sixteenth-century aldermen were likely to be Merchant
Adventurers, a century later officers of the great trading companies, and a

century after that, directors of the Bank of England, East India Company, and insurance companies. All of these positions yielded easily the property qualification of £10,000. Each alderman was responsible for one of London's wards, although in practice he need not live there and increasingly delegated his authority to a deputy or a committee (see later discussion). Taken collectively, the Court of Aldermen had immense power. They appointed the recorder and subordinate officers, issued orders regarding the public health, granted alehouse licenses, approved guild orders, and governed London's prisons. The lord mayor and Court of Aldermen also acted as the Commission of the Peace for the City and so could preside as judges in sessions of the peace (for misdemeanors) at the Guildhall and in other London courts. Finally, they had the right to set the agenda for Common Council and for much of the period could veto any legislation it passed which they did not like.

Common Council consisted of the lord mayor, 25 aldermen, and 210 councillors (234 counting deputy aldermen), the last of whom were elected annually on December 21 by London's free ratepayers (taxpayers) on a ward-by-ward basis in a popular court called the *wardmote*. These men, although not as prosperous as the aldermen, were all substantial citizens, shopkeepers, and master craftsmen, nominated by their parish vestries in consultation with the aldermen: circa 1600, 84% were members of the twelve great companies. Nevertheless, they tended to be more populist and less conservative than the Court of Aldermen: during the seventeenth century they inclined to be Puritans; by the early eighteenth they were Tories and Jacobites. Called by the lord mayor usually five or six times a year, Common Council was originally intended to be consultative, its decisions subjected, as we have seen, to veto by the Court of Aldermen. But from 1642 to 1683 and again from 1688 to 1725, the aldermanic right of veto was repealed, and Common Council asserted itself, claiming the right to legislate for London. The Court of Aldermen contested this, especially in the latter period. In 1725 the Walpole government passed the City Election Act (11 Geo. I, c. 18), which restricted the franchise to householders worth £10 (thus expelling 3,000 poor freemen from the rolls) and reconfirmed the aldermanic right of veto. Nevertheless, the opposition to Walpole gradually gained control of the Corporation in the 1730s, and this as much as the statute could explain why Common Council became moribund for twenty years: who needs Common Council when you control the mayoralty and Court of Aldermen? In 1746, with a new national government in power, the 1725 act was repealed. From this point, Common

Council revived, increasingly operating as a sort of House of Commons for the City, responsible for regulating markets; street lighting; repairing the wall, gates, and conduits; and paving and other necessary services.

In theory, each ward was run by its alderman assisted by the ward inquest, which was supposed to look after the poor, lighting, paving, and public morals, in the last case by closing down unlicensed ale, gambling, and bawdy houses. But from about 1600 and accelerating after 1700, the responsibilities of the inquest were fulfilled in some wards by an executive committee consisting of the alderman assisted by his deputy, and the common councilmen assisted by a beadle. The beadle was an ancient officer who roamed the streets supervising the watch, inspecting houses for unauthorized inmates, looking out for abandoned children, policing hawkers, enforcing alehouse hours, compiling tax roles and muster lists, and checking poor people's fuel stocks. In other wards these responsibilities were left to individual parishes.

Each of the City's 26 wards was divided into precincts (242 at the beginning of our period) and parishes (111). Each ward, precinct, and parish had an army of subordinate officers, some paid, some unpaid. Annually at the wardmote, in addition to the ward's alderman (on a vacancy by death) and common councilmen, between one and three hundred local offices were elected, in this case by all male ratepayers. These included constables, criers, and night watchmen to maintain the peace, rakers and scavengers to clear the streets of refuse, keepers of grates, diggers of conduits and ditches, meal weighers, garblers (to regulate the purity of spices), sealers, and packers. Perhaps 3,000 men were elected annually to local office in wardmotes, with a further 1,500 or so serving at the behest of the parish or livery company. This meant that at any given time, as many as one out of ten adult men in the City was active in local government.

It also meant that London was in some ways the most democratic place in Europe. The highest expression of democratic will in the City was Common Hall, the body of citizens who elected London's lord mayor, sheriffs, and four members of Parliament. This electorate had once encompassed all the freemen of the City, but by the fifteenth century (confirmed in the City Election Act of 1725) it was restricted to the liverymen, maybe 2,500 men in late Elizabethan London, 4,000 in 1641, 6,000 in 1680, and 8,200 in 1710. In Westminster, an even larger electorate chose its two MPs on a franchise based on those who paid certain taxes, called "scot-and-lot." As the West End expanded, the number of residents paying scot and lot came to 14,000 in the early eighteenth century. In short, London and Westminster amounted to the two largest borough electorates in the British Isles. Characterized by one historian as "suspicious, jealous and stubborn,"[22] they were impossible to bribe or frighten. The City elite sought to prevent democracy from running amok by carefully chore-ographing elections, nominating candidates for offices, usually in strict rotation by seniority among those who had not served. Ideally, nominees faced the electorate only when deals had been struck so that there were no opposing candidates. Often, the Crown interfered in City elections by pressuring the aldermen to admit courtiers to the livery and thus a vote. Elizabeth's chief minister, William Cecil, Lord Burghley (1520–1598), con-structed a solid clientage network among the governors of London and Westminster, and Charles II set aside electoral results he did not like.

The key piece of metropolitan government, the one that impinged most frequently on most Londoners' lives, was the parish. The City of London had 111 parishes in the sixteenth century. These tended to be small, averaging 3.9 acres and 137 households apiece. The dozen or so suburban parishes were much larger: for example, St. Dunstan Stepney, founded when the medieval population beyond the walls was tiny, stretched from the walls of the City to the River Lea in the East, from the Thames to Hackney in the north. As London burst its bounds, this one parish grew to have a population of 47,000 in the 1690s, larger than any other city in England! Each parish was governed by a body known as the vestry. The vestry nominated officers to be voted on in the wardmotes, maintained the fabric of the church, managed the parish properties and school, and oversaw the Poor Law. In some big suburbs where there was no immediate higher government authority, like Marylebone and St. Pancras to the northwest, they took on lighting and paving as well.

A vestry could be open – meaning every rate-paying male parishioner had a right to attend its meetings – or closed, meaning that parish affairs were run by a select committee, usually thirty to fifty former officers (i.e., constables, scavengers) who tended in practice to be the wealthiest and most long-standing male householders. Most London vestries started out open and remained so, but as the period wore on, at least a quarter moved to more restricted participation, including some of the city's wealthiest. The reason was simple: a large, open vestry was harder for a small elite to control or dominate. In 1736, the respectable parishioners of Whitechapel were shocked by the "clamorous proceedings and irregular behaviour of the great multitude of persons" that attended its meetings.[23] The alternative was to confine authority to "exclusive and self-perpetuating oligarchies."[24]

The new and fashionable West End parish of St. George Hanover Square provides an extreme example: when it was established in 1725, its vestry included seven dukes, fourteen earls, two viscounts, and seven barons.

The most important vestry officials were the churchwardens. Usually former constables, they managed the parish finances, collected rates and special taxes, levied soldiers, policed parish moral standards, maintained the streets, settled arguments, and determined the hierarchy of the parish by deciding where people sat in church. This was often a source of dispute. Early in the period, men and women sat separately, with the vestry toward the front, lesser members of the parish behind. Eventually, whole families simply rented pews, with more or less the same effect: the wealthy up front. Churchwardens had usually come to know their parishes as constables, responsible for law enforcement. In addition, other parishioners served as surveyors of the highways, responsible for paving. Overseers of the poor distributed poor relief. Women could serve as searchers, hunting out anyone who had died or was suffering from a contagious disease. Because local officers often had to cross the boundaries of their parishes to do their duties – chasing criminals, returning the poor to their parish of origin, conferring with other officers – their horizons sometimes encompassed wide swaths of London.

There was much potential for conflict in this system. The lord mayor and aldermen represented the interests of the rich oligarchs who dominated overseas trade and finance. For most of the period, they had strong connections to the court, but from 1641 to 1661 they tended to be Puritans, and after 1680, Whigs. By the 1720s, these Whig oligarchs were once again firmly allied with the government, led by Robert Walpole and later the Pelhams. In contrast, Common Council represented, and Common Hall consisted of, tradesmen and craftsmen of more modest means. They too tended to be Puritans before the 1690s, but as Whig aldermen in rich central City wards drew closer to the court after the Revolution of 1688/89, the rank and file in poorer wards beyond the walls and down by the river started to vote Tory. By the 1720s Common Council and Common Hall came to be dominated by staunch Anglicans, Tories, and later Jacobites. Their interests often clashed with those of the national government, lord mayor, and aldermen, not least because the mayor could call and dismiss them at will, and for much of the period the aldermen could veto the legislation they wanted. From the mid-seventeenth century on Common Council and Common Hall therefore demanded a wider franchise, the direct election of the lord mayor, and the abolition of the aldermanic veto.

In the meantime, there was one more way in which ordinary Londoners could express their will, persuade or intimidate their betters, and have an impact on national politics: by acting as a mob. We will address the London crowd in Chapter 7.

These conflicts and divisions notwithstanding, the governors and governed of London shared much common ground when it came to the good of their city. The aldermen, assistants in companies, and closed vestries did more than pay lip service to paternalistic ideals; there is plenty of evidence that they gave attention and effort to the grievances of craftsmen and householders, the plight of poor widows and orphaned children, and the price of bread. Perhaps this is not surprising: because of the social mobility and population density discussed in Chapter 2, many of London's rulers had risen from, yet still lived cheek by jowl with, ordinary people.

In any case, the elaborate machinery of City government described earlier applied to less than one quarter of the area and people comprising greater London in 1750. The most important metropolitan area outside the City of London was, of course, Westminster. Before the Reformation, it had been governed as a manor owned by the dean and chapter of Westminster Abbey. Following the Dissolution of the Monasteries in 1545, it was given a high steward chosen by the Crown to represent royal interests. Subsequent attempts to establish Westminster as an incorporated borough from 1585 to 1633 all failed, but in 1585 a Court of Burgesses was established, chosen by the dean and chapter in cooperation with the steward: as this implies, the Crown had a great deal more influence on how Westminster was governed than it had in the City. Each burgess with his assistant presided over one of Westminster's twelve wards. Acting something like a Court of Aldermen, the Court of Burgesses made legislation, looked after markets and streets, and urged the big Westminster parishes (like St. Margaret Westminster or St. Martin-in-the-Fields) to suppress new building and the subdivision of old, send vagrants to the Westminster Bridewell, and look after the poor. In fact, even more than in the City, the real work of Westminster local government was borne by the parishes.

The Court of Burgesses also acted something like a bench of JPs for misdemeanors, which brought it into conflict with the king's Palace Court, from 1611 the Court of the Verge. This court was responsible for anything that happened within a twelve-mile radius of the king, but in practice its jurisdiction extended only to the palaces of Whitehall and St. James's and the royal parks. Violent crime and major felonies, as in the City, were handled by the Central Criminal Court at the Old Bailey. Westminster

finally got its own JPs in the late seventeenth century, holding sessions of
the peace for misdemeanors at Hicks' Hall, Clerkenwell. The burgesses
declined in importance from the 1720s on, because their authority and
responsibility came to be assumed by the vestries of the nine Westminster parishes and the Middlesex JPs. From the 1760s they were mostly
ceremonial positions.

As London expanded in the seventeenth century, several large unincorporated suburban districts emerged, for example Kensington, Chelsea,
Marylebone, and St. Pancras to the north and west, Stepney to the east,
Bermondsey and Rotherhithe to the south. These communities were run
by their parish vestries. Elsewhere, vestries had to follow the orders of an
ever-expanding bench of Middlesex and Westminster justices. Because
by the eighteenth century substantial citizens rarely wanted to serve, these
new JPs were often minor professionals and petty tradesmen, that is,
poorer than London common councilmen. Contemporaries called these
men "trading justices," in the sense of JPs who were mainly tradesmen, not
gentlemen, but also in the sense of justices who were more likely to work
out a deal or take a bribe than a gentleman would do. Unlike aristocratic
justices of independent means, they charged for justice, exacting a fee for
every service they performed. The temptation to promote business "by
hindering justice or by maintaining"[25] was too great for many, but such
justices nevertheless often performed a necessary service for poor people
who could not afford to see a case go to trial.

London would not begin to see metropolitan-wide government until
the institution of the London County Council in 1888. It would not
elect a citywide mayor until 2000. But the tendency toward centralization
was already being felt during the second half of our period. Increasingly, the City took over responsibilities previously left to individuals or
small groups, while Parliament passed legislation for the metropolis as a
whole. Take street lighting, paving, and sanitation. At the beginning of the
period, London was far behind other capitals. For example, at night, light
was provided by the moon and candles in windows. In 1416 Parliament
required householders to hang lights on moonless nights from Michaelmas
(September 29) to Lady-Day (March 25) between sunset and curfew (8
PM), enforced by ward beadles and the vestry. Individual householders
were also responsible for paving the street immediately in front of their
houses and sweeping it every Wednesday and Saturday, although refuse
was theoretically the province of parish rakers and scavengers. Nevertheless, prior to 1660, most streets were dark as pitch after midnight, badly

paved and piled high with trash, all of which facilitated shady activities and discouraged the development of a night life patronized by the respectable classes. Instead, Londoners feared what one Star Chamber witness called "the dead time of the night when all good subjects should be at quiet taking their natural rest in their beds."[26] Constables arrested nightwalkers and idle persons who could not explain themselves just for being out after curfew.

Most of these arrangements were reconfirmed by Act of Parliament at the Restoration. As late as the early eighteenth century, Lincoln's Inn Fields was a veritable garbage dump, the Fleet remained disgusting, and both were also thought of as dangerous. When out at night – an increasing possibility as a night life began to develop after 1660 – one could hire linkmen to light the way with flambeaux, portable torches dipped in tallow. But according to John Gay's (1685–1732) *Trivia: Or the Art of Walking the Streets of London* (1716), they were not to be relied upon:

> *Though thou art tempted by the Link-Man's Call,*
> *Yet trust him not along the lonely Wall;*
> *In the Mid-way he'll quench the flaming Brand,*
> *And share the Booty with the pilfering Band.*

Part of the problem was that in the late seventeenth century the City was experiencing a financial crisis and could not afford to pay for services itself; the alternative was to sell monopolies on such services to entrepreneurs. Thus, in 1683 John Vernatti (fl. 1680s) was allowed, over the opposition of the tinsmiths and tallow chandlers, to set up convex lights in Cornhill. These lamps had lenses and reflecting glasses that cast their glow widely. Two years later, Edmund Hemming (fl. 1680–1699) was granted a monopoly on London street lighting on the condition that he place lamps at every tenth house on main streets between 6 PM and midnight from September 29 to March 25. In 1694 the City contracted with the Convex Light Company to provide lamps. Finally, in 1736, it was allowed to raise taxes specifically to pay for globular lamps to be kept lit until sunrise year round. Lincoln's Inn Fields was enclosed by Act of Parliament in 1735 and the Fleet Ditch filled in by order of Common Council in 1747. From the mid-eighteenth century on, commissions were established to take over such services as street lighting, paving and cleaning, and drainage. In 1760 London began a street-widening program that saw the demolition of the City gates. These were all City measures, however: Southwark, Westminster, and so forth remained dark and full of potholes. Here, the turning point came with the Westminster Paving Act of 1762 (2 Geo. III, c. 21), which was followed by a series of citywide (not City-wide) statutes designed to improve London street life by paving with Purbeck stone, deepening gutters, clearing stalls and other obstructions, and numbering houses and shops. By the 1780s, Westminster's major streets were paved with Aberdeen granite and lit with oil lamps. Gas lighting was introduced at the beginning of the nineteenth century. The city's population, the environmental problems associated with it, and the pace of reform would pick up in the nineteenth century, but that is a subject for another book.

4. Fine and Performed Arts

*I*f you were an artist or merely a lover of the arts and living in London in 1550, you had two main sources of patronage, inspiration, or entertainment: the court or the Church. From the Middle Ages to the dawn of our period, those two institutions dominated the world of high culture. First, the court and the Church had the vision to provide artistic programs and subjects for artists in London. Second, they commanded the financial resources to pay for both occasional commissions to artists in the form of buildings, paintings, statues, music, and literature, and to give them regular by-employment when new projects ran scarce. Thus, most of the great musicians of the day such as Thomas Tallis (c. 1505–1585) and William Byrd (c. 1543–1623) had positions as gentlemen of the Chapel Royal choir, or in one of the two great cathedral choirs in London, those of the Abbey or St. Paul's. Later in the century, stage players like William Shakespeare would be sworn into the service of the monarch or one of his great courtiers. Finally, the court and the Church provided large, national audiences, which led in turn to more attention for artists, wider dissemination of their works, and more commissions among the nobility. So, if you were a sixteenth-century artist and wanted to make a splash, you headed for London, and more specifically, to Whitehall, the Abbey, or the Cathedral.

But there was a price to be paid. What the court and Church gave with one hand, they limited – in subject matter, content and style – with the other. That is, the court and Church censored the arts: monarchs regulated their own images tightly, all printed works had to be approved by the bishops, and the Elizabethan stage was monitored by the master of the Revels in the lord chamberlain's office. Artistic expression in mid-sixteenth-century London, like trade, was unfree. It is thus perhaps fortunate that, although these institutions remained important cultural patrons throughout the period, their monopoly on subject matter and patronage was eroding. First, even before the Reformation, the great age of church building in London was largely over. After it, there was no more call for saintly statuary or stained glass; rather, these were removed on the orders of the Crown. During the Civil Wars of the mid-seventeenth century the Puritan/parliamentary regime abolished the cultural power of the Church of England, disbanded the court, closed the public theaters, and suppressed most of the visual and performing arts, breaking long-standing relationships and traditions. But they also lifted censorship on the printed word, resulting in an explosion of public writing.

After the Restoration the government made some attempt to revive censorship, but the last Licensing Act expired in 1695. The result was another London-sourced flood of print: by 1724 there were more than 100 publishing houses in the country, 75 of them based in the capital. They produced the first regular newspapers, literary magazines, novels, and collections of poetry. Because of the Commercial and Financial Revolutions, and London's prosperity generally, an increasingly flush and sophisticated general public could support a restored public theater, and new institutions like the concert hall, public masquerade balls, and a burgeoning literary market. At the same time, the financial decline of the court and the intellectual division of the Church made way for a vibrant public sphere of artistic and political discourse, no longer dependent on the approval or patronage of a king or archbishop but rather on the wealth and interest of literate Londoners. It can thus be argued that London gave birth to public patronage of the arts in England, pioneering new methods for the production and dissemination of culture that provided the blueprint for our own. Once again, the metropolis was at the forefront of the creation of the modern world. At the same time, it is argued later in this chapter that insofar as much of this art was not only created in but inspired by the metropolis, it was also important in creating Londoners.

1550–1640

Prior to the Reformation, the principal patron for English art was the Catholic Church. Sunday and holiday services were probably where most Londoners encountered great art: the Gothic arches, vaulting, and tracery of the churches themselves, their walls painted in geometric patterns, their statuary and stained glass, in the larger churches the sounds of chant and

Renaissance polyphony, and above all the sonorous ceremonial of the Latin mass itself. London was filled with medieval abbeys, priories, and churches – more than 100 in the square mile of the City alone – of varying architectural pretensions. We have already noted the vaulted magnificence of Westminster Abbey and the ramshackle greatness of Old St. Paul's; to this might be added the Norman splendor of St. Bartholomew the Great in Smithfield. At the other end of the scale were modest parish churches like St. Olave Hart Street (see Chapter 1) and tiny chapels of ease. All of these had been built by 1550. Many were lost in the Great Fire or the Blitz; indeed, some were lost twice, having been destroyed by both. Others have since met the wrecking ball at the hands of developers. Even those few pre-1666 churches surviving today look very different from their late medieval or early Tudor appearance, partly because both the Protestant Tudors and the godly Parliamentarians ordered the removal of much elaborate decoration. As this book opens, the Edwardian regime had just launched another such wave and was moving to proscribe elaborate Church music. The result was plainer churches and simpler services.

Simpler but not unbeautiful – Edward's regime also mandated that services use the *Book of Common Prayer* in 1549, revised in 1552. Composed by Archbishop Thomas Cranmer, the Book of Common Prayer re-cast the liturgy in magnificent English prose. After a five-year return to Catholic style liturgy and decor under Mary, the new, English service became permanent under Elizabeth in 1559, with a further revision in 1662. The result was a plainer, cleaner, more immediately eloquent experience to which many became devoted. Cranmer's beautiful prayers notwithstanding, for the first century of the Anglican settlement, the centerpiece of this new Protestant service was the sermon. The Chapel Royal and, before the Civil Wars, Paul's Cross were especially known for good sermons. Famous preachers, like Hugh Latimer and Nicholas Ridley (c. 1502–1555), Bishop of London in the sixteenth century, or John Donne, Dean of St. Paul's and vicar of St. Dunstan-in-the-West at the beginning of the seventeenth, held their listeners spellbound for hours, combining theological and social concerns, Biblical scholarship, and stupendous oratory. Often, they attacked prodigal London as a new Babylon, a second Sodom. Puritans especially valued the Word of God and its exposition in sermons, which they much preferred to the poetic ritual of the Prayer Book. When, in the 1590s and 1630s, High Church bishops purged parish livings of Puritan clergy, sympathetic London merchants banded together to endow lectureships and fill them with like-minded preachers. All through the period, intellectuals of varying degrees of religious enthusiasm, like John Evelyn and Samuel Pepys, followed preachers like modern-day fans follow actors or sports figures. Thus, on March 16, 1662, Pepys wrote "This morning, till Churches were done, I spent going from one church to another and hearing a bit here and a bit there."[1]

If the Reformation was hard on the visual arts, it was a boon for literature. Protestantism, with its emphasis on the Word, required literacy, which promoted schooling and a hunger for books that Fleet Street was happy to satisfy after Edward VI relaxed the censorship laws in 1547. Many books were sent from London presses to the great libraries of the universities, nobility, or gentry, but others found their way into the hands of the city's increasingly literate merchant class and some trickled down to the very lowest levels of society as chapbooks. But after the Edwardian experiment with a free press, the government reinstituted censorship in 1549. In 1554, Parliament specified the penalty for writings critical of the sovereign to be the loss of the author's right hand. In 1581, after Catholic plots against Queen Elizabeth and Puritan attacks on bishops, these prohibitions became capital. To enforce them, Star Chamber decreed in 1586 that all printing presses had to be based in London apart from those of the two universities, that every press had to be licensed by the Stationers' Company, and that no book could be printed unless it had first been examined and licensed by a bishop. Despite these restrictions, Fleet Street presses worked overtime: whereas 800 books had been published in the decade from 1520 to 1529, 3,000 appeared between 1590 and 1600. London housed a raft of polemicists who railed in poetry and prose, print and manuscript, against the defects of Church, state, and city in learned treatises, cheap pamphlets, and one-page broadsides. The authorities could respond harshly: in 1593 John Penry (1562/63–1593) was first imprisoned in the Poultry Compter and then executed for his role in publishing a series of Puritan tracts critical of the bishops.

In the wake of the Reformation, as the power and wealth of the Church declined, the court in London became the primary center for the production of culture. The monarch's propaganda needs, personality, and activities, and those of his or her entourage, provided the subject matter for art. Fashions in art or dress either originated or made their debut from Europe at Whitehall. And when the sovereign was too cheap or too poor to commission art directly, the court's concentration of blood and money made it the best place to catch the eye of an alternative patron. For example, apart from the presentation of tournaments, pageants, processions, and revels, especially on Elizabeth's Accession Day (November 17), Queens Mary and Elizabeth seldom commissioned works of art. Although Elizabeth I and James I were themselves writers of some note, they paid few artists directly, apart from the musicians of their Chapel Royal. Rather, it was Crown ministers like Thomas Cromwell, the Duke of Somerset, Lord Burghley, and the Duke of Buckingham who kept stables of writers busy, often supported by jobs at court, producing entertainments for the monarch and propaganda in favor of their policies, just as the City employed poets and musicians to sell its message while entertaining the citizenry in the lord mayor's show and other pageants. In general, the Stuarts were less peripatetic than the Tudors, more profligate, and did, as we shall see, collect and commission art. These factors facilitated the development of a distinctive court culture, the rise of the London season, and the growth of the idea of "urban gentry" at the beginning of the seventeenth century. This development was not without controversy. The early Stuarts worried that the attractions of London were draining the countryside of its aristocratic leadership and therefore threatening order. In 1632 the lord keeper described the new urban rhythms to aristocratic life while complaining about gentlemen who:

> go from ordinaries [restaurants] to dicing-houses, and from thence to play-houses. Their wives dress themselves in the morning, visit in the afternoon and perhaps make a journey to Hyde Park, and so home again.[2]

Needless to say, repeated proclamations ordering the elite back to their country estates were mostly ineffective against London's increasing attractions.

The most dramatic and expensive peacetime activity in which kings engage is building. Henry VIII was a great builder and renovator of royal palaces, but his children were too short-lived or too poor to follow his lead. As a result, the royal housing stock left in London by Henry VIII at his death provided the bulk of royal residences throughout the period: here as in so much else, it was "Great Harry" who set the parameters for subsequent monarchs. There were important renovations of Whitehall under James I, Charles II, and James II; Greenwich under James I; and St. James's under Queen Anne. But even in the eighteenth century, the king's houses were essentially Tudor. Prior to 1640, the most important additions to the Tudor palaces were made by James I, who although no

wealthier than Elizabeth I, was far more willing to go into debt. He commissioned Inigo Jones to build the Banqueting House at Whitehall and the
Queen's House at Greenwich. Jones had studied the neoclassical designs
of the Italian architect Andrea Palladio (1518–1580), and so his buildings
represented a radical departure from the Gothic style in vogue until the
mid-sixteenth century. But the late Tudor and early Stuart monarchs did
not have enough money to sustain the effort on a grand scale like St.
Peter's in Rome or the Louvre in Paris. Jones also added a magnificent but
incongruous neoclassical portico to Old St. Paul's and erected the first
large-scale housing development, the prototype of the London square, for
the Earl of Bedford at Covent Garden. This last, rather than his tinkering
with the palace and cathedral, pointed to London's architectural future. In
fact, most of the great buildings put up in London from 1547 to 1640 were
aristocratic, not royal, for example, Somerset House, Northumberland
House, and several other new townhouses along the Strand; the Earl of
Salisbury's New Exchange on the Strand and residential development of
St. Martin's Lane; or the Earl of Clare's development of Drury Lane near
Covent Garden. Still, the monarchy hoped to make London a showcase
of order and uniformity by regulating the number, size, and style of new
buildings between 1580 and 1640. One contemporary complained in 1619:
"We have every week almost a new proclamation for buildings."[3] Fortunately, the Crown was largely ignored or bought off with the payment
of fines. Finally, at the opposite end of the scale, contemporary tourists
were often charmed by the late Tudor tumbledown houses of the pre-Fire
metropolis.

The later Tudor court produced no painter of the quality of
Hans Holbein the Younger, who had served Henry VIII. Indeed, Queen
Elizabeth probably set portraiture in England back half a century by having
her Privy Council regulate her image to ensure that she always appeared
as she was early in her reign. That image was disseminated in a wide
variety of portraits with complex iconographical programs: the Sieve Portrait, the Armada Portrait, or the Ditchley Portrait by Marcus Gheeraerts,
commissioned by the courtier Sir Henry Lee (1533–1611), which shows
her emerging, like a tree, from the patchwork of English counties. But
none of these pictures give much psychological insight into their subject,
and no single portraitist dominated commissions at her court as Holbein had done at her father's. It was not until the Jacobean period that
the visual arts received really effective royal and aristocratic patronage.
This began in a court circle that grew up around James I's son, Prince

Charles (1600–1649), and included George Villiers, Duke of Buckingham, and above all Thomas Howard, Earl of Arundel (1585–1646). The
prince encouraged his father to bring over and patronize prominent continental artists, notably Peter Paul Rubens and Anthony van Dyck. This
patronage resulted in masterpieces such as the former's ceiling for the
Banqueting House, *The Apotheosis of James I*; and the latter's series of
portraits of the royal family. As king, Charles I assembled one of the great
art collections in Europe by ordering his diplomats and aristocrats on the
Grand Tour to purchase desirable items. Courtiers, led by Buckingam
and Arundel, emulated the king by filling their residences with the finest
paintings, sculpture, furniture, metalwork, woodwork, porcelain, embroidery, and tapestry hangings the continent had to offer. At Arundel's death
in 1646, his house in the Strand contained 37 statues, 128 busts, and 250
inscribed marbles. Because there were no public art galleries, the only way
to experience such visual splendor was to go to court or visit a nobleman's
house. Fortunately, such buildings were generally open to the gentle,
who could see the owner's greatest treasures by paying the staff a small
gratuity. Indeed, these treasure houses were *meant* to be shown, as royal
and aristocratic collecting (as well as elaborate dress and room decor)
was intended to impress important visitors with the patron's wealth and
lineage, a projection of power and status.

Toward the end of the reign of Elizabeth I, the court began to combine
all of the art forms available circa 1600 in formal choreographed pageants,
or "masques," with allegorical or mythological plots, spoken lines, elaborate sets, costumes, and music. The court masque achieved its greatest
sophistication, splendor, and expense under James I and Charles I thanks
to the pen of Ben Jonson and the scenic designs of Inigo Jones, in whose
Banqueting House they were often performed. Their usual themes were
the dangers of political and social chaos, the virtue of order, and the enno-
blement of conjugal love. Their point was usually to glorify the monarch
and reinforce the Great Chain of Being. First, the theater was set up so
that the king and queen had the best view of the masque, whereas the rest
of the audience had a good view of *them* watching it. Second, the typical masque began with comic or antic dances illustrating the devastating
effects of chaos (the anti-masque). A member of the royal family would
then appear to compose all differences in a dance celebrating order, love,
and so forth (the masque itself). Charles's queen, Henrietta Maria (1609–
1669), appeared often, as did Charles himself on occasion, to the scandal of
Puritan preachers. In fact, few would have witnessed the spectacle because

Charles aimed his artistic message almost solely at the court elite. He kept a much more formal and exclusive court than his father or his son, and as a consequence only courtiers were allowed to attend the king's masques and view his paintings. Most Londoners, let alone the English people as a whole, were never exposed to this propaganda or such sophisticated art generally, and the early Stuarts had little interest in the sorts of street pageants and cavalcades that contributed to Elizabeth's popularity (see Chapter 3). Whatever propaganda value Charles's masques and paintings possessed was lost on the vast majority of his subjects.

Still, court styles in art did have an influence beyond Whitehall. During the 1630s, with the rise of the High Church movement under Archbishop Laud and the strict enforcement of what they called "the Beauty of Holiness," there was a revival of elaborate religious ceremony and music in London churches, beginning at the Chapel Royal. The king's chapel was the premier center for the production of Church music and the anthems and services composed and performed there by the likes of Orlando Gibbons, Henry Lawes (1596–1662), and Thomas Tomkins (1572–1656) were borrowed by cathedral and church choirs around the country. The court also produced instrumental dance music for balls, masques, and madrigals, and lute or keyboard music for quiet hours from William Byrd, John Dowland (c. 1563–1626), Thomas Campion (1567–1620), and William Lawes (1602–1645). This music was often published for performance in aristocratic, gentle, and mercantile households. Beyond the court, the City maintained trumpeters and waits (a band of public musicians) to perform on ceremonial occasions. Ordinary Londoners sang hymns and carols in church, and folk songs and printed ballads in taverns and in the streets. These were sometimes borrowed, arranged, and embellished (as we saw in the cases of the cries of London) by "high culture" composers like Gibbons and Thomas Morley (1557–c. 1602). As we will see in Chapter 5, the line between high culture and popular culture was thus a porous one.

The art form for which Elizabethan and Jacobean London is best known was arguably the theater. The first plays in the English language were medieval mystery and mummers' plays, mounted on religious feast days, but these were outlawed at the Reformation. During the sixteenth century, strolling bands of players presented short secular interludes in private houses, market squares, and the courtyards of inns and taverns like the Boar's Head in Eastcheap. There were also bands of boy players, often based in ecclesiastical establishments and choir schools like the Chapel Royal. The Children of Paul's, who began life in the choir of St. Paul's

Cathedral, performed at court repeatedly in the late sixteenth century. During this period, full-fledged five-act plays began to be mounted by young men at the universities and London's Inns of Court. The greatest of these "university" wits was Christopher Marlowe (1564–1593), who wrote *Tamburlaine the Great* (1587), the *History of Edward II* (c. 1592), and *Dr. Faustus* (c. 1589; published 1604). The queen occasionally experienced such productions while attending the Christmas revels of the Inns of Court. She enjoyed these plays so much that she began to encourage their performance at court. In 1583 twelve actors were made grooms of the chamber, giving them the status and legal protection of household servants. She also gave royal protection to a company of actors, the Queen's Men, as did Leicester and other court peers. This allowed such companies to mount plays for paying audiences.

Such protection was necessary because the law was hostile to roving bands of masterless men: in particular, the Poor Law of 1572 outlawed "common players in interludes & minstrels, not belonging to any baron of this realm" (14 Eliz. 1, c. 5). Actors ran into the stiffest opposition from the civic authorities of London. As high-ranking members of the trading and livery companies, the lord mayor and aldermen were keenly aware of the economic impact of large numbers of ordinary people – their employees – idling away their time watching plays. Moreover, big crowds of any sort were thought to be dangerous: politically, because of the potential for unsupervised speech and riot; legally, because theater audiences were targets for pickpockets; socially, because of the mix of classes and genders; hygienically, because of the potential to spread disease. It did not help that once theaters were established in the suburbs of Shoreditch and Southwark (see later discussion), they tended to be surrounded by brothels. Finally, many of London's civic leaders were Puritans and therefore ill-disposed toward the sometimes shocking activities portrayed onstage. Under Elizabeth, they repeatedly asked the queen, the Privy Council, and the Archbishop of Canterbury to restrain the stage. In 1577, Rev. Thomas White (1550–1624) summarized their position succinctly in a Paul's Cross sermon: "[T]he cause of plagues is sin, if you look to it well, and the cause of sin are plays, therefore the cause of plagues are plays."[4]

This municipal and clerical hostility explains why the earliest theaters were established in the suburbs and liberties, outside the City's jurisdiction. The advantage of a purpose-built theater was that it clarified the financial relationship between player and playgoer: instead of passing the hat around a square or courtyard and hoping for the best, the players could charge patrons a set fee on entry. The first was the Red Lion, built east of the City in Whitechapel in 1567. In 1576 James Burbage (c. 1531–1597) established an open-air public playhouse called, appropriately enough, the Theatre, in the north London suburb of Shoreditch. This was followed by the Curtain in the same neighborhood in 1577. In 1597 Burbage reopened the hall at Blackfriars, down by the Thames, as an enclosed theater, implying higher ticket prices and a more exclusive clientele. In 1587 the open-air Rose was established across the Thames near Paris Garden and the Bankside Bear Garden. The location must have been convenient: the Rose was followed by the Swan in 1596, and the Globe, built out of materials brought from the now defunct Shoreditch Theatre, in 1598. The Fortune Theatre, built north of the City at Cripplegate, followed in 1600. In the ensuing century these open-air venues were joined by more hall theaters: the Cockpit, Drury Lane in 1616 and Salisbury Court in 1629. Their capacity was several hundred, their repertory and clientele tending to be more upper-crust.

More reminiscent of inn courtyards and bear-beating arenas, the open-air theaters were generally of three stories, their galleries roofed with thatch (see Illustration 4.1). One advantage to playing alfresco was that it was more conducive to the sort of spectacle the crowd loved: in 1613, during a performance of *Henry VIII*, the Globe's thatch roof caught fire from the kind of special effect that was only possible outdoors, a firing cannon. Fortunately, the most serious injury was that of a man who found "his breeches on fire that would perhaps have broyled him if he had not with the benefit of a provident wit put it out with bottle ale."[5] A second advantage to the outdoor theaters was their capacity: as many as 3,000 Londoners could come together in the afternoon to see the latest play, munch on apples and nuts, and drink bottle ale sold during the performance. Yet, even here the Great Chain obtained: the wealthy sat in upper boxes for 3 pence, the middling orders below them on benches for 2 pence, and ordinary people in the pit, the large open area on the ground level, for a penny – hence their designation as "groundlings" or "penny stinkards."

There has been much debate as to how popular Elizabethan audiences truly were. On the one hand, a penny was about a fifth of a day's wage for a laborer in the late sixteenth century – a reasonable expense on occasion. In 1613, an Italian diplomat attended the Curtain surrounded by "a gang of porters and carters."[6] On the other hand, it is hard to see how journeymen, apprentices, and servants could have cut work very often, in contrast to their masters and their wives, watermen, or students at the

Inns of Court. Certainly, the indoor hall theaters like Blackfriars, where the general admission was 3 to 6 pence, tended to attract the courtly elite; merchants, craftsmen, and fishwives patronized the Rose or the Globe. Particularly privileged patrons, for example, young aristocrats desperate to be seen, might demand to sit on the stage at a hall theater, or above it in the gallery overlooking an open-air theater (see Illustration 4.2). The stage itself jutted into the pit, giving a ground's eye view to the groundlings. It had a trap door, leading down to "hell," from which, for example, Banquo's ghost in *Macbeth* could suddenly appear onstage. Above the rear of the stage was a platform called "heaven," above which was a balcony from which Juliet could await her Romeo, defenders of towns in the *Henry VI* plays could shout imprecations at rebels, musicians could play before curtain time, or powerful aristocrats could show off their place in the Great Chain of Being. At the back of the stage were three doors for entrances and exits from the "tiring house," where players costumed and awaited their entrances.

Theaters like the Globe clearly represented a new form of artistic patronage: that of the paying public. Indeed, the rise of a paying audience in the 1580s is one of the great developments in English cultural life: Andrew Gurr goes so far as to argue that Elizabethan and early Stuart drama "was the only major medium for social intercommunication, the only existing form of journalism and the only occasion that existed for large numbers of people other than sermons and executions" to gather before, say, 1640.[7] It was public taste, not that of the court or the Church, that dictated whether a new play succeeded or failed. That taste tended to divide along class lines: spectacles, heroic plays, and farces at the more plebeian open-air theaters, more allusive and abstract plays full of classical references like Webster's (c. 1580–c. 1638) *Duchess of Malfi* (pre-1614; published 1623) or Jonson's *The Alchemist* (1610) for the courtiers and aristocrats of the indoor theaters. Plays for elite audiences often made fun of city merchants as greedy simpletons: Francis Beaumont's (1584–1616) *Knight of the Burning Pestle* (1607) begins with a London grocer, called "Citizen," rising from the audience with his wife, called "Wife," to demand that the players "present something notably in honour of the commons of the City," like *The Legend of Whittington* or *The Life and Death of Sir Thomas Gresham, with the Building of the Royal Exchange*. Here, the citizens' taste for plays about London's past worthies is ridiculed. But as we noted in Chapter 3, playwrights writing for a citizen audience were happy to return the favor by lampooning court favorites and fops.

Still, to be performed at all, that play had to get past the master of the Revels, who might forbid or censor it. As this implies, the theater, like so much of late Tudor and early Stuart government, had not yet entirely gone "out of court." The theater companies all gave command performances there, and all relied on a royal or noble patron to stay on the good side of the civic authorities: hence the Earl of Worcester's Men, the Admiral's Men, and so forth. All wore livery and badges just like other royal and noble servants but also like craft guilds. Like the guilds, their privileges were protected by the Crown. Today, when one sees the word *Royal* in the name of some artistic or charitable institution, this is a vestige of that need for such protection. From 1593 there were only two such companies, the Lord Chamberlain's Men, patronized by the first and second Lords Hunsdon (1526–1596; 1548–1603), and the Admiral's Men, patronized by Charles, Lord Howard of Effingham (1536–1624). In 1602, Edward, Earl of Worcester (c. 1550–1628), Elizabeth's master of the Horse, was granted a chartered company to play at the Boar's Head Tavern, Whitechapel. Under James I the Lord Chamberlain's Men became the King's Men, playing at the Globe in summer, Blackfriars Theatre in winter from 1609 to 1642; the Earl of Worcester's became the Queen's Men, based at the Cockpit, Drury Lane; and a new company arose, Lady Elizabeth's Men, patronized by James's daughter (1596–1662), the future Queen of Bohemia. The word *men* was of course operative, because women were not allowed on the stage before 1660.

The Globe was the original home base of the Lord Chamberlain's Men. At least six actors were shareholders in the company and the theater itself, with the builders Cuthbert (1565–1636) and Richard Burbage (1588–1619) holding double shares. Actors not only took on many parts but also were expected to write if necessary. Among the playwright-player-shareholders in the Lord Chamberlain's Men was a young immigrant to London from Stratford-upon-Avon, Warwickshire, named William Shakespeare. For more than twenty years, preeminent among a host of talented authors including Marlowe and Jonson, Shakespeare produced a series of comedies (*A Midsummer Night's Dream* [c. 1596], *Much Ado About Nothing* [c. 1598], *Twelfth Night* [c. 1600], *The Merry Wives of Windsor* [1602]); histories (*Richard II* [c. 1595], *Henry IV, Pts. 1 and 2* [1597–1598], and *Richard III* [c. 1594]); and, above all, tragedies (*Romeo and Juliet* [c. 1595], *Hamlet* [c. 1601], *King Lear* [c. 1605], and *Macbeth* [c. 1606]), which delighted Londoners then and continue to speak to humanity today. Although few of his plays are actually set in the metropolis, there would have been no Shakespeare without London: its inhabitants provided not only his audience but also the models for many of his characters, especially the working-class types in his comedies or the crowds in his history plays.

Thus, if London was not only a venue for the arts and a source of patronage, it was a subject for the arts as well. In Chapter 1 we noted that foreign printmakers like Claes Visscher and Wenceslaus Hollar came to draw its sights, culminating in famous panoramas of the Thames-side city. Orlando Gibbons was inspired by the music of London speech to set the *Cryes of London*. Poets, encouraged by City commissions for royal entries and mayoral pageants, celebrated the metropolis, including London's own "water poet," the bargeman John Taylor. But satirists like Joseph Hall (1576–1656), John Marston (1576–1634), and Everard Guilpin (b. c. 1572; fl. 1595–1600) followed the Roman models of Horace and Juvenal in attacking "all the City's luscious vanity." According to Guilpin, "The city is the map of vanities, /The mart of fools, the magazine of gulls, /The Painter's shop of antics."[8] Dekker's *Gull's Handbook* of 1609 is a satirical guide to elite living in London. Above all, London is a frequent setting for plays by Thomas Dekker, Thomas Heywood (1573–1641), Ben Jonson, Thomas Middleton (c. 1580–1627), Philip Massinger (1583–1640), and occasionally Shakespeare (*Henry IV, Pts. 1 and 2*, and, indeed, court scenes in all of the History plays). By the late sixteenth century an entire genre of "city comedy" had developed, satirizing the pretensions of Whitehall courtiers, warning of the tricks of London criminals, and celebrating the honesty of City merchants, the resourcefulness of their apprentices, and the cleverness of London serving girls. Examples include Jonson's *Bartholomew Fair* (1614), Heywood's *Four Prentices of London* (published 1615), or Dekker's *The Shoemaker's Holiday*, which premiered at the Rose in 1599. The protagonist of the last is a master shoemaker who presides over a chaotic household of journeymen and apprentices such as we might meet anywhere in the old City. The audience must have been pleased when the play's lovers marry happily and the shoemaker is elected lord mayor á la Whittington. Middleton's *A Chaste Maid in Cheapside* (1611) is the daughter of a London goldsmith.

Not all city comedies were so innocuous or complimentary to the city; others concern genuine urban problems. Middleton's *Your Five Gallants* (1608) is about a pimp, a pickpocket, a cheat, a pawnbroker, and a whoremonger. Middleton and Dekker's *The Roaring Girl* (1610) portrays Mary Frith (?1584–1659), better known to her fellow Londoners as the pickpocket Moll Cutpurse. Middleton and Dekker also teamed up to write *The Honest Whore* (1604, 1630), whose final wedding scene takes place in Bedlam, the City's mental hospital outside Bishopsgate. The court responded with satire of its own: Ben Jonson's *Epicoene or the Silent Woman* (1609) and, as noted previously, Beaumont's *Knight of the Burning Pestle* ridicule Londoners affecting the airs and lifestyle of courtiers. In these plays Londoners and courtiers did more than see themselves. As Jean Howard has argued, they worked out the tensions in London life between the classes and the genders, between court and City, crime and safety, truth and deception, the promise of London and the breaking of that promise in so many individual lives. Although clearly a branch of high culture, the early London theater was popular as well; indeed, it could be argued that it was one of the institutions that helped Londoners to acclimate to and identify with their new urban existence and to cope with "the shock of the new." Thus, the art that both celebrated and criticized London assisted men and women in becoming Londoners.

1640–1660

The crisis that precipitated the Civil Wars (see the Introduction and Chapter 7) was a crisis for the arts in London as well. During the Personal Rule 1629 to 1640, when Charles I refused to call Parliament and so cut himself off from extraordinary funding, he cut back on his collecting, and the last masques were performed at court in January 1640. When the king left the city in 1642 he took a skeleton household with him, including several court artists. Production in London practically ceased during the English Civil Wars (1642–1649), which was just fine with the City's and Parliament's Puritan authorities. The public theaters were closed by parliamentary order on September 2, 1642 and most fell into disrepair over the next few years. Charles I's execution and the ensuing abolition of the monarchy and court in 1649 eliminated at one stroke the nation's chief patron, clearinghouse for new styles, and meeting point for connoisseurs. The king's art collection was sold off, although some pieces were kept because Whitehall would remain the seat of government. What was left of the Chapel Royal and musical establishment were disbanded, as were the cathedral choirs. Anglican worship, in particular the *Book of Common Prayer*, was suppressed. Balls, dancing, and Christmas revelry were banned, most effectively under the Protectorate.

All this has generally been seen as a disaster for the performing and visual arts; for those who loved plays or Church music, or lived to perform them, it certainly was. But it also opened up new opportunities: for example, the sale of the king's art treasures led to a brisk art market. The suppression of sacred music did not extend to secular music, and many Church musicians turned to the growing domestic music market, much of it supplied from the mid-seventeenth century by the publisher John Playford (1623–1687). He compiled *The English Dancing Master* (1650), a hugely popular collection of dance tunes, mostly folk but some new, which went through many editions into the 1720s. Continuing the Elizabethan tradition, gentlemen amateurs like Samuel Pepys could perform such music at home with friends singing or playing the virginals or lute. Even Oliver Cromwell loved music and as lord protector kept a regular band.

Nor was it possible to suppress the traditional arts entirely. Actors continued to give secret performances, not unlike the way Catholic priests had continued to offer mass for recusants over the previous 80 years. By the mid-1650s, an acting troupe based at the Red Bull Theatre, Clerkenwell was gamely defying the authorities. Like clandestine Catholic masses, these productions were often broken up by soldiers and the actors arrested, but they refused to give in. William Davenant (1606–1668) got around the ban on plays by performing the first operas in England, really semi-operas, like *The Siege of Rhodes* (1656), in which speeches were given as recitative. This reminds us that Londoners have never been scrupulously law-abiding: Parliament could close the theaters and ban plays repeatedly, but the frequency with which they did so indicates the futility of the exercise.

Above all, the Puritan emphasis on the Word channeled artistic energies in different directions, for example, preaching, diary keeping, news writing, and pamphleteering. In 1641 the bishops' right of censorship was abolished, opening the floodgates to a relatively free press, much of it based in Fleet Street. In the two decades leading up to the war, the public's hunger for news had been satisfied by handwritten newsletters and printed *corantos*; during the war, newspapers appeared in large numbers for the first time, many of them one-issue wonders (see Chapter 5). The number of political and religious pamphlets published each year mushroomed. One surviving collection alone, assembled by a London bookseller named George Thomason (c. 1602–1666), holds nearly 23,000 items from 1641 to 1662. Most expressed traditional, conservative sentiments, but others aired radically new opinions. John Milton (1608–1674) celebrated this flowering of ideas in *Areopagitica* (1644), his classic defense of free speech. He also wrote about religious reform and defended divorce.

At the Restoration in 1660, many of these writers went underground and retreated from great public issues, as the restored Crown reinstated censorship. Milton produced his great epic poem, *Paradise Lost*, in 1667. The first part of the first great novel in English, John Bunyan's (1628– 1688) *The Pilgrim's Progress*, appeared in 1678. Whereas the former was composed in the capital by a native Londoner, the latter was written in Bedfordshire. One further significance of the Puritan ascendancy and the explosion of publishing activity it entailed was that it tended to de-emphasize London. Prior to 1642, one could see Shakespeare plays or hear the Chapel Royal only in the metropolis, and thereafter most of the printing presses remained in London, but writers could write, and readers could read, newspapers, pamphlets, poetry, and novels anywhere in the country. Taste could therefore be set from anywhere, although it still flowed through the capital. To that extent, "the Puritan moment" was, on the one hand, a democratizing one. On the other, both Milton and Bunyan were part of a movement that really thought that it could remake the world in God's image and remake London into a "city on a hill" by expounding the Word and banning plays, dancing, and Christmas celebrations. Given London's appetite for pleasure and demand for attention, their efforts were bound to fail.

1660–1750

In 1660 and 1661, the monarchy, the court, and the Anglican Church were restored to much of their former power and glory. This was accompanied by a strong reaction across the country against the Puritan worldview. The court revived the theater, although on the north bank this time; the *Book of Common Prayer* was revised and mandated in all services of the Church of England by the Act of Uniformity of 1662 (13 & 14 Chas. II, c. 4), and censorship was once again imposed by the Licensing Act of 1662 (13 & 14 Chas. II, c. 33), which condemned "heretical, schismatical, blasphemous, seditious and treasonable books, pamphlets and papers." This time, the censor was no longer a bishop but an official government licensor, Sir Roger L'Estrange (1616–1704), whose sympathies were entirely Royalist. The early 1660s therefore represent a shift in cultural power back to the court and Church, the performing and fine arts, and away from the Word. But could the clock really be turned back?

The Restoration regime certainly tried. Anglican ceremony, organs, and sacred music were revived in churches all across the country. Ecclesiastical courts once again prosecuted nonconformists, their powers strengthened by a series of anti-Puritan statutes that came to be known as the *Clarendon Code*. At Whitehall, the court of Charles II defied its shaky financial situation to reestablish its cultural leadership through artistic patronage, as well as the aforementioned regulation. For example, the king attempted to buy back as much of his father's art collection as possible. Once again, connoisseurs like John Evelyn could walk the palace galleries admiring his Dutch and Italian masters, as well as new commissions by Sir Peter Lely, and later Sir Godfrey Kneller and Antonio Verrio, all of whom were given court posts. Charles II also loved music and restored the Chapel Royal and the band of musicians to their previous size and supremacy. Evelyn, Pepys, and other music lovers could thus hear the voluntaries and anthems of the young John Blow (?1648–1708), Pelham Humfrey, and Henry Purcell. At the king's order, Sunday services were accompanied by his 24 Violins, virtually the only permanent orchestra in the British Isles, various permutations of which also played for his dinner and moonlighted with theater work. Their music was Baroque: contrapuntally complex and heavily ornamented, it was thought to complement the awesome power of absolutist monarchs.

The Baroque style had its architectural counterpart in the imposing designs of Hugh May (1621–1684) and Sir Christopher Wren at Whitehall and other palaces; the elaborate carving of Grinling Gibbons (1648–1721), and the ornate allegorical ceiling painting of Verrio. In fact, the greatest buildings put up in London between 1660 and 1714 were royal commissions: Charles II's establishments of Chelsea Hospital and Greenwich Hospital designed by Wren and others, Charles II's and James II's extensive renovations to Whitehall, and above all Wren's commission, given after the Great Fire by Charles and finished under Anne, to rebuild St. Paul's Cathedral. It might be argued that the new St. Paul's, designed in a neoclassical style and topped by a great dome 365 feet high, was less London's church than the old medieval cathedral, more the nation's. As if to make up for this, Wren also designed some fifty exquisite parish churches to replace those destroyed by the Fire, each a small masterpiece (see Chapter 8).

Once again, the Chapel Royal featured "excellent Preaching . . . by the most eminent Bish[ops] & Divines of the Nation,"[9] such as Francis Atterbury (1663–1732), Ralph Bathurst (1620–1704), Thomas Ken (1637–1711),

John Sharp (?1645–1714), Edward Stillingfleet (1635–1699), and John Tillotson (1630–1694), all of whom rose from court chaplaincies to become bishops. As this implies, Charles II was always on the lookout for new talent: thus Evelyn recommended the carver Grinling Gibbons to Wren, who introduced him to the king. Charles paid to send the young Pelham Humfrey to France to learn the latest musical styles. His court also provided jobs in the Chamber and Bedchamber for many of the famous literary "wits" of the time, including George Villiers, second Duke of Buckingham (1628–1687); Charles Sackville, Earl of Dorset (1643–1706); John Sheffield, Earl of Mulgrave (1647–1721); John Wilmot, Earl of Rochester (1647–1680); Henry Guy (1631–1711); Thomas Killigrew (1612–1683); and Henry Savile (1642–1687). Notice by the court might lead to commissions (both royal and aristocratic) but also to offices, pensions, or lands. The artistic result was a flood of "inside" art: courtiers were painted in the Baroque style by Lely and Kneller; their conversation celebrated in the new comedy of manners written by other court wits such as Sir George Etherege, Sir Charles Sedley (1639–1701), or William Wycherley (1641–1716); their politics and sexual escapades satirized alike by court poets like Rochester and opposition figures like Andrew Marvell (1621–1678). Admittedly, many aspiring artists (e.g., John Dryden [1631–1700] and Samuel Butler [1613–1680]) found the king and his court far more interested intellectually than financially in their careers. Moreover, the fact that the Restoration court was a world unto itself renders it *in* London, but not always *of* London.

Still, it cannot be denied that Charles II restored the court's traditional leadership as an artistic patron and a clearinghouse for new styles after the Interregnum. For example, it was in his reign that St. James's Park and Mall, laid out or improved on his instructions, became a fashionable place to promenade in one's best attire while the Ring in Hyde Park once again became the place to "cruise" in one's coach and six. The Restoration court has also been credited with introducing or popularizing in Britain the French taste in music, dancing, furniture, costume, and table manners; Dutch taste in architecture, painting, silverwork, and embroidery; the man's vested suit; periwigs for both men and women; the guitar; champagne; tea; and ice cream. This made the court attractive not only to those with political, financial or artistic ambitions but also to anyone interested in what was new, fashionable, or fun. In the winter of 1662–63 the French ambassador reported to Louis XIV that "There is a ball and a comedy every other day; the rest of the days are spent at play, either at the Queen's or at the Lady Castlemaine's, where the company does not fail to be treated to a good supper."[10] No wonder that Sir Ralph Freeman (d. 1667) rented another courtier's lodgings at Whitehall that spring, while the latter was away on a diplomatic mission, "to accommodate his daughter, who desired to see the Court entertainments, as balls and plays, which have been frequent this last winter."[11]

Perhaps the Restoration regime's most important artistic interventions came on behalf of the dramatic arts. Soon after Charles II returned to London, he demonstrated his love for the stage by ordering its reopening; his love for women by demanding that they appear in female roles; and his love for order by reviving the censorship powers of the lord chamberlain's office. He also followed Tudor precedent by restricting theatrical performances to two licensed companies. The King's Company, run by Thomas Killigrew, and the Duke's Company, run by Sir William Davenant, were both granted otherwise exclusive privileges within weeks of the Restoration, on July 9, 1660. Because the patents granted in 1660 were hereditary, there were never more than two licensed companies between 1660 and 1750.

As previously, both companies were amphibious between court and city, giving evening command performances at the Great Hall and later at a theater fitted out in Henry VIII's Cockpit at Whitehall, after playing in the afternoon for paying audiences at their own theaters in the West End. The King's Company, claiming descent (spuriously) from the prewar company of the same name, got the rights to all the pre-1642 repertory. It acted first at the Red Bull Theatre, then in a converted tennis court in Vere Street, before moving into the new purpose-built Theatre Royal in Bridges Street, off Drury Lane, in 1663. After this house burned down on January 25, 1672, the king appealed for donations through the nation's parish churches to build a new Theatre Royal designed by Wren: there could be no clearer indication that Puritan attitudes were in eclipse! The Duke's Company performed a brand-new repertory in another converted tennis court in Lincoln's Inn Fields outfitted with large stage machines able to provide the elaborate special effects that Restoration audiences demanded (see Illustration 4.3). This company moved out to a new, bigger theater designed by Wren in Dorset Gardens, off of Fleet Street, in 1671. In 1682 the two companies, each suffering from terrible management, were merged for thirteen years, performing at the Theatre Royal.

Because these indoor theaters were small, holding 500 to 1,000 people, and elaborate effects cost more, they charged much higher fees than their Elizabethan and Jacobean predecessors: 4 shillings for a seat in a box, 1 shilling for a seat in the upper gallery. As a result, the audience for Restoration theater was mostly aristocratic or fashionably mercantile. The groundlings were shut out. This did not produce better audience behavior, however. Restoration and Augustan audiences were notoriously rowdy and self-regarding. Aristocrats still insisted on being seen, sitting and even walking, onstage. Orange girls sold fruit, audibly, during the performance, and fights or even duels might break out. As before, the theaters were ensconced in an urban low-life culture of gambling dens and bawdy houses, especially along Drury Lane.

When they could see and hear what was going on, Restoration audiences enjoyed Elizabethan, Jacobean, and Caroline works, often in "modernized" versions. But they also saw themselves dramatized in two new styles of drama, both written by courtiers with a court audience in mind: the Restoration comedy of manners, written by the Duke of Buckingham, Etherege, Sedley, Wycherley, and later William Congreve (1670–1729); and rhymed heroic drama written by Buckingham, Dryden, and Thomas Otway (1652–1685). The former style might be seen as related to the tradition of city drama from the beginning of the century, but plays like *The Country Wife* (1675) or *The Man of Mode* (1676) were set more frequently at court or in country houses and addressed the tensions between the artificial standards of behavior that reigned there and carnal human desires. They also showcased the wit of the Restoration court: bad behavior could be made palatable by charming expression. City merchants, if they appeared, were ridiculed as pretentious, greedy, or vulgar. The heroic plays, drawn from historical and legendary figures, often set in exotic locations, revolved around issues of duty, loyalty, and royal power that had wracked the English ruling class for two generations. In each case, therefore, it was the preoccupations of the court and not the city that prevailed. Writers still had to be careful, because prior to 1700, the lord chamberlain's chief goal was to avoid political controversy.

The Restoration court's cultural hegemony was never exclusive, nor was it long-lasting. Even at the height of its glory and fame under Charles II, the royal household began to face political, social, and financial difficulties that progressively undermined its attractiveness. First, the accessibility, diversity, and cosmopolitanism of the court declined from the early 1660s on, as first Dissenters and then Catholics became unwelcome there. This process was accelerated by generational change: toward the end of the seventies, the small circle of court "wits" that had dominated the artistic and social life of the capital began to die, drift away, or become submerged in the political struggle beginning to grip the nation. Finally, the Crown's chronic financial troubles affected the quality of court life. As early as 1662–63, Charles II was forced to suspend payments of pensions for one year and abolish the tables of hospitality that had provided free meals for courtiers for centuries. Subsequent retrenchments led to fewer balls and plays and the elimination of the king's French and Italian musicians.

James II launched an even greater retrenchment from 1685 to 1686, cutting the size and expense of the household by about two-fifths. Admittedly, the early years of James's reign still saw frequent balls and plays. His sponsorship of Wren's extensive renovations at Whitehall, which cost £35,000, almost rendered that palace worthy of its mission. In particular, the Catholic chapel he designed was filled with new commissions by continental Catholic artists like Benedetto Gennari (1633–1715), Willem Wissing (1656–1687), and Verrio, introducing styles of art and worship heretofore little known in England. But whatever their aesthetic merits, James II's Catholic style and attempted Catholic restoration drove away Protestant courtiers and provoked his ouster. After the Revolution of 1688/89, Catholics were permanently banned from court, the Catholic Chapels Royal that Pepys found so interesting were closed, and much of their artwork removed because they were given over to French Huguenot and German Lutheran worship.

Under William and Mary there was a brief revival of court life, largely owing to Mary's artistic patronage and fun-loving personality. Mary was a child of the Restoration court, and so she liked going to the theater, hosting court balls and drawing rooms, and even visiting London shops and fairs. She collected delftware, revived the tradition of needlework among English court ladies, and patronized Henry Purcell for magnificent birthday odes. Her sudden death from smallpox in December 1694 resulted in a magnificent state funeral that paralyzed the streets of London, but thereafter, the court grew quiet. William III's poor health, lack of social graces, and obsession with the war with France led him to prefer seclusion at Kensington or Hampton Court to the sooty throng at Whitehall. In subsequent reigns, Anne's poor health and conversation and George I's desire to be left alone meant that drawing rooms were few and far between. Simultaneously, the "rage of party" followed by the post-1714 Whig ascendancy dictated that at any given time, one-half of the political world felt unwelcome at court, while the diversion of government revenue toward a succession of European wars left it less able to sustain patronage of the arts and finer pleasures. The coup de grâce was delivered on January 4,

1698 when the palace of Whitehall burned down. This disaster eliminated at one stroke both the Crown's principal venue for the pursuit of art and pleasure and the one royal palace capable of housing a good percentage of their courtly audience. The conflagration both sealed and symbolized the court's social and cultural decline. A century would pass before the monarchy once again possessed a great palace in London.

The failure to rebuild or replace Whitehall marked the Crown's abandonment of any pretensions to maintain a continental-style Baroque monarchy. None of this is to say that the monarch ceased to be an important patron in the eighteenth century: today, royal palaces are filled with the evidence to the contrary. In particular, the court's patronage of the visual arts, including painting, furniture, metalwork, and ceramics, remained important. Members of the royal family attended the theater and concert hall and bestowed the prestige and protection of royal sponsorship on academies of music and art. Despite occasional periods of revival, however, the court could no longer claim to be the engine or leader of fashion, "the focus where everything fascinating gathered, and where everything exciting centred,"[12] to use Walter Bagehot's phrase.

From about 1680 and accelerating after 1700, the focus moved to the metropolis itself. First, the leading aristocratic townhouses provided their own hospitality and culture that at times bested the court. The period from 1660 to 1750 was a great age for townhouse building. During this period, important noble families erected Buckingham House (1702–1705), Burlington House (1664–1665, remodeled according to the Palladian style 1717–1720), Devonshire House (1734–1737), Montagu House (1678; rebuilt 1686), and perhaps most spectacular of all, Marlborough House (1709–1711), designed for the Churchills by Wren to be more magnificent than the palace (St. James's) next door. These mansions were filled with elegant decor, old masters, sculpture, delftware, and curiosities brought back from the Grand Tour by their aristocratic owners, as well as new commissions by leading painters like Kneller, and later Thomas Gainsborough (1727–1788), William Hogarth, Phillippe Mercier (?1691–1760), and Sir Joshua Reynolds (1723–1792). Montagu House hosted concerts, and at various points in the eighteenth century Marlborough House and Leicester House provided a sort of anti-court for opposition politicians.

Aristocratic landlords also rebuilt much of London after the Fire and developed the West End. We have already seen how the Russell family, Earls of Bedford, developed Covent Garden. After 1660, that development became the model for other aristocratic projects such as Bloomsbury,

St. James's Square, Devonshire Square, Grosvenor Square, Leicester Square, Red Lion Square, and so on commissioned by the Wriothesleys, Jermyns, Grosvenors, and others (see the Conclusion). The London square provided a new urbane model for aristocratic and middle-class living that offered security, ventilation, green space, and proximity to the court and theater. It also provided a new economic model for development. Most of these families had been granted their land by the Crown after the confiscations of the sixteenth century, either as outright gifts, advantageous purchases, or at long (99-year) leases. Although some aristocratic speculators, like the Grosvenors, kept everything in their own hands, most would in turn sublease their land to builders for 10 to 30 years. It was these builders, the most famous of whom was Nicholas Barbon (c. 1637–1699), who erected London's new physical plant. Barbon was the son of Praise-God Barbon (c. 1598–1680), a Puritan leather seller and preacher in Fetter Lane who became a London MP in the "Parliament of Saints" of 1653 and was nearly sent to the Tower for opposing the Restoration in 1660–61. Young Nicholas, originally named "If Jesus Had Not Died For Thee Thou Wouldst Be Damned," went another way. He fled London, changed his name, and studied medicine at Leiden and Utrecht, where he also encountered Dutch house architecture. On his return in the early 1660s, he launched a career of speculation, development, and building in which one complex deal financed the next, and no one made out better than Barbon. Specifically, he would contract with builders and carpenters to erect a shell on the land that he leased and pay him the ground rent. The builder would sell the house; it was up to the owner to finish it by contracting with painters, joiners, and plumbers. Often, Barbon would end up owing far more money than he was owed; ultimately his deals caught up with him, and he died penniless. Still, it was Barbon who built much of Soho and transformed the Strand from a row of dilapidated medieval palaces into a modern streetscape of brick houses and shops.

Clearly, the relative decline of *court* culture in London did not mean the decline of metropolitan *elite* culture. The ruling class had always amused itself at the public theater, taverns, cock matches, and horse races; after the Restoration, the concert hall, the pleasure garden, the coffeehouse, and the all-male club also competed for its patronage (see Chapter 5). These institutions offered their clientele all that the royal household could offer and more – including food, drink, news, gossip, conversation, and companionship – without the formality necessitated by the royal presence. This occurred all day, every day at the patron's convenience – not merely on a thrice-a-week schedule when the sovereign was well and the treasury full. Moreover, London taverns, coffeehouses, pleasure gardens, and sporting events mixed aristocrats with monied men, merchants, and professionals. As a result, it was increasingly in these venues, and not at court, that art and literature were commissioned, business transacted, political plans laid, and one's newly fashioned self could be put on display. Elite women helped to shape the new urban sociability at balls, musical assemblies, promenades, and frequent visits to the homes of other elite women.

Aristocrats also supported artists individually. In 1710, the German musician George Frideric Handel, the greatest opera composer of the age, came to London hoping to work for the English Crown. A few big royal commissions did come his way, most famously the *Water Music* of 1717 and the *Music for the Royal Fireworks* of 1749. The first was composed to accompany a vast water party organized by the court for the evening of July 17 and 18, 1717. According to the *Daily Courant*, as King George I sailed majestically in the royal barge to Chelsea for a picnic supper, returning to Whitehall at 3 AM:

> Many other Barges with Persons of Quality attended, and so great a Number of Boats, that the whole river in a manner was cover'd: a City Company's Barge was employ'd for the Musick, wherein were 50 Instruments of all sorts, who play'd all the Way from Lambeth . . . the finest Symphonies, composed express for this Occasion, by Mr. Hendel; which his Majesty liked so well, that he caus'd it to be plaid over three times in going and returning.[13]

The *Music for the Royal Fireworks* was written to celebrate the signing of the Treaty of Aix-la-Chapelle, ending the War of the Austrian Succession, in 1749. It was to be the aural accompaniment to a magnificent fireworks display in Green Park by the theatrical designer Giovanni Niccolò Servandoni (1695–1766). The frame was 410 feet long and 114 feet high. The musicians played from a raised gallery above a statue of Peace surrounded by Mars and Neptune, and a relief showing George II presenting Peace to Britannia. Overlooking all was a sun. Unfortunately, on that night, this sun exploded amid a general and unplanned conflagration. The result was a spectacular fiasco in the short term, but since then both the *Water Music* and the *Royal Fireworks Music* have become indelibly associated with the vigorous spirit of eighteenth-century London.

Handel found such royal commissions rare. By the middle of George I's reign he was also composing anthems for the immensely wealthy James

Brydges, Duke of Chandos (1674–1744), whose suburban estate at Cannons, Middlesex, featured a full orchestra. John, Lord Somers (1651–1716) supported the early careers of Swift, Addison, and Richard Steele (1672–1729), whereas Lord Halifax promoted the playwright William Congreve. Lord Treasurer Oxford and Sir Robert Walpole employed stables of writers, the former including Swift and Defoe, to support their administrations: a talented writer was a valuable asset in the propaganda wars fought between the two parties. Oxford also assembled a magnificent collection of books and manuscripts at his London residence, which later became part of the nucleus for the British Museum.

As we have seen, the new wealth flooding into later Stuart London enriched not only the elite, but also merchants and professionals, who spent some of it on the arts. The theater was already a "public" venue at the end of the sixteenth century; a little more than a century later great entrepreneurial producers, like John James Heidegger and Christopher (1647–1714) and John (c. 1692–1761) Rich, knew how to appeal to changing popular tastes. For example, in the 1690s the clergy attacked the comedy of manners as immoral (see Chapter 5), and the lord chamberlain began to crack down on plays for their sexual rather than political content. As Restoration comedy fell out of favor, producers turned to revivals of Shakespeare and the new Italian opera, first performed in London with elaborate sets and stage devices in 1705. John Rich added the after-performance pantomime, another Italian practice. His company acted at Lincoln's Inn Fields, where his most notable success was John Gay's satire on the Walpole administration, *The Beggar's Opera* (1728), said to have made "Gay rich, and Rich gay." Rich's company moved to the new Covent Garden Theatre, Bow Street – London's sixth theater – in 1732, where he mounted Handel's oratorios, most notably the *Messiah* (1742), for a paying public. In the 1690s there was also a theater in Sadler's Wells, and from the 1720s several new companies appeared, playing in Goodman's Fields and the great and little theaters at the Haymarket. These put on everything from serious plays to circuses, rope dancing, and gymnastics, to more biting satires of the Walpole administration. The satires explain why in 1737 the government established an examiner of plays (10 Geo. II, c. 28) who censored the stage until 1968. Playwrights also wrote for the puppet play booths at Bartholomew Fair, May Fair, and Southwark Fair. By 1711 the first masquerade balls were being held in London; from 1715 to 1743 they were dominated by Heidegger, who put them on at the Haymarket Theatre. Attendees could transcend their own class and personal reputation by hiding behind their masks: a well-dressed army officer or tradesman could flirt with a countess. These balls thus epitomized Londoners' capacity for reinvention and duplicity in microcosm.

Sometimes artists banded together to support each other or to act as their own impresarios. Sir Godfrey Kneller founded an academy for painters in Great Queen Street in 1711. This was succeeded in the 1720s by Sir James Thornhill's (1675/76–1734) school. Thornhill's son-in-law, William Hogarth, opened a new academy in St. Martin's Lane in 1734 that provided the nucleus for the Royal Academy, founded in 1768. A half-century earlier, John Banister (1624/25–1679), a royal musician disgruntled at his uncertain pay, organized the first public concerts in Europe at his house in Whitefriars from December 1672 to 1678, charging a fee of one shilling. His efforts were succeeded by Thomas Britton (1644–1714), a music-loving coal merchant who presented professional musicians in the room over his shop in Clerkenwell from 1678 until his death in 1714. Conditions were not ideal: the room was "not much bigger than the Bunghole of a Cask."[14] But Britton's concerts featured the best artists of the day, including Handel, and they were patronized by the nobility. By the time of Britton's death in 1714 public concerts occurred frequently, and London was very much on the circuit of European capitals that a touring musician had to conquer. Concerts were given at York Buildings, Villiers Street, and Hickford's Rooms, James Street, Haymarket (later moved to Brewer Street). Music clubs like the Castle Society, founded circa 1720, met in places like the Castle Tavern, Paternoster Row. In 1719 a Royal Academy of Music was founded to produce opera, and in 1726 a rival Academy of Ancient Music (which met in the Crown and Anchor Tavern, the Strand) was established to revive English classics like Purcell. The pleasure gardens provided another public venue for music: just a few days before the disastrous command performance of the *Fireworks Musick* in 1749, Handel led a series of rehearsals at Vauxhall Gardens that attracted 12,000 people, stalling traffic on London Bridge for three hours.

The literary equivalent of a Heidegger or a Britton was the publisher and Kit-Cat Club member Jacob Tonson (1656–1736). He made a fortune (£50,000) selling the works of Addison, Congreve, Dryden, Milton, Prior, Swift, Vanbrugh, and Wycherley, either at his shop at the Judge's Head, Chancery Lane (just off of Fleet Street), or to London's 150-plus other bookshops, or directly to readers through subscription lists, whereby sponsors would undertake to support publication collectively. More occasional work – newspapers, essays, almanacs, political broadsides, advice books, travel books, and true crime narratives – was churned out by an army of hack writers who congregated in the area around Moorfields known as "Grub Street" (see Chapter 5). As this implies, a ready market for literature of all kinds replaced the court as an author's chief means of support. Writers like Aphra Behn (?1640–1689) and Alexander Pope (1688–1744) relied almost exclusively on sales (again, sometimes by Tonson) to an appreciative public, whereas Daniel Defoe largely abandoned political writing for fiction. Of his four great novels, *Robinson Crusoe* (1719), *Moll Flanders, Journal of the Plague Year* (1722), and *Roxana* (1724), the last three are virtual journalistic exposés of London life ranging from City to court and back again.

Increasingly after 1660, members of the merchant and professional classes could afford to imitate their betters and so create demand in other areas of consumption as well, by having a portrait painted, purchasing maps and prints, or outfitting themselves with clocks and watches. Even the lower middle and working classes of London were increasingly able to afford something to decorate their digs: the prints that Hogarth made from his paintings and engravings, costing as little as 6 pence apiece, were directed at this market, and it made him a wealthy man. Hogarth's famous prints, like Defoe's novels, frequently depicted the follies of London life – *A Harlot's Progress* (1732), *A Rake's Progress* (1735), *Industry and Idleness* (1747), and *Beer Street* and *Gin Lane* (1751; see Chapter 5). For all of their exaggeration, they depict a London full of stories and types that contemporaries would have recognized.

As this suggests, London was even more a subject of art during the second half of our period than in the first. For example, the painters Leendert Knijff, known in England as Leonard Knyff, and Giovanni Antonio Canal, better known as Canaletto, followed the pre-Civil War example of Visscher and Hollar and came to London. Knyff painted views of royal palaces, many of them engraved by his fellow Dutchman Johannes Kip (c. 1653–?1721) for his collection *Britannia Illustrata* (1707) and sold from his house in St. John's Street, Westminster. The Italian Canaletto had long supplied his cityscapes to English aristocrats on the Grand Tour before setting up shop at 16 Silver Street in London itself from 1746 to 1755. The result was forty famous views capturing the eighteenth-century grandeur of the city on the Thames.

It is perhaps significant that Knyff and Canaletto were foreigners, because eighteenth-century Londoners tended to be less celebratory and more satirical in portraying their city. The prints of Hogarth, the novels of Defoe, and the works of city poets describe a sometimes tawdry, dangerous London, anything but the city of dreams that immigrants might have expected. The anonymous *Hell Upon Earth* (1729) portrays "a great, wicked, unweildy [sic] overgrown Town, one continued hurry of Vice and Pleasure; where nothing dwells but Absurdities, Abuses, Accidents, Accusations" though also "Admirations, Adventures."[15] This was, of course, a common theme in the literature on cities dating back to Babylon, Athens, and Rome. The aptly named Augustan Age had a great admiration for the achievements of Rome in particular, and both John Dryden and Samuel Johnson made the comparison with the Eternal City explicit when they translated the Third Satire of Juvenal, a biting exposé of Roman life, into its London equivalent. Johnson's is called, innocuously enough, "London: a Poem" (1738). The satire warns readers that the streets of eighteenth-century London were dark, dangerous and full of shady characters:

> *Prepare for Death, if here at Night you roam,*
> *And sign your Will before you sup from Home.*
> *Some fiery Fop, with new Commission vain,*
> *Who sleeps on Brambles till he kills his Man;*
> *Some frolick Drunkard, reeling from a Feast,*
> *Provokes a Broil, and stabs you for a Jest.*

Welcome to London! And yet, the overall effect of the ensuing poem is a wry celebration of London's chaos: after all, if its problems are as bad as Rome's, then it must be as great as Rome.

Johnson's use of an old form and a classical model was typical of the Augustan Age. London poets adapted other traditional styles to the urban experience. One such form was the pastoral, celebrating the placid joys of country living. Represented here by Thomas Otway's "Morning" from his play, *The Orphan* (1680), such poems would seem to have no relevance to London life:

> *Wished Morning's come! And now upon the plains*
> *And distant mountains, where they feed their flocks,*
> *The happy shepherds leave their homely huts,*
> *And with their pipes proclaim the new-born day.*
> *The lusty swain comes with his well-filled scrip*
> *Of healthful viands, which, when hunger calls,*
> *With much content and appetite, he eats,*

To follow in the fields his daily toil,
And dress the grateful glebe, that yields him fruits.
The beasts, that under the warm hedges slept,
And weathered out the cold bleak night, are up,
And, looking towards the neighboring pastures, raise
The voice and bid their fellow-brutes good-morrow
The cheerful birds, too, on the tops of trees,
Assemble all in quires, and with their notes
Salute and welcome up the rising sun.

Otway's morning dawns on an ordered and peaceful rural landscape in which all are happy and all needs met.

Jonathan Swift's London day begins rather differently. His "Description of a Morning" (1709) subverts these clichés into an alternative urban "pastoral":

Now hardly here and there a hackney-coach
Appearing, show'd the ruddy morn's approach.
Now Betty from her master's bed had flown,
And softly stole to discompose her own.
The slip-shod 'prentice from his master's door
Had pared the dirt, and sprinkled round the floor.
Now Moll had whirled her mop with dextrous airs,
Prepar'd to scrub the entry and the stairs.
The youth with broomy stumps began to trace
The kennel-edge, where wheels had worn the place.
The small-coal man was heard with cadence deep;
Till drowned in shriller notes of "chimney-sweep."
Duns [creditors] *at his lordship's gate began to meet;*
And brickdust Moll had scream'd through half a street.
The turnkey [jailer] *now his flock returning sees,*
Duly let out a-nights to steal for fees.
The watchful bailiffs take their silent stands;
And schoolboys lag with satchels in their hands.

The humor arrives forthwith in the prosaic sound of "hackney-coach," but it resides mainly in the contrast between the ideal pastoral world described by Otway and the reality of London life described by Swift: Otway's "lusty swain" versus Swift's "slip-shod prentice"; the sound of Otway's shepherd's pipes, lowing livestock, and cheerful "quires" [choirs] of birds versus the call of Swift's small-coal man and the chimney sweep; the hard-bitten images of "brickdust Moll" and the turnkey, who performs the same morning office for his "flock" of thieves that Otway's happy shepherd does for his sheep. Far from having a restful night, it is clear that Betty – the stereotypical name for all maidservants – has spent the wee hours in "her master's bed" and that it is part of her morning ritual to "discompose her own" to make it appear that she slept in it. London is depicted as a place where nature and proper morality are inverted, the Great Chain lying in tatters. On the one hand, a poem like Swift's stands as a warning of what can happen to society in the urban cauldron, but for the most part it invites Londoners to "'ave a larf" at the seeming disorder of their lives. Poems like this must have fostered a knowing solidarity among readers, a recognition among veteran urban dwellers that, indeed, "London is like that." At the same time, such poems may have provided a valuable warning to the literate newcomer. Thus, publications like Swift's "Description of a Morning" or Johnson's "London: a Poem" were yet another way in which Londoners learned how to be Londoners.

In fact, the early eighteenth century saw a plethora of poems and prose that mocked London life to old residents, while warning of it to new ones. These works do not merely entertain, however; they enlist readers into the common culture of the city and assist them, by their advice or by their humor, to cope with London's sometimes unprecedented challenges. Swift's "Description of a City Shower" (1710) offers the city equivalent of country advice, explaining, for example, that bad weather is sure to follow when "Returning home at night, you'll find the sink (i.e., London's gutter-sewers)/ Strike your offended sense with double stink." Thus natural country knowledge is replaced by city experience. Similarly, Richard Steele's essay for *The Spectator* No. 454, "The Hours of London" (1712), replaces the seasons of the year and hours of the agricultural day with the different rhythms and populations of the city:

> The Hours of the Day and Night are taken up in the Cities of London and Westminster, by People as different from each other as those who are born in different Centuries. Men of Six a Clock give way to those of Nine, they of Nine to the Generation of Twelve, and they of Twelve disappear, and make Room for the fashionable World, who have made Two a Clock the Noon of the Day.[16]

Once again, the natural world of the village seems inverted as the most elevated creatures rise the latest.

John Gay's *Trivia: Or the Art of Walking the Streets of London* (1716) is, on one level, yet another "How to" guide for the uninitiated. But by painting in vivid colors the sheer variety of London's streets and portraying them as contested space, full of challenges facing the unassuming rambler, it turns the seemingly "trivial" business of perambulation into a heroic act, worthy of celebration in an epic poem in three books, in imitation of Homer or Virgil:

> *Through Winter Streets to steer your Course aright,*
> *How to walk clean by Day, and safe by Night,*
> *How jostling Crouds, with Prudence to decline,*
> *When to assert the Wall, and when resign,*
> *I sing: Thou, Trivia, Goddess, aid my Song,*
> *Thro' spacious Streets conduct thy Bard along;*
> *By thee transported, I securely stray*
> *Where winding Alleys lead the doubtful Way,*
> *The silent Court, and op'ning Square explore,*
> *And long perplexing Lanes untrod before.*

"I sing" is a consciously ridiculous echo of the opening of Virgil's *Aeneid* as translated by Dryden. Clearly the heroic age is past and country wisdom useless: to walk the streets of London is to brave dangers demanding new urban skills.

Partly for this reason the second half of our period saw the publication of numerous prose guidebooks to London, like today's Michelin or Fodor's guides. Some, like Robert Seymour's *A Survey of London, Westminster, &c.* (1734), based on Stow's early seventeenth-century guide, give the "official" story, the equivalent of a Knyff or Canaletto view, heralding the antiquity, history, size, and public splendors of a well-ordered city: "London is the Metropolis of Great Britain, the Seat of her Monarchs, the largest in Extent, the fairest built, and most populous, and best inhabited City in Europe, or perhaps the whole World . . . ", etc., etc. By the 1730s, London's size and variety, the consequences of a burgeoning economy, were seen as good things, points of favorable comparison with Paris or Rome. But other works, such as Ned Ward's *London Spy* (1698–1703), or the anonymous *Hell Upon Earth* (mentioned earlier), or *A Trip Through the Town, Containing Observations on the Humours of the Age*, portray a different London: raw, unexpurgated, satirical. Following in the footsteps of Guilpin and Marston, they take the reader to places like Bedlam, Wapping, or Rag Fair. Ward claimed a didactic purpose:

"Wherein Young Gentlemen may see the Vices of the Town, without their dangerous experience; and learn the better to avoid those Snares and practicable Subtleties which Trappen [trick] many to their Ruin."[17] But when *A Trip Through the Town* (1735) informs the reader that "We have a Play-House to every Parish, and more than a thousand Taverns, and Brothels, to one Church,"[18] the tone is neither indignant nor celebratory, but matter of fact: the reader is assumed to be an adult and can make up his or her own mind. This too seems modern.

Finally, from the mid-seventeenth century on, London offered to the prosperous one more amusement: leaving it. That is, road and carriage engineering had improved to the point that, if a moderately successful merchant or government official grew sick of the "Crouds of miserable People" described in *A Trip Through the Town*, he could easily make an occasional day trip into the country, as Samuel Pepys observed at the end of one such excursion, to Epsom, on July 14, 1667:

> Mrs. Turner mightily pleased with my resolution, which I tell her is never to keep a country-house, but to keep a coach and with my wife on the Saturday and to go sometimes for a day to this place and then quite to another place; and there is more variety, and as little charge and no trouble, as there is in a country-house. Anon it grew dark, and as it grew dark we had the pleasure to see several Glow wormes, which was mighty pretty.... [19]

Thus, the brave new London of the second half of our period offered something for every taste – even for those who did not like the place. Its culture had broken free from court and church to cater to aristocratic, middle-brow, and popular tastes. The result was a truly uncontrollable public sphere in which original thought and artistic creativity could have free rein, so long as they sold. We can see this development even more clearly if we focus on a new branch of the literary arts that arose and flourished in London during our period: the press.

5. The Public Sphere and Popular Culture

*I*t should be obvious that the lines dividing one social or economic group from another in early modern London were porous. Londoners of all ranks frequently had encounters – in church or in the street, at the market or over the shop counter, standing nearby at an outdoor sermon, play, or a bear baiting – with people whose ambitions and sensibilities were quite different from their own. Such interaction, the mixing rather than disintegration of social groups, was a hallmark of metropolitan life in the early modern period. This chapter explores London's tendency to bring people of different backgrounds and ranks together in three contexts: the evolution of the news trade; the proliferation of venues for social interaction such as taverns, coffeehouses, and clubs; and popular cultural formations that often crossed class and gender lines.

NEWS BEFORE PRINT

The notion of a public press began in Europe in the fifteenth century, in printing centers like Amsterdam and London. For most of our period, however, this was not necessarily a free press in the modern sense; rather, a debate arose between two different kinds of press. Does a national press exist to inform the public of the establishment's "case," the "official" version put out by the government or Church hierarchy; or should it broadcast the "truth" as its authors see it, independent of governmental or ecclesiastical authority? In early modern England, the power structure favored the former; but the latter erupted periodically and ultimately proved impossible to suppress. The result, aided and abetted by institutions of relatively free social interaction like the coffeehouse, was to create a public sphere of relatively free common discourse whose headquarters was London.

How did Londoners get the news before the development of either kind of press? Great events, like the proclamations of kings and declarations of wars, were announced by heralds and other government officials at Whitehall or (from 1702) St. James's Palace, at Paul's Cross, on the steps of the Guildhall, and other significant public places. If the king or Church wanted people to know something less momentous, they heard it in Sunday or holiday services, during the sermon. From 1556 London also employed bellmen and criers whose job it was to give people necessary information, including notice of missing persons, the weather, and other news. Thus, on January 16, 1660, Pepys "sat up till the bell-man came by with his bell, just under my window as I was writing of this very line, and cried, 'Past one of the clock, and a cold, frosty, windy morning.' I then went to bed.... "[1] These institutions should be added to the list of factors that linked Londoners together.

Literate people wrote letters full of court and city news. Although an effective national postal system did not emerge until the seventeenth century, carters and carriers were happy to transport mail into the countryside. Thus, nobles, country gentlemen, and their wives away from the capital relied on friends who were there. If they lacked friends sufficiently trustworthy or nosy, by the early seventeenth century they could commission professional writers to gather information, hand write it, and send it to them in the form of regular newsletters. Some newsletter writers supplied scores of clients, thus representing a bridge between traditional, personal methods of news dissemination and the newspapers that appear at the end of the century. Their business was spurred by English interest in the Thirty Years' War (1618–1648): for example, *The Weekely Newes* featured continental news from 1621 to 1625. The 1620s also saw the first printed *corantos*, one-sheet summaries of foreign news that appeared when there was news to report, priced at about four pence, supplied by printers in both Amsterdam and London. Eventually they grew to sixteen and twenty-four pages but continued to appear irregularly and stuck with foreign news to avoid government censorship. On a more local and personal level, anyone with access to a servant could get letters delivered anywhere in London within minutes. Indeed, great aristocrats sometimes carried on virtual conversations (the closest equivalent to text messaging or e-mail today) by notes delivered by their footmen. Finally there was gossip, picked up from foreign travelers or one's next-door neighbor, spread in gathering places like the Royal Exchange and Westminster Hall, inns, taverns, at the front stoop, or across the back garden wall. Historians exploring legal records have discovered a distinct lack of privacy in London, where overcrowding and flimsy buildings made neighbors' business readily accessible.

Each of these news sources might have its own ax to grind, and objectivity was not a value. Official sources – government proclamations, the pulpit, even the town crier – mostly stuck to the establishment line, not least because clergymen and minor officers could be sacked if they failed to do so. Courtly newslettermen tended to slant their information toward the inclinations of their clients. Gossip was less easy to control, but even here there were laws against libel and scolding intended to curb speech. Historians have come to realize that these laws were applied mostly to women, often by other women, the net effect of which was to reinforce traditional gender roles. When London housewives stood at their front doors or in the market discussing the affairs of the neighborhood, their conversation was not idle. In effect, they were regulating communal moral standards, enforcing neighborliness, and holding reputations up to approval or scorn based on how other women ran their households and sex lives. The word *whore* was particularly incendiary and could lead to a defamation suit, at once rending a community yet also reaffirming its social norms. Perhaps the most dramatic example of the power contemporaries attributed to language are the Tudor treason statutes, which made some kinds of speech capital crimes: questioning the succession or calling the sovereign a heretic could have you hanged, drawn, and quartered.

REGULATION OF THE PRESS

This method of informing the public of just what it needed to know and no more had "done" for a millennium in England before anything new appeared. Even the arrival of the printing press in the late fifteenth century did little at first to crack the monopoly of the Crown and the Church on information. Although the new technology made wider dissemination of thought possible, these institutions exercised strict control over the number of presses licensed, the importation of books, and the content of those books allowed to be printed (see Chapter 4). When it suited the Crown's purposes, these restrictions were loosened briefly under Henry VIII and Edward VI. Under Mary and Elizabeth they grew tight again. The classic example of how dangerous it could be for a writer to defy

Elizabethan government censorship is offered by the career of John Stubbe (c. 1541–1590). In 1579 he wrote a pamphlet questioning a proposed French marriage for Queen Elizabeth. After being dissuaded from her initial idea of executing him, the queen ordered the public removal of his right hand in Westminster Market. Following the necessary three blows, he managed to shout "God save the Queen" before fainting. He was then deposited in the Tower until 1581, when the Act against Seditious Words and Rumours Uttered against the Queen's Most Excellent Majesty (23 Eliz., c. 2) was passed. This made the publication of any book deemed seditious a felony and thus made the world even less safe for men like the unfortunately named Stubbe. In 1586, an order of Star Chamber required presses to be licensed and restricted to London and the universities of Oxford and Cambridge; anything they printed had to be approved by a bishop. In 1637, Star Chamber imposed the strictest censorship yet: new books had to be licensed by the Stationers' Company of London, printers were required to enter a bond of £300 in pledge that they would print only licensed books, and the number of master printers was limited to twenty.

As we have seen, all of this changed in the 1640s. The abolition of the court of Star Chamber and the coercive power of the bishops in 1641 unleashed a flood of new publication flowing outward from London, some 20,000 pamphlets and newspapers over the next 20 years. There were two reasons for this. First, Royalists, Parliamentarians, political, religious, and economic thinkers all wanted to put their case to the literate public as to what the new England should look like. Second, that public was hungry for news of the wars. The opinion came mostly in the form of partisan pamphlets, ranging from two pages to small books. Further commentary and perhaps some news arrived in woodcuts and prints, generally with satirical intent. But most news came from early newspapers or "intelligencers," usually generated from London. Despite sporting grandiose titles like *The Flying Eagle, Communicating Intelligence both Fare and Neere* (1652), they tended to have very short runs, many appearing in only one edition. What they lacked in longevity, they made up for in variety. There were newsletters for every taste: for example, *The City Scout* (1645) offered city news, whereas *The Informator Rusticus: or, the Country Intelligencer* (1643) catered to those interested in rural affairs. Consistent with the classical roots of this culture, there were innumerable *Mercurius's*: *The Mercurius Belicus* (1647–1648) and the *Mercurius Pacificus* (1649); the *Mercurius Dogmaticus* (1648) and the *Mercurius Impartialis* (1648); the *Mercurius Censorious* (1648), *Mercurius Melancholius* (1647–48),

Mercurius Pragmaticus (1649), and the helpfully titled *Mercurius Civicus: London's Intelligencer, or Truth Impartially Related Thence to the Whole Kingdom, to Prevent Mis-Information* (1646). Because the early newspaper was a new form, the notion of a concise banner or quick headline had obviously not yet become standard. For every *True Informer* (1644–1646), there were titles like *New News, Strange News, True News, and Upon the Matter, No News* (1648) or *Mistris Parliament Presented in her Bed, after the Fore and Ravaile and hard Labour which She endured last weeck in the Birth of her Monstrous Off Spring, the Childe of Deformation* (1648).

Once the Civil Wars were over and an effective government settled on the nation, it took steps to curtail the unfettered dissemination of news. Thus the Cromwellian regime shut down all but pro-government newspapers in the 1650s. In the 1660s the restored Stuart monarchy attempted to control information even more tightly. It did so in two ways: one traditional, one innovative. First, it restored censorship. As we have seen, the lord chamberlain resumed his power to regulate the stage in 1660. In 1662 Parliament reestablished print censorship in England by the Licensing Act (12 and 13 Chas. II, c. 33). Once again, the number of master printers in Britain was restricted to twenty, with a larger but still limited number of journeyman printers. All presses had to be reported to the Stationers' Company, and all publications were required to carry the name of the author and printer. This time all publications had to be approved not by the bishops but by a government censor known as the *licensor of the press*. From 1663 until the expiry of the act in 1679, and then again at its restoration from 1685 to the Revolution of 1688, that man was the Royalist journalist Sir Roger L'Estrange.[2] L'Estrange had no problem with the news so long as it was reported by the government; he regarded a free press as tantamount to "making the Coffee-Houses, and all the Popular Clubs, Judges of those Counsels and Deliberations which they have nothing do withal."[3] To prevent such an outrage, L'Estrange employed a messenger of the press, that is, a human bulldog to ferret out not only unlicensed writers and printers but also founders, smiths, and joiners (carpenters) who worked on presses; bookbinders, stitchers, and stationers who made the books; hawkers, peddlers, mercury-women, ballad singers, porters, carriers, hackney coachmen, and even sailors who distributed them. L'Estrange and his messenger went after the whole economic web of clandestine publication in London.

The Restoration regime did more than try to quash information; it sought to provide it as well. In 1661, the Crown took over the old

Parliamentary Intelligencer and renamed it *The Kingdom's Intelligencer.* This was succeeded in 1663 by L'Estrange's own *Publick Intelligencer.* Finally, in 1665, when the court had moved to Oxford because of the plague, the regime founded *The Oxford Gazette*, renamed *The London Gazette* when the court returned to Whitehall in February 1666. *The London Gazette* is the oldest continuously publishing newspaper in Great Britain. From its initial issue on November 7, 1665, the *Gazette* gave the news (mostly foreign, some domestic) "by Authority," that is, as the government saw it, providing notices of royal proclamations, royal appearances, and court appointments "for the use of some Merchants and Gentlemen, who desire them."[4] In fact, an appointment so noted soon came to be said to have been "gazetted."

Between the Licensing Act and the *Gazette*, the Restoration regime aimed to be the principal conduit for news and information in England, but its monopoly was never complete. The horde of London newsletter writers and private correspondents was impossible to regulate, although the secretaries of state could and did open the mails, especially from foreign parts. There was also a great deal of what has been called *scribal publication* during the Restoration period, that is, the circulation of manuscript poetry and prose, much of it highly critical of Charles II and his court. One-off pamphlets and woodcuts selling for a penny or two in the streets covered every conceivable matter: a murder in Yorkshire, a storm in London, the king's bedfellows, political and actual. Francis Maximilian Misson (c. 1650–1722), a Frenchman writing for a continental audience, was shocked at the relative freedom enjoyed by English writers:

> England is a Country abounding in printed Papers, which they call Pamphlets, wherein every Author makes bold to talk very freely upon Affairs of State, and to publish all manner of News. I do not say that every one does with Impunity speak his own Thoughts, but I say, they take great Liberties. A Friend of mine affirm'd to me, that in the Reign of the late King Charles, he heard the Hawkers cry about the Streets a printed Sheet, advising that Prince to quit [his mistress] the Dutchess of Portsmouth, or to expect most dreadful Consequences. The extreme Mildness of the Government gives Room for this Licentiousness.[5]

Of course, Misson's idea of mildness was derived from the standard set by Louis XIV; in fact, L'Estrange and his masters worked tirelessly to stanch the flood.

The Licensing Act lapsed in 1679 just as the Exclusion Crisis began and an opposition Whig Parliament was elected (see the Introduction and Chapter 7). This led to another explosion of publications – tracts, poems, and prints – debating the respective power of Crown and Parliament. Many of these were coordinated by the Whig leader, Anthony Ashley Cooper, Earl of Shaftesbury (1621–1683), who took advantage of London's concentration of literary talent and the lapse of censorship to mount a sophisticated propaganda campaign. Writers like John Locke (1632–1704) and Algernon Sidney (1623–1683) argued for Parliament's right to bar Charles II's Catholic brother, James, Duke of York, from the throne. The Tories, defending the Duke's right to succeed, countered with propaganda of their own, such as John Dryden's masterful satire "Absalom and Achitophel" (1681).

When the Duke of York ascended the throne as James II in 1685, he secured from Parliament a renewal of the Licensing Act for seven years (1 Jac. II., c. 17), with censorship once again exercised by L'Estrange. Although William of Orange evicted James from the throne and L'Estrange from his office three years later, the Licensing Act remained. The Williamite regime tried first a Whig, then a Tory licensor, which meant that each side felt itself oppressed. Charles Blunt (1654–1693) and others revived Milton's arguments against censorship, circulating them hand to hand under the licensor's nose. Meanwhile, the booksellers, bookbinders, and printers petitioned Parliament, arguing that the Licensing Act stifled trade and yet had not succeeded in suppressing offensive materials or defusing political discord. The act was renewed again for just two years in 1693 (4 & 5 Will. III and Mary II, c. 24), but when it lapsed in 1695 the House of Commons resolved, over the intentions of the Lords, not to renew. It did not do so because of any widespread conviction that the press ought to be free or that censorship per se was a bad thing: both Whigs and Tories saw its uses, especially in time of war, although each would of course censor the other. Rather, censorship was clearly inefficient and inconvenient in practice: the Commons complained that the licensor's fees were too high, that foreign books interdicted at the Custom House lay there so long waiting for licensing that their pages mildewed in the damp riverside air, and no one liked the possibility of having his house or place of business searched by the messenger of the press. Thus did such practical concerns as commerce, convenience, and privacy lead London to pioneer another hallmark of modernity, a free press. Whatever the reason, the Victorian historian T. B. Macaulay (1800–1859) thought that the series of votes allowing the Licensing Act to lapse in 1695 had "done more for liberty and for civilisation than the Great Charter or the Bill of Rights."[6]

THE FIRST REGULAR NEWSPAPERS

Certainly, with the Licensing Act wiped from the books, the presses started producing, if not a flood, then a rising tide of newsprint. It is from this point that London began to be served by regular newspapers. Over the next twenty years, more than twenty newspapers, including *The Flying Post* (1695–1731), *The Post Boy* (1695–1728), and *The Post Man* (1695–1730), offered their own slant on the news three times a week. By 1704, some 44,000 copies of newspapers were sold weekly; by 1712, 70,000. On March 11, 1702, just three days after the accession of Queen Anne, London's first daily newspaper, *The Daily Courant* (1702–1735), began publishing from rooms above the White Hart tavern in Fleet Street. Not all periodical publications were strictly news oriented. John Dunton's (1659–1732) *The Athenian Mercury* (1690–1697) answered questions on any and all subjects, popularizing the latest ideas in science and philosophy (see later discussion). The period also saw the first journals of opinion. Defoe's *Review* (1704–1712) told readers that its essays sought "to wheedle them in . . . to the knowledge of the world."[7] Swift's *The Examiner* (1710–1711) offered political commentary, whereas Addison and Steele's *The Tatler* (1709–1710) and *The Spectator* (1711–1712 and 1714) delivered social and cultural criticism in brilliant prose essays that did much at once to perfect the English language, establish standards of urbanity and politeness, and entertain the literate reader (see later discussion). All this was available at least three times a week for just a penny.

What were these first newspapers like? There were no newspaper boxes in turn-of-the-eighteenth-century London; instead, the easiest way to acquire a paper was at a coffeehouse (see later discussion). There the newshound usually had a choice of several; paying his penny for *The Daily Courant*, what he held in his hand bore striking similarities to and differences from a modern newspaper (see Illustration 5.1). Like *The Times* of today, *The Daily Courant* sports its title, or banner, in bold print at the top, or masthead, along with its issue number and date. But there are no headlines. That would take up too much space in a production that, again in contrast to a modern broadsheet, amounts to only two pages, the front and back of a sheet, divided into just two columns. This would be the standard layout of a London newspaper to the end of the period. The space problem, combined with the fact that most London newspapers were written by one person, also dictates that there are almost never any pictures, graphs, or charts. Of necessity, the London newspaper had to rely on the printed word. Like their modern counterparts, these early newspapers give a place of origin and dateline for each story (Naples, February 22, etc.). But unlike the modern practice, they do not give a byline or name a correspondent. The reason for this was not primarily space. The reporters and sources for early eighteenth-century newspapers were a small and competitive fraternity that included Abel Boyer (?1667–1729), Arthur Maynwaring (1668–1712), Abel Roper (1665–1726), George Ridpath (d. 1726), John Tutchin (?1664–1707), and the essayists Addison, Defoe, Dunton, Swift, and Steele. They had to maintain anonymity because journalism remained a dangerous activity even after the expiration of the Licensing Act.

First, the government retained the ability to prosecute any journalist whose work it did not like on a charge of seditious libel. In 1703, Defoe was sent to Newgate and put in the public pillory for a satirical attack on Anglican attitudes toward Puritans entitled *The Shortest Way with Dissenters*. For three successive days at the end of July he was pilloried, first outside the Royal Exchange, then near the Conduit in Cheapside, and finally at the Temple Bar end of Fleet Street – right in the face of the publishers and booksellers. According to legend, the crowd threw flowers instead of fruit. Ever the entrepreneur, Defoe used the occasion to hawk additional copies of *The Shortest Way* and a poem written especially for the occasion, "A Hymn to the Pillory." Still, he was subject to harassment and arrest for the rest of his life. Boyer, Ridpath, Tutchin, and others were also prosecuted repeatedly. Although they often managed to win their cases, the legal fees and suspension of publication alone could put a writer out of business. Just how dangerous a profession print journalism could be was illustrated in 1719, when John Matthews (?1701–1719) became the only printer in English history to be executed on a charge of seditious and treasonous libel. His crime was publishing a Jacobite pamphlet with the insubordinate title *Vox Populi, Vox Dei* ("The voice of the people is the voice of God"). Offered his life if he would reveal the author, Matthews refused, was sent to Newgate in September, tried in October, and hanged at Tyburn, in the rain, on November 6, 1719. Defying the Whig regime, other Jacobite printers produced five different versions of Matthews's reputed dying speech, all of which reaffirmed his loyalty to the exiled Stuarts.

Nor was the government the journalist's only foe. This period has been characterized by "the Rage of Party." Most aspects of public life were divided into Whig and Tory sides, and print culture was no exception. Nearly all newspapermen and their productions sided with one party or the other, and because all were in competition with each other, they sometimes attacked each other with stronger weapons than quills and newsprint. Both Dryden and Tutchin were beaten within an inch of their lives on the streets of London by gangs set on them by rival writers. Abel Roper, the editor of *The Post Boy*, used to get material out of the death threats he received.

Finally, most writers made a very poor, hand-to-mouth living. The best could survive fairly well on the profits of their newspapers (both sales and advertising): the editor of *The Post Man* took in £600 a year, whereas the writer of *The London Gazette*, a paid government employee, made anywhere from £60 to £300. But more occasional contributors to the *Gazette* could expect just £7. Moreover, the newspaperman had to reserve part of each penny he made for printers, carriers, and anyone else who was instrumental in producing and distributing his work. Many writers hired themselves out as polemical hacks, churning out pamphlets for whichever of the two parties happened to be paying. By the first decade of the eighteenth century, the government kept a stable of writers on hand: as secretary of state and then lord treasurer, Robert Harley, Earl of Oxford employed both Defoe and Swift. Subsequently, Robert Walpole kept a less distinguished battery of writers at his service. Like any other profession, journalists even had their own precinct of the town: many of them congregated around Grub Street, just north of the wall, in the poor Moorfields area. In the eighteenth century, "Grub Street" came to mean the Gentlemen of the Press, with even less complimentary connotations than the term "Fleet Street" today.

The necessity for authorial circumspection was reflected in the subject matter of early newspapers. Most were born in war and that, combined with the avid interest of merchants and financiers in the shipping news, meant that they were filled with foreign intelligence: battles, ships, and cargoes lost to French privateers, diplomatic initiatives, ceremonies at continental courts. It could be argued that this steady diet of information about affairs beyond England helped create the cosmopolitan mind-set of what was fast becoming a world city. Foreign news was also safer to print. This is in contrast to contemporary political pamphlets, which took on domestic issues avidly, although even here the particulars were often disguised with allegorical or foreign names to avoid trouble: thus *The Secret History of Queen Zarah and the Zarazians* (1705 and 1711) is a thinly veiled satire on Sarah, Duchess of Marlborough.

When domestic news was reported, it was presented in a partisan fashion. In general, *The Daily Courant* adhered to the middle of the road, *The London Gazette* was pro-government, *The Post Boy* Tory, and *The Flying Post* Whig. Take the following story from 1713. Three years before, the Rev. Henry Sacheverell (1674–1724), a firebrand High Tory preacher, had been impeached by Parliament for delivering a sermon in 1709 attacking the Revolution of 1688 (see Chapter 7). His sentence was to be suspended from preaching for three years. The Tory *Post Boy* reported the end of his suspension as follows:

> On *Sunday* last, in the Afternoon, the Doctor preach'd the First time, after the Expiration of his Sentence, at his Church of *St. Saviours Southwark*. The prodigious Multitude of his Congregation is inconceivable to those who did not see it, and inexpressible by those who did; As was the Excessive Joy which was shewn by so many Thousands at his returning to the Exercise of his Function. He preach'd a most Excellent Sermon, which his worst enemies must praise, if they have any Shame in them.

The Whig *Flying Post* reported this differently:

> Last Sunday Dr. Sacheverall preached his first publick Sermon, since he was silenc'd, at St. Mary Overy's Church in Southwark, on Luke 23 v. 32. *Father forgive them for they know not what they do.* There was a very great Mob to hear him, and his Sermon lasted above two Hours.[8]

On the surface, each reports the same event, but the contrast in language is obvious enough: to the Tory reporter, Sacheverell's auditors are a "prodigious Multitude" and a "Congregation"; to the Whig, "a very great Mob," implying lower-class origins and possible violence. To the Tory, his sermon was "most Excellent"; to the Whig, it "lasted above two Hours." So much for the hard news, objectively reported!

A final obvious difference between a modern newspaper and that of 1704 is the proportion of its content devoted to advertisements: obviously, sales to readers were not enough to keep these publications afloat by themselves. The ads are a window onto the London economy and the preoccupations and worldview of their readers. First, they impress with the incredible amount and variety of entertainment possibilities in London. The papers were full of ads for plays, concerts, horse races, foot races, cock fighting, bear baiting, and other public events. The ads also reveal London's emergence as the capital of a wordwide trading empire. The bored Londoner, sitting at the epicenter of that empire, could purchase exotic wines and fruits, coffee and port, and luxury fabrics, or view animals heretofore unknown in Britain.

> At the Duke of Marlborough's Head in Fleet Street is to be seen these Rarities following: 1. The noble and majestick Lion, lately brought from Barbary, which for its most surprizing Largeness, and its being so wonderful tame, far exceeds any that was ever seen in the World. . . . 3. the noble Panther, lately brought from Egypt, one of the beautifullest Creatures in the World for variety of Spots of divers Colours; a creature much admir'd by all the Gentlemen and Ladies that ever saw him. The noble Pelican or Vulture, lately arriv'd from America, 3 foot high, nine over. The Head like a Griffin, Neck like a Swan; the like never seen in this Kingdom before; With several other Rarities too tedious to insert here. To be seen from 8 in the Morning till 7 at night.[9]

It could be argued that, in a society that provided education catch-as-catch-can, London's newspapers, operating in close cooperation with taverns and inns, offered a portal not only to products but also to knowledge, linking impresarios and their productions with a curious audience. By reading a newspaper, the average Londoner could acquaint himself with the world and perhaps even acquire some of it. Admittedly, most probably examined the ads out of mere curiosity rather than acquisitiveness or some dispassionate scholarly impulse. We see this in the many advertisements for viewings of monstrous births, deformed animals, and other freaks of nature.

Perhaps the principal way in which London's newspapers became both a literal marketplace for ideas and a school for the populace was in advertising the other products of the printing press. Following the lapse of the Licensing Act, the ad pages filled with notices for books and pamphlets, sermons, poems, and maps. Many of these productions were perfectly conventional works of theology and history such as the good bishops might very well have allowed a century before. Not every published opinion was orthodox, however: we have already noted how Defoe's *Shortest Way with Dissenters* mocked the Anglican hegemony. There was also a great deal of satirical poetry, most notably several collections of *Poems on Affairs of State*, that would never have been allowed before. Finally, as in any modern bookshop, we also find advertisements for books of self-improvement of mind and body: books on how to learn Latin, how to make wine, how to be an effective secretary, how to write poetry. There were numerous ads for beauty aids, including the first known promotions for weight loss remedies: early in 1710, just after the Christmas feasting season, we find advertisements for *Pilula contra Obesitatem*, which "if taken according to the Directions given with each Box, never fail'd carrying off Fatness."[10] This reminds us that London was about self-fashioning. Thus, the ad for *Instructions for Gentlemen to Know Whether a Picture be well Design'd, well Painted and an Original* (1707) is symptomatic of four great metropolitan developments: first, the rise of a London art market; second, the new wealth flowing through the metropolis, which enabled minor gentry and prosperous merchants to develop a collection; third, the possibility of fraud as unscrupulous sellers took advantage of buyers with no artistic training; and fourth, the increasing emphasis on *affecting* the manner of a gentleman in a society in which social rank was increasingly negotiable. Nothing could be more modern.

It is significant that these ads offered the possibility of what amounted to private instruction; no one need ever know that the reader did not, heretofore, know how to tell a good painting. If London were a place to reinvent oneself, this was because it offered both information and anonymity: it cannot be overstressed how necessary was such easy and discreet access to knowledge for a population of immigrants, unmoored from local customs, support networks, or trusted counsel. The need for knowledge discreetly acquired was nowhere more important than in the area of health. We have already noted that London was insalubrious, yet few had the money for a physician's care, and so most people self-medicated. One way to plot a course of health care was to follow the ads in the paper because, long before the Internet, London newspapers provided discreet information about, and access to, medicines and practitioners. There were ads for cures of gout, king's evil, toothache, and venereal disease. In the last case, especially, the anonymity provided by newspapers must have been a relief to anyone afflicted with so stigmatic an illness. Thus the ad for *A Practical Scheme of the Secret Disease* (1713) stresses its ability to effect a cure "without Sip-Slops of Physick, Suspicion, Confinement, or telling their Case to anyone."[11] In this sense, the London newspaper became a trusted friend and advisor, an oracle in a world devoid of other readily available authorities. But its authority was never ironclad, for its very anonymity also facilitated fraud and deception. In the village one could have had a personal relationship with the elder or wise woman dispensing medicines or advice. In the city, authority and trust were conferred by institutions, credentials, and common fame:

> These are to give Notice, That Mary Kirleus, Widow of John Kirleus, Son of Dr. Tho. Kirleus, a Collegiate Physician of London, and sworn Physician in Ordinary to K. Charles II is the only Person that sells (exactly prepared) his famous Drink and Pill, which is eminently experienced to cure all Ulcers, Sores, Scabs, Itch, Scurfs, Scurvies, Leprosies, Venereal and French Disease, Running of the Reins, and all such Malignities, though never so Inveterate, in all Constitutions at all Seasons of the Year. . . . [12]

The idea of newspapers providing a sort of informal open university for London reached its apogee in the 1690s with John Dunton's *The Athenian Mercury*. This early periodical offered to answer readers' questions, taking on issues of religion, science, law, health, and love, with a view "to open the avenues, raise the Soul, as it were, into Daylight, and restore the knowledge of Truth and Happiness, that had wandered so long unknown, and found out by few."[13] The last few words cannot help but remind us of all of those immigrants who had wandered to London in search of a better life. As with all early newspapers, there was no byline, but this one claimed to be written by a blue-ribbon panel of experts, the Athenian Society, which, according to Dunton, included Richard Sault (d. 1702) in mathematics and Samuel Wesley (the father of the founders of Methodism) in divinity (1662–1735). In Volume X, No. 18, Dunton was asked how long it took blood to circulate through the body; in No. 26 what he thought of the New England (Salem) witches. Some questions were more practical: Volume XVII, No. 17 addresses "Gent, what will maintain him in Inns of Court." Others wrote simply asking for advice, as we do today to agony aunt (i.e., advice) columns. Thus, on February 21, 1693, a young man wrote in to ask what he should do, given that he and his father disagreed on his course in life:

> Query, if I may not without his leave remove to some place where I am not known, and there take up an honest (though inferior) Employ to maintain my self? Or what Course will you Advise me to take, to keep

my self from Starving? And for my satisfaction, if ever I should be able, am I by Duty Obliged to repay him the Charge of my Education?

Predictably, the committee's answer chose the wisdom of age over the enthusiasms of youth, tempering a traditional view of parent–child relations with humanity and practicality:

> As Youth is more subject to error than Old Age; so 'tis very probable your father is a better Judge of the Figure you ought to make in the World than your self: 'Tis not a certain Argument that you really want a thing, because you desire it. . . . But supposing you are not mistaken in your Judgement, We think you ought not to remove yourself without your Fathers Knowledge, because your Body is his proper Goods; You should make use of the Interest of Friends to represent the Case to him; . . . [14]

Overall, the aim of *The Athenian Mercury* was the encouragement of virtue. It was thus part of a larger Reformation of Manners movement begun in the 1690s by Anglican and Dissenting clergy and encouraged by both Mary II and later Anne (see discussion later).

The aspiration toward mutual aid that characterizes the *Athenian Mercury* can also be seen in the "community bulletin board" aspect of early newspaper adverts. For example, there were frequent notices of missing persons or pets:

> Lost the 20th Instant between St. James's Square and the Old Palace-Yard, a little Cross-Shap'd Dog, of the Lurcher Kind, of a yellow brown Colour. 'Twas taken up by an ill-look'd Fellow, a notorious Dog-Stealer, and led by a Blue String towards York-Buildings. He answers to the Name of Bugg, and leaps over a stick. Whoever brings him next Door to the Great House in Dean's Yard, shall have Two Shillings Reward. [15]

Indeed, newspapers provided eighteenth-century Londoners with their principal "lost-and-found" service. Watches were a common item. Their importance to early modern people was considerable, especially as status symbols. They were frequently lost because, being valuable and dangling from decorative chains, they were frequently stolen. One does not require a suspicious mind to think that most of the watches, walking sticks, and jewelry listed as "found" in contemporary newspaper ads had, in reality, been stolen from their owners. As we shall see in Chapter 6, it was standard practice for a thief to sell his ill-gotten goods to a fence, who would then place an ad in a London newspaper and offer to return the booty, for a small fee.

Early newspapers thus provided far more than news. They were repositories of general knowledge and advice. They were counselors, mouthpieces, and community bulletin boards. They provided periodicity; that is, their daily or thrice weekly appearance gave Londoners a rhythm to the days of the week. For readers not directly involved in, say, the plight of the potentially prodigal son or the loss of poor Bugg, they must have provided the sorts of often trivial subjects of discourse that people seem to need to maintain cordiality and smooth social relations – what we today call water-cooler talk. Insofar as they offered guidance to those new to the metropolis, they formed one of the institutions that helped immigrants to become Londoners, while knitting all of its inhabitants, old and new, together. Robert Kirk, the visiting Scotsman, concluded of the metropolis that "Few in it know the fourth part of its streets, far less can they get intelligence of the hundredth part of the special affairs and remarkable passages in it." But he also saw the potential unifying influence of the press – "unless by public printed papers."[16] Newspapers thus had the potential to provide a degree of social cohesion, of common experience otherwise lacking in the great conurbation: knowledge was shared through the medium of newsprint from Londoner to Londoner, many of whom gathered together in small groups to hear it read at their local coffeehouse. This is rather different from the parish church, but it provided some of the same sense of community – when it did not divide people into Whigs and Tories.

THE ESSAY MAGAZINE

Perhaps the ultimate example of how the new public sphere of print gave meaning, provided shared experience, and in general made Londoners is offered by yet another literary invention of the Augustan Age, the essay magazine. The first regular essay magazine was Roger L'Estrange's *The Observator*, in which he purported to answer questions, anticipating the *Athenian Mercury*, between 1681 and 1687. But L'Estrange's periodical was purely political and he made up the questions himself. The next decade saw both the *Athenian Mercury* and Pierre Motteux's (1663–1718) *The Gentleman's Journal* (1692–1694), which offered cultural news from London in a general magazine format. The genre reached its early peak with two magazines that appeared at the end of Queen Anne's reign: *The Tatler*, edited by Richard Steele from April 12, 1709 to January 2, 1711, and *The Spectator*, edited by Joseph Addison, which appeared from March 1, 1711 to December 6, 1712 and again from June 18 to December 20, 1714. *The Tatler* claimed to relay news gleaned from the coffeehouses, but in reality both reported on topics of general interest devised by their authors, for the most part Addison or Steele or Addison's cousin Eustace Budgell (1686–1737). Both periodicals sought to "enliven Morality with Wit, and to temper Wit with Morality."[17] Both purported to be written within a frame device by an anonymous, Olympian observer of London life, *The Tatler's* Isaac Bickerstaffe and *The Spectator's* Mr. Spectator.

This frame device was a brilliant inspiration and a prime attraction for contemporary Londoners. First, these fictional *personae* provided the anonymity that all Augustan journalists required. Second, they added an element of intrigue to the whole enterprise: who *was* Mr. Spectator, inquiring readers wanted to know. Might he be walking down the same street or sitting in the same coffeehouse as the reader at the very moment that the latter was scanning his paper? Third, they humanized the narrators of the two magazines, making them characters with their own preoccupations, quirks, and foibles. *The Spectator* went even further by creating a circle of characters around Mr. Spectator to represent different types in Augustan Society. There was Sir Roger de Coverley, an old-fashioned country gentleman; an unnamed lawyer from the Inns of Court; Sir Andrew Freeport, a London merchant; Captain Sentry, a retired military man; Will Honeycomb, a gallant; and finally a clergyman who "visits us but seldom."[18] All of these types would have been recognized by contemporary readers. They represent a variety of crucial London interest groups with which prosperous readers might identify. Thus Addison draws his readers in and creates the atmosphere of a club.

Note who is omitted from the club: there are no craftsmen, laborers, or servants. Indeed, working London is almost entirely absent, because this publication is intended for smart society. There is no real politician: although Addison and Steele were both Whigs, they were careful to avoid blatant partisanship, because that could only have cut down on their readership. There were other essay magazines for that. Above all, although the *Tatler* eventually introduced the narrator's sister, Mrs. Jenny Distaff, *The Spectator's* club contained no women. Rather, the tone is sometimes misogynistic, for example No. 102, which satirizes women's deployment of fans as a weapon in the battle of the sexes:

> There is an infinite Variety of Motions to be made use of in *the Flutter of a Fan*. There is the angry Flutter, the modest Flutter, the timorous Flutter, the confused Flutter, the merry Flutter, and the amorous Flutter. Not to be tedious, there is scarce any Emotion in the Mind which does not produce a suitable Agitation in the Fan.[19]

In response, "Phoebe Crackenthorpe," probably Steele's occasional nemesis Delarivier Manley (c. 1670–1724), penned *The Female Tatler*, which sometimes addressed Mr. Tatler directly during its run from July 8, 1709 to March 31, 1710. In 1744, Eliza Haywood (1693–1756) launched *The Female Spectator* (1744–1746), equally dedicated to women's issues and concerns. Thus, by the end of our period, middle-class women had enough purchasing power to sustain their own magazine.

Addison's cast of characters allows him to express several different points of view without having to give away his own. Moreover, their presence tends to personalize the essays, turning them from arid philosophical discourses to a running serial on London life, with some of the characteristics of a high-class literary soap opera. As with a soap opera, the reader is encouraged to identify with one or more characters. One can imagine a male reader, at any rate, finding something to anticipate, someone to cheer for in the character most like him. Above all, *The Tatler* and *The Spectator* create a sense of community among their chosen audience by tattling or spectating on things that any Londoner might experience. A typical example is afforded by *Spectator* No. 5, which appeared in the coffeehouses on Tuesday, March 6, 1711. The subject of this essay is the Italian opera in London. Italian opera – more stagy and featuring flashier singers than the native variety – had only recently come to the English metropolis. It was very popular, but because it was not a native-born product, it was also highly controversial. Critics saw it as an alien, foreign art, more superficial than English semi-opera or stage plays. Addison himself had tried his hand at an English opera libretto, *Rosamond* (1707), with music by Thomas Clayton (1673–1725), that had failed miserably at the box office. Mr. Spectator was therefore in fact anything but an impartial observer in this case: Addison could be expected to loathe the Italian opera's reliance on showy effects as opposed to the beauty of the English language. His essay throws down the gauntlet against such superficiality immediately by beginning, as he always did, with a Latin epigram, this time from Horace: "Spectatum admissi risum teneatis?" Left untranslated in the original, this opening marks its readers as an exclusive and well-educated group. It is therefore an in-joke, intended to set the tone for what follows: "Admitted to the sight, would you not laugh?"

Typically, the essay proper begins with a general principle, seemingly unobjectionable, but really subversive:

> An Opera may be allowed to be extravagantly lavish in its Decorations,
> as its only Design is to gratify the Senses, and keep up an indolent
> Attention in the Audience.

Phrases like "*extravagantly* lavish" and "*indolent* attention" leave no doubt as to the author's sympathies. The paragraph then asks what the wits of Charles II's time would have made of "painted Dragons spitting Wild-fire, enchanted Chariots drawn by *Flanders* Mares, and real Cascades in artificial Land-skips." This is followed by an Aristotelian assertion of the need for reason and verisimilitude on the stage: "Shadows and Realities ought not to be mix'd together in the same Piece." So far, so good. Were the essay to stop here, it would be a superior example of the countless opinion pieces that flowed from Grub Street on every topic from the Treaty of Utrecht to the best way to cure the pox.

In the next paragraph, however, Addison does something brilliant. Rather than continue to pontificate on abstract principles, *The Spectator* takes the reader to the streets of London: "As I was walking in the Streets about a Fortnight ago, I saw an ordinary Fellow carrying a Cage full of little Birds upon his Shoulder. . . . " It is this encounter that really sets the essay in motion. Everything that follows has that much more force because it claims to be rooted in real life, the life of London's crowded thoroughfares. Addison continues the fiction (if it was a fiction) of happenstance, the luck of the streets:

> and as I was wondering with my self what Use he would put them
> to, he was met very luckily by an Acquaintance, who had the same
> Curiosity. Upon his asking him what he had upon his Shoulder, he
> told him, that he had been buying Sparrows for the Opera. Sparrows
> for the Opera, says his Friend, licking his lips, what are they to be
> roasted? No, no, says the other, they are to enter towards the end of
> the first Act, and to fly about the Stage.

This manner of discovering the use of the birds is necessary because part of the frame device of *The Spectator* is that Mr. Spectator is an anonymous unnoticed observer; therefore, any Londoner might encounter or be observed by him without knowing it. The mistaken supposition that the birds are to be eaten highlights the absurdity of using real birds for the opera as opposed to doing something more practical with them – like eating them. It is important that someone other than Mr. Spectator make this suggestion because, being a philosopher as well as a reporter, his mind is bent on more elevated things than eating!

The chief characteristics of Mr. Spectator are curiosity, keen observational powers, and a sense of irony. The first compels him to buy a ticket, where he discovers that the birds are only there for show, their music being provided by human musicians. So much for verisimilitude! In fact, this is only the beginning of the absurdity:

> I found by the Discourse of the Actors, that there were great Designs on foot for the Improvement of the Opera; that it had been proposed to break down a part of the Wall, and to surprize the Audience with a Party of an hundred Horse, and that there was actually a Project of bringing the *New-River* into the House, to be employed in Jetteaus and Water-works. This Project, as I have since heard, is post-poned 'till the Summer-Season; when it is thought the Coolness that proceeds from Fountains and Cascades will be more acceptable and refreshing to People of Quality. In the mean time, to find out a more agreeable Entertainment for the Winter-Season, the Opera of *Rinaldo* is filled with Thunder and Lightning, Illuminations, and Fireworks; which the Audience may look upon without catching Cold, and indeed without much Danger of being burnt; for there are several Engines filled with Water, and ready to play at a Minute's Warning, in case any such Accident should happen. However, as I have a very great Friendship for the Owner of this Theater, I hope that he has been wise enough to *insure* his House before he would let this Opera be acted in it.

Here we see the Spectator's talent for irony and exaggeration. Part of the humor derives from the fact that much of this is only just implausible, and in fact Mr. Spectator here mixes real occurrences – *Rinaldo* was an opera by Handel that received its triumphant premier just days before, on February 24 – with the fantastical and exaggerated, thus holding up the whole world of opera to ridicule. (Given the opera's success, he may also be revealing some professional jealousy.) The joke seems to be that people, who should normally suspend their disbelief for an evening in the theater, need ever more realistic and spectacular effects to enjoy themselves. This should sound familiar to modern filmgoers. Subsequent paragraphs build on this by reporting ever-wilder rumors that John Rich is contemplating intruding a real cat and the requisite number of mice into the tale of Dick Whittington; and that "there is a Treaty on Foot with *London* and *Wise* (who will be appointed Gardeners of the Play-House) to furnish the Opera of *Rinaldo* and *Armida* with an Orange-Grove." George London (d. 1714) and Henry Wise (1653–1738) were famous gardeners who had done work for William III and Queen Anne at Hyde Park, St. James's, and Kensington. Once more the Spectator roots his humor in the real experience of Londoners by dropping names that his readers would have known.[20]

In one sense, *The Tatler* and *The Spectator* established for periodicals the tradition of smart cultural observation peppered with in-jokes for the natives and *cognoscenti*, such as one might read in the modern *Private Eye* or *The New Yorker*. They also anticipate the sort of "man-in-the-street" observational column that would be practiced in the twentieth century by journalists like Jimmy Breslin (b. 1930) in New York and Mike Royko (1932–1997) in Chicago, or in the twenty-first by an infinite number of bloggers. As any reader of those productions knows, part of their attraction is in providing water-cooler talk, a communal reading experience based on shared familiarity with the city that transcends class and education: we can all take part in the conversation because we have all been to that corner, shopped in that store, or drunk in that bar. Finally, there is something exciting about one's own familiar haunts being held up to the world. It validates one's own taste and experience and increases one's self-importance – no small thing in the modern, anonymous metropolis. So here, once again, the press brought Londoners together in a shared experience, creating a sense of community among its readership every third day, but only certain Londoners: as in a guild or a London club, women and most workers were shut out.

Some idea of the degree to which essay periodicals could create community is indicated by *Spectator* No. 8, March 9, 1711, which purports to print letters to the editor. The qualification arises from the suspicion that the letters were written by Addison himself, for what they reveal about their authors is ridiculous:

> I Am one of the Directors of the Society for the Reformation of Manners [a real organization in Augustan London: see discussion later], and therefore think my self a proper Person for your Correspondence.

Read quickly, this opening seems innocuous enough; read carefully, it reveals a correspondent puffed up with pride. The faint whiff of hypocrisy becomes a strong odor in the next few sentences:

> I have thoroughly examined the present State of Religion in *Great-Britain*, and am able to acquaint you with the predominant Vice of every Market-Town in the whole Island. I can tell you the Progress that Virtue has made in all our Cities, Boroughs, and Corporations; and know as well the evil Practices that are committed in *Berwick* or *Exeter*, as what is done in my own Family. . . .

The reader is left to wonder precisely which vices *are* performed in the correspondent's own family! If the author is in fact Addison, he seems to be sending up the reformers of manners, Anglican and Dissenting clergymen and vestrymen, JPs, and general busybodies who would seek to regulate the stage, the printed word, and personal behavior, in London especially:

> I am no less acquainted with the particular Quarters and Regions of this great Town, than with the different Parts and Distributions of the whole Nation. I can describe every Parish by its Impieties, and can tell you in which of our Streets Lewdness prevails, which Gaming has taken the Possession of, and where Drunkenness has got the better of them both. When I am disposed to raise a Fine for the Poor, I know the Lanes and Allies that are inhabited by common Swearers. When I would encourage the Hospital of Bridewell, and improve the Hempen Manufacture, I am very well acquainted with all the Haunts and Resorts of Female Night-walkers.[21]

In short, the man is an expert on vice, which allows him to offer crucial lessons, discreetly imparted, in how to be a Londoner.

The Spectator was a great success. It was only partially in jest that Addison wrote in issue No. 10, March 12, 1711, that "I hear this great City inquiring Day by Day after these my papers, and receiving my Morning Lectures with a becoming Seriousness and Attention."[22] In this issue, he informs the reader that his publisher prints 3,000 copies a day. Allowing 20 readers per issue, that comes to 60,000 pairs of eyes, or one-tenth of the population of London. Although Addison and Steele became exhausted and retired Mr. Spectator by the end of 1714, they launched, separately or together, additional essay magazines like *The Guardian* (1713), *The Englishman* (1713–1714), and *The Freeholder* (1717–1718). Others did so as well. Defoe's *Review* and Swift's *Examiner* were unabashedly political. To stifle this new and potentially unruly public sphere, the Harley government introduced a Stamp Duty in 1711 (10 Anne, c. 18) that effectively doubled the price of newspapers to two pence or more. Still, people bought them. Two decades later Henry St. John, Viscount Bolingbroke's letters to *The Craftsman* (1726–1750), at 10,000 copies a printing, were a constant thorn in the side of Prime Minister Walpole. Walpole was sometimes known as "the Poet's Foe," because he used whatever means the government had at its disposal to prosecute and silence opposition writers. These included establishing an Examiner of Plays and reviving the Stamp Act to again double the price of periodicals. In 1743, hawkers selling unlicensed newspapers were targeted, but the flood could not be stemmed. In 1724 London had three daily papers, seven that appeared three times a week, and six weeklies. Between 1730 and 1750, there were six morning papers and six evening papers.

In short, by 1750 the genie was well out of the bottle. Political and cultural figures had to put up with the fact that the gentlemen of the London press could write what they wanted and their readership would lap it up. But the first relatively free press in the world did more than simply bring down the powerful or amuse the masses. It offered assistance, advice, entertainment, civilization, even a sense of belonging to those who might otherwise have felt adrift in the big city. The press was therefore one of those crucial institutions of London life that served to ameliorate the worst aspects of the modern urban experience and turn men and women into Londoners. It did so in close conjunction with another set of London institutions: inns, taverns, coffeehouses, and clubs.

DINING AND DRINKING OUT IN LONDON

London had a voracious appetite and a prodigious thirst. The provision of food and drink was one of the city's major industries: according to a 1749 poll book, of 9,465 voters listed in Westminster, 1,441 (15%) were victuallers, butchers, bakers, or distillers. We have already noted the many feasts that punctuated the ritual year for the lord mayor, guildsmen, and parish. On the surface, these would appear to have fostered community and a sense of identity, not to mention full bellies and good humor. But nearly all these occasions also divided the community, both by excluding lesser members and (usually) women, and presumably by the order in which people sat. Historians of cooking like Sara Pennell have demonstrated the unifying and dividing potential of the hearth and kitchen, a gendered space if there ever was one, and how the possession of a kitchen and/or the utensils necessary to cook indicated status. Political historians like Newton Key have shown how Whigs and Tories used ritual feasting in the late seventeenth century as a tool to advance their agendas by associating the values of community and hierarchy with the feasters, and anarchy and disunity with those not invited. Eating and drinking in early modern London therefore had class, gender, and party dimensions.

Historians have also learned to listen carefully to the conversation and social interaction that happened over food and drink. Talk became a self-conscious activity in eighteenth-century London, with witty, erudite, and polite conversation especially prized. For aristocratic women, this took place on visits to other women. The great age of the bluestocking and aristocratic salons really began just as our period ended, but as early as the 1680s, Louis de Kéroualle, Duchess of Portsmouth (1649-1734), one of Charles II's mistresses, turned her lodgings at Whitehall into an alternative to court drawing rooms. In the 1720s and 1730s, Lady Mary Wortley Montagu (1689-1762) maintained a social network that included many of London's best and brightest. For aristocratic men, such sociability took place in inns, taverns, coffeehouses, and clubs.

Between 1550 and 1750, as the cityscape changed and expanded, traditional meeting places like the inn and the tavern were joined by the coffeehouse, the club, and the pleasure garden, products of London's burgeoning economic reach and fluid social scene. The result was an informal network of institutions that provided some of the conviviality and emotional support that many had left behind in the village. London's watering holes played a crucial role in welcoming and acclimating new Londoners, while sustaining community among old ones. Indeed, as the established Church, the craft guild, and the neighborhood parish lost some of their influence in the expanding metropolis, these secular institutions filled some of their social function. But, as with guild and parish, none provided community for all Londoners at all times and places. To repeat, eating and drinking are class- and gender-based activities: where, with whom, even when you ate were determined by your status. Inns and taverns were expensive and exclusive, attracting an upper, middling, and in the case of taverns, mostly male clientele. Membership in clubs was restricted to elite men. Alehouses attracted a lower class and more localized clientele of both sexes. Coffeehouses are sometimes said to have been more democratic than say, taverns, but their customer base tended to divide across occupational lines and probably excluded the poorest Londoners and most women. In other words, if Londoners sought companionship at such establishments, they did so selectively, along class, gender, neighborhood, and occupational lines. At board or bar, at least, London echoed the hierarchical and sometimes divisive world of the village.

INNS

Early modern London inns operated like today's full-service hotels, offering accommodation, stabling, food, drink, even entertainment in the form of occasional plays in their open courtyards. There were about 200 of them in the metropolis by the 1730s. Many were very old. Some began life as bishop's or abbot's palaces that changed hands at the Reformation: in the Strand, the abbot of Glastonbury's house became the Dolphin; that of Lewes, the Walnut Tree; that of Peterborough, the Bell. Before the arrival of the railways, inns were London's transportation hubs, located at the termini of major roads and stage lines into the countryside. For example, in the eighteenth century, the Bath and Bristol coaches to the west started and ended at the Chequer, Charing Cross. This is perhaps one reason that Samuel Johnson thought "the full tide of human existence is at Charing-cross."[23] Other western passengers boarded or alighted at inns along the Strand, Fleet Street, or Holborn. Passengers for the northwest and midlands started off at inns in Aldersgate; those for the north and east at inns in Bishopsgate like the Bull, with thirty-three hearths; or the Dolphin, which served East Anglia. Inns congregating around Borough High Street, Southwark like the George (still in operation today) and the Tabard, linked to the Dover Road and accommodated passengers for the south and east. Innkeepers were prosperous businessmen, and by the 1750s many had diversified, investing in their own stage coach lines; in the nineteenth century, railroads would expand on the concept, building massive hotels attached to their termini. As all this implies, inns were significant structures, rising two, three, or four stories. Often, they presented a plain, narrow front to the street. It was beyond that, in their galleried courtyards, that coaches stopped, passengers alighted, horses were taken to stables, and entertainments could be staged (see Illustration 5.2). The ground floor would have a tavern and shops as well, forming a smaller version of the Royal or New Exchanges.

The great London coaching inns catered to an elite clientele: gentlemen, wealthy merchants, prosperous tradesmen, and their wives and daughters. A new immigrant of more modest means might also spend the money for a decent room to get a good start in his new home among people from the old. That is because inn guests tended to come from the region at the other end of the road and coaching line that terminated at the innkeeper's door. Often, the innkeeper himself was an expatriate from the same region, and he might employ his fellow countrymen at the inn. Both experienced businessmen and new immigrants in a strange town must have found it comforting and helpful to hear accents familiar from home and to network with people from their own "country." Here one could make valuable business and employment contacts, and receive mail and news from home. Inns were traditional sites for livery company feasts, and some sponsored annual banquets for the London expatriates from a particular county, not unlike college and school reunions today. Thomas D'Urfey (?1653–1723) wrote and Henry Purcell set the Yorkshire Feast Song "Of Old, When Heroes Thought it Base" for precisely such an event in March 1690, although the expected turnout for England's largest county necessitated its being held at Merchant Taylors' Hall. Such events were not only convivial; they were also charitable, because proceeds often went to a worthy cause.

The inn was therefore one of those institutions, like the newspaper and essay magazine, that made London more welcoming and negotiable for strangers, but it did not tend to make London more integrated. Its clientele was not diverse, and it tended to look outward and backward, not toward the city. A newcomer was well-advised to look beyond the inn as soon as possible. He needed to find his local.

TAVERNS, ALEHOUSES, AND ORDINARIES

Toward the end of our period London boasted some 500 taverns. Taverns were, like inns, very old institutions; some, like the Bear at Bridge Foot in Southwark or the Ship in Lime Street, had been around since the Middle Ages. The Devil Tavern in Fleet Street was famous throughout the seventeenth century, whereas the Mitre a few doors east was patronized by Sam Pepys in the 1660s, William Hogarth 60 years later, and Samuel Johnson a few decades after that. In fact, it was here that Johnson had his first extended conversation with his future biographer, James Boswell, over two bottles of port, until one in the morning. This tavern made last call only in 1788.

Taverns mainly provided wine: until the eighteenth century the most popular were claret (from the French *clairet*), a pale red wine from France, and sack (from the Spanish *secco*), a dry white wine from Spain. Following the passage of high tariffs on French wine in 1678 and the Methuen Treaty with Portugal in 1703, malaga, sherry, and port became the preferred drinks of the upper classes. Like inns, taverns were substantial structures, usually operating primarily on the upper floor of a large house, often with shops or a spacious barroom on the ground floor. Taverns offered additional services, including food and rooms for accommodation or for meetings. Indeed, their multiplicity of rooms – the Pope's Head just off Lombard Street had fifteen – meant that, once the potboy or drawer brought the drinks, patrons could have some privacy. This was crucial to anyone with an assignation to make or a plot to hatch. Both Pepys and Boswell engaged with women, in the latter case prostitutes, in tavern rooms. The wits of Charles II's court found seclusion, unavailable at Whitehall, at Locket's, Charing Cross, the Rose in Russell Street, or the Cock in Bow Street. During the Exclusion Crisis, the King's Head Tavern, on the corner of Fleet Street and Chancery Lane, hosted the meetings of the Whig Green Ribbon Club: one wonders if the tavern were chosen ironically, given its name. The plans for the Rye House Plot, to assassinate Charles II and his brother the Duke of York, were hatched in the back rooms of taverns like the Angel near the Royal Exchange, or the Five Bells in the Strand. On a lighter note, oyster girls sold their wares and musicians performed in taverns. Thus, on March 27, 1661, after dinner at the Dolphin Tavern, Tower Street, Pepys recalled:

> a great deal of mirth. And there stayed till 11 a-clock at night. And in our mirth, I sang and sometimes fiddled (there being a noise of fiddlers there) and at last we fell to dancing – the first time that ever I did in my life – which I did wonder to see myself to do.[24]

As this implies, taverns provided a degree of connection and convivi- ality – innocent and illicit – that had the potential to take the edge off of the hustle and bustle of urban life. Thus Samuel Johnson, as much a tavern man as Pepys was, opined to his biographer, James Boswell:

> There is no private house, (said he,) in which people can enjoy themselves so well, as at a capital tavern. . . . at a tavern, there is a general freedom from anxiety. You are sure you are welcome: and the more noise you make, the more trouble you give, the more good

things you call for, the welcomer you are. . . . No, Sir; there is nothing which has yet been contrived by man, by which so much happiness is produced as by a good tavern or inn.[25]

As much as any modern urban dweller, the early modern Londoner needed a place "where everybody knows your name." Precisely because of their ability to bring together people who might not normally associate, the national and civic authorities tried to regulate taverns and alehouses. A 1553 statute (7 Edw. VI, c. 5) required London taverns to be licensed and guests restricted to forty in number. They could not possess bowling greens or skittle alleys – associated with gambling – because these were restricted to inns. During the sixteenth century, tavern keepers were even prosecuted for putting up lodgers. By the mid-seventeenth century, however, these proscriptions were not being enforced: any member of the Vintners' Company could open a tavern, and nonmembers could obtain licenses easily from the Commissioners of Wine. As a result, there were more than 400 taverns in London by 1638. A survey of 1620 found 100 along the Strand between Temple Bar and Charing Cross alone.

Some taverns, like the King's Head, Charing Cross, included full ordinaries, that is, restaurants. Samuel Pepys records a particularly memorable meal of leg of veal, bacon, two capons, sausages, and fritters at the Bell in Westminster. Stand-alone restaurants made their first appearance early in the seventeenth century. They were most popular for dinner (i.e., the mid-day meal) and so early modern Londoners, like those of today, might find themselves cooling their heels waiting for the lunch rush to subside: on one occasion, Pepys reports waiting two hours to be served. Ordinaries could also host and cater wedding receptions and other occasions, such as the feasts of livery companies: the Half Moon in Cheapside played host to the Wax Chandlers in the 1680s, the Clockmakers in the 1690s, and the Wire Drawers from 1741 to 1802. Some specialized in a particular cuisine: the most prestigious restaurants in London then as now were French. In Pepys's day, Chatelin's was a fashionable French restaurant in Covent Garden where meals ran 8 shillings 6 pence. In Swift's London the place to go was Pontack's in Abchurch Lane, where a good dinner cost two guineas! Those on a budget could buy a "dirty dinner" at an average tavern or ordinary for as little as 1 shilling for a fixed meal of two dishes. To save time or money, a cheap meal could be had in a Smithfield cookshop or ordered take-away (although this terminology came after our period), or one could supply one's own food – say, meat bought at Smithfield or a fish bought at Billingsgate – to be cooked at the local tavern. In the eighteenth century, steak- or chophouses were popular: Boswell particularly liked Clifton's near the Temple and Dolly's near St. Paul's in Paternoster Row. On December 15, 1762 Johnson's biographer "had a large, fat beefsteak" at Dolly's and then attended a cock fight in St. James's Park.[26]

Alehouses like the Cock in the Strand operated on a far less grand scale than taverns or ordinaries, providing just beer and ale, period. In 1722 porter, a strong, dark, bitter beer, was introduced and soon became Londoners' preferred potable. These drinks, often flavored with sugar, spices, or cherries, were staples in London because the water was not entirely safe to drink. Indeed, because ale can be brewed easily at home, in theory, anyone could open his or her place of residence to the public as an alehouse, hence the contemporary term *public house*, shortened by the end of the eighteenth century to *pub*. As this implies, alehouses tended to be smaller and more ad hoc than taverns: there were many of them (some 6,000 by the 1730s), but they tended to have much shorter histories than the great Cheapside or Strand establishments, coming and going at the whim of their owners. They also attracted a localized clientele: unlike inns and taverns, alehouses looked not outward but inward, to the neighborhood. The cheap price of beer and ale, a penny a pint, 2 or 3 pence for a quart, meant that they attracted a more casual, lower-class clientele, which tended to drive away their betters.

In fact, there were many reasons for the upper classes to shun ale-houses, especially during the first half of the period. The very clientele of the alehouse – undiluted, unsupervised, and lower class – was, within the context of the Great Chain of Being, dangerous. Alehouses brought crowds of such people together and allowed them to engage in unregu-lated, unmonitored speech. The government feared treasonous speech, the established Church worried about heresy and the mixing of the sexes, and both were uneasy about the emboldening effect of alcohol. Worse, as Thomas Dekker indicated in his plays, alehouses were thought to be the familiar haunts and crucial points of exchange for thieves and fences, pimps and prostitutes. Respectable contemporaries shuddered at the mis-chief supposedly planned or undertaken there. According to William Vaughn, "here breed conspiracies, combinations, common conjurations, detractions, defamations."[27] The government of Edward VI ordered JPs to require alehouses to take out licenses. That effort was renewed in the seventeenth century by Puritan justices in particular. This was part of a larger campaign against disorder, but it was always unsuccessful, especially in London. As we saw with taverns, elite and Puritan notions of social order stood not a chance against Londoners' needs for companionship and alcoholic lubrication: in 1614, there were more than 1,000 alehouses within the walls; in 1634, 285 alehouses in the parishes of St. Margaret's and St. Martin's alone. In fact, the authorities need not have worried: Peter Clark's study of the English alehouse has found relatively little evidence that they hosted crime or sedition. Rather, the London alehouse provided a social center for people who might not otherwise have had one, a more modest equivalent to "the throne of human felicity"[28] that Sam Johnson saw in his tavern chair. This was especially true as the capital grew, because there were not enough parish churches to serve London's expanding population. Even if there had been more churches, thanks to the Reformation, they could no longer provide many of the convivial activities (i.e., wedding receptions, church-ales) so beloved of the late medieval parish. In London, those entertainments could be found in the neighborhood pub.

As the early modern period wore on, the drinks trade became more commercialized and industrialized. Big London breweries, some of which are still in existence, began to supply inns and taverns. The Anchor Brewery in Southwark was founded in 1616 and was in the eighteenth century owned by the Thrale family, friends of Dr. Johnson. The Truman family built the Black Eagle Brewery in the 1720s, but it would be surpassed in 1742 when Samuel Whitbread (1720–1796) and Thomas Shewell (fl. 1742–1765) founded a brewery that by 1760 would be the largest in London, delivering 64,000 barrels annually. Homebrew came to be replaced by commercial brew, leaving the distill-it-yourself market to gin.

If alehouses grew more respectable in the eighteenth century, it was both because they began to offer more services (commercially brewed beer, pub food, lodgings, credit, newspapers) and because doss-houses and gin shops – usually just a counter sans benches or tables – replaced them in the nightmares of the upper classes. Gin is supposed to have been brought from Holland at the end of the seventeenth century by William III and his courtiers. Because it was new, there were no gin taxes or licensing requirements. It was also easily made, readily available at barbershops, tobacconists, street vendors, and doss-houses, and infamously cheap: the inscription over the gin cellar in Hogarth's *Gin Lane* reads: "Drunk for a penny. Dead drunk for twopence. Clean straw for nothing." The result was the Gin Craze of the 1730s and 1740s. Between 1727 and 1735, gin sales rose from 3.5 to 6.5 million gallons, and by 1739 there were more than 8,000 spirit-houses in London. The death rate also rose: gin addiction helped make the 1740s the deadliest decade of our period. In 1751, William Hogarth satirized the effects of gin in his two prints *Gin Lane* and *Beer Street*. On Beer Street (see Illustration 5.3) everyone is happy and healthy; business prospers, apart from the pawnshop and coffin maker; babies are about to be made. Clearly, the alehouse had lost its stigma. In contrast, on Gin Lane (see Illustration 5.4) everyone is sickly and near death; only the pawnshop and coffin maker prosper, while, in a fundamental violation of human nature, a gin-besotted mother neglects her child.

COFFEEHOUSES

By the 1650s, London's economic reach produced a new institution, cheaper than the tavern and more respectable than the alehouse, where its male inhabitants could congregate: the coffeehouse. Coffee was introduced to England by Levant merchants in the mid-seventeenth century. It is therefore surprising that the first recorded coffeehouse in England was established well inland, at Oxford, in 1650. Its proprietor, one Jacob, moved to London two years later and set up what some claim was the first such metropolitan establishment at Holborn. Others credit Pasqua Rosée (fl. 1651–1656), an immigrant from Smyrna, Turkey, who opened the Smyrna coffeehouse (not to be confused with a later establishment of the same name in Pall Mall) in St. Michael's Alley, Cornhill in 1652. Rosée, with a good Londoner's entrepreneurial sense, promoted the exotic new beverage in a handbill as a health drink, effective against headaches, dropsy, gout, scurvy, miscarriages in pregnant women, "the spleen, hypocondriack winds, or the like." He was more accurate in asserting that coffee "will prevent drowsiness and make one fit for business."[29] Perhaps because the drink was much stronger then, with a heavy narcotic effect, it was an immediate hit. By 1663 there were eighty-two coffeehouses in London, all of which paid one shilling a year for their licenses. By 1739 their number exceeded 550. Coffeehouses not only provided Turkish coffee and London newspapers, but also tea from China, chocolate from the West Indies, and tobacco from Virginia – the nascent British commercial empire brought to your table. Above all, like the other institutions described in this chapter, they offered Londoners conversation, companionship, and relaxation. Misson describes the new coffeehouse sociability:

> These Houses, which are very numerous in London, are extreamly convenient. You have all Manner of News there: You have a good Fire, which you may sit by as long as you please: You have a Dish of Coffee; you meet your Friends for the Transaction of Business, and all for a Penny, if you don't care to spend more.[30]

The newspapers were an important part of this nexus. Coffeehouses were established during the Interregnum, just when the London press experienced its first burst of relative freedom. Their golden age occurred during the wars with France from 1689 to 1713, when the public was eager for foreign news. Proprietors saw newspapers and pamphlets as a way to attract custom, and they vied with each other to provide the best selection. They also provided bulletin boards on which notices might be posted and long tables at which newspapers could be shared and passed around (see Illustration 5.5). The Frenchman César de Saussure (1705–1783) thought London coffeehouses dirty and smoky, but he saw why Londoners found them indispensable circa 1726:

> What attracts enormously in these coffee-houses are the gazettes and other public papers. All Englishmen are great newsmongers. Work-men habitually begin the day by going to coffee-rooms in order to read the latest news. I have often seen shoeblacks and other persons of that class club together to purchase a farthing paper. Nothing is more entertaining than hearing men of this class discussing politics and topics of interest concerning royalty. You often see an Englishman taking a treaty of peace more to heart than he does his own affairs.[31]

De Saussure's condescension notwithstanding, it is clear that the London proletariat was well-informed and opinionated. No wonder that the authorities worried about the connections among coffeehouses, print journalism, and popular opinion. In December 1675, Charles II issued a proclamation closing the coffeehouses of London. Fortunately, no royal proclamation was more doomed to failure than this one, and it was withdrawn within a few weeks. Still, the government might go after individual owners just as it did authors and printers: in 1677 Edmund Chillenden (fl. 1631–1678), a Puritan coffeehouse keeper in Leadenhall Street, was accused of publishing and disseminating false and seditious news. Consistent with their two-pronged offensive of censorship and "official" news, the Restoration regime also sometimes tried to use the coffeehouses to broadcast its own case. Thus, during the Second Anglo-Dutch War, Samuel Pepys was told to go to the coffeehouse to spread rumors of Dutch mistreatment of British prisoners in the hope that such stories would "spread like the leprosy."[32]

Coffeehouses were thought to be even more corrosive of the status quo than inns and taverns because, as de Saussure suggests, their low admission price made it possible for almost anyone to go there. At the turn of the eighteenth century, the French Ambassador, Camille, Comte de Tallard (1652–1728), was mildly astonished at the resultant mix of patrons:

> Nothing is so different from the manners of former times as the present style of living among noblemen. They have no intercourse with one another after they quit the House; most of them go to dine at some tavern; and afterwards they repair to places called coffee-houses, *where everybody goes without distinction* [our italics]. Of these there is an infinite number in London, and there they remain till they return home.[33]

Historians debate the degree of real social mixing that took place in coffeehouses, but it is suggestive that according to a contemporary set of "Rules and Orders of the Coffee House," no man was expected to give place to someone "Finer." Thus did Roger L'Estrange's worst fears come true: in the haze of tobacco and coffee fumes the Great Chain blurred and its links tangled, as landed aristocrats, merchants, small tradesmen, apprentices, carriers, and possibly the occasional woman rubbed shoulder to shoulder, imbibing strong coffee, reading the papers, and becoming "Judges of those Counsels and Deliberations which they have nothing do withal." None of this boded well for hierarchy or deference.

Admittedly, coffeehouses grew less open and communal as time went on. At the beginning, patrons sat around large tables, papers spread out before them. But as coffeehouses became more established, more elaborate, and more of a resort for people with particular interests and friends, they began to install smaller tables and booths. If inns divided according to the county roads they served, and alehouses by neighborhoods, individual coffeehouses served particular professions. Indeed, just as particular trades once gathered around specific churches and guildhalls, men of a similar vocation or avocation now met at the coffeehouse. We have already noted that Garraway's, Jonathan's, Lloyd's, and the Jamaica, all on

Cornhill, catered to particular business interests (i.e., auctioning, stock-jobbing, shipping, and slaving, respectively). The St. James's, just beyond the gates of the palace of that name, was the place for politics and foreign news; the Grecian, near the Temple, for lawyers, students at the Inns of Court, and other scholars (including meetings of the Royal Society); White's Chocolate House, also near St. James's Palace, for gallants. Coffeehouses went in and out of fashion. In the late seventeenth century, poets gathered at Will's, 1 Bow Street, near Covent Garden, where Pepys found "all the wits of the town" assembled on February 3, 1664.[34] During the later years of his life the poet John Dryden would hold court by the fire, listening to and encouraging younger poets. But with Dryden's passing in 1700 the literary scene moved down Russell Street to Button's, of which Joseph Addison was a part owner. By 1713, when he, Steele, and others were working on *The Guardian*, the house's famous lion's head postal slot opened "its Mouth at all Hours for the Reception of such Intelligence as shall be thrown into it" by those who wished to communicate with "the Guardian."[35] Legend has it that anyone wanting to see the authors, John Arbuthnot (1667–1735), Pope, or Swift in person could find them there in the evening. Button's lasted until about 1751, by which time much of the literary world had moved across Covent Garden to the Bedford. By Johnson's time, this was the great rendezvous for writers and actors taking a break from their work in the theaters nearby: here one might run into Henry Fielding (1707–1754), David Garrick (1717–1779), Alexander Pope, Richard Brinsley Sheridan (1751–1816), Tobias Smollett (1721–1771), or Horace Walpole over a cup of coffee.

CLUBS

The increasing specialization of coffeehouses and the abandonment of long tables for booths suggests that Londoners were willing to trade conviviality and diversity for privacy and association based on similar interests. Eventually, many of London's most famous coffeehouses went the way of Lloyd's: linked to one particular interest, perhaps increasingly uncomfortable with a diverse clientele that might include pickpockets and con men, they evolved into exclusive clubs. By the mid-eighteenth century, for example, White's Chocolate House became an aristocratic gambling club whose members included every prime minister from Sir Robert Walpole to Sir Robert Peel (1788–1850); powerful men continue to wager there in the twenty-first century. The Cocoa Tree and the

St. James's also became exclusive. There were middle- and lower-class clubs too, which explains why Johnson's famous definition is so broad: "an assembly of good fellows, meeting under certain conditions."

Both livery companies and religious fraternities might be seen as medieval clubs, but it was the genius of early modern Londoners to divorce most such assemblies from work and religion. Early in the seventeenth century, Ben Jonson organized a literary society, the Apollo Club, that met at the Devil Tavern, Fleet Street. The impulse for mutual society seems to have grown acute from the end of the seventeenth century as the court declined and the Reformation eliminated avenues of sociability; by the early eighteenth century London had some 2,000 clubs. Many early clubs were political: parliamentary tavern clubs during the 1640s; the Rota, which met at the end of the Protectorate at Miles's Coffee House, Westminster; or the Green Ribbon Club, which helped coordinate Whig propaganda during the Exclusion Crisis. The Royal Society started life as an informal scientific club at Oxford. Chartered by Charles II in 1663, and assembling mostly at Gresham College near Bishopsgate, its meetings brought together some of the most eminent scientists of the day (Boyle [1627–1691], Halley [1656–1742], Hooke [1635–1703], Newton [1642–1727], Wren [1632–1723], et al.) with gentlemen amateurs like Dryden, Evelyn, and Pepys. Under Queen Anne, the Tories had several clubs: the October Club (after October ale, associated with country values), which met at the Bell Tavern, Westminster; the March Club, more radical than the October; and the Scriblerians, a literary society that included Arbuthnot, Gay, Pope, Swift, and Thomas Parnell (1679–1718). Arbuthnot was a physician to Queen Anne and an accomplished satirist; the club met for occasional dinners in his lodgings at St. James's and Windsor, an example of the transition from court society to club society. Encouraged by Lord Treasurer Oxford and held to the highest literary standards by Swift, the Scriblerians produced some of the best political satire of the early eighteenth century. Half a century later, beginning in 1764, Samuel Johnson founded the nonpartisan "Club" that met at the Turk's Head Tavern, Gerrard St. and included many of the leading cultural figures of the day: Boswell, the naturalist Sir Joseph Banks (1743–1820), the politicians Edmund Burke (1730–1797) and Charles James Fox (1749–1806), the actor Garrick, the poet Oliver Goldsmith (?1728–1774), the painter Reynolds, the playwright Sheridan, and the political economist Adam Smith (1723–1790).

In short, if you wanted to engage with the most talented men in London during the last 50 years of our period, you were more likely to find them at the coffeehouse or club than at court. We see this clearly in the case of the most famous club of the Augustan era, the Whig Kit-Cat Club. The origins of the Kit-Cat are shrouded in mystery. According to the historian John Oldmixon (1673–1742), the club began just before the Revolution of 1688/89, when Whig politicians gathered secretly at a tavern near Temple Bar to relax. According to another tradition, the Kit-Cat was born of the friendship of the well-connected publisher and bookseller Jacob Tonson and Christopher Cat (fl. 1688), a pastry cook who ran a bakeshop, The Cat and Fiddle, in Gray's Inn Lane. In both stories, his mutton pies, called "kit-cats," were the initial attraction. Arbuthnot refers to the club custom of toasting the most beautiful women in London. It was the Kit-Cat that originated the use of the word *toast* as a noun to describe such women, whose names were famously engraved on glasses from which the toasters drank. The toasts, who, as far as we know never attended meetings, included an impressive roster of the famous beauties and political operatives of the time, including all the daughters of the Duke and Duchess of Marlborough, the wives of important politicians, Catherine Barton (1679–1739, Lord Halifax's mistress), and the wit Lady Mary Wortley Montagu.

The Kit-Cat's membership was equally impressive. Tonson and Cat brought together some of the leading Whig politicians of the day: most of the members of the Whig Junto (Somers, Wharton [1648–1715], Halifax), which had governed in the mid-1690s, the Dukes of Devonshire (1671–1729), Dorset (1688–1765), Grafton (1683–1757), Kingston (c. 1667–1726), Newcastle (1693–1768), Richmond (1672–1723), and Somerset (1662–1748); assorted lesser peers; Lord Treasurer Godolphin (1645–1712) and Robert Walpole; and great writers like Addison, Congreve, and John Vanbrugh (1664–1726). Early in Anne's reign the club moved to the Fountain Tavern on the Strand, and then at its height to special rooms – a clubhouse – at Tonson's estate, Barn Elms, in the leafy western suburb of Richmond. During the summer, the club met at the Upper Flask on Hampstead Heath. These venues became the setting not only for aristocratic sociability and political plotting but also for cultural patronage. Tonson's leading role resulted in numerous commissions and publications. Perhaps the Kit-Cat's greatest achievement was in the world of painting. Sir Godfrey Kneller, the king's principal painter, was also a member; arguably his most significant body of work was the series of forty-two portraits of Kit-Cat members, many of which now hang in the National Portrait Gallery in London. In effect, the Kit-Cat Club was a kingless court, toasting a roster of beauties who, a few years earlier, might have been painted by Lely or Kneller for a royal patron.

Most clubs were less ambitious. The interests of the Beefsteak Club should be self-evident. There was the Society of Kings, made up of men whose last name was *King*. Similarly, the Georges met on St. George's day at the sign of the George. If Addison can be believed, there were street clubs in London that mitigated somewhat the exclusivity of upper-class clubs and even parish culture by welcoming anyone who lived on a certain street. Although unskilled workers could not technically form guilds, at the beginning of the seventeenth century the water bearers, street porters, and laborers established fraternities. Mid-eighteenth-century workers organized by trade, joining friendly societies and "box clubs," meeting in alehouses to provide mutual support and plan industrial action: the tailors did so in 1721, 1744, 1752, 1764, and 1768.

Many clubs offered a further advantage that poses a difficulty for the historian: privacy. Some were secret, and few kept records of any kind. Much of our information about particular clubs comes from occasional mentions in correspondence, or appearances in *The Spectator*, which, as we have seen, moves seamlessly between reality and fantasy. In fact, so many clubs proliferated with such specialized interests that it is not always clear which ones really existed and which were invented by Augustan satirists. Take the infamous Calves-Head Club, which purportedly met to eat a calf's head every January 30th in profane celebration of the execution of the Royal Martyr, Charles I. All of our information about this supposed club of radical republicans comes from scandalized (or scandal-creating) Tory propagandists. If such a club really existed, its members were understandably careful not to leave traces of what was in effect a desecration of the dead king's memory. As a consequence, its existence and membership remain one of the great mysteries of Augustan history.

The secrecy associated with certain clubs was understandable, because many were, as we have seen, sites of political opposition. The whole business of that secrecy – clandestine meeting places, passwords, and handshakes – along with their competition with the court, unnerved those in authority. The very idea of concentrating, single-mindedly, on some secular pursuit, be it eating, dueling or just keeping mum, was suspicious. But by the early eighteenth century the public sphere was too well established – in the tavern, in the coffeehouse, in print – for the government to have any chance of suppressing its secret adjuncts. Clubs continue to play a major if controversial role in London life today. The controversy derives not from their secrecy, but their exclusivity, as the oldest and most prestigious have, true to their origin, tended to remain bastions of upper-class male privilege. Their association with establishment values indicates that they have come full circle from the days when they were considered dangerous precisely because they were open to the discontented.

PLEASURE GARDENS

There was one more type of watering hole, specific to London, that provided entertainment, conviviality, and a necessary form of privacy throughout the period: the pleasure garden. Already, in our 1550 visit to Southwark, we noted one of the first, Paris Garden. This was replaced around 1660, but farther south along the riverbank, by the New Spring Garden, later known as Vauxhall Gardens (see Illustration 5.6). Vauxhall would persist, in one form or another, to 1859. It was the "New" Spring Garden because there had been a Spring Gardens between Charing Cross and St. James's Park that operated as "the usual rendezvous for ladies and gallants"[36] from the late sixteenth century to the Restoration. To confuse matters further, from 1702 to the mid-1760s there was also a New Spring Garden in Stepney to the east. Londoners could also patronize Marylebone Gardens north of the city from 1650 to 1778, and Ranelagh Gardens near Chelsea to the west from 1742 to 1803. To this we might add the *Folly*, a river pleasure barge moored in the middle of the Thames from the 1660s to 1720. It was visited by Pepys and rather more controversially by Mary II, for by the 1690s it was degenerating into a floating brothel. Madame Tussaud's had an eighteenth-century predecessor in Fleet Street at Mrs. Salmon's Waxworks, patronized by Hogarth and Boswell. Finally, the outskirts of the city were dotted with smaller pleasure gardens, tea gardens, beer gardens, bowling alleys, and natural wells, to which the middle and working classes could stroll of an evening.

What, exactly, was a pleasure garden? A pleasure garden was an early modern version of an amusement park – for adults. Patrons could saunter along meandering walks behind high hedges, stroll beautifully manicured gardens, retreat to secluded booths where they could order dinner and drinks, gamble, listen to the latest music, and as twilight descended, be enchanted by the fires of numerous small lamps. Samuel Pepys recounts the delights of Vauxhall on a May night in 1667:

> [B]y water to Foxhall and there walked in Spring-garden; a great deal of company, and the weather and garden pleasant; that it is very pleasant and cheap going thither, for a man may go to spend what he will, or nothing, all as one – but to hear the nightingale and other birds, and here fiddles and there a harp, and here a jew's trump, and here laughing, and there fine people walking, is mighty divertising.[37]

Spring Gardens had a bowling alley, as did Marylebone, which also boasted dog and cock fights, bull and bear baiting. Above all, this was a perfect location for amorous intrigue or an elicit assignation: as *A Character of England* said of Spring Gardens "... it is usual here to find some of the young company till midnight; and the thickets of the garden seem to be contrived to all the advantages of gallantry."[38] Because they were such mazes, even "the most experienced mothers often lost themselves in looking for their daughters."[39]

Pleasure gardens grew more exclusive at about the same time that clubs arose. Jonathan Tyers (1702–1767), whose family ran Vauxhall from 1728 to 1821, imposed a shilling entry fee and introduced the *ridotto*, a combination of concert and masquerade dance, imported from Italy, for a guinea admission. He also built a pavilion for nightly concerts, supper boxes adorned with paintings, a replica of the ruined temple of Palmyra, Syria, and cascades, all lit with 1,000 gas lamps. Much of this was an attempt to compete with Ranelagh Gardens, opened in 1742. But Ranelagh's magnificent rotunda and music from the greatest composers of the day caused the elite to flock there in droves, "from my Lady Townshend to the kitten," leaving Vauxhall deserted.[40]

Patronizing pleasure gardens was not the only kind of outdoor activity enjoyed by London's elite. In the sixteenth century, noblemen liked to host banquets in St. James's and Hyde Parks. In the 1620s Ben Jonson noticed the growing custom of aristocrats parading in coaches around the Ring in Hyde Park. The park was also a popular venue for horse and foot races. We have already commented on the popularity of strolling in St. James's Park: from the 1700s the Mall at the northeast side of the park was the place to see and be seen. More like the coffeehouse than the club, these venues may have had aristocratic cachet, but they were not exclusive. Although St. James's Park, for example, was gated, it was notorious that thousands of keys had proliferated and that it was a common rendezvous for libertines and ladies of pleasure.

This section argues that inns, taverns, alehouses, coffeehouses, clubs, and pleasure gardens did more than merely provide food, drink, accommodation, and entertainment in the narrow sense. Much of what the guild and parish represented at the beginning of the period, these institutions had come to represent at its end: crucial venues of hospitality and nexuses of patronage, providing an element of identification and neighborliness more often associated by historians with the cosier confines of the English village. These functions give the lie to the old idea that London was of necessity devoid of cohesiveness, coherence, or warmth. There might have been a shortage of parish churches in some parts of the growing city and the reach of livery companies rarely extended far beyond the walls, but these watering holes and the newsprint they provided did much to bring comfort and structure to city life. But whereas newspapers and prints, if they were not too partisan, could unite their readers to each other and the city as a whole, these institutions tended to divide people: by place of origin (inns), neighborhood (taverns and alehouses), occupation (coffeehouses) and politics, interests, and class (clubs). Finally, although none of these institutions attracted people of both genders and all classes equally, the lines dividing them from each other were porous: clubs like the Kit-Cat met in taverns; the Royal Society adjourned its meetings to the Grecian Coffee House, or dined at the Crown Tavern, Leadenhall Street. Patrons flitted from one type to another, and many establishments within a type: Samuel Pepys visited 100 taverns during the 10 years covered by the *Diary*.

POPULAR ENTERTAINMENTS: WHAT ORDINARY LONDONERS DID FOR FUN

In Chapter 4 we examined the opportunities for artistic entertainment enjoyed by the elite. As we have seen, some of them, plays in particular, were equally available to ordinary people prior to 1642. Some historians have argued that the Reformation initiated and the Civil Wars accelerated an increased separation of elite and popular culture. The movement of popular feasting and holiday celebration from the church to the alehouse is one example of this. The closing of the public theaters in the 1640s and their revival at a higher and more exclusive price at the Restoration is another. Aristocratic distance and increased hostility toward popular entertainments was also a reaction to new ways of having fun. As this book opens and for many years before, those at the top of the Chain had, in fact, approved of certain traditional country pastimes as innocent pleasures that might also improve the usefulness of their tenants. In particular they encouraged the practice of archery, as English yeomen and husbandmen archers were the backbone of English armies during the medieval wars with France. Thus, ordinary Londoners would practice shooting in the open fields surrounding the early modern city to the east, north, and west. Prior to 1600, there were also quintains (upright posts with a crossbar on a pivot with a sandbag hanging down to attack) in Cornhill and Paris Garden for those who wished to practice jousting.

As the gun replaced the bow, archery lost its military relevance, and as London expanded, its open fields were built over. This explains why the Artillery Ground was set up bordering the northern part of the City, although it was reserved for the use of the Honorable Artillery Company and the Tower Ordinance, not ad-hoc groups of residents. In any case, ordinary people increasingly preferred to use the open space available to them to engage in other country pastimes that did not lead directly to military skills. They played football, wrestling, bowls, draughts, cudgels, or skittles; they attended prizefights and footraces in Hyde Park. In fact, football (what Americans call soccer) was still played by London boys in the very streets, which Stubbe found "a bloody and murthering practice."[41] Indoors, people liked to gape at unusual humans: in 1581 a Dutch giant-and-dwarf duo – the one seven feet tall, the other but three feet – took London by storm. Although London's first circus would be established after our period, in 1769, Restoration and Augustan newspapers tell us that its inhabitants also loved animal acts: dancing bears, learned pigs, the royal menagerie in the Tower. For those who actually hated animals, there was cock fighting or bear baiting in Southwark, Hockney-in-the-Hole, Saffron Hill, and Tothill Fields on the northern or western outskirts. Pepys sampled both, providing more evidence that when it came to pleasure, Londoners did not stay within class lines:

> being directed by sight of bills upon the walls, [I] did go to Shooe Lane to see a Cocke-fighting at a new pit there – a sport I was never at in my life. But Lord, to see the strange variety of people, from Parliament-man (by name Wildes, that was Deputy-governor of the Tower when Robinson was Lord Mayor) to the poorest prentices, bakers, brewers, butchers, draymen, and what not; and all these fellows one with another in swearing, cursing, and betting. I soon had enough of it. . . .[42]

The Thames afforded fishing (a source of food as well as entertainment), and during the cold winters of the seventeenth century, when the river actually froze above London Bridge, skating and sledding. Those frozen out of the public playhouse after 1660 could fall back on street theater and puppet plays. Finally, as we have seen, there was cheap ale to be drunk in alehouses or, later, cheaper gin in gin-shops, possibly followed by the patronage of brothels and prostitutes, both of which London had more of than any other place in the country.

One might expect to see the sex trade in the chapter on crime, but brothel keeping was only recently made illegal as this book begins, and prostitution remained a gray area throughout the period. In fact, the London sex trade makes a good case study of the ambiguities that make nonsense of simple distinctions between legal and illegal activity, and elite and popular culture. Brothels had been established on the south bank as long ago as Roman times. During the Middle Ages, the Church and the Crown took the view that such activity could not be eradicated altogether, so they sought to restrict, regulate, and profit from it by confining it to the Southwark liberty of the Clink, supervised by the Bishop of Winchester. The Church and the Crown divided the revenue, and St. Thomas's Hospital looked after the health of the girls. This broad-minded arrangement changed only at the Reformation: when the Crown dissolved the monasteries it also moved against liberties and confiscated extramural sources of Church revenue, closing the Bankside stews. At the same time, Protestant reformers urged the City authorities to crack down on this activity, as they were to do on plays and alehouses.

Ironically, the net effect of these measures was to drive prostitution both underground and all over: by the late 1570s there were more than 100 established bawdy houses in London, and prostitutes could be found throughout the metropolis. Before the Civil Wars, brothels were concentrated on the outskirts of Southwark to the south; Clerkenwell, Aldgate, Bishopsgate, and St. John Street to the north; Shoreditch to the northeast; and St. Katherine's and Whitechapel to the east. After 1660, heterosexual brothels and homosexual molly houses followed the politicians to St. James's and Pall Mall, the sailors to Whitechapel and Shadwell, and the actors to Covent Garden and the nearby theater district around Drury Lane, hence John Gay's advice in *Trivia*:

> *O! may thy virtue Guard thee through the Roads*
> *Of Drury's mazy Courts and dark Abodes. . . .*

Because prostitution was mostly condemned by the authorities, we might be tempted to place it in the "illegal" category. Certainly many contemporaries – Puritan preachers, merchants and JPs in particular – saw consorting with prostitutes as violating the law, both God's and man's. Recall, however, that they also thought the same way about stage plays and Christmas celebrations. It is true that ordinary Londoners seem to have agreed with upper-class moral standards to the extent of using the language of sexual incontinence to insult their neighbors, especially women: the most common form of epithet toward women in early modern court records is "whore." Sexual reputation was crucial for women and under constant scrutiny by their (mostly female) neighbors. Apprentices too seem to have acted according to conventional notions of right and wrong when they periodically attacked and pulled down bawdy houses. This suggests some congruence between official and ordinary attitudes.

But whatever the law or the pulpit might say, in real life the lines separating fornication, adultery, and prostitution were blurry at best. Not everyone who found companionship and intimacy in the street, the park, or the pub engaged in a financial transaction. Although canon law in particular criminalized all three of the aforementioned activities, and Puritan authorities made them felonies during the Interregnum, that does not mean that ordinary people agreed. Contemporaries tended to distinguish these activities by motivation, not payment. A "whore" was someone who enjoyed sex beyond marriage, whether paid or not; nor should we assume that an ordinary Londoner paying for sex or visiting a brothel was any more conscious of doing something wrong than one attending an alehouse or a play. As in the case of riot in early modern London (see Chapter 7), Londoners had their own moral economy for these things.

Even after the Reformation, moreover, the signals sent by the ruling elite were decidedly mixed. Many brothels paid rent or a cut to important courtiers, for example, the early seventeenth-century Earl of Worcester (c. 1550–1628), just as they did to the early sixteenth-century Bishop of Winchester. Friends in high places prevented serious prosecution, and the authorities often backed off from campaigns against brothels and prostitutes as soon as they stepped on important toes. At the turn of the seventeenth century, Black Luce of Clerkenwell carried on in her work for years without interruption; John Honman, who kept a Southwark brothel patronized by "very Auncyent folkes and welthye," also evaded trouble for two years.[43] Others were bound for good behavior by a respectable patron. No wonder that William, Marquess of Winchester (1483–1572), opined that "when the court is furthest from London, then is there the best justice done in England."[44] There really was not much difference between upper- and lower-class sexual behavior: Faramerz Dabhoiwala's study of the Westminster quarter sessions of 1713 discovered that both prostitutes and clients represented a typical cross-section of Augustan society: bakers, tallow chandlers, footmen, soldiers, innkeepers, gentlemen, and tourists and their wives.

In fact, historians have come to realize that most prostitutes were not professional in the sense of having chosen the sex trade as a vocation and then pursuing it with single-minded dedication. Chapter 2 discusses the limited choices for female immigrants to London, and the dark option of prostitution. The average prostitute was more likely to be a young girl fresh from the country or frustrated with her position, a domestic servant between situations, or an abandoned housewife or widow, thrown into the streets, trying to keep body and soul together by selling the one and ignoring the other. Naturally, people in these situations were vulnerable to being taken up and "looked after" by a mother midnight like the notorious Sarah Jolly (fl. 1724) or Winifred Lloyd (fl. 1729; see Illustration 5.7). In Chapter 2 we also noted Boswell's encounter with seventeen-year-old Elizabeth Parker, fresh from Somerset. Dabhoiwala's study offers additional archetypal examples. In the late 1720s, Hanna Smith, a fourteen-year-old apprentice, ran into Mrs. Lloyd while in St. James's Park and made the mistake of accepting an invitation to her lodgings. Lloyd hooked her up with a "Squire Jensen," who "was very fond of this Deponent and called her pretty Girl," gave her several sums of money, and eventually had his way with her for 10 shillings. Lloyd used the money to buy Smith shoes and stockings and kept the rest, pimping her out to Jensen, who said "he would make a Woman of her for ever." During the same period, Anne Bond found herself "out of Service, and sitting at the Door of a House where she lodged, a Woman, who was a Stranger to her, came to her, and ask'd her if she wanted a Place? and told her, she helped Servants to Places." The inquisitive woman turned out to be another infamous bawd, "Mother" Needham (fl. 1727–d. 1731), who turned her over to the equally infamous libertine Colonel Francis Charteris (c. 1665–1732). Failing to gain Bond's compliance after imprisoning her for ten days, he raped her and threw her back onto the streets. Representing the abandoned or impoverished spouse is Mary Price, a poor tallow chandler's wife who lived in a tavern in Mayfair, begged for a living in Chelsea, Kensington, and Hammersmith, and was caught having sex in a field with the aged and prosperous, if too aptly named, Francis Gotobed. According to the court record, she stated that "she had had many a shilling and sixpence of him and had it not been for him she should have been half-starved." Financial desperation explains why some women used the enticement of sex in a dark corner to practice the skills of the pickpocket or cutpurse. Lurid and heart-rending stories like these inspired reforming JPs like John Fielding (1721–1780) and Saunders Welch (1711–1784) to found societies to rescue prostitutes from their otherwise hopeless situations, culminating in the establishment of the Magdalen Hospital, Whitechapel, in 1758.

Admittedly, some women clawed their way up from the streets to become famous and prosperous madams, like Mother Needham, or courtesans like Fanny Murray (1729–1778) and Sally Salisbury (?1692–1724), both of whom lived high for a while from affairs with prominent noblemen. Certainly, running a brothel could be profitable: circa 1600 brothel keepers were assessed on tax roles at the same rate as prosperous craftsmen and small retailers. According to early seventeenth-century Bridewell records, one Mrs. Maye made £100 in three years from keeping a bawdy house near Aldgate. Mrs. John Shaw earned £4 10 shillings in a single night. But for every businesswoman entrepreneur, there were hundreds of girls like Hanna Smith or Anne Bond: Mr. Shaw had a network of 23 prostitutes working in a chain of five brothels around the city. The fees and fortunes of the prostitutes themselves ranged widely, from the £10 Thomasine Breame earned for one afternoon's work in the early seventeenth century, down to the 2 pence that a poor apprentice might pay to an even poorer streetwalker. The average in the early seventeenth century was about 2 shillings. Most of these women almost certainly felt that they had little choice of career:

> those Stroling Gilts which are whippt in Bridewel, do often Complain with Tears in their Eyes, that it is for want of Employment, and to get bread that they betake themselves to or continue in that abominable Course of Life.[45]

The sex trade may have given Londoners pleasure and income, but like so much of urban life, it had its winners and losers.

THE FESTIVE CALENDAR: HOW LONDONERS ORDERED THEIR YEAR

London's festive calendar was yet another source of amusement and relaxation for some, conflict and disapproval for others. Like so many other London traditions, it was the product of a cross-pollination among elite, civic, mass, and folk culture. Calendar rituals are crucial for all people: they mark time, giving a rhythm to the year. They also provide a sense of anticipation, and once they arrive, opportunities for merriment, relaxation, community, and reflection on life and the passage of time. They might have been especially important to urban dwellers, divorced as they were from the natural rhythms of the agricultural year. For most people in medieval and early modern England, the calendar was set by two great factors in their lives: the demands of agriculture and the rubrics of the Church. For country people, planting and harvest were the two big agricultural seasons, punctuated by ancient pagan festivals like May Day (May 1) and Midsummer's Eve (June 24). Following the early medieval Christianization of England, the Church overlaid Advent, Christmas, Epiphany, Lent, Easter, and Ascension onto the agricultural year and therefore co-opted many of the pagan agricultural festivals. May Day, the ancient Floralia or Beltane, became the Feast of Saints Philip and James. The summer solstice festival of Midsummer's Eve became the feast of St. John-the-Baptist. The best known such takeover was the transfiguration of the pagan harvest festival of Samhain into All-Hallow's Eve, or Halloween.

The result was a pre-Reformation calendar that mingled the sacred and the profane. Its red-letter celebrations began with New Year's Day, on which people wished each other well and exchanged gifts, possibly also engaging in ritualized hunting. Then followed Epiphany or Twelfth Night on January 6, the end of the Christmas season when the wassail bowl was last passed around. In some parts of England this was followed by Plough Monday, when farm implements were blessed. Candlemas, or the feast of the purification of the Virgin on February 2, was traditionally celebrated with candle-lit processions. St. Valentine's Day came after that, on the 14th, followed by Shrovetide. This season just before Lent saw Londoners imitate their rural countrymen, flocking to the open fields surrounding the city for wrestling matches, football, stoolball, cock fights, or cock throwing, that is, the throwing of sticks at tethered cocks. London apprentices were especially rowdy on Shrove Tuesday (see Chapter 7). John Chamberlaine wryly observed in 1611: "our 'prentices were very unruly on Shrove Tuesday and pulled down a house or two of good fellowship."[46] The next day, Ash Wednesday, began the 40 days of Lent, during which people were supposed to refrain from meat and getting married; doing the former was a way for mid-sixteenth-century London Protestants to defy the Church.

Spring began with Lady Day, named for the annunciation of the Blessed Virgin Mary on March 25. This was the day on which the year changed and was the traditional start for agricultural contracts. Palm Sunday, Maundy Thursday, Good Friday, and Easter Sunday marked the high point of the Church year. In some pre-Reformation London parishes, the Easter season was also marked by Hock Monday, on which the males of the parish chased the females and only freed them from capture on payment of a ransom, which was donated to the Church. On Hock Tuesday, the sex roles were reversed. St. George's Day, April 23, was a popular occasion for parish plays about his slaying of the dragon. Ascension Thursday, 40 days after Easter, took place at the end of Rogation week, the traditional time for the whole parish to "beat the bounds," that is, to assert the parish boundaries ritually by processing along them behind the crucifix and parish banner in what one historian calls "an outdoor springtime frolic."[47] These processions, led by the churchwardens, one or two parish elders, and the children of the parish singing psalms and prayers, took place on the Monday, Tuesday, or Wednesday before Ascension. Seven weeks after Easter followed Pentecost or Whit Sunday and Whitsun Week (accompanied by Whitsun ales), then Trinity Sunday, and on the Thursday after that, Corpus Christi celebrations, usually involving a major civic procession and plays.

In the middle of these Church festivities came the traditional first day of summer, May 1 or May Day. In the country, May Day arrived just as seeding was completed, and so people usually got the day off. On this obvious fertility festival, both country and city people traditionally Morris danced around maypoles and crowned a May Queen. They also famously underlined the phallic significance of the poles by engaging in amorous adventures. The delights of Midsummer's Day followed, marked by bonfires, and St. Bartholomew's Day (August 24), the excuse for London's most famous fair. St. Michael's Day, or Michaelmas, on September 29 was the traditional end of the fiscal year, when all rents came due, as well as the day when civic officials were elected. All Hallows' on October 31 marked the end of harvest season and was commemorated with bell ringing. All Saints' Day on November 1 and All Souls' Day on

November 2 commemorated the dead – very important to Catholics who still believed in the intercession of saints and the punishment of sinners in Purgatory. St. Cecilia, on November 22, was associated with musicians. The Advent and Christmas seasons marked the end of the ritual year. Finally, there were scores of saints' days celebrated with varying degrees of ritual throughout the year. This calendar fit a Catholic country in which the bulk of the population was engaged in agriculture.

In London, many of the religious holidays had a civic expression: processions down Cheapside to St. Paul's by the lord mayor and aldermen on New Year's Day, Epiphany, Candlemas, Easter, Ascension, Pentecost, Corpus Christi, and All Saints'. Sheriffs were elected at Midsummer, houses were decorated with greenery, and prior to 1541, Londoners marched in the Midsummer Watch, a sort of "beating the bounds" for the whole town. Moreover, many traditional festivals were associated with individual London parishes and their patron saints. For example, the parishioners of St. Olave Silver Street commemorated St. Olave's Day in 1557 with "a stage play of [goodly matter]" lasting from 8 PM to midnight when "they made an end with a g[ood song]."[48]

All of this should have changed for Londoners after 1550. The Reformation stripped the official calendar of scores of saints' days, leaving only the major ones. Church-ales, the fraternities that sponsored them, and the Midsummer Watch were suppressed. Londoners were slow to abandon favorite religious holidays, however. For example, they continued to beat the bounds of their parishes on Ascension Thursday, omitting only the crucifix and banner at the head of the procession. This ritual was so important, given the legal and fiscal significance of parish boundaries, that even Puritan-leaning parishes still performed it. St. Bartholomew's continued to be associated with an annual cloth fair in Smithfield, held over the 24th and 25th of August; with the return of traditional revelry under Charles II it was extended to two weeks. By this time, the religious and commercial significance of London fairs was negligible. People went for the plays, puppets, wax works, rope dancers, and famously, the consumption of mountains of roast pork – a perfect end-of-summer festival.

Londoners also continued to celebrate St. Valentine's Day, minus its religious significance. In the seventeenth century, English adults and children drew names the night before. On that day, women in particular either wore the names as favors (later to evolve into the valentine card), or if seeking the element of surprise, would deposit them in a secure pectoral location (i.e., their cleavage) for convenient retrieval when the named one approached. The lady then demanded of her valentine a present or money. Another popular tradition that had nothing to do with the Church was that the first person you saw in the morning of February 14 was your valentine. This explains the following entry from the *Diary of Samuel Pepys*:

> Up early and to Sir W[illiam]. Batten's [?1601–67]. But would not go in till I had asked whether they that opened the doore was a man or a woman. And Mingo [Batten's black servant] who was there, answered 'a Woman', which, with his tone, made me laugh.[49]

In 1665 Sam tried some gender bending of his own, hiding under the covers, pretending to be his wife so as to surprise Richard Penn (d. 1673), Sir William's second son, but young Dick would not take the bait.

Protestant reformers were no more keen on pagan agricultural festivals than they were on saints' days; one would expect these to be abandoned in any case as migrant villagers became Londoners. After all, what was the point of Plough Monday if, as in Swift's poem, city dwellers moved dirt with a broom and a mop? Midsummer bonfires and household greenery, however, suggest that Londoners were nostalgic about their collective rural past right up to the Civil Wars, at least. On May Day, London milkmaids dressed in their best, adorned with borrowed silver plate instead of their usual milk pails, going door to door accompanied by musicians and chimney sweeps to demand a handout. Similar to their country cousins, Londoners danced around maypoles on May Day. St. Andrew Undershaft in Leadenhall Street was virtually named for its annual maypole, but after the Evil May Day Riot of 1517 (see Chapter 7) the offending totem was taken down and stored in Shaft Alley. In 1549 it was burned at the instigation of a reforming clergyman. Another famous maypole near St. Mary-le-Strand (in the street of that name) survived the sixteenth century to become a favorite target of Puritans in the seventeenth. It was cut down during the parliamentary ascendancy on their order in 1644 but replaced again at the Restoration with a mammoth 134-foot example, "at which the little children did much rejoice and the ancient people did clap their hands, saying golden days begin to appear."[50] The golden days lasted until the second decade of the eighteenth century, when Sir Isaac Newton bought the Strand maypole to re-erect it in Wanstead to support a great telescope. Thus did metropolitan culture give way not to reform or religious zeal but to the rational scientific impulse of the eighteenth century.

Londoners also celebrated May Day at May Fair. Today, this name denotes a posh West End residential district, but it derived from a fair held there from May 1 to 15. Thus, the London summer was bracketed by May Fair and St. Bartholomew's Fair, until the former was suppressed in 1764. Finally, throughout the period, Londoners gathered to watch the parades of papier-mâché giants, dragons, and green men of the lord mayor's pageant on October 29. There is evidence that the lord mayor's show grew more elaborate and assertive of the City's rights just as the Midsummer Watch and other popular liturgical feasts were abolished. London's popular calendar therefore was a nostalgic refusal to let go of the old civic, church, and country traditions.

In contrast, the upper-class London calendar revolved around but one season – *the* season (see Chapters 3 and 4). The elite celebrated some of the same days (e.g., Valentine's Day, Easter, Christmas) as ordinary Londoners, but as part of a different ordering of the year: the court and artistic season, the law terms at Westminster, and the meetings of Parliament, all of which usually began in the autumn. In the seventeenth century the government promoted a new, patriotic, and Protestant calendar to which all could subscribe. Its red-letter dates were January 30, the Feast of the Royal Martyr Charles I; May 29, King Charles II's birthday and the anniversary of his Restoration; November 5, Gunpowder Treason Day; and November 17, the anniversary of the death of the Catholic Bloody Mary and accession of the Protestant Elizabeth. In addition, building on the tradition of Elizabeth's Accession Day tilts, it became the custom under the Stuarts to celebrate the reigning monarch's birth, accession, and coronation days. On all of these occasions, sermons were delivered, processions were made, church bells were rung, bonfires were lit, houses were illuminated, and sometimes effigies of unpopular figures were burned in mass demonstrations (see Chapters 3 and 7).

Perhaps because these celebrations were imposed from above, there were drawbacks to this calendar as a means of unifying the nation. For starters, the patriotic year split into a Tory spring and a Whig autumn; that is, those who tended to commemorate the execution of Charles I and Restoration of his son were likely to oppose those who would "Remember, remember the 5th of November!" and the accession of Elizabeth. The former were anti-Puritan and so Tory holidays, the latter anti-Catholic and so Whig ones. The Whigs made much of the November anniversaries during the Exclusion Crisis (see Chapter 7), and the Tories never failed to throw January 30 in Puritan faces. Moreover, Whigs and Tories celebrated the current monarch's anniversary days more or less enthusiastically depending on whether they were in power. Thus, early in Anne's reign, when the

Tories were in the ascendancy, Whigs liked to commemorate the birthday of William III on November 4. Mid-reign, when the queen chose Whigs to run her ministries, they were happy to celebrate Anne. When she threw them out of power again from 1710 to 1714, they tended to boycott her birthday celebrations on February 6. In the next reign, that of the Hanoverian George I, Anne's birthday, as well as that of the Pretender (June 10), were celebrated by Tory and Jacobite crowds as a way of showing their distaste for the current regime. Often these anniversaries provided the excuse for a good riot. Clearly, like newspaper and pamphlet literature, the new calendar could be used to send very potent messages from one political group to another, and like them, it was much less successful at bringing such groups together.

Thus, the new patriotic Protestant calendar was capable of rousing the masses in times of political tension but not necessarily to demonstrate their loyalty. On a deeper level, it failed to do what more popular calendar rituals did: unite Londoners in celebration of the landmarks of the year, and perhaps give them a temporal mooring to replace the one left back home in the country. Once in the metropolis, an immigrant could no longer regulate his or her year or day by the agricultural season or by the sun. Rather, the London calendar was mostly vestigial and its daily routine artificial, having little to do with the Earth or the sun: that is why Steele's "Hours of London," Gay's *Trivia*, and Swift's London poems are at once funny and informative. London's popular calendar provided the landmarks, the sense of temporality and periodicity that newcomers to London must have craved. Insofar as its great days brought people together, it also provided that sense of belonging and community of which, we have surmised, early modern Londoners were in particular need.

THE REFORMATION OF MANNERS

Throughout the period, some Londoners tried to reform and regulate the pastimes and habits of others. Why? First they saw plays, alehouses, gambling dens, and brothels as essentially sinful. At the very least, these pastimes and locations drew attendance away from Sunday church services: a good seventeenth-century Christian was expected to attend several services for the sermons and to not play bowls on the green. Second, prior to 1650, activities like bowling and gambling were also thought to tear young men away from the approved practice of archery. Third, the authorities saw the time spent in these pursuits as economically destructive: a playhouse full of porters and barmaids was hardly getting the work of the city done, and idle journeymen and apprentices took money out of the pockets of their masters. Moreover, these activities taught apprentices bad habits and made the poor poorer by separating them from their money. Fourth, City officials also worried about the health effects of large crowds gathered at playhouses and small ones gathered at brothels; indeed, fear of venereal disease from the patronage of brothels and prostitutes, and what to do about it if contracted, is a recurrent theme among correspondents of the second century of our period. Finally, the authorities feared that any activity drawing large crowds bred crime and civil disturbance. After all, the period from 1603 to 1642 saw rioting on twenty-four Shrove Tuesdays and eight May Days. But as we shall see (Chapter 7), large-scale riots were just as often provoked by accidents in the streets: after all, London was *always* a crowd.

What could the authorities do about activities of which they disapproved? There were several tiers of authority regulating entertainment in London: the central government at Westminster, the Church in Convocation, and the lord mayor and aldermen at the Guildhall made the law. The Central Criminal Court at the Old Bailey; the Court of Aldermen and governors of Bridewell in the City; Middlesex and Surrey assizes, quarter sessions and JPs; Westminster burgesses; and the consistory and archdeacon's courts of London, Middlesex, and Winchester (for the southern suburbs) adjudicated it. The City marshals, constables, and churchwardens of individual parishes enforced it. Just as this book opens, the reformist Protestant administrations of Thomas Cromwell, the Duke of Somerset, and the Earl of Northumberland tried to do something about public licentiousness. In 1553 Northumberland's government banned brothels and free-standing bowling alleys and tried to limit social drinking. The statute of that year limited bowling to inns and private homes and set the number of taverns in London at no more than forty. In 1556, the governors of Bridewell were given broad powers to search and seize brothel keepers, prostitutes, lewd and idle persons, and vagrants. They met as a court and were empowered to hand down summary justice, usually a term of incarceration in Bridewell or at least a whipping within prison walls. Under Elizabeth I, as we have seen, theaters were strictly regulated and theater companies required a royal or noble patron, or their players were regarded as vagrants subject to arrest. Felonies were handled at the Old Bailey (see Chapter 6), whereas bastardy, bigamy, and incest were handled by Church courts. Another way of regulating unsavory activities was to require licenses. After the royal proclamation of January 19, 1619, taverns and alehouses were to be licensed by the Vintners' Company. Owners had to pay a recognizance of £10 and provide two sureties (today we would call them cosigners) who themselves entered bonds of £5 apiece.

Unfortunately, the authorities might not agree on which pastimes were criminal or how far to go to eradicate them: as we saw in Chapter 4, under Queen Elizabeth and James I the court regulated but also encouraged stage plays, although the civic authorities detested them. We also noted earlier how campaigns against bawdy houses ran aground on the interests of their aristocratic landlords. Bridewell's charter might have given it sweeping powers, but they were never backed by statute, and some resented the attempt at social control by its Puritan directors. In 1618, while Puritan authorities across the nation were trying to crack down on bowling greens and stage plays, and the City was clearing the streets of vagrants, whore-mongers, and lewd women, James I issued the *Book of Sports*, a directory of approved Sunday pastimes that included May games and maypoles, Morris and other forms of dancing, leaping and vaulting, and other tra-ditional pastimes that conservatives and High Church Anglicans thought harmless. It banned only bowling and bear and bull baiting. In so doing, and again when Charles I reissued the book in 1633, the Stuarts drew a line in the sand over which forms of popular culture were acceptable. Puritan magistrates pursuing the reformation of manners found themselves on the other side of that line. This lack of ruling class unity meant that everything depended on the scruples of your local JP, constable, or churchwarden. In London, the first attempted reformation of manners therefore largely failed. We have already noted the thriving Elizabethan, Jacobean, and Restoration public theater. In 1616 London boasted thirty-one *authorized* bowling alleys, fourteen tennis courts, and forty gaming houses; who knows how many more operated under the radar? Two years later it had at least 5 or 6 theaters and 400 taverns, ten times the number allowed by the 1553 statute. During the Puritan regime of Oliver Cromwell, dancing, provocative fashions, and Christmas celebrations were banned but came back again with a vengeance at the Restoration.

From 1660, most of the legislation restricting entertainment and festival (as opposed to printing) was repealed or ignored, leading to an explosion of both, taken advantage of by the likes of Samuel Pepys. The 1690s, however, saw the renewed dislocations of war, economic depression, an upsurge of poverty, and clerical complaints about the "licentiousness of the times": all led to a revived reformation of manners movement. This time it was supported by Queen Mary II and later Queen Anne, as well as both High and Low Church clergy and justices. In general, the movement concentrated on spreading the gospel and stifling profanity, immorality, and the lasciviousness of the stage. In particular, the Society for the Reformation of Manners, founded in 1691, declared war on what it considered to be the most objectionable aspects of metropolitan culture. Members patrolled the streets identifying Sabbath breakers, blasphemers, drunkards, and prostitutes, encouraged constables to apprehend them (prosecuting between 200 and 900 prostitutes alone a year), and published lists of offenders known as the "Black Rolls." Clergymen like Jeremy Collier (1650–1726) railed from the pulpit and press against the licentiousness of the theater. The theater reformers succeeded for a time, as the Lord Chamberlain's Office cracked down on the comedy of manners, stifling the work of playwrights like William Congreve and George Farquahar (c. 1677–1707). But none of these movements succeeded in eliminating maypoles or brothels, especially from London. Rather, local London communities seem to have resented manners informers as busybodies. After 1725, prosecutions by the Society declined sharply.

Why did reform fail? The obvious reason is that it is impossible to stop great masses of people from doing what they like. We know this from the testimony of upper-class participants like Pepys and Boswell, but it was "the rabble" that kept the doors open and often attacked arresting officers. In a world that stressed hierarchy and control, it was perhaps inevitable that many would persist in pastimes that allowed them freedom, relaxation, and enjoyment. But proscription and regulation also failed because of structural factors specific to early modern London. First, it was too big to control given the part-time nature of metropolitan law enforcement. City constables and parish officers were overwhelmed by the task: they had to seek out offenders and look out for such establishments on their own time. There were simply too many venues, too many offenders, and too few officers. Moreover, if enforcement was less than strict, it was in part because the would-be enforcers often had a vested interest in keeping the taverns and brothels open. Just as the medieval Church derived handsome profits from such establishments on their land, so did the aristocrats and courtiers who succeeded them as London's landlords. For example, when Covent Garden declined into an assemblage of brothels, bagnios, and Turkish baths in the middle of the eighteenth century, its rents flowed just as freely into the pockets of the Duke of Bedford as had those paid by more respectable tenants a century earlier. On a lower social level, JPs and constables could do very well for themselves by obstructing a prosecution or warning brothel keepers of a raid. At the turn of the century, Bernard de Mandeville (1670–1733) argued in *The Fable of the Bees, or, Private Vices, Public Benefits* (1714) that the money spent on shady pleasures was good for the nation's economy. Finally, as *The Spectator* implied earlier, Londoners resented the sheer hypocrisy of the Reformation of Manners movement: according to Defoe, "Your annual lists of Criminals Appear/But no Sir Harry or Sir Charles is here." Ordinary Londoners voted with their feet, crossing the blurry line between elite and popular culture, respectable and illicit amusement repeatedly.

6. The People on the Margins

$\mathscr{T}$he challenges faced by metropolitan London's governors – the perennial concerns of cities everywhere, such as poverty, crime, crowd control, disease, fire, and the maintenance of order generally – became more complex as the population increased. These problems were probably as old as the city itself, but their growing scale stretched the existing governmental system to the breaking point. Among these challenges, poverty and crime became particular obsessions for Londoners, partly because they seemed to contemporaries to go hand in hand.

THE PROBLEM IN MACROCOSM: THE LONDON POOR IN AGGREGATE

There are two ways to examine any great human problem: from the macroscopic point of view of statistics and policy, and from the microscopic, that is, its effect on individual people. As with most such problems, poverty engulfed people in a situation created by massive forces and long-term trends beyond their understanding, let alone their control. In the case of early modern English men and women, much depended on the demand for, and supply of, labor. For two centuries after the appearance in England of the Black Death in 1349, the resulting population shortage meant that agricultural labor was in relatively high demand, all the more so because the English cloth trade was usually vibrant. What we would today call "unemployment" seems to have been fairly minimal and manageable in the later Middle Ages.

Moreover, there was a long-standing medieval Catholic tradition of providing for the poor. Theologically, the poor were regarded not only with pity but also with a certain amount of benevolent approval, even affection. Unfortunate in this world, their humble lot virtually guaranteed salvation in the next. Indeed, the prayers of poor people were thought to be especially efficacious, which is one reason that they were popular guests at Catholic funerals: in return for their prayers, the deceased often bequeathed them gifts of food, gloves, or other alms, or if wealthy enough, endowed whole monasteries and almshouses. These acts of posthumous charity were intended to relieve the benefactor's soul of time in Purgatory. This helps to explain why London had so many religious foundations. Prior to the Reformation, the metropolis boasted a network of monasteries, priories, hospitals, and guilds that provided assistance to the poor and the sick, including St. Bartholomew's in Smithfield; St. James's, Westminster (a leper hospital that was the predecessor of St. James's Palace); St. Katherine's east of the Tower; St. Mary Bethlehem (Bedlam, for the mentally ill) and St. Mary Spital, both north of Bishopsgate; and St. Thomas's in Southwark.

By the sixteenth century, many of these institutions seem to have been in a state of decline, but it was the Reformation that delivered the coup de grâce. One of the major tenets of the new Protestant theology was the elimination of Purgatory and therefore the idea of praying for the souls of the dead; behind this was the idea that no human being could ever merit salvation through anything he or she did, including the performance of charity and other good works. This did not mean that the English people stopped being charitable: indeed, historians now realize that private charity to schools and almshouses continued unabated throughout the period. In London it rose 54% in real terms by the end of Elizabeth's reign, raising twice as much money as the Poor Rate in the 1590s. A century later, the charity school movement endowed 132 educational institutions for London's poor by 1734. But Protestantism did remove the theological underpinnings from older endowed institutions like monasteries, chantries, hospitals, and schools, helping to justify three waves of royal confiscation in 1536, 1539, and 1547/48. These measures fundamentally altered both landowning and charitable patterns in London, replacing Church landlords with the Crown and later their nobles and favorites, while eliminating the chief providers of social services to the city's populace.

Just as the Reformation swept away the Church's social safety net, the problem of poverty was growing worse. As we have seen, the principal reason for this was demographic. The population of England was already expanding before this book begins, from about 2.3 million souls in 1500, to 3 million in 1550, and then 5.2 million in 1650. In a modern economy, a rising population is a stimulus for demand and therefore economic growth. But the Tudor economy was not flexible enough to absorb the added numbers: land was not being cleared fast enough, the cloth industry stagnated, and there were no other industries of a sufficient scale to absorb the added labor. As a result, more and more workers competed for too few jobs on farms or in towns, too many renters for too few cottages, and too many mouths for too little food. So England's demographic expansion produced a decline in real wages between 1550 and 1650 as the labor market flooded and landlords raised rents and prices on food. Admittedly, the average annual rate of inflation of prices was low by modern standards, between 0.05 and 2% a year. But since most workers' wages were not rising at all, even such minimal inflation meant a relentless, inexorable decline in real wages. The result, exacerbated by mid-Tudor recoinages and wars that raised taxes and hurt trade, was a slow-going disaster for those with modest incomes such as husbandmen, cottagers, and laborers. A series of bad harvests such as occurred in the mid-1590s could force them first to go into debt, then to sell their land and become cottagers, and finally to "break" (i.e., go broke) entirely and join the ranks of landless laborers. It has been estimated that at the end of the Tudor period something like 10% to 20% of the general population could not meet their expenses out of their income.

For many, the next step was to hit the London road in search of work. They often failed to find it, not least because of the stagnant wool trade. In any case, whether tramping through the City gates or congregating on its street corners, the new poor were highly visible and deeply disturbing to those unused to seeing so many masterless men and women. Recall that by 1600 nearly 6,000 new faces were appearing on the streets of London every year. Starting in the mid-sixteenth century, official records betray ever-greater alarm at the rising tide of humanity. Parish vestries complained to the City authorities, and City authorities complained to the king. For example, after the confiscations of 1538/39, the lord mayor and aldermen petitioned Henry VIII about the loss of monasteries and hospitals, leaving "the poor, sick, blind, aged and impotent persons . . . lying in the street, offending every clean person passing by with their filthy and nasty savours."[1] The plight of abandoned children, increasingly common in a city full of migrants and young people forbidden to marry, was especially heartrending: in 1587 John Hawes lamented how the "manye lytle prettie children, boyes and gyrles, doe wander up and downe in the stretes, loyter in Powles [St. Paul's], and lye under hedges and stalles in the nights."[2] Poignant as these stories were, even Tudor officials recognized that they were anecdotal evidence. At the dawn of the Age of Reason they also tried to get a handle on the problem – and provide compelling evidence of their plight to the Crown – by counting the poor. A survey of poverty in 1552 found 2,100 City residents in need of relief: 300 orphans, 600 sick or elderly, 350 "poor men overburdened with theire children," 650 "decayed householders," and 200 vagrants without employment. The problem would get worse. A 1595 survey, in the middle of four years of high food prices, listed 4,014 City householders as needing relief. Three years later one contemporary bewailed "the poor and miserable people within this city who for want of food and like do daily perish."[3]

Shocking as this testimony might seem, these numbers represent only a small percentage of the metropolis, which by 1600 amounted to about 200,000 souls. Admittedly, the size of the problem also depends on how one defines poverty or more specifically, whom one categorizes as "poor." London authorities spent much time labeling people as vagrants, prostitutes, or lewd people – but this might tell us more about their worldview and their need to fit people into it than about the lives of those so labeled. Ian Archer, extrapolating from the surveys of a few Elizabethan parishes, suggests that perhaps 14% of the metropolitan population was poor, defined as the working poor who needed only an occasional handout to keep going and the destitute reliant on parish relief. Other historians have looked at tax records, because the working poor were often made to pay at reduced rates and the destitute were absolved of payment altogether. Broken down by district or parish, these records make clear that poverty rates varied across the metropolis. For example, the 1664 Hearth Tax returns indicate that most City residents (i.e., within the twenty-six wards) could pay some tax, but in some western suburbs nearly a quarter could not do so. In outlying suburbs to the north like Aldgate, Shoreditch, and Shadwell, those unable to pay amounted to 50%, in eastern Whitechapel, 70%.

Clearly, the problem of poverty looks very different depending on where in London one looks. Even these averages obscure the fact that poverty often existed cheek by jowl with wealth. This makes perfect sense: out-of-house servants lived near their masters, and beggars targeted the rich. We have already noted the colonies of thieves and beggars in Westminster (see Chapter 1). As soon as Covent Garden was built in the 1630s there were complaints of nearby slums; as the rich moved west, the slums moved with them. We would expect 18.6% of the householders of Southwark to need occasional relief and 7.4% to be utterly destitute according to a survey of 1622. It is more surprising to learn from a survey of 1603 that the comparable numbers for the fashionable West End suburb of St. Martin-in-the-Fields were 18.8% and 7.9%.

To make matters worse, after the Reformation many Londoners felt threatened by the poor. The jobless, hanging about church steps and street corners by day, roaming the streets and alleys at night, were regarded as vagrants and potential criminals, masterless men and women who, by dropping out of the Chain of Being, threatened the social order. In 1601, the lord mayor ordered a crackdown on "the great numbers of idle, lewd, and wicked persons flocking and resorting hither from all parts of this realm, which do live here and maintain themselves chiefly by robbing and stealing."[4] They were greatly feared – and why not when an early seventeenth-century vagrant like Edward Mopine could tell the lord mayor "it was a good dede [deed] to knock out the braynes of those that apprehended rogues"?[5] The clash of haughty rich and abject poor jostling each other on London's streets could be incendiary, sparking insults and bloodshed. It is thus not surprising that official records from the period from 1580 to 1630 convey an air of crisis. Everyone from the Crown and Privy Council down to the lowliest vestryman worried that the "overflow of people . . . [of the] meaner sort . . . [can] hardly be fed and susteyned or preserved in health or governed."[6]

The Problem in Microcosm: To be Poor in London

What of the individuals caught up in this vast socioeconomic tide? As in any city, one does not have to look far to find them. The streets of London were full of poor people, both the working poor and the utterly destitute. Thus in the early 1760s, at the beginning of another downturn in the metropolitan economy, James Boswell frequently encountered beggars and other characters, such as this patron of a London pub:

> Close by the fire sat an old man whose countenance was furrowed with distress. He said his name was Michael Cholmondeley, that he was a day-labourer but out of work, that he had laid out a penny for some beer, and had picked up a bit of bread in the street which he was eating with it. . . . He then told me he was a sad dog in his youth, run off from his friends to London, wrought here some time, and at last, wanting money, he had sold himself for a slave [indentured servant] to the [American] Plantations for seven years . . . [for £20].

In fact, Cholmondeley had liked his life there; it was only on his return to London after a period at sea that his lot turned sour "and often, even in severe weather, [he] has been obliged to lie in the streets."[7] The sight that this conjures up will be familiar to any modern urban dweller, but Cholmondeley's story further reminds us that, in the early modern period, poverty was often simply a consequence of old age, that is, of having outlived one's ability to do hard physical labor.

Imagine being poor. Imagine being compelled to leave your home in the village, taking to the roads and arriving in London, bereft of means and relatives, circa 1600. Imagine that you cannot afford even one night in a fine inn; in its absence, you will have to forgo the postal and employment services that might have kept you in contact with your old world and helped you to make your way in your new one. How could you "make shift" to live? For poor, unskilled laborers of both genders, menial service was probably the most common choice; the trick was to catch a gentleman or a prosperous tradesman when he needed a porter, a chambermaid, or a cook. If a man, you might head for St. Paul's, to that column in the nave famous as a hiring point for potential masters and servants, or to the nearest street corner to hire yourself out for construction work because there always seemed to be new building in London. Poor women, if they had a dwelling, took in lodgers, washing, spinning, or sewing, set themselves to wet-nurse, or took in children from the parish. If you lacked lodging, you might go door to door offering ad-hoc cleaning as a charwoman. You might apply to be a barmaid or be taken up by a mother midnight. Others hawked fish or fruit or chapbooks or toys on the streets, told fortunes, or entertained as street musicians and ballad singers. Children became linkboys, shoeblacks, or chimney sweeps. Londoners associated street people with crime, conning, and loose living. Thus John Reeve stopped on a pleasant spring evening in 1722 "to hear the ballad singers in St. Paul's Church Yard between 9 and 10 at night" – and had the wig box stolen from under his arm.[8] The authorities thought fishwives an especial problem, so they faced incessant hounding.

If you found accommodation, it might not be very sheltering. London grew so fast that buildings were thrown up or subdivided hurriedly, which explains their unfortunate tendency to collapse. When cheap housing stayed up, it was crowded. A 1582 survey of St. Margaret Westminster, in the very shadow of the court, found for example that the Catherine Wheel, possibly a former inn in Tothill Street, had been divided into seventeen tenements with a total of fifty-three lodgers. A 1637 survey found a ten-room tenement in Silver Street near the wall occupied by "10 several families, diverse of which also had lodgers"; another house in riverside All-Hallow-the-Less contained eleven married couples, seven widows, and eight unmarrieds.[9] The worst districts were all beyond London's ancient wall. Circa 1600, these included, going clockwise, Gray's Inn Road to Bunhill Fields, Clerkenwell, Shoreditch, and East Smithfield to the north; St. Katherine's, Wapping, and Stepney to the east; Rotherhithe to the south and east; and upper Westminster and St. Giles's to the west. To offer a more specific example, in the mid-seventeenth century, the parish of St. Botolph Aldgate, just northeast of the wall, filled up with tenements built five and six stories high along narrow alleys and sunless courts, like Red Lyon Alley, with twenty or thirty units crammed in, all at a rent of between £1 and £3 a year. By the eighteenth century, the areas around Holborn and St. Giles's to the northwest, Spitalfields to the northeast, and the docklands of the East End had the highest concentrations of poor slums.

If all else failed, you could beg. The practice had been outlawed by statute in 1601, yet beggars were everywhere in early modern London. Strangely, not everyone seems to have noticed them. Samuel Pepys, for all his interest in street life, hardly ever mentions being accosted by beggars. The following passage from the *Diary* is nevertheless helpful. It reminds us that there was no age of entry to being poor, that the category included many working poor, that a gentleman such as Pepys could command the assistance of nearly any poor Londoner, albeit probably for a small fee, and finally, that poor people "made shift" by means of an ingenious underground economy:

> So homewards and took up a boy that had a lanthorn, that was picking up of rags, and got him to light me home. And had great discourse with him how he could get sometimes three or four bushels of rags in a day, and got 3*d.* [pence] a bushel for them. And many other discourses, what and how many ways there are for poor children to get their livings honestly.[10]

In fact, there was an entire market, Rag Fair in Smithfield, to facilitate this makeshift economy.

Male beggars most commonly chose their stations at busy street corners, the doors of churches and palaces, and the stiles that formed the entrances to squares like Covent Garden. Women, the majority of London beggars, tended to go door to door (see Illustration 6.1). Many, like Cholmondeley, had a compelling story to tell, whether true or no: recently historians have stressed that, just as the authorities manufactured identities for the poor, labeling them to fit their preconceptions, so did the poor find it necessary to forge compelling competing *personae*, fitting more positive preconceptions, by sympathetic stories and appearances. According to a cynical observer from 1729:

> If any Person is born with any Defect or Deformity, or maimed by Fire or any other Casualty, or by any inveterate Distemper, which renders them miserable Objects, their Way is open to London, where they have free Liberty of shewing their nauseous Sights to terrify People, and force them to give Money to get rid of them.[11]

In fact, there was a repertory of pitiful stances and demeanors, gambits and supplications well known to long-time practitioners. Because beggars with children were effective sources of sympathy, they might be rented or loaned – one temporary solution to the problem of unwanted youngsters. All of this implies organization and teamwork; indeed, older beggars sometimes taught younger ones the ropes or helped forge passports and other papers. Beggars occasionally worked or bedded down in groups. Londoners on the margins could thus sometimes rely on each other for crucial knowledge about survival on the streets and presumably to alleviate some of the coldness and loneliness to be found there. Perhaps here, as in the alehouse, one might find an alternative society to that of respectable London.

Often, respectable Londoners were annoyed: in 1700 an anonymous pamphleteer complained:

> The number of Beggars increases daily, our Streets swarm with this kind of People, and their boldness and impudence is such that they often beat at our Doors, stop Persons in the ways and are ready to load us with Curses and Imprecations if their Desires be not speedily answer'd.[12]

But others were moved to pity. Thus Boswell responded to Cholmondeley's story, above: "I paid for his meal and gave him a penny. Why such a wretched being subsists is to me a strange thing."[13] Boswell's interactions with Michael Cholmondeley also illustrate the difficulties with such spontaneous charity and the culture clash that could ensue when the two worlds met. Anyone who gave money might wonder if it were used for the purposes for which he gave it, or whether, with so many clamoring for a handout, any one particular object of charity was the most worthy. In fact, the poor themselves seem to have imbibed the distinction between deserving and undeserving; the following passage tells us a little of their culture and worldview.

> ... upon Thursday I went to Michael Cholmondeley and gave him four shillings, three from the Kellie family and one of my own. The creature did not seem so thankful as I could wish. An old woman who stood by (for I gave him it in a little court) grumbled that I might have bestowed my charity better, and presently a young one said that people who had both been worthless and would be idle should not be encouraged. Michael's choler rose, he raged in blackguard exclamation. The young jade said that he had fifty wives or thereabouts, and such as encouraged him would choose to have the like. By this time a number of miscreants was gathered round us. I was sorely beset, and stood like the unhappy stag at bay, considering how it should come about that I should be thus rendered uneasy when in the exercise of that most Christian grace, charity.

Boswell attempted to defend himself by articulating a modern, enlightened view of charity:

> "You see," said I, "this poor old man. We shall not dispute whether his conduct has been good. But you see him ragged, hungry, and cold; and surely I did right in trying to relieve a fellow-creature in such circumstances." I then stole away slowly from them.[14]

Civic Remedies

Not everyone was as sympathetic as Boswell. The early modern period largely predates the modern understanding of economics, and so almost nobody grasped the connections among population, demand, and unemployment. Rather, those who made policy assumed that, apart from the lame, the sick, children, or the elderly, any able-bodied poor man could work if he wanted to do so. Those who did not work were obviously shirkers – or worse. Thus, when the government of Henry VIII attempted to take some responsibility for the poor who could no longer go to monasteries, the first Poor Law of 1536 distinguished between the "deserving" or "impotent" poor, that is, those unable to work as noted previously, for which relief was to be supplied by voluntary subscriptions, and the able-bodied souls who apparently refused to work, popularly known as "sturdy beggars." Their seeming refusal suggested that they were lazy, shiftless, and probably up to no good. According to popular myth, they went about the country in roving bands, robbing, assaulting, and in general intimidating honest, respectable folk. Therefore, the proper governmental and social response to the poverty of sturdy beggars was punishment.

In fact, as early as 1495 Parliament ordered beggars placed in the stocks for three days, whipped, and then sent back to their home parishes.[15] The Vagrancy Act of 1547 (1 Edw. VI, c. 3) designated anyone leaving his or her home parish or refusing to work a "vagrant," to be branded with a "V" and enslaved for two years. This law was unenforceable and soon repealed, but previous draconian legislation stayed on the books. In 1572 Parliament ordered vagrants to be whipped and bored through the right ear as a punishment for a first offense, taken into service or branded a felon for a second offense, and hanged for a third. Many communities refused to enforce such harsh punishments, but as a last resort London did: between 1572 and 1575 the Middlesex JPs branded forty-four vagrants, put eight to service, and hanged five. The death penalty for vagrants was abolished only in 1597.

The authorities had other, somewhat less draconian, strategies at their disposal. As we have seen, the Privy Council attempted to restrict new and subdivided building, and it periodically ordered the City to crack down on inmates, vagrants, big-bellied (i.e., pregnant but unmarried) women, idle and loose livers, bawds and pimps, nightwalkers, bear baitings and bowling alleys, and so forth. The reformation of manners campaigns of the early 1590s filled Bridewell to capacity. Still, vagrants could evade the crackdowns by fleeing to the suburbs, which were always short of constables. In the mid-seventeenth century, John Graunt complained that in the "greater out-parishes ... many of the poor parishioners through neglect do perish and many vicious persons get liberty to live as they please, for want of some heedful eye to overlook them."[16]

Fortunately, there was a countervailing tendency in dealing with the so-called deserving poor. First, the parliamentary acts of 1572 (14 Eliz. I, c. 5) and 1576 (18 Eliz. I, c. 3) allowed for certain legitimate conditions (migration for farm work; discharge from service) that excused, temporarily, the able-bodied unemployed from the harsh penalties noted earlier. Second, they made support of the deserving poor compulsory by a local tax on parishioners which came to be known as the *Poor Rates*. These were to be administered by local justices assisted by churchwardens who collected them and overseers of the poor who distributed them. In London, funds from wealthy parishes were shared with poorer ones – a recognition that conditions in the neediest parishes had consequences for the whole city. The funds subsequently distributed, averaging about sixpence a week per recipient in London circa 1580, were known as "outdoor relief": that is, poor parishioners could receive aid and stay in their own houses as opposed to going to the parish almshouse or workhouse ("indoor relief"). Although this was more than people received in the country, it was still only about one-half of what a single poor woman required to live, and there were few or no cost-of-living adjustments. We know little of the attitudes of those on the receiving end, although it is suggestive that Moll Flanders regards "going on the parish" as a last resort. Others seem to have regarded it as a right. To demand it, you literally knocked at the vestry door of the nearest parish church. There, the churchwarden would look you up and down to try to determine if you were a deserving object of charity. For once in early modern England, female gender was a positive advantage – but only if you were alone. An unwed pregnant woman or a single mother with children was generally unwelcome because of the additional mouths that the parish would have to feed. Some parishes provided a childbed to expectant mothers, but others shunted them to the next parish, sent them to Bridewell for a whipping, or paid them sixpence to get lost.

The hard times of the 1590s resulted in further parliamentary statutes of 1598 (39 Eliz. I, c. 3) and 1601 (43 Eliz. I, c. 2) authorizing parishes to erect dwellings for the infirm and provide schooling or purchase apprenticeships for poor or orphaned children. But most parishes required residence for at least three years before they would entertain an application. Finally, the Act of Settlements and Removals of 1662 (13 & 14 Chas. II, c. 12) allowed overseers of the poor, with the approval of a local JP, to ship the impoverished back to the parishes of their birth if they were not apprenticed or occupying a tenement renting for at least £10 a year. The result, when it did not discourage applications for relief, was a constant trafficking of poor people across parish boundaries: the poor, seeking a generous parish; less generous parishes, desperate to avoid an increase of their tax burden, sending the poor away, possibly employing informers, constables, and churchwardens to escort pregnant mothers, even those in labor, to the parish next door. Neighboring parishes sometimes posted guards to prevent such dumping. Parish vestries increasingly used the bestowal or withholding of poor relief as a means of social control. Those who received it and were housed in parish almshouses or were paid pensions out of doors had to behave well and wear badges.

Finally, what of those who were too poor, too sick, unknown to the parish, or too badly behaved for outdoor relief? The petitions by the lord mayor and aldermen noted earlier in the chapter persuaded the government of Edward VI to sell the hospitals of St. Bartholomew's, Christ's, St. Thomas's, and St. Mary Bethlehem to the Corporation of London. In addition, Edward VI granted the otherwise unsuitable Bridewell Palace to the City in the hope that it might be used to aid the poor. Thus, between 1546 and 1553 a cooperative system of five hospitals was created to deal with the City's social problems: St. Bart's and St. Thomas's for the sick north and south, respectively; Christ's for orphans and abandoned children; Bethlehem (Bedlam) for the insane; and Bridewell for vagrants, ill livers, and the deserving poor. Altogether, some £60,000 was poured into the endowment of hospitals after the abolition of Church-run charity in the mid-sixteenth century. Because this was a Protestant initiative, Mary I was hostile. She refounded the Savoy Hospital on the Strand in 1556 for the poor on the site of yet another ruined palace, but because of mismanagement, it was the least successful London hospital. In any case, being west of Temple Bar, it was never part of the City's social safety network. Once Elizabeth I ascended the throne in 1558, the Protestant foundations were secure.

Of these foundations, the most innovative and imitated was Bridewell. The answer to those who thought parish outdoor relief too generous was the Act of 1576, which authorized parishes to put the homeless poor, including sturdy beggars, into workhouses. Bridewell became the model and eventually the generic name for other workhouses, including the "Rounde House" of St. Margaret Westminster and its successor in Tothill Fields (1622), St. Martin-in-the-Fields (1604), Clerkenwell (1614), and Bishopsgate (1699). By the 1720s most parishes had access to a workhouse. Their governing boards thought that the poor could be reformed through work, and that they should repay the community with their labor. Workhouse inmates cleared ditches, spun thread, beat hemp, threaded beads, and made buttons, gloves, nails, pins, caps, hats, and tennis balls from dawn into the night, with Sunday off for worship. During the Civil Wars, when London was ruled by Parliament, Puritan leaders initiated another scheme to put the impoverished to work, entitled the Corporation of the Poor, which they would revive in 1698.

These initiatives were as much about saving the soul as saving the body. The poor were to be improved as well as fed, corrected as well as preserved. This explains why some contemporaries called Bridewell a hospital; others called it a prison. Most inmates knew what to call it. Stays in Bridewell might involve whipping and hard manual labor, but they were rarely long, usually lasting three days to a week. In the workhouse, families were broken up, husbands separated from wives, parents from children. Infants were sent into the country to be wet-nursed. A parliamentary commission of 1767 inspired by the philanthropist Jonas Hanway (1712–1786) found that only 7% of workhouse infants survived three years, and those who did were often sold into apprenticeships. Their masters viewed them as cheap labor and put them to hard, menial work as chimney sweeps, or hawking milk or fruit on the streets, making stockings, or domestic service. Teen-aged and adult males might be drafted into the army or navy. Alternatively, from 1618 homeless boys and girls and adult vagrants, thieves, and troublemakers might be transported to the American colonies. Officially, these arrangements were voluntary, but the pressure to agree was great; refusal might mean continued incarceration. In 1638, Geffray Mynshul (1594–1668) described Bridewell as "a grave to bury men alive" and "a little world of woe."[17] Indeed, poor conditions, an intensification of those in the slums, made protracted workhouse stays deadly. At the end of our period, Hanway called the workhouse for St. Giles-in-the-Fields and St. George Bloomsbury "the greatest sink of mortality in these kingdoms, if not on the face of the whole earth."[18]

The practical goal of institutions like Bridewell was thus threefold: first, to give the poor a usable skill; second, to get them to pay for their own relief; and, third, to make the experience of going to the workhouse so unpleasant that no one would want to resort to it. Neither the workhouse nor the larger poor relief system of which it was a part ever produced the desired result. Rather, the number of poor people and the expense of relieving them continued to rise. Taxpayers grumbled, and those who administered the Poor Law generally served their year without much enthusiasm. Since their accounts were audited by no authority higher than the vestry of which they were a part, dishonesty and corruption could flourish, as was discovered at St. Martin-in-the-Fields in 1714. Funds earmarked for relief might be spent on beer for the churchwardens and overseers; the dead might be added to the lists and their relief funds pocketed; friends might be given lucrative contracts. Above all, the whole system encouraged vestry officials and ratepayers to see the poor as a problem, an expense to be cut. Some parish officials did everything they could to drive the poor away, using the Act of Settlement and Removals as an excuse to reduce their tax rolls. Others were more lax, even welcoming and generous to the unfortunate, but their generosity could not eradicate poverty.

If the Poor Law's combination of carrots and sticks was often cruel and inefficient, it still represents one of the first attempts to provide government relief since Roman times. Its recognition that the nation as a whole had a responsibility to care for its least fortunate members, and that local government should be the state-mandated vehicle for that care, was remarkably advanced for its time, far ahead of anything on the continent. Most of the evidence uncovered by historians about the Poor Law suggests that it operated, like welfare does today, not to create a permanent underclass, but to tide people over who genuinely wanted to work. Most people who came on the poor rolls eventually went off, although they might come back when older or during breaks in seasonal employment. Hypocritical, inconsistent, and inadequate as the Poor Law may seem to modern eyes, it probably did sustain people through a crisis, and it might even have given some poor Londoners a stake in their parish by promising some minimal relief from their neighbors. Still, it is hard to see how London's patchwork of guild and parish communities could have kept up with the influx and outflow of new residents, or how the residents themselves could have provided much neighborliness beyond basic relief. Here, among the homeless and unwanted poor, is where urban anomie may have reigned.

Healing the Sick and Sparing the Child: Health care and Child Welfare 1660–1750

Economic conditions improved in the third quarter of the seventeenth century as both national population growth and inflation slowed down. Famine became a thing of the past after the 1620s. It is true that the wool trade never really recovered, and there were cloth depressions in 1689, 1693/94 and 1696/97. But, as we have seen, other aspects of foreign trade took up the slack in what came to be called the *Commercial Revolution*. Admittedly, the wars of the seventeenth and early eighteenth centuries were hard on the economy. For example, London streets were flooded with demobilized soldiers after Buckingham's wars in the 1620s, the Civil Wars in the 1660s, the Dutch Wars of the 1650s to the 1670s, and again after those with Louis XIV ended in 1713 (157,000 in the last case). Soldiers from the earlier wars established camps in Moorfields, a City manor just north of the wall, harassing officials, ripping notices of vagrancy laws from walls, and roving about in gangs. In the later wars, French privateers disrupted seaborne trade. The 1690s in particular saw very hard times thanks to the Nine Years' War, bad harvests, cloth depressions, and a necessary recoinage in 1695 that wiped out many people's savings. After 1700, despite overall prosperity, ordinary people still lived hand to mouth and faced almost certain poverty as they aged. In London, where opportunity was greatest and wages highest, so were prices: it has been estimated that a working family required £54 10 shillings 4 pence per annum to subsist in 1734. A skilled craftsman might earn £3 a week (£156 *per annum*) in the eighteenth century, but an unskilled laborer was more likely to make 10 shillings a week (just £26 *per annum*), and many unskilled jobs paid even less. Some contemporary commentators feared that the London poor had become a permanent underclass. Rather than seek to eliminate them, they worried about their morals (the Reformation of Manners movement), their health and hygiene, their excessive drinking, and their treatment of children.

Take health, for example. As we have seen, the 1720s saw the rise of cheap gin, far more potent than ale and beer, as Hogarth's famous prints illustrate. The resulting Gin Craze killed thousands into the 1740s. Bad food and water killed perhaps more. Even in the 1750s, Londoners were prone to fevers and agues that often devastated the poor population. Most health care was dispensed within families. What if you became ill and had no family to nurse you? If your condition was temporary, or chronic but not life threatening, you could turn to your livery company or parish. The latter might use Poor Law funds to pay for a nurse, probably an elderly woman herself in need of some relief. Those without even this resource or requiring specialized care could seek admission to one of London's hospitals. As initially established in the Middle Ages, most of these institutions looked after the poor, orphans, and travelers as well as the sick. As we have seen, however, the Reformation had eliminated all but the four largest London hospitals: St. Bartholomew's, St. Thomas's, Christ's, and Bedlam, to which was later added the Savoy. Once refounded, they specialized, the first two for the physically ill, the third for children, the fourth for the mentally ill, and the last for the homeless and wounded soldiers.

The implied degree of coordination notwithstanding, London's hospital network was for the most part overwhelmed by the magnitude of these problems. St. Bartholomew's bed count was supposed to be 120, but hit 180 by 1588; St. Thomas's had a capacity of 100, but rose to 140 by 1561.

By 1634 it was 240 in summer, 280 in winter. St. Bart's' first physician, Dr. Roderigo Lopez (c. 1517–1594), was appointed in 1568 at £2 a year, with a house and garden. He was skillful in gunshot wounds and advice on diet and purging, but was hanged, drawn, and quartered in 1594 on the charge of having tried to poison Queen Elizabeth. Far more distinguished was the career of the celebrated William Harvey (1578–1657), who was chief physician from 1609 to 1633. St. Thomas's got its first physician, Henry Bull (d. 1577), in 1566 at £13 6 shillings 8 pence. Both of these older hospitals also had three surgeons apiece. In contrast, St. George's Hospital, Knightsbridge, a later foundation, housed 250 patients, ministered to by 6 physicians, 3 surgeons, and 20 nurses in 1745.

How good was the medical care dispensed in these institutions? After all, bringing sick people together in an age before antibiotics might seem to make them vectors of disease rather than of cure. Still, even in our period the staffs of these foundations understood some basic principles of good health: they grew herbs for the hospital tables and emphasized fresh air. St. Bart's had medical students on site by 1662 and in 1722 the physicians and surgeons petitioned for a dissecting room and hot and cold baths for the patients. The aforementioned St. George's Hospital was founded in 1733 near Hyde Park Corner specifically so that patients might enjoy the benefits of fresh air:

> ... which in the general opinion of the physicians would be more effectual than physick in the cure of many distempers, especially such as mainly affect the poor, who live in close and confined places within these great cities.[19]

As in Bridewell, and particularly after the Reformation, there was a strong moral dimension to health care: patients were required to attend chapel services or they would not be fed. Although St. Thomas's had long treated the poor prostitutes who worked in the Bankside stews, in 1561 the new Protestant regime turned away unmarried pregnant women on the grounds that the hospital now existed for the care "of honest persons and not of harlottes."[20] Sometimes it is difficult to separate moral rules from hygienic ones: from 1752 St. Thomas's regulations forbade the admission of incurable patients or those with infectious diseases, readmission of any patient for the same disease, or the accommodation of more than one patient per bed. They also specified that inmates could be expelled for suspicious talk, entering wards set aside for the opposite sex, or contracting matrimony. This last reminds us that one of the goals of the London charitable system was to avoid the production of more people who would have to be added to its rolls.

Of early modern London's major hospitals, Bethlehem, shortened in London speech to "Bethlem" or "Bedlam," is easily the most infamous. Founded as a priory in 1247 just outside of Bishopsgate, there was an attached hospital by the mid-fourteenth century. We know that lunatics were treated there within a generation, and this continued to be Bedlam's function when bought by the City in 1547. Robert Hooke designed a beautiful new building for the hospital in 1675/76 in Moorfields, to which London's artistic community also contributed. For example, at the entrance stood two statues by Caius Gabriel Cibber (1630–1700), *Madness* and *Melancholy*, both modeled on inmates. In part because of the art, but mostly because inmates were chained in cells along galleries like animals in a zoo, Bedlam became one of the must-see attractions of early modern London. It was only after our period that the inmates ceased to be put on display, and treatment became more humane.

Christ's, dependent on rates levied on the parishes, took care of 550 to 650 orphans at a time in the late Elizabethan period. Children of freemen received preferential treatment, but 10% of the population were foundlings. Christ's provided an elementary education and sent some inmates off to grammar school; some received vocational training; others were made apprentices. Conditions were not ideal: by 1564 Christ's had admitted 1,916 children, of which 733 had died.

Finally, the Savoy operated like a modern homeless shelter, taking in those without a roof for the night, but it was mismanaged and became associated with corruption and crime. In 1581 Recorder Fleetwood called it the "chief nurserie of evil men."[21] The Savoy was frequently confiscated by the government to treat wounded soldiers.

Astonishingly, these six (including Bridewell) were left to serve the ever-growing metropolis until the early eighteenth century. After 1700 there was an expansion of private charity and a boom in hospital building inspired by Enlightenment ideals and paid for by the wealth from the Commercial and Financial Revolutions. All of the existing hospitals saw significant renovation, and prosperous merchants and professionals contributed to the establishment of new facilities. St. Bart's was rebuilt over the period from 1730 to 1759 according to designs by James Gibbs (1682–1754). The London artistic community got involved: in particular, William Hogarth served as a governor and painted the *Good Samaritan* and *The Pool of Bethesda*, still in the hospital's possession. Toward the beginning of the eighteenth century, St. Thomas's was rebuilt thanks to the generosity of Sir Robert Clayton (1629–1707), a former lord mayor and president of the institution. Thomas Guy (c. 1644–1724), a successful printer and London sheriff who had built a fortune on South Sea Company stock, worked closely with St. Thomas's celebrated chief physician, Sir Richard Mead (1673–1754), to improve conditions. At Guy's death in 1724 he left funds to endow the 100 bed Guy's Hospital across the street from the older institution. In 1744, Guy's added a lunatic asylum. Westminster Hospital was founded in 1715 entirely out of voluntary contributions as the result of a meeting at St. Dunstan's coffeehouse, Fleet Street. St. George's Hospital, Knightsbridge, was founded in 1733, as we have seen. To this were added the London (1740), the Middlesex (1745), and specialized hospitals like the German Street Maternity Hospital (1730) and London Lying-In Hospital (1749); Thomas Coram's Foundling Hospital (1741); the Lock Hospital for venereal disease (1746); and St. Luke's (1751) for the mentally ill.

The new philanthropy and enlightened goals of the eighteenth century, as well as their pitfalls, are perhaps best illustrated by Coram's Foundling Hospital. "Excess" children were a chronic and especially heartbreaking problem in early modern London. As we have seen, they could be viewed as an encumbrance to the poor and a cause for the denial of relief. Many were simply abandoned. Carriers from the countryside often brought children to the city for a fee but might not do more for them: thus, in 1595 eight-year-old William Candy was found crying in the cloisters of Christ's after having been left there by a carrier from Northamptonshire. In 1749 the eleven-year-old Mary Howell ran away to see the fireworks in Green Park for the peace of Aix-la-Chapelle (see Chapter 4). Her experience of "sleeping rough" must have been typical:

> For several nights that I staid in town, I was forced to creep under bulks or any where, to hide myself from the watchmen: and as soon as day brake, I went in to the market, to pick up rotten apples, or cabbage-stalks; as I had nothing else to support nature.[22]

It is fortunate that otherwise callous carriers and desperate mothers seem to have been careful to leave children in places where they might soon be discovered; still, contemporaries tell us that thousands of unwanted infants were left on the streets of London to die.

Thomas Coram (c. 1668–1751) set out to do something about this. Coram was a successful merchant, first in Massachusetts, then in London.

Living from 1720 in maritime Rotherhithe, walking into the City for business, Coram was appalled at the sight of infants abandoned to the streets in the greatest city in the British Empire. Technically, these children were not orphans and had little chance of being accepted to the overburdened Christ's Hospital. Resolving to save them but getting nowhere with Parliament or the municipal authorities, Coram tried the court, specifically the wives of great peers who might have charitable impulses, plenty of free time, and influence (if not control) over their husbands' pocketbooks. It took him seventeen years, but he eventually persuaded twenty-one ladies "of Nobility and Distinction" and their husbands to petition George II to grant a royal charter for the Foundling Hospital. Said to be the world's first incorporated charity, Coram's brainchild opened in some houses in Hatton Garden in 1741 before moving to a permanent site of fifty-six acres beyond London's congestion in Lambe's Conduit Fields, north of the Russell properties.

Almost immediately, the hospital was flooded with demands for places from all across Britain, necessitating some system of selection. In 1742 the directors decreed that on arrival with their children, mothers would pick a ball out of a leather bag. A white ball meant admission for their child; a black ball, rejection; and a red ball, a place on a waiting list should an "admitted" child be turned away as diseased on medical examination. A contemporary print gives some idea of the anguish involved for all concerned: the "unlucky" mothers and children who had been rejected, and the "lucky" ones who were to be separated (see Illustration 6.2). The mothers were required to provide tokens, often a coin split into halves, to be redeemed if the child were ever to be claimed back. The Foundling Hospital Trust still owns many of these tokens, a mute yet poignant testimony to the sacrifice made by these mothers.

Once accepted, children were sent out to wet nurses in the countryside until the ages of four or five. They were then returned to the London facility, separated by gender, and trained in crafts intended to provide useful employment in the world beyond Lambe's Conduit Fields. At the age of fourteen, the boys took up apprenticeships arranged by the directors, and then most entered the armed forces. Girls trained to be lady's maids. The blind children sang in the hospital choir for Sunday services. By 1756, 1,384 children had been admitted. Although 724 (52%) subsequently died, this was a far better survival rate than the parochial alternative. Encouraged by these results, Parliament voted an additional £10,000 in that year so that the hospital could take in all comers. Over the next four years, 15,000 children were admitted, but the hospital was overwhelmed and two-thirds of them died. This led to the restoration of selection. Despite the best of intentions, however, mortality in the Foundling Hospital ran at more than 30% in its best eighteenth-century years.

Like all charitable organizations, the Foundling Hospital was in constant need of support. One fund-raising strategy took advantage of elite Londoners' desire for sociability by holding ladies' breakfasts; on one occasion, more than 1,000 attended. William Hogarth and his wife Jane (c. 1709–1789), with no biological offspring, took in foster children and dedicated themselves to the work of the hospital. Hogarth painted Coram's portrait and came up with a scheme to promote art and benefit the hospital. He encouraged his fellow artists in the St. Martin's Academy to join him in donating portraits to the Governor's Room, turning it into a showcase for their work. Hogarth, Sir Joshua Reynolds, and Thomas Gainsborough were among the contributors. The idea was that members of the upper class would be drawn in to see the art but would also encounter the children and the good work of the hospital, thus further encouraging their generosity. This led eventually to an annual exhibition at a time when artists had few public outlets for their work, which, in turn, evolved into the Royal Academy of Arts, founded in 1768. George Frideric Handel also patronized the Foundling Hospital, writing a Founding Hospital anthem, donating an organ for the chapel, and mounting periodic performances of his *Messiah* for its benefit. After 1749, annual performances at Eastertime became a tradition, and at his death Handel bequeathed an autographed fair copy of the piece to the hospital.

The enthusiasm of some of the greatest artists of the eighteenth century for the Foundling Hospital speaks not only to Coram's vision or even Enlightenment ideals of public philanthropy but also reminds us that, despite its size, early modern London had a remarkable ability to bring together the best and the brightest in common endeavor. Admittedly, Coram's brainchild could house only a few hundred children at a time and so barely made a dent in the problem of infanticide and abandonment, let alone London's poverty in general. But as part of a series of reforms culminating in the 1767 Act for Keeping Children Alive (7 Geo. III, c. 39), it can be credited with helping to lower London's infant mortality rate. Nor should we discount its symbolic importance, because the Foundling Hospital represents the eighteenth-century London mind-set at its best: enlightened, charitable, corporate, and cultured. Still, Londoners also had their own security at heart, because poverty was thought to lead inevitably to crime.

DROWNING IN A CRIME WAVE?

Imagine sitting down to your accustomed brew in Button's coffeehouse, Covent Garden on the crisp morning of January 5, 1706, opening your *Flying Post* and reading this:

> London. We hear that on Tuesday-night last five House-breakers broke into Sir Charles Thorn's House near Bedington in Surrey, and having Jagg'd [gagged] his Servants, got into his Bed-chamber. At their Entrance, Sir Charles fir'd a pistol at them, which unhappily miss'd doing Execution; upon this they bound and jagg'd him, and afterwards one of them attempted to Ravish his Lady; at which Sir Charles being exasperated, with much Struggling he got his hands at liberty, and flung a Perriwig-Block at the Villain's Head; who, in revenge stabb'd Sir Charles, then cut his Throat from Ear to Ear, and left him dead on the spot: They afterwards ransack'd the House, and it's said, carried off to the value of £900 in Money and Plate. The Lady Thorn is so ill by this barbarous Treatment, that her Life is despaired of.[23]

The resultant feelings of shock, horror, and pity, but also perhaps fatalistic indifference, are familiar to any modern urban dweller. As we have seen, Johnson urged his fellow Londoners to "Prepare for Death, if here at Night you roam/And sign your Will before you sup from Home," but clearly even "home" could be a dangerous place. No wonder that, for much of our period, Londoners thought their city a virtual combat zone.

But was it? The obvious place to start to measure the impact of crime on a city and its citizens is by calculating its rate against the size of its population over time. The records of London's criminal courts resist the computation of a simple crime rate, however. Setting aside for the moment the bewildering array of courts (e.g., Old Bailey, Westminster, Middlesex, and Surrey sessions) and jurisdictions noted in the previous chapter, we still find a problem of documentation. It is true that we possess nearly complete records of indictments, but not every accused criminal was indicted (see later discussion). For purposes of calculating a crime rate, it would be far more useful to have a complete series of depositions and examinations, the statements given by accusers, accused, and witnesses to magistrates toward the beginning of the legal process. Because these survive haphazardly, we have no way to determine the number of crimes reported to the JP or constable, but for which no one was indicted. Nor do we know how many crimes were never reported at all, or for which no perpetrator was ever caught – the so-called dark figure of criminal activity. Therefore, when the most distinguished historian of London crime, John Beattie, reports that the Central Criminal Court of the Old Bailey was handling 500 to 600 felonious property offenses a year between 1725 and 1750 (a rate of roughly 1 per 1,000 Londoners), that might represent only a fraction of the number of crimes actually committed. When his figures show spikes in prosecutions for property crimes committed within the City in the 1670s, the 1690s, from 1713 to 1716, the 1730s and 1749/50, that might tell us only that the system was more responsive in those years, not necessarily that more crimes were being committed. For example, we know that periodic expansions in the number of moral offenses being prosecuted had more to do with occasional Reformation of Manners campaigns than they did with Londoners' fluctuating sinfulness (see Chapter 5). The spikes in indictments noted here might indicate genuine crime waves, and they do correspond to contemporary complaints about crime. But they also might reflect more efficient law enforcement in response to those complaints – or even more efficient record keeping. All that we might be counting is the assiduity of court clerks! In short, the quantitative evidence with which to measure the *true* incidence of crime over the course of the period does not exist. As a result, much of the history of crime remains speculative.[24]

Of course, there is plenty of impressionistic and anecdotal evidence about London crime. For example, a 1585 account blames London's growth and "general concourse" for overcrowded courtyards and back alleys that led in turn to "soondry great Murders, Ryottes, Routes, fraies, roberies.... Adulteries and oder [other] incontynente [incontinent] lief [life] ... and many oder the lieke [like] shamefool synnes."[25] A century or so later, newspapers like the *Flying Post* and poems like Johnson's "London" (see Chapter 4) catalogue a litany of assaults, robberies, and mishaps arising from the simple act of venturing the city's streets. Certainly, just as one encountered more people in London than in the village, so the possibilities to perpetrate, or be victimized by, crime increased in absolute terms. Put simply, Londoners *were* murdered, raped, assaulted, robbed, burgled, pocket-picked, conned, and propositioned for sex in greater numbers than could have happened elsewhere in England. Whereas the

Old Bailey was handling 500 to 600 cases of property crime a year from 1725 to 1750, the county of Sussex was dealing with 30, a discrepancy that cannot be explained by differences in record keeping alone.

Property crimes appeared most frequently on Old Bailey calendars and generated the most attention in contemporary sources. Unlike the village, where food was the commodity most likely to be filched, London's commercial activity and concentration of wealth provided motive and opportunity for crimes against all sorts of property, edible and inedible: food, drink, money, cloth, clothes, household goods, watches, jewelry, and so forth. Daniel Defoe's novel *Moll Flanders*, grounded in his keen observations of city life, sometimes reads like a how-to manual, as his heroine recounts in detail her life as a thief: "Our principal Trade was watching Shop-Keepers' Compters [counters], and Slipping off any kind of Goods we could see carelessly laid any where, and we made several good Bargains as we call'd them at this Work."[26] The open-air nature of most London shops and stalls made shop-lifting easy: thus in Leadenhall Market in 1668, Samuel Pepys "did see a woman ketched, that had stolen a shoulder of mutton off of a butcher's stall, and carrying it wrapped up in a cloth in a basket."[27] London's congestion gave ample opportunity to pick pocket, waylay, or con an innocent citizen. Like a city dweller of today, Pepys was fatalistic when in 1663 his wife, Elizabeth, experienced the equivalent of a modern urban smash and grab:

> So home, and there find my wife come home and seeming to cry; for bringing home in a coach her new Ferrandin waistecoat, in Cheapside a man asked her whether that was the way to the tower, and while she was answering him, another on the other side snatched away her bundle out of her lap, and could not be recovered – but ran away with it – which vexes me cruelly, but it cannot be helped.[28]

Theft was far more common than assault, but murder captured the public imagination. Foreign visitors thought the English especially hot-headed, and the evidence of indictments and other court records indicates that when Londoners did kill each other, they did so spontaneously, in the heat of an argument after a few drinks, rather than in cold blood after careful planning. Pepys records several instances of ad-lib violence. One example from 1660, borne of frustration over a London traffic jam, reads like a seventeenth-century version of road rage: "In King-streete, there being a great stop of coaches, there was a falling-out between a drayman and my Lord Chesterfield's coachman, and one of his footmen killed."[29]

Still, murder seems to have been an uncommon occurrence in London. In 1632, the Bills of Mortality list 628 deaths from old age, 1,797 from consumption, and 1,108 from fever, but only 7 murders. More Londoners "made away with themselves" (15) or were killed by "Planet" (13). John Graunt's *Summary of the Bills* for the years 1629 to 1636 and 1647 to 1660 lists the number of murders as exceeding single digits only twice, in 1659 and 1660, when 70 and 20 people respectively fell victim to the breakdown of order just before the Restoration. During these two periods there were slightly more than a dozen poisonings, despite the frequent depiction of that method on the Jacobean stage. Given the size and nature of the metropolis in the seventeenth century, these figures do not seem to indicate a particularly dangerous place.

Still, one possible reaction to the report of the Thorn murder and robbery might be to think that such things *seemed* to be happening more frequently by 1706. Thus, the anonymous author of *Hanging not Punishment Enough* (1701) had "with great Concern for some years last past observed the Lamentable Increase of High-way Men, and House-breakers among us."[30] Contemporaries seemed convinced not only that their city was the very capital of crime, but that they were experiencing a crime wave, especially in the 1690s and the period from 1710 to 1725. One obvious explanation was that this was roughly the period of the two great wars with France, at the ends of which London's streets were filled with demobilized soldiers, trained in violence, poorly paid for their service, and with few job prospects. The aftermath of previous wars (Elizabeth's in 1604, Buckingham's in 1629, the Civil Wars in 1660, the Dutch Wars, especially the one ending in 1668) were also thought to have led to increased crime.

Professor Beattie offers another explanation for the *perception* of a crime wave in Augustan London: the increase in reportage that came with a free press. Londoners had always been fascinated by crime. Beginning under Henry VIII with Robert Copland's (fl. 1508–1547) *Hye Way to the Spyttal-House* (1536), a steady diet of books and pamphlets fed their curiosity about the tricks of thieves and con men. One Elizabethan best-seller, Thomas Harman's *A Caveat for Common Cursitors* (1567), described a whole alternative social structure of vagrants and criminals with its own slang, rules, and occupational hierarchy (e.g., pickpockets outranked cutpurses). The 1590s saw a rash of rogue literature depicting the latest backstreet horror or Fleet Street con. The London depicted in its pages was a veritable Ship of Fools, crewed by lowlifes ready to take advantage of the unwitting newcomer, the careless shopkeeper, or the gullible maid.

One of the most popular plays of the late sixteenth century, the anonymous *Arden of Feversham* (1592), dramatizes the infamous true story of the murder of a prosperous London merchant. Petty criminals figure prominently in Shakespeare's plays, often as the henchmen for ambitious men contemplating crimes against the state. As we have seen, Middleton and Dekker's *The Roaring Girl* (1610) brought to the stage the legendary pickpocket Mary Frith, better known as Moll Cutpurse. Dekker hit this theme again in his best-selling pamphlet guides to London's underworld of 1608, *The Belman of London* and *Lanthorne and Candle-Light*. For those who could neither read nor attend a play, crude woodcuts depicted notorious crimes and gave warning of the dangers of listening to con men – yet another example of the press taking on the role that parents and friends might play in the village.

The volume of material on crime grew after the Restoration and exploded with the end of Licensing in 1695. In particular, beginning in the 1670s and with official blessing from 1678, the Proceedings of the Old Bailey (also known as Sessions Papers) were printed for public consumption. On top of this, the bookstores of London were flooded with breathless popular accounts of the adventures of legendary city criminals, often based on their own testimony as recorded by the ordinary (chaplain) of Newgate just before their hanging. Grub Street stoked popular fears by churning out an endless stream of sensationalist newspaper reports (e.g., that of the Thorn murder) and crime literature, including compendia such as *A Complete Collection of Remarkable Tryals of the Most Notorious Malefactors* (1718–1721) and Captain Alexander Smith's (fl. 1714 to 1726) *History of the Lives of the Most Noted Highway-men, Foot-pads, House-Breakers, Shoplifters and Cheats* (1714). The most famous of these collections, the first *Newgate Calendar*, did not appear until 1774, but it recorded crimes going back to 1700.

No wonder that prominent London criminals, like the thief and escape artist Jack Sheppard (1702–1724), the highwayman Dick Turpin (1705–1739), or the thief-taker Jonathan Wild (1683–1725), became national celebrities and folk heroes. Sheppard was a model for the antihero, Macheath, in John Gay's fabulously popular *The Beggar's Opera* (1728). Macheath is, of course, the original for the Berthold Brecht (1898–1956)–Kurt Weill (1900–1960) and later artists' *Mack the Knife*, and so Sheppard is still being sung in one form or another. Turpin was portrayed in ballads, novels, stage, and film, including more recently the egregious *Carry On Dick!* (1974). Wild was later immortalized in a novel by Fielding and was one of the models for the character Peachum in *The Beggar's Opera* (see later discussion). The reputed "boss" of the London criminal underworld in the first quarter of the eighteenth century, Wild himself took advantage of the new medium of the regular newspaper to advertise his services in recovering stolen goods – which had been filched by his own gang! Yet another implication of the rise of a free press was that Londoners knew more and more about crime as the period wore on. Bombarded as they were, like the modern viewer of cable news, by an endless flood of information from plays, novels, and newspaper stories like that of Sir Charles Thorn's grisly end, it is not to be wondered that readers feared that crime was increasing. The evidence for that increase as bewailed by the author of *Hanging not Punishment Enough?*: "our Sessions-Papers Monthly and the Publick News daily."[31]

LONDON CRIMINALS AND LONDON CRIME

Thanks to Grub Street, the heavily embellished stories of underworld "stars" like Sheppard, Turpin, and Wild naturally dominated the popular imagination and became archetypal. Typically, the London criminal was supposed to be a poor boy who had trouble making ends meet in the big city. The mirror image of Dick Whittington, he either drifted or was forced into a life of crime, often under the baleful influence of a loose or wicked woman. Thus, in both George Lillo's (c. 1693–1739) *The London Merchant* (1731) and Hogarth's *Industry and Idleness* (1747), an apprentice (George Barnwell and Tom Idle, respectively) turns to robbery and murder after consorting with "a common prostitute." In fact, Turpin, Wild, and Sheppard did fall into crime from respectable backgrounds, the last two in the company of women. Having resorted to the criminal life reluctantly, the protagonist of our story should affect the air of a gentleman, treating his victims with courtesy: both Dick Turpin in the 1730s and James MacLaine (1724–1750) in the 1740s became famous in the popular imagination for their almost chivalrous treatment of their victims. If caught, the criminal antihero was expected to perform a daring escape, as Sheppard did repeatedly. Failing that, he should mount the scaffold with either a becoming remorse or a dashing defiance: in fact, Sheppard was charming; Wild, as we shall see, disappointing.

Still, the archetypal narrative clearly had some basis in fact, particularly in showing how circumstances could force poor men and women into illegal activity. Admittedly, the fictional Moll Flanders seems to have been born to a life of crime, having entered the world in Newgate Prison, where her mother was incarcerated. But she too becomes a criminal only later in life, after having been widowed out of a comfortable existence. Her example reminds us that women were particularly vulnerable in the early modern economy, which may explain why they formed one-third of all those accused of property crime. The implication that most criminals were driven to it through necessity or bad company may help to explain why the public, including those who faced many of the same trials and temptations in London, was often surprisingly sympathetic to offenders.

Those temptations were popularly associated with particular times and places. As we have seen, prior to the development of reliable street lighting, Londoners thought the night to have been particularly unsafe: "Prepare for Death if here *at Night* you roam." They also knew, from reading the newspaper, that the most crowded resorts were the most dangerous. Dryden and Johnson warned about London's streets, but you could have your pocket picked in the king's own chapel. Other "popular" places to lose a pocketbook or a watch were St. Paul's, the "Change" (Royal Exchange), the playhouses, the parks, Bartholomew Fair, and of course, any house of drink or ill-repute, where prostitutes were notorious for supplementing their clients' fees with some of their belongings. As seen in Chapter 5, London newspapers are littered with ads advertising watches lost on the steps of such and such a church, while one was exiting the theater or walking in St. James's Park.

Perhaps another reason for the perception of a crime wave in the first half of the eighteenth century is that Londoners were not only more aware of crime, but also of a wider variety of crimes than before. Between 1550 and 1650, they would have heard from their pastor, or read in newsletters or the Bills of Mortality, about treasons, murders, and thefts. Neighborhood rumor would have publicized rape, debt (treated like a crime in early modern law), and the need to beware of con men and prostitutes. After the Civil Wars, however, innovative cons and transgressions, associated with the modern age, began to appear. In particular, the Commercial and Financial Revolutions necessitated new kinds of communication and paper, instruments of credit, and so forth. This led to the possibility of forgery and embezzlement, yet another reason that stock-jobbers were held in such low regard.

London's criminals could be very resourceful in taking advantage of new opportunities for crime and the new media as a tool for enhancing their take. This implies a high degree of planning, which in turn brings us to another historiographical controversy. Was crime in London organized? Elizabethan rogue literature portrayed a thriving alternative underground society made up of gangs of thieves and murderers, mirror images of the guilds, with their own captains, schools, apprentices, language, and rookeries where they were safe from the law. Thus, Robert Greene thought that they "have a kind of corporation, as having wardens of their company, and a hall . . . where they confer of weighty matters touching their workmanship."[32] More than two centuries before Dickens's Fagin and Co., in a 1583 report to Lord Treasurer Burghley, London's recorder, William Fleetwood (c. 1525–1594), describes a sort of criminal apprenticeship and cursus honorum:

> . . . one Wotton a gentilman borne, and sometyme a merchauntt man of good credyte [credit], who falling by tyme into decaye, kepte an Alehowse att Smarts keye [quay] neare Byllingesgate, and after, for some mysdemeanor beinge put downe, he reared upp a newe trade of lyffe [life], and in the same Howse he procured all the Cuttpurses abowt this Cittie to repaire to his said howse. There, was a schole howes sett upp to learne younge boyes to cut purses. There were hung up two devises, the one was a pockett, the other was a purse. The pockett had in yt [it] certen cownters [counterfeit coins] and was hunge abowte with hawkes bells, and over the toppe did hannge a litle sacring-bell [rung at the elevation of the host]; and he that could take owt a cownter without any noyse, was allowed to be *a publique ffoyster*; and he that could take a peece of sylver out of the purse without the noyse of any of the bells, he was adjudged *a judiciall Nypper*. *Nota* that a foister is a Pick-pockett, and a Nypper is termed a Pickpurse, or a Cutpurse.[33]

Liberties like Alsatia, off Fleet Street, were thought to be safe havens for criminal society; in 1601 Sir Stephen Soame (c. 1544–1619) attacked them in Parliament as "the very sink of sin, the nurcery of a naughty and lewd people, the harbour of rogues, theeves and beggars, and maintainers of idle persons; for when our shops and houses be robbed, thither they fly for relief and sanctuary."[34] Some evidence for this assertion is provided by the fact that, where we know locations, almost 55% of the petty criminals sent to Bridewell from 1604 to 1658 were caught in the two Farringdon wards surrounding Fleet Street. Early in the seventeenth century, Richardson's alehouse in St. Mary-at-Hill, the Blue Boar, Thames Street, and assorted alehouses in Southwark were also thought to be popular hangouts for thieves.

A century later, Londoners worried about gangs of highwaymen, like Dick Turpin's notorious Gregory Gang, or Mary Young's gang of pickpockets, as well as youth gangs, such as the aristocratic Mohocks or the plebeian Black Guard. The Mohocks were a group of wealthy young men circa 1712 who purportedly relieved their boredom with swordplay in the streets of London, slitting the noses, cutting off the ears, and rolling the bodies of respectable citizens downhill in barrels. In the 1740s the Black Boy Alley Gang, based in Chick Lane, Smithfield, was said to have had 7,000 members, reputedly controlling much of Southwark and the area around St. Giles-in-the-Fields. People still thought that such gangs provided mutual support and instruction: when Defoe's Moll Flanders begins her training in the "art" of shoplifting, she refers to her mentor as a "school-mistress." As depicted in the novel, pickpockets tended to work together in the streets, and this is borne out by the techniques of Young's Gang. Mary Young (c. 1704–1741), aka Jenny Diver, "one of the most artfullest Pick-pockets in the World," was another London criminal immortalized in the *Beggar's Opera* and *Mack the Knife*.[35] One of her tricks was to fake pregnancy by stuffing a pillow under her dress and then fainting in a public place. This enabled her gang to swoop in and rob those distracted Londoners who came to her aid. Female shoplifters, masquerading as serious shoppers, worked in pairs: while one occupied the shopkeeper by haggling or asking to see more merchandise, her partner filched the goods and hid them in her dress. Finally, London's bawdy houses also necessitated planning and organization.

Historians who have spent time with criminal records (i.e., indictments, depositions) have found little evidence for elaborate criminal societies or long-standing gangs, however. According to William Maitland (c. 1693–1757), the Mohocks were, in fact, an invention of the London press: "This Rumour gaining universal Credit, struck such a Terror among the Credulous and Timorous that at the Approach of Night many durst not stir abroad, for Fear of being Mohock'd," and yet, "it does not appear that ever any person was detected of any of the said Crimes."[36] The Gregory Gang and the Young Gang certainly did exist, but they represented shifting alliances of criminals, coming together and breaking apart as opportunity and necessity dictated, not permanent organizations. Honor soon dissipated among thieves if turning king's evidence could save one's neck.

This was true even of the greatest criminal organization of eighteenth-century London, that of Jonathan Wild. Wild was born in 1682 at Wolverhampton, Staffordshire, to a respectable family of tradespeople. After serving his apprenticeship with a Birmingham buckle maker, he returned to Wolverhampton about 1705, married, and set up in trade. Within two years, however, he abandoned his wife and young son and made for London. Within months, he was arrested for debt and imprisoned in Wood Street Compter. For most people, this would be a career-ending disaster, as it was very hard to pay off a debt from prison; in fact, because there was almost no concept of incarceration as punishment in and of itself in early modern England, debtors were just about the only long-term prisoners in the City's jails. But his first imprisonment made Wild. His quick mind and fluent tongue earned him the respect of both the keepers and the kept, mostly petty criminals and prostitutes. The former gave him the "liberty of the gate," that is, the freedom to come and go, and the office of "underkeeper." From the criminals he took lessons "of the sharping and thieving world."[37] Clearly, London's underworld did have schools: the prisons themselves.

Having completed his "training" and been released in 1712, Wild took up with Mary Milliner, the first of his five London wives, starting off in a house (possibly of ill-repute) in Lewkenor's Lane, moving later to Cock Alley, Cripplegate. Apparently tutored by one Charles Hitchen, a disgraced former City marshal accused of fencing, Wild soon began to establish himself as a dealer in stolen goods. Thus, if the prisons were the nursery of criminals, their professors were not only fellow criminals but also law enforcement officials. Put another way, much of London crime was facilitated by those on the interface with it. It was Wild's genius to exploit this to the full. Audaciously moving house to be near the Old Bailey itself, Wild placed ads in London newspapers offering to find stolen goods. To avoid falling under a 1706 act banning the possession of such goods (5 Anne, c. 31), he undertook never to keep them in his own house and at first charged no fees: he took his cut from the thieves themselves. To show just how honest and respectable he was, he also set up as a thief-taker, that is, handing in the very thieves with whom he was working. For example, in 1716 he was celebrated for apprehending the killers of a lady who had been murdered in the course of a robbery.

Obviously, this was a very delicate balancing act, playing all the principals off against each other – not unlike the way Barbon built houses. Later we address the vagaries of London law enforcement, but in the meantime, a sign of Londoners' powerlessness to avoid crime is that many saw Wild as performing an unpleasant but necessary public service. He became semi-respectable, assumed esquire status, wore a sword, and identified himself in the newspapers as "Thief-catcher General of Great Britain." Thus he was at once an example of how a poor country boy could remake himself in the City, the alternative social structure of the criminal world, and the entrepreneurial possibilities provided by the new medium of newspapers. Soon it emerged that Wild was playing the system, corrupting judges and other law-enforcement officials to secure verdicts of innocence for thieves and pickpockets who were still useful to him, guilty for those who had outlived their usefulness. This continued despite the passage in 1718 of the Transportation Act (4 Geo. I, c. 11), popularly known as the Jonathan Wild Act, which made it a felony to accept payment for stolen goods without prosecuting the thief. In fact, Wild concentrated increasingly on thief taking, encouraged by a proclamation granting a reward of £100 for the conviction of anyone who had committed theft in the vicinity of London, but this was his undoing. In 1724 he went too far when he facilitated the hanging of two of London's most celebrated – and popular – criminals: Jack Sheppard and Joseph "Blueskin" Blake (1700–1724).

Jack Sheppard was a thief who became famous for his escapes from Newgate and other prisons. He was a native Londoner, born in Spitalfields in 1702 to a respectable carpenter and his wife. Educated at Mr. Garret's School, St. Helen Bishopsgate, he was apprenticed in 1717 to a carpenter in Drury Lane. Unfortunately, Sheppard frequented the Black Lion Alehouse, situated nearby in Lewkenor's Lane, one of Wild's old haunts. There he met the prostitute Elizabeth Lyon, who encouraged him in "a train of vices as before I was altogether a stranger to."[38] Sheppard became an accomplished burglar but was more celebrated as an escape artist. One of his greatest escapes, with Lyon, was from the hold of the New Prison in Clerkenwell:

> . . . after he had sawed through his fetters and removed an oak muntin and an iron bar from the window the couple descended 25 feet to the yard below by means of a rope fashioned from a sheet, a blanket, and Lyon's gown and petticoat, and then surmounted a 22 foot perimeter wall.[39]

Like Wild, Jack Sheppard became a media star, but his refusal to join Wild's gang prompted the latter to inform on him, leading to several more incarcerations and a series of spectacular escapes. During his last imprisonment, his jailors made more than £200 by showing him off to visitors (including the ever-inquisitive Daniel Defoe) and he was sketched several times by Sir James Thornhill, the king's serjeant painter. His execution took place before a vast crowd on November 16, 1724; two weeks later, a play about him opened in Drury Lane.

Blake was thought to have been reared in the criminal life by Wild himself before joining Sheppard in highway robbery in 1724. When Wild informed Blueskin, in prison, that he would not lift a finger to help him, his former charge slit his throat, but Wild survived. In both cases, Wild's role in their hangings was viewed as an act of the most cynical betrayal: Londoners expected honor among thieves. In February 1725, in response to public pressure, Wild was finally arrested on eleven counts, including having "form'd a kind of Corporation of Thieves" and of having "often sold human blood, by procuring false Evidence."[40] Convicted in May, Wild's courage deserted him. He avoided the traditional final religious service in Newgate Chapel, fearing insult from fellow thieves whom he had betrayed, and attempted suicide the night before his hanging by swallowing a massive dose of laudanum, which served only to make him violently ill. As a result, his procession to Tyburn and subsequent hanging was anything but the bravura performance that might have been expected. Wild was stoned in both senses of the word, gave no scaffold speech, and was dispatched with a minimum of ceremony.

As should be obvious, Londoners handled metropolitan life by telling stories about it. Despite his whimpering end, Wild's story seemed to capture for contemporaries the depths of their society's corruption. The conniving jailor Peachum in John Gay's "Newgate pastoral," *The Beggar's Opera* (1728), is clearly modeled, in part, on Wild. Henry Fielding's satire, *The Life of Jonathan Wild the Great* (1743), equates his protagonist's amoral and treacherous behavior with "greatness." In both, Wild is conflated with the prime minister, Sir Robert Walpole, to make the point that the world of Westminster politics was no less corrupt than that of London's infamous prison. Each work can be connected with long-standing London genres: Gay's with city drama, Fielding's with Elizabethan satire, both of which harp on trickery and false appearances in London. What is new here is that both draw an explicit parallel between the organized corruption of London's criminal underworld and what many saw as the political corruption at the very top of the Walpole regime, which relied on a patronage spoils system, bribes for MPs, and extensive propaganda to maintain its ascendancy (see Introduction). The very first song in the play is a salvo against the corruption and duplicity of the times, flouting community, and taking the professional specialization we noted in coffeehouses and Mr. Spectator's cronies to vicious extremes:

> *Through all the Employments of Life*
> *Each Neighbour abuses his Brother;*
> *Whore and Rogue they call Husband and Wife:*
> *All Professions be-rogue one another:*
> *The Priest calls the Lawyer a Cheat,*
> *The Lawyer be-knaves the Divine:*
> *And the Statesman, because he's so great,*
> *Thinks his Trade as honest as mine.*

Like the Elizabethan satirists and Puritan preachers a century earlier, both works argue that in London's perverted moral system, white is black, and black, white.

The Beggar's Opera was the hit of the 1728 theater season. When it premiered at Lincoln's Inn Fields, the prime minister was in the audience, and famously and seemingly good-humoredly laughed at the last line of the following song:

> *When you censure the Age*
> *Be cautious and sage,*
> *Lest the Courtiers offended should be:*
> *If you mention Vice or Bribe,*
> *'Tis so pat to all the Tribe;*
> *Each cries – That was levell'd at me.*

London legend has it that Walpole stood up in the theater and loudly repeated the last line, making the audience roar at his ability to take a joke. But his government refused a license for Gay's sequel, *Polly*, in 1729.

London Law Enforcement

Perhaps another reason why some Londoners might have been so fearful of crime and cynical about authority was that, as in the case of disease, the latter had so few remedies for the former. Observers then and now have emphasized that London law enforcement before the nineteenth century was an ad hoc, amateur affair, hardly adequate to the task of policing a great city. To understand the problem, imagine yourself walking the streets of London at midday. As you are strolling down the Strand, you see the crowd bunched up before, say, Temple Bar. Suddenly, you are jostled. Reaching down for your pocket watch, you find it gone. Looking up, you can just make out a head in the crowd moving up Fleet Street rather more briskly than the others. Today, you might pull out your mobile phone to call the police, but in early modern London, not only are there no mobile phones; there are no police. There were two reasons for this. First, professional police forces cost money, and Londoners, already grumbling under the Poor Rates, were in no mood to see their taxes raised. Perhaps more important, however, is that professional police forces, like standing armies, were seen as instruments of state coercion and therefore dangerous to freedom. Contemporaries knew that absolute monarchs like Louis XIV had secret police to spy on opponents, stifle religious dissent (read Protestantism), and seize the property of their subjects. Thus, after our period, the *Daily Universal Register*, the progenitor of *The Times*, thundered that its readers "would rather lose their money to an English thief, than their liberty to a *Lieutenant de Police.*"[41] As a result, London had no professional constabulary until the establishment of the Metropolitan Police, at the instigation of Sir Robert Peel (1788–1850), in 1829. In the meantime, Sir Charles Thorn's fate notwithstanding, neither the English ruling class nor the English people were ready to sell "the rights of an Englishman" for a little security.

Rather, during the early modern period, London's citizens policed themselves under the supervision of the local JP. Thus, the first recourse for the crime victim was to "raise the hue and cry" by yelling the time-honored but today utterly ineffectual "Stop! Thief!" In those days the point of this ejaculation was not, of course, to actually persuade the miscreant to come to a halt, but to alert one's fellow perambulators. If you were fortunate, some of them would take off after the thief: others would know where to find the local constable. Thus, policing the streets was very much a community matter, and there was a great deal of room for maneuver before the law became involved. If there were no fatalities, the victim could choose whether to report the crime to the constable. Sometimes, the crowd in the street acted as arbitrators between the parties. Even in London, good neighbors tried to work things out without resorting to the law, and a crowd could put pressure on one side or another. Alternatively, a passing gentleman like Boswell might intervene. If the crime was egregious, the crowd might set matters to rights on their own by what was sometimes called "the justice of the streets," or, more accurately, "the rage of the streets," by beating the accused, pillaging a dishonest shop, or dowsing a pickpocket under a pump.

Failing the crowd, you hoped for the constable. The City's policing arrangements had been laid down in 1285 by the Statute of Winchester (13 Edw. I, cc. 1 and 4) and the Statute Civitatis of London. Although the City's marshals, established under Elizabeth I, and the ward's beadles were expected to patrol and had wide powers of arrest, the centerpiece of London law enforcement was the night watch, organized on a ward-by-ward basis, in which all householders were obligated to participate. In 1643 there were 543 watchmen in the City, raised to 672 in 1737. About the same number patrolled Westminster and urban Middlesex. Watchmen were supposed to turn up with halberds from 9 PM to 7 AM in winter, 10 PM to 5 AM in summer. After being assembled by the "constable of the night" and inspected by the beadle, they worked in pairs, carrying staffs and lanterns. While one patrolled the beat, the other remained in a designated spot, alternating these duties hourly. After about 1640, London was dotted with watch boxes where the stationary watchman could find some shelter and the citizen could find the watchman. Vagrants, prostitutes, and so forth would be rounded up and deposited in watch houses, that is, small holding jails, for examination by a JP in the morning. Extra watchmen could be added at times of crisis: Wyatt's Rebellion of 1554, the Gunpowder Plot of 1605, or Bartholomew Fair annually. Turbulent wards always had more watchmen: Farringdon Without, containing Alsatia and Fleet Street, needed 130 in the early seventeenth century. For daytime law enforcement, the wards were split into 242 precincts, each with a constable. Every tax-paying City freeman had to serve one year as constable, beadle, and scavenger, and afterwards on ward watch. Westminster's system was like the City's. In 1663 the number of City constables was reduced to just twenty-six (one per ward) and watchmen got pay. From the 1730s, this pay came out of parish rates, which meant that wealthy West End parishes like St. James Piccadilly, St. George Hanover Square, and Marylebone had the best paid and most effective constables.

For the most part, London's constables and watchmen did not have a high reputation. According to one sixteenth-century complainant, the watch was notorious for:

> abusing the time, coming very late to the watch, sitting down in some common place of watching, wherein some falleth on sleep by reason

of labour or much drinking before, or else requireth a rest in the night. These fellows think every hour a thousand until they go home, home, home, every man to bed.[42]

In fact, court records indicate that in the early seventeenth century most constables were respectable citizens drawn from the top third of the tax roles. Increasingly, however, busy freemen sent substitutes, usually the old and unemployable. A century later, wealthy wards like Cornhill still called on solid citizens (i.e., shopkeepers, linen drapers), but poor outer wards were less well served. Absenteeism seems to have been a problem. In the 1720s César de Saussure saw no evidence of a night watch, "either on foot or on horseback as in Paris, to prevent murder and robbery" apart from the bellman or crier:

> The only watchman you see is a man in every street carrying a stick and a lantern, who, every time the clock strikes, calls out the hour and state of the weather. The first time this man goes his rounds, he pushes the doors of the shops and houses with his stick to ascertain whether they are properly fastened, and if they are not he warns the proprietor.[43]

Court records reveal plenty of cases of constables who were incompetent or corrupt, taking bribes, giving advance warning to criminals, shielding (or running) bawdy houses, fencing goods, or exchanging freedom for sex. But it is equally clear that most were trusted figures in the neighborhood who made a significant effort to keep it safe, sometimes undertaking herculean efforts to clear the streets of vagrants, lewd persons, ballad singers, and big-bellied women, or bravely breaking up assaults and burglaries.

Alternatively, wardmote inquests and, increasingly, deputy aldermen could also present offenders to the Court of Aldermen. For moral offenses (i.e., adultery, fornication, nonattendance at services, blasphemy, and some forms of debt) parish officials (e.g., churchwardens and sidemen) could present to ecclesiastical courts, or the victim him- or herself could bring the offender to a JP.

In other words, for most of the period, London law enforcement, at least in the early stages of the legal process, was a local matter in which the community worked together to police itself. This became more difficult as the city grew: while the village or parish community was small and close-knit, London was, as we have seen, a vast sea of people within which one could hide easily. Thus, Moll uses London's maze of streets to evade detection: "I went thro' into *Bartholomew Close*, and then turn'd round to another Passage that goes into *Long-lane*, so away into *Charterhouse-Yard* and out into *St. John's-street*, then crossing into *Smithfield*, went down *Chick-lane* and into *Field-lane* to *Holbourn-bridge*, when mixing with the Crowd of People usually passing there, it was not possible to have been found out."[44] At the same time, she could not count on staying unrecognized for long, because any street crime would be witnessed by scores of people. Thus Moll moves from district to district and keeps her place of residence secret even from her fellow thieves in an attempt to avoid running into the same people twice. It is a tribute to London's vast size and anonymity that these moves are rarely more than half a mile, yet with each one, she assumes a new identity.

Given the difficulties facing the authorities in keeping an eye on it all, Londoners were encouraged to police themselves in yet another way. As we have seen, privacy was hard to come by in the London street, and guilds, parishes, and other authorities paid people to watch each other. Early in the seventeenth century these informers began to evolve into thief-takers, usually thieves themselves, who, in hopes of saving their necks and/or obtaining a reward, informed on other thieves. By the late seventeenth century the City itself increasingly offered rewards to private – and none too respectable – operators like Jonathan Wild, for apprehending criminals and recovering stolen goods. Indeed, thief-takers soon received statutory legitimacy: from 1693 the reward for apprehending a highwayman was £40. This was subsequently extended to coiners, counterfeitors, burglars, and housebreakers.

Thief-takers, inhabiting the hazy margins between the law and the law-less, solicited their rewards by taking out ads for "found" goods, or offering to find "lost" ones. Some hinted at their illicit connections quite brazenly. Take this example from the thief-taker Jack Bonner (fl. 1690–1710):

> This is to give notice that those who have sustained any loss at Stur-bridge Fair last, by Pick Pockets or Shop lifts: If they please to apply to John Bonner in Shorts Gardens, they may receive information and assistance therein; also Ladies and others who lose their watches at Churches, and other Assemblies, may be served by him as aforesaid, to his utmost power, if desired by the right Owner, he being paid for his Labour and Expences.[45]

Londoners seem to have welcomed the chance to recover their property and were only too happy to turn to the services of newspapers and thief-takers in place of the watch, constables, and JPs. Perhaps readers regarded the fees they paid as the price of living and doing business in the metropolis.

The man who did the most to fight the rewards system was Henry Fielding. Readers will know him as the author of picaresque novels like *Joseph Andrews* (1742), *Jonathan Wild* (1743), and *Tom Jones* (1749). If you lived in the fashionable but crime-ridden Bow Street area of mid-eighteenth-century London, which included Covent Garden, however, you knew him as the local justice of the peace, resident at No. 4, two doors down from Will's coffeehouse. In *The Life of Jonathan Wild the Great* he satirized the practice of thief-taking; in *An Enquiry into the Causes of the Late Increase of Robbers* (1751), he attacked the rewards system as "the dirtiest money on earth." As a magistrate, he established a group of six volunteer thief-takers in 1749 that evolved into the Bow Street Runners, a proto-professional police force. At his death in 1754 Fielding was succeeded as justice at no. 4 by his brother John, another vigorous judge, who was knighted in 1761. Although blind, Sir John was said to be able to recognize more than 3,000 thieves from their voice alone. He established foot patrols on main roads in and out of the capital. London continued to tinker with this system until 1829.

If the system worked and the suspect was apprehended, he was brought to the JP, ideally a London gentleman or a prosperous merchant. It was the duty of the JP to interrogate the accuser, accused, and witnesses, and decide, with the concurrence of the first, whether to make out a recognizance to bind them over to appear at the next assizes at the Old Bailey. Because there was no district attorney, the victim of the crime was in effect the prosecutor and had a choice whether to pursue the case and under which statute to do so. The victim or the justice might also undervalue the goods stolen so as to render a felony theft a misdemeanor and so avoid the possibility of capital punishment. In that case the justice might try to resolve the matter out of court, either by delivering summary justice (usually a term in Bridewell or the pillory) or by getting the parties to agree to a settlement. Out of court settlements were especially common for minor property crimes and crimes against the peace (e.g., riot, defamation): in these cases the recognizance would bind the offender to make restitution or keep the peace. Summary justice was also favored in the case of misdemeanors like brothel keeping, unlicensed alehouses, drunkenness, prostitution, and, as we have seen, vagrancy. In some cases an apology or payment of a fine sufficed. Because the victim bore the expense of prosecution, he or she might feel that informal restitution was less troublesome.

In short, while the London policing system might not have been professional, it was flexible, taking individual circumstances and local conditions into account, and, in so doing, could be said to have served the needs of the populace. But as we have seen, toward the end of the seventeenth century, it became harder and harder to draft substantial gentlemen as London and Middlesex JPs. They came to be replaced by petty tradesmen and shopkeepers, "blue-apron men" or trading justices. Precisely because these men were not of independent means, they had to rely on fees to dispense justice, and this led to a reputation for corruption and bribery. A trading justice might be a virtual illiterate, with no knowledge of the law. He might take a bribe to launch a malicious prosecution, grant a license to an alehouse of ill-repute, or keep a brothel open. On the other hand, he might also know his neighborhood and have real sympathy for its inhabitants. To the extent that this was true, London's confederation of communities was not so cold or ineffective.

If both justice and victim-prosecutor agreed to charge a felony, then the suspect was "bound over" (held for trial) and a recognizance and indictment drawn up. At this point, accuser and accused would present their cases to a grand jury, composed of minor but respectable merchants and tradesmen. These representatives of the community determined whether the indictment was a "true bill" and should proceed to trial, or they could render a verdict of "ignoramus" and throw it out. If the latter, the accused went free. If the former, the case was tried at the London assizes in the Old Bailey before a regular or "petty" jury, which would pass judgment of innocence or guilt. It was up to the assize judges to pass sentence, in the case of a capital crime, of mercy or death.

Trial and Sentence: The Greatest Show in Town

Clearly, early modern Londoners lacked much of the modern apparatus for crime detection and law enforcement. All they really had at their disposal were the habits of mind instilled by the Great Chain of Being (weaker in London than elsewhere), community loyalty, and deterrence, the sheer fear of the consequences of breaking the law. It was this last recourse that explains many of the heads posted at the City gates: one foreign visitor counted nineteen or twenty on London Bridge alone in 1661 (admittedly, a banner year for executions because of Civil War treason). Moll Flanders expresses the appropriate "terror of mind" after she commits her first theft: "why, I shall be taken next time and be carry'd to Newgate and be Try'd for my Life!' and with that I cry'd again a long time, and I am sure, as poor as I was, if I had durst for fear, I would certainly have carried the things back again."[46]

The cultivation of such fear, the presumed deterrent effect of capital punishment, only begins to explain a series of remarkable facts that have puzzled historians of English law and crime ever since. First, the number of capital offenses, that is, crimes for which one could be hanged, expanded enormously in England during the second half of our period. Between 1688 and 1820, Parliament raised the number of capital felonies from around 50 to more than 200. In particular, during the hard times of the late seventeenth century, increasing attention was paid to crimes against property: highway robbery, shoplifting, burglary and housebreaking, forgery, clipping and counterfeiting coins. Much of the new legislation stipulated hanging for new offenses like forging of documents, but other new laws raised the stakes to death even for petty theft, shoplifting, or pocket-picking of goods of even very small value. For example, from 1691 receiving stolen goods became a felony (3 & 4 Wm. III & Mary II, c.9); in 1699 it became a capital crime to shoplift goods worth more than 5 shillings, a quarter of a pound sterling (10 & 12 Wm. III, c. 23); in 1713, stealing goods worth more than 40 shillings (£2) from a house became a hanging offense (12 Anne, c. 7).

Traditionally, this tightening of the law has been interpreted as an attempt to deter crime by instilling fear. Indeed, the notices of hangings printed in London newspapers were pretty fearful:

> London, Dec. 19. The Sessions at the Old Baily did not end till Monday last; and it has not been known for many Years, that so many Persons receiv'd Sentence of Death at one time, there being then condemn'd 23 Persons, being 6 Women, and 17 Men, two of which are Richard Keele, and William Lowther, for the late Notorious Riot and Murder of Edward Perry, the late Turnkey at Clerkenwell-Bridewell; 7 for Burglary, 5 for Shop-lifting, 4 upon the late Statute for Entring of Houses, and Stealing Goods above the value of 40s. [shillings] and the rest for several Capital Offences.[47]

Perhaps the most remarkable thing about this sad roll call is that it is reported as being unusually long. Although the number of criminal statutes for which an English man or women could be hanged quadrupled in the eighteenth century, the full extent of the law was rarely applied. Overall, about one-half of those indicted for capital crimes were convicted, but only a fraction of those were put to death. Indeed, the latest research indicates that the number of hangings declined steadily in England as a whole, and London in particular, both absolutely and per capita, from 1550 to 1750. About 150 felons were executed annually in London in the early seventeenth century; this fell after the Civil Wars to 25 a year in the late seventeenth century, then to about 6 a year from 1701 to 1750, before rising again to 25 a year in the 1760s. These numbers are horrific, but they represent a smaller bloodbath than we might expect from a ruling class bent on terrorizing the mob. In fact, Beattie has found evidence of numerous experiments by Parliament, judges, and JPs to come up with effective intermediate noncapital punishments: transportation, military service, committal to Bridewell, and so forth. Why would a nation so fearful of crime pass what has been called the bloodiest criminal code in Europe, and then choose to enforce it so sparingly? Part of the answer might lie in the tension between national policy and local sentiment: contemporaries observed that juries hated to convict on these draconian laws, and most Londoners would probably have agreed with "the simple cuntryman and woman . . . [who] are of opynyon that they wold not procure a mans death for all the goods yn the world."[48]

In the 1970s and 1980s, several historians of the law such as Douglas Hay and Peter Linebaugh offered another answer. They argued that the eighteenth-century legal system's split personality – draconian laws; flexible, even merciful outcomes – was actually a coldly calculated ruling-class conspiracy to intimidate the lower orders using a kind of theater of power that emphasized the law's majesty, justice, and mercy. If so, then the first act of the play was set at Newgate Prison. Newgate might not have been exactly majestic, but as one contemporary wrote of the new, post-Fire building: "the sumptuousness of the outside but aggravated the misery of the wretches within." First, with a capacity of 150, Newgate was always overcrowded, averaging 228 prisoners during the sample period from May 1696 to December 1699. According to the *London Encyclopaedia*, "the wretches within" also encountered the following: "The water supply was quite inadequate, the ventilation almost non-existent, the stench appalling; and during the frequent outbreaks of gaol-fever, a virulent form of typhoid [sic.], the fumes bore the germs of the disease into every cell of the prison." A well-heeled prisoner could alleviate his misery by paying the notoriously corrupt keeper for better accommodation, and for more and better food. But for those with no money, there was the Stone Hold, which one prisoner described as: "a terrible stinking dark and dismal place situate underground into which no daylight can come. It was paved with stone; the prisoners had no beds and lay on the pavement whereby they endured great misery and hardship." Even the poorest inmate had to pay the keeper for food, water, candles, and liquor, as well as other optional sums to be released from his irons or to come near a coal fire in winter. People passing by all of London's prisons and compters were accosted by the sights, sounds, and smells of prisoners at the grates of their underground holds begging "Bread and meat for the poor prisoners." No wonder that Fielding called Newgate a "prototype of hell." If Hay and Linebaugh are correct, it was intended to be so, a psychological weapon in the class war that raged in early modern England, its reputation spread abroad by the numerous pamphlets for sale at London bookstalls retelling the experience as told to the Newgate ordinary.[49]

The law achieved its greatest level of majestic intimidation at trial. London's felony trials took place at the Old Bailey, originally a nondescript Tudor appendage to Newgate. Named for a nearby street, the courthouse burned down in 1666 and was rebuilt in 1673 in a "fair and stately"[50] Palladian style. The Justice Hall was built with one wall open to the elements to increase fresh air and prevent its officers from contracting the "gaol fever" that infested Newgate. This side of the hall opened onto the Sessions House Yard, where attorneys, clients, witnesses, and spectators gathered in a sort of amphitheater; indeed, foreign visitors were impressed with the openness of the proceedings, in contrast to much continental practice. Unfortunately, this made trials more raucous and easily disrupted by spectators who were thought to intimidate juries. It was even alleged that criminals gathered here to anticipate prosecution and defense strategies. When the court was remodeled in 1737 it was enclosed again, resulting in proceedings that were more decorous but also more deadly. The typhus outbreak of 1750 killed 60 people, including the lord mayor and two judges.

Cases were tried in clumps, and individual trials rarely took more than a half hour, allowing an average of 15 to 20 a day circa 1700. The accused stood in the dock facing the witness box, while on the opposite side of the room sat the judge, elevated on a dais – a clear sign of his superiority (see Illustration 6.3). The judge, wearing scarlet robes and a full-bottomed white wig, was a human embodiment of the majesty of the state. If anyone missed the point, he sat under the royal arms. Because it was the victim who prosecuted, making his or her case before the court, lawyers were a rarity; when present they wore black robes and shorter wigs. Jurors sat in boxes to the right or left of the accused until 1737, when they were united in a box to his right. For the accused and possibly for jurors and spectators in the Sessions House Yard, the impressive architecture, unusual dress, arcane legal terms, and even the upper-crust accents of the officers of the court must have seemed alien, even godlike. They would have served to emphasize their distance from those officers – and the officers from normal human concerns generally.

The trial process placed the defendant, already hungry and dirty from living in Newgate, at a disadvantage. For example, while the prosecutor could hire a lawyer, prior to the mid-1730s the defendant was not entitled to counsel and was allowed to call witnesses only at the judge's discretion. Trials were carried on in a technical legal language that must have seemed baffling to novices, although sharp characters like Wild probably picked up its salient points quickly enough. Before the trial began, the accused entered a plea to the charge. The clerk then read the charge, and the victim-prosecutor stated his or her case. Witnesses were called; then the accused made his or her case. In the absence of lawyers, the judge and the defendant performed the cross-examination. There was no presumption of innocence; defendants were expected to disprove the case against them. Before the case finally went to the jury, the judge gave a summation in which he was likely to indicate his own view and give instructions on the law's fine points, all in measured tones, no doubt.

Still, the jury's hands were not tied. Composed mostly of moderately prosperous shopkeepers and small tradesmen, they might acquit the accused on the evidence, or even their own feelings of neighborliness. According to Professor Beattie, Old Bailey juries acquitted about 45% of defendants in property crimes from 1660 to 1689, and 31% from 1689 to 1713. They also might render a partial verdict, for example, of manslaughter instead of murder, or by declaring a shoplifting or burglary simple theft, which carried no capital penalty, or by devaluing goods to render the crime a misdemeanor. Even if found guilty, all was not lost for the accused. A female defendant might "plead her belly," that is, claim pregnancy, as Moll's mother did. This gave her a reprieve until the birth of her child, or until she was exposed as a fraud. Many felons escaped via benefit of clergy. This was an ancient custom dating back to the Middle Ages, during which clergy could not be punished by civil courts. To prove that he was a cleric, the accused was asked to read, because during the Middle Ages few non-clerics could do so. Although literacy increased steadily throughout the early modern period, this loophole remained on the books, so that anyone who could read selected portions of Psalm 51, popularly known as the "neck verse," literally saved his or her neck! A defendant could only resort to benefit of clergy once, however, and anyone who had escaped punishment in this way would be branded on the thumb, or, later, transported to the colonies. Finally, toward the end of the period judges had increasing discretion to sentence a convicted felon to transportation or military service. But if a judge decided in favor of death, the theatrical spectacle of the courtroom rose to a fever pitch. After donning white gloves and the black cap of judgment, he might then give a long speech, expounding on the age and wisdom of the law, the enormity of the crime, the threat to the social order, and the sad necessity of capital punishment. The sentence always concluded, ritually, with the same words, which served to cement his superhuman persona: "and may the Lord have mercy upon thy soul!"

The many opportunities for defendants to escape punishment and the judge's care to defend the law's fairness remind us that the system would not have worked if it was perceived to be unjust. That is, the law was promoted to the English people as impartial, applying equally to everyone. It is certainly true that English law did not, generally, differentiate offenses and punishments by social rank, as did some contemporary continental law. But eighteenth-century commentators went further, arguing that the law was applied more or less equally to all *in practice*, thus making equal access to the law part of the "rights of an Englishman." They made much of the case of Laurence, Earl Ferrers (1720–1760), hanged at Tyburn in 1760 for murdering his servant. On the other hand, they tended to omit numerous counter-instances, such as that of Charles, Lord Mohun (?1675–1712), who committed several murders without suffering capital punishment.

Mohun's example supports the argument that the notion of the law's fairness and impartiality was a sham, part of the propaganda designed to keep the lower orders in their place. First, a poor man or woman might very well have been forced into crime by poverty, stealing to put food into his or her children's mouths. Second, the world of the law and the courtroom were probably far more alien and threatening to an ordinary person than they were to his or her social superiors: the elite spent a great deal of time at litigation and so tended to be familiar with courts. Many elite men would have picked up some knowledge of the law at the Inns of

Court or while serving as a sheriff or JP. Finally and above all, the law was an expensive proposition to a poor man, even more so to a poor woman. Admittedly, neither rich nor poor defendants were allowed counsel in a felony trial, but one can be sure that, in practice, any peer or gentleman accused of a capital crime would have pulled in any marker, given out any bribe, enlisted any friend he had in high places to derail his prosecution. Jonathan Wild's career of corruption was sensational not perhaps because of the level of malfeasance it exposed, but because its protagonist was so common.

For the wretch condemned to death at trial all hope was not yet lost, because, as we have seen, mercy might be bestowed by the judge at sentencing: about 35% of those convicted of property crimes in London from 1663 to 1689 were given noncapital sentences. The king might also, at the recommendation of the judge or the recorder of London, issue a pardon at any point before a sentence of death was carried out: in the eighteenth century 50% to 60% of those so sentenced, many of them first-time offenders, were reprieved. As this implies, discretion, community feeling, and an awareness of individual circumstances were part of how the law was carried out: victims prosecuted, JPs indicted, and juries convicted as much on the reputation and circumstances of the accused as they did on the evidence. Old or violent offenders suffered the ultimate penalty; new ones tended to be reprieved. For some historians, mercy, circumspection, and discretion represent the third element of the law intended to restrain the power of the masses; that is, the cold calculation that it would be unwise to hang *every* criminal found guilty, because that might lead to a worse reaction on the part of the populace. In other words, it was important for the drama to kill just the right number of offenders and no more. The alternative would have been counterproductive: a level of slaughter likely to produce a rebellion or revolution in reaction. In this interpretation, the real point of it all was not so much to actually exercise mercy as to avoid "overdoing it" and so to enhance the godlike perception of the ruling elite by making clear that, like the Supreme Being, they had the power to condemn or reprieve, damn or save. After all, which act made the king or his magistrate seem more godlike: to execute the prisoner or to reprieve him at the last moment? Other historians are skeptical, not only because there is no hard evidence of a *conscious* upper-class conspiracy but also because the victims of crime and the juries that decided guilt or innocence were most commonly ordinary Londoners themselves.

Perhaps the theater of the law was at its most raucous, shocking, and difficult to interpret as it reached the final act. Those to be hanged were taken back to Newgate to live out their last few days or weeks in the Condemned Hold, perhaps the worst part of the prison. Although the prisoners were theoretically segregated by gender, a female might still try to make a connection with a male inmate to "plead her belly" and be reprieved for a few months. Throughout their final stay, the ordinary (the chaplain) of Newgate worked on them to repent – and to dictate their adventures to him for future sale. These accounts, on sale from every London bookseller and street pedlar, like the infamous conditions of the Condemned Hold itself, were part of the theater of the law, intended to deter those who would follow the crooked trade.

There were about eight execution days a year. Always a Monday, what came to be known as a "hanging match" began with a chapel service at which the condemned sat next to their own coffins. In a perverse take on the marriage ceremony,

> He that is to be hang'd . . . first takes Care to get himself shav'd, and handsomely drest, either in Mourning or in the Dress of a Bride-groom; . . . Sometimes the Girls dress in White, with great Silk Scarves, and carry Baskets full of Flowers and Oranges, scattering these Favours all the Way they go.[51]

Lord Ferrers actually wore his satin wedding suit with silver embroidery. A particularly popular male might be handed a bouquet of nosegays by the prostitutes gathered in front of the Church of the Holy Sepulchre, across the street from the prison. After chapel the procession of carts set off, carrying the condemned, tied two by two, and their coffins. They were accompanied by the ordinary (still preaching repentance), officers of the court, constables, javelin men on foot, and, if trouble was anticipated, mounted troops. For two hours this party made its way through the streets of London, from the prison, down Snow Hill to Holborn Bridge onto Holborn, east to Broad Street, St. Giles, then along Oxford Street to the northeast corner of Hyde Park, close to where Marble Arch stands now, but which, in those days, was the site of Tyburn Tree. The procession stopped periodically at taverns along the route, and always at St. Giles-in-the-Fields, so that the condemned might be fortified with drink. The three-mile route was lined with crowds who turned out to see the condemned, to cheer antiheroes like Sheppard or jeer recognized villains like Wild.

Indeed, hanging days were regarded as holidays and generated a carnival-like atmosphere. In 1727 Jonathan Swift satirized the scene:

> *As clever Tom Clinch, while the Rabble was bawling,*
> *Rode stately through Holbourn, to die in his Calling;*
> *He stopt at the George for a Bottle of Sack,*
> *And promis'd to pay for it when he'd come back.*
> *His Waistcoat and Stockings, and Breeches were white,*
> *His Cap had a new Cherry Ribbon to ty't.*
> *The Maids to the Doors and the Balconies ran,*
> *And said, lack-a-day! he's a proper young Man.*
> *But, as from the Windows the Ladies he spy'd,*
> *Like a Beau in the Box, he bow'd low on each Side;*

No wonder that de Saussure compared the cavalcade to the lord mayor's show.

Once the parade reached Tyburn, the tension must have been excruciating as the condemned looked out at the crowd of as many as 30,000 (see Illustration 6.4). There was always great suspense to hear the "dying speeches," and in particular whether the prisoners would indeed repent or go out defiantly. Tom Clinch chooses the latter course after objecting to the common practice of printing and selling made-up dying speeches to the crowd:

> *And when his last Speech the loud Hawkers did cry,*
> *He swore from his Cart, it was all a damn'd Lye.*
> *The Hangman for Pardon fell down on his Knee;*
> *Tom gave him a Kick in the Guts for his Fee.*
> *Then said, I must speak to the People a little,*
> *But I'll see you all damn'd before I will whittle* [confess].
> *My honest Friend Wild, may he long hold his Place,*
> *He lengthen'd my Life with a whole Year of Grace.*
> *Take Courage, dear Comrades, and be not afraid,*
> *Nor slip this Occasion to follow your Trade.*
> *My Conscience is clear, and my Spirits are calm,*
> *And thus I go off without Pray'r-Book or Psalm.*
> *Then follow the Practice of clever Tom Clinch,*
> *Who hung like a Hero, and never would flinch.*

Indeed, de Saussure marveled at some real life criminals "going to their death perfectly unconcerned, others so impenitent that they fill themselves full of liquor and mock at those who are repentant."[52] The only unacceptable choice was Wild's: he simply gave up and so failed to put on a show. The suspense mounted, because a royal pardon could come at any time.

If no fast rider approached, the hangings proceeded, yielding the most grotesque scene of all. Hanging is at best an inexact science: the condemned now stood on a large cart under the gallows. The gallows were simply a triangular wood frame from which were suspended the nooses through which their heads were slipped by the hangman. At a signal, he shooed the horses, which pulled the cart, leaving the condemned to fall. The result was an agonizing death by asphyxiation, hastened – if the prisoner had friends – by their rushing the scaffold and pulling down on his or her body so as to snap the neck and have done with it. They might then have to fight off the agents of medical schools that wanted the bodies for dissection. Others jostled to touch the corpses because of an ancient folk belief that such contact could cure disease. The clothes of the hanged belonged to the hangman, who might engage in a brisk trade under the gallows, selling them to loved ones or bargain hunters. Still others made quick cash by carrying the bodies to friends and relatives waiting with coaches and carts to carry them away.

De Saussure found "the noise and confusion unbelievable," but what are we to make of it all? Why would an establishment that normally feared crowds and a civic authority that had little use for staged drama encourage such a show? What was being said, by whom, to whom, and to what effect? At first glance, it would seem that the entire production fulfilled efficiently the needs of the ruling elite by making an example of a relatively small number of criminals before the largest possible audience of ordinary Londoners. On one level, the authorities would seem to have been soliciting the same kind of approval for their actions that a Tudor might do at a royal entry. By doing so, they could claim that the law remained an expression of shared values, enforced by the community. On another level, the lurid spectacle could be seen as just retribution, a ritual settling of scores, a poetically apt response to the shock horror theater of the Thorn murder that set things right again. As with Tudor displays of power, however, it was also clearly meant to overawe as much as to heal, to deter terror by inducing it in would-be offenders. Certainly the whole Tyburn ritual shocks and fascinates modern observers and has been used on Web sites arguing against the death penalty.

But if these rituals were intended to convey the majesty, fairness, and mercy of the law or strike terror into the hearts of the populace, how do we account for the fact that crime continued? Perhaps the most significant part of Moll's frenzied meditation on the consequences of her criminal acts, quoted earlier, is its end: "but that went off after a while."[53] She then persists in her trade. Robert Shoemaker, studying misdemeanors, has detected a lack of respect for the law and its officers among ordinary people in the late seventeenth and early eighteenth centuries. Indeed, if the public execution of felons was intended to frighten and intimidate, how do we account for the party atmosphere of the procession to Tyburn? Is not the mob saying something *back* to the ruling elite? What do we make of the apparent theatrical push back by the prisoners themselves, and their discourse with the crowd? It would appear that if capital punishment in London was a play written by the ruling class, the audience of London groundlings saw no reason why they could not cheer and jeer at will, turning the production into a dialogue in which they too could have their say.

The popular rituals that grew up around hangings continued a medieval tradition of misrule, inversion, and mocking of forces (e.g., death, disease, the law) that were normally beyond people's control. There may have been a certain amount of fatalism in this, but also perhaps resistance. The Tyburn crowd seems to be saying to the upper classes that they do not entirely accept, or accept only provisionally, their dominion over them. Rather than bow down to the awesome power of the law, they treat the serious business of a hanging like a party. On a more basic level, the crowd might be said to be reminding the elite, by their very presence, of their latent power: after all, they far outnumbered their betters and they could easily turn into a mob, threatening elite control and, in special circumstances, manipulating or diverting it. In the next chapter, we spend more time with the London crowd.

7. Riot and Rebellion

*L*ondon liked to portray itself as a loyal, royal city, but also as the bastion of English liberties. It was that second description that worried the authorities. Quite simply, there were too many Londoners to control, and the city's wealth, size, location, and administrative importance ensured that it played a decisive role in the rise or fall of rulers and dynasties. No wonder that both the court at Whitehall and the Corporation at the Guildhall took alarm at even the hint of riot, let alone rebellion. The last chapter addressed how the authorities tried to maintain order, and how they reacted when individual Londoners violated that order. In particular, we noted the difficulties facing metropolitan governors who lacked a police force or any of the modern technology of surveillance or law enforcement. The regime was even more vulnerable to disorder when Londoners acted en masse, because the state had no standing army until the Civil Wars of the 1640s. From 1660 to 1685 the army was small and barely able to cope with localized rebellion; thereafter it was mostly away fighting continental wars and so unavailable for domestic security. In any case, Englishmen and women hated standing armies for the same reasons that they hated urban police forces: they were expensive and a threat to liberty.

Instead, during the reign of Henry VIII, London established a militia, the trained bands, which was easily the most formidable military force in England before 1650. Trained by the Artillery Company on the Artillery Ground just north of the ancient wall, they numbered at least 4,000 under Elizabeth I and expanded to 10,000 during the Civil Wars. The nine wartime regiments of trained bands distinguished themselves in the defense of London at Turnham Green in 1642 and the relief of Gloucester in 1643. But these amateur soldiers, shopkeepers, and tradesmen in their day jobs could not be relied on to fire at fellow Londoners. Indeed, the active enlistment of ordinary Londoners in their own policing as soldiers, constables, and watchmen seems to have promoted a sense of identification with, and ownership of, law and custom that ironically encouraged some of them to riot.

RIOT

Historians are fascinated by riots. It is easy to see why. On the most obvious level, crowd action, public demonstration, riot, and their protracted cousin, rebellion, were the most dramatic spectacles that early modern London had to offer short of the Great Fire. They had the potential to gather more Londoners in one place than perhaps any other type of occasion, and for that reason alone they inspired a cold terror in the hearts of London's rulers, both civic and national. Of course, that fear stemmed first from the violence against people and property to which the crowd could turn. But on a deeper level, riot and rebellion would seem to represent a prima facie breakdown of the social order, threatening it, even on those occasions when their participants claimed to be defending it, by enacting, if only temporarily, mob rule, which is the very antithesis of the Great Chain of Being. Mass demonstrations thus threatened the chain by their very existence; riots exposed its tensions; and rebellions broke it. Indeed, crowd action may be the one situation in which London's classes clashed overtly, in which the cold war between social groups became hot.

This brings us to a deeper reason for historians to fixate on riots. On the face of it, *riot* would seem to be an economical word for people running amok in a moment of collective hysteria, committing random and indiscriminate havoc as the spirit moves them. This was sometimes the case: take the behavior of London's apprentices. There were some 30,000 apprentices in the city in 1600, roughly 15% of the population, most of them single young men with time on their hands. Attracted to radical religion and jealous of their rights, following the tradition of the hue and cry, called out by shouts of "'Prentices and clubs!" or "Shovels and spades!," apprentices were frequently at the head of political and religious demonstrations (see discussion later). But they also engaged in tumults that had nothing do with principled challenges to authority. Thus, in July 1599 the lord mayor bewailed "troops" of "riotous and unruly apprentices" armed with

"long staves and other weapons" who hung about near Hackney on summer evenings,

> setting men's corn growing in the fields on fire, breaking down glass
> windows and signs hanging at men's doors, thrusting down of bricks
> with their staves from the tops of brick walls, pulling up of gates and
> stiles, breaking into orchards and stealing of fruits, beating of Her
> Majesty's watches, and diverse other rebellious parts.

Such pranks have led one historian to conclude that "the disorderly
behaviour of young men in sixteenth-century London was hardly ever
organized or purposeful, at least not consciously."[1]

Beginning in the 1950s and '60s, historians such as George Rudé
and E. P. Thompson began to argue that most riots *were* organized and
purposeful, and that in fact they served as a form of communication from
those at the bottom of the social scale to those at the top. Londoners who
had no vote and no institutional outlet for their views could as a last resort
demonstrate to call on those in authority to remember their paternalistic
obligations to their inferiors, and thus to preserve the traditional social
and economic order generally. Trained in the custom of *communal* law
enforcement, London rioters tended to believe that they had a *right* to riot
and that when they did so they were engaging in the legitimate enforcement
of community standards and their ancient right of petition for redress of
grievances. In keeping with this, London rioters usually had specific
objectives, which they articulated in a variety of ways, and were often
careful to limit violence to specific targets. Thus, when ordinary – and
ordinarily anonymous – Londoners rioted, marching en masse toward
some specific goal, they provided clues to their mental universes. Often,
in the course of airing their grievances, they spelled out their theory of
order, their sense of their rights, and their views on church and state, both
vocally and in the rituals and symbols with which they rioted. It is true
that rebellions were even more likely to produce statements of grievances
and rituals of resistance, but these were almost always written up by elite
rebel leaders. Riots are perhaps more interesting to historians because
they had the potential to be the only time that ordinary people publicly
acted in great numbers, *of their own accord*, to express their views. They
therefore provide yet another kind of theater, this one largely popular, as
dramatic and moving as that of the law, which may tell us a great deal about
how rank-and-file early modern Londoners conceived of their world and
situation in it.

But historians have also taught us to be careful of the fact that riot-ers deployed symbols and engaged in rituals, elected captains, marched behind colors, attacked some places and not others, and above all pro-duced cogent statements of grievance. All of this tells us that riots were not *entirely* spontaneous. Like rebellions, they could be inspired, even manip-ulated by elite politicians for their own purposes. Even when they were not directed from above, rioters in London and elsewhere acted within long-standing traditions of how to behave in a proper riot. Indeed, so acting was thought to be one of the requirements to get their grievances heard, and heard they often were. Arguably the most interesting discovery of the recent historiography concerns the elite response to early modern riots. Perhaps because they were outnumbered; perhaps because there was no standing army and the trained bands were an ineffective tool against their own neighbors; perhaps because, as good paternalists, they saw the riot-ers' point of view, judges, JPs, and other authorities rarely suppressed or punished them forcefully. Rather they often seem to have tacitly assented to a right to riot by listening to and even redressing the rioters' grievances. In most cases they limited punishment to a few ringleaders, if anyone, and sometimes chastised those against whom the rioters were grieving. In short, the theater of riot, like the theater of the law, was interactive between actors and audience. Like the law, it had time-honored rules and traditions for those on both sides of the social divide. Its study can tell us much about how London worked.

What qualifies as a riot, exactly? The Riot Act of 1715 (1 Geo. I, c. 5) famously (and tautologically) defined a riot as any assemblage of twelve people "unlawfully, riotously, and tumultuously assembled together." Anciently, however, even three or more people engaged in such activity – say, shouting at an unpopular constable – could be deemed a riot if the authorities so decided. This loose definition gave them and subsequent historians tremendous leeway in declaring what was a riot and what was not. Along these lines, they might be tempted to call those three people, and certainly those twelve, "a crowd" or, more pejoratively, "a mob." The word *mob* arrived in the English language as a term of upper-class derision during the political turmoil of the 1680s (see below) and was short for the Latin *mobile vulgaris*, that is, "the people on the move." Any reader who has paid attention to this book knows what feelings of unease "the people on the move" would cause in the hearts of civic authorities.

Londoners had many reasons for rioting in the early modern period, and historians have been tempted to divide riots up accordingly. There were riots over harsh or scandalous words and behavior (especially sexual behavior); economic riots over the price of bread, working conditions, unpaid wages, or in defense of native products; xenophobic or religious riots, often led by apprentices, against some national, ethnic, or religious group; calendar riots associated with particular festivals and times of year, also popular with apprentices; and finally political demonstrations that could shade into or be part of a larger rebellion. Most riots had multiple causes, straddling categories: thus the Evil May Day Riots of 1517 exploited a calendar festival to attack foreigners, whereas the Sacheverell Riots of 1710 had political, religious, and economic roots.

Before examining various types of riot in detail, it might be worth asking just how often Londoners rioted. In an important article published in 1987, Robert Shoemaker compared the total number of recognizances and indictments for riot at Middlesex Quarter Sessions (thus excluding the City and portions of Southwark) during the period from 1663 to 1721 to figures from the early seventeenth century.[2] He found that while the population of Middlesex quadrupled between 1614 and 1720, the number of prosecutions for riot multiplied by twenty times, from less than 10 a year to nearly 200. Of course, it is possible that these figures are inflated by increased reportage: as the passage of the Riot Act indicates, the national and civic authorities grew less tolerant of riot as the period wore on and so probably defined more disturbances and demonstrations as riots than before. But given that something so dramatic as a riot was unlikely to go completely unnoticed, Professor Shoemaker's upward trend seems convincing.

Who started riots in London? Who joined? Who watched? Who attempted to stop them? Tim Harris found no evidence of upper-class manipulation for the Bawdy House Riots of 1668, but the Exclusion Crisis demonstrations from 1679 to 1681, both addressed later, were clearly orchestrated by the Whig and later the Tory elite. In both the May Day Riots of 1517 and the Sacheverell Riots of 1710, inflammatory sermons increased tension and gave the impression that the established Church was, in effect, pro-riot. There is also some eyewitness testimony of the presence of Tory gentlemen along the sidelines in 1710 and of planning at the Rose and Crown tavern. Years later the Duke of Newcastle not only approved but also claimed to have led the Whig mug-house rioters of 1715: "I love a mob. I headed a mob once myself. We owe the Hanoverian Succession to a mob."[3] But Nicholas Rogers has discounted upper-class influence for these riots, arguing that although Whig and Tory crowds from 1714 to 1716 certainly embraced the party struggle, these demonstrations were authentic expressions of popular sentiment. It would appear that, even with political riots, there was no simple rule of upper-class encouragement: some were instigated from above, but others were genuinely popular in origin.

Turning to the rioters themselves, Shoemaker detected four types of participants in the legal records that he examined. First, there were the instigators, often, when not members of the elite, known hotheads and community leaders, usually singled out for prosecution after a riot had run its course. Then there were premeditated participants, people who did not organize a riot but planned in advance to take part in it. Perhaps more interesting were the spur-of-the-moment participants, bystanders who decided to join in. Finally, there were the spectators. It is difficult to slot people into these categories neatly: London's streets were always crowded, and the pedestrian traffic in London was sometimes referred to as "the mob." One might be carried away by a crowd and participate against one's own will.

What kinds of people participated? In Shoemaker's broad survey of legal records, about 10% of all male rioters were gentlemen, 14% yeomen or skilled craftsmen, 44% unskilled tradesmen, and 33% poor. Women participated in one-third of the riots and disturbances reported, and formed on average one-third of all rioters bound over by recognizance, but increased their presence over the period from 20% to 44% by its end. They mostly rioted over scandalous words and behaviors, and were far less likely to participate in political riots. Geoffrey Holmes's examination of the ninety-one Sacheverell rioters whose occupations are known breaks this down to reveal various occupations, from ten gentlemen or esquires, through professionals (two lawyers, a physician, a barber), several shopkeepers and small tradesmen, down to servants, footmen, coachmen, soldiers, sailors, even one of the queen's watermen. Clearly, in this case at least, party loyalty crossed class lines.

As indicated earlier, many riots and demonstrations were meant to grab the attention of the ruling elite, whether informing them of a grievance, reminding them of their paternalistic duties, or intimidating them with sheer numbers. They were *not* meant to unhinge the prevailing social order: rural enclosure rioters sometimes carried copies of royal proclamations against that hated practice and they often petitioned the local lord or JP for redress. Similarly in 1592, when about forty parishioners of St. Margaret Westminster and St. Martin-in-the-Fields tore down fences and gates surrounding what they claimed as common land, they were led by parish officers and substantial citizens. They also "had divers

Constables with them, to keep Her Majesty's Peace,"[4] and claimed the support of the lord treasurer and Privy Council. In fact, many of the enclosers were well-connected members of these parishes as well, but in the end the authorities listened to the wider community: an inquest in December found for the protesters. The following year, Parliament forbade enclosures within three miles of London. In this case, the parish community asserted itself and in the short term won.

Riots over Words and Behavior

Perhaps the most common form of riot, and the one least likely to unhinge the social order or alarm the authorities, was the disturbance that started with cross words or an insult in a house, shop, or tavern that spilled out into the streets. Technically not even a riot was the "rout" that ensued when someone stood in the street, shouted insults outside a neighbor's house or place of business, and so gathered a crowd out of mere curiosity. Thus when Richard Woodley went to Tom's Coffee House, Southwark one day in 1720 to demand payment of a debt, "Hot words . . . occasioned some people to come together about the coffee house door."[5] Court records are full of disturbances that began with "Hot words": a man in a tavern calling another "rogue" or "dog"; a woman in the market insulting another as "whore," "bitch," or "bastard-bearer." If the issue were taken to court, the result might be a defamation suit; if taken to blows, an assault; if taken to the streets, a riot.

In each case, the speaker might claim to be enforcing community standards by calling out deviance, especially around gender roles and sexuality. Sexual behavior was a common instigation to demonstration, most famously in the tradition called "charivari." In the country, villagers had long been accustomed to bang pots and pans under the windows of a house thought to contain people who did not abide by community norms: a notorious wife- or husband-beater, a cuckold and his wandering spouse, a "shrew" who hen-pecked her husband. Although "rough music" at windows seems to have been dying out in London, brothels and prostitutes, adulterers and bastard bearers might still get the treatment. Both John Stow and Maximillian Misson report examples from the streets at either end of the seventeenth century. Thus Misson:

> I have sometimes met in the Streets of London a Woman carrying a
> Figure of Straw representing a Man, crown'd with very ample Horns,
> preceded by a Drum and follow'd by a Mob, making a most grating

Noise with Tongs, Grid irons, Frying-pans and Sauce-pans: I ask'd what was the Meaning of all this; they told me that a Woman had given her Husband a sound beating, for accusing her of making him a Cuckold and that upon such Occasions some kind Neighbour of the *poor innocent injur'd Creature* generally perform'd this Ceremony.[6]

Far from being crude or random, these street demonstrations followed a script with a clear purpose: to shame transgressors of community standards of marriage, household, and gender. As with the calendar, that script retained elements of rural traditions, suggesting that early modern Londoners might not have been so different from their country cousins after all. But we must be careful about assuming that all Londoners shared these values: in the early eighteenth century they were just as likely to rescue prostitutes and attack Reformation of Manners constables trying to arrest them. In short, "the" London crowd was really many crowds, none of them predictable.

Economic Riots

Economic disagreements and transgressions might also provoke disturbances of the peace, as when shop or tavern keepers haggled with a patron over a price, a bill, or a transaction gone bad. Shoemaker cites two women, possibly dissatisfied customers, who were accused of "making a riot" in 1719 by driving other patrons away from a market stall. A scab worker might be ridden, on a rail or in a wheelbarrow, in an urban skimmington as a warning to his fellows. If riot were a form of communication and a weapon in the arsenal of ordinary people, it was a blunt weapon, sometimes expressing no more than class resentments, as when apprentices and gentlemen's servants clashed around the Inns of Court in the 1580s.

In the early modern period, just as there were no trade unions in the modern sense of the word, there was no orderly picketing. Instead, industrial action tended to degenerate into riot, often involving workers ruining products with which they were competing or attacking new machinery or techniques designed to cut labor costs. Thus in August 1675, the weavers of London – wearing Leveller green – broke machine looms that threatened to reduce their workforce. Even this violence was targeted and often aimed to persuade a higher authority to fulfill its customary responsibilities. In 1595, Huguenot weavers were attacked because they flouted guild rules by introducing a new, less labor-intensive, type of loom, and sold door to door. There may have been a xenophobic aspect to these demonstrations, but we should recall that the alien weavers could not have established themselves in the metropolis without the support of English weavers who sought to take advantage of their skills. The petitions and pamphlets accompanying the riots seem, instead, to have been aimed primarily at the guild officers, who had turned a blind eye to violations of company regulations. Thus the point of the riot was to force the authorities to enforce their own rules, not to abandon them. The silk weavers in 1689 and 1697, the framework knitters in 1711, and the shoemakers in 1714 demonstrated to demand protectionist legislation from Parliament. In the Calico Riots of 1719/20, supporters of Spitalfields weavers ripped clothes made of imported Indian fabrics from the backs of the women who wore them. They also put pressure on Parliament, gathering "in extraordinary Numbers in the Old Palace Yard, Westminster . . . begging the Lords as they passed" into the House of Lords "to commiserate the poor Weavers." When the Horse Guards were called out, the weavers dispersed peacefully – but not before they "unrigg'd a few Callico Ladies."[7] So this was at once a crude attack on a foreign-made product designed to intimidate English consumers and a calculated appeal to the authorities, alternately groveling and threatening, to protect English manufactures. Such demonstrations sometimes got results: the Calico Act of 1721 (7 Geo. I, c. 7) banned the wearing of this fabric.

What all such demonstrations have in common is their attempt to maintain the status quo. After cheap Irish labor began settling in London in the 1730s, riots erupted in 1736 in Spitalfields, Shoreditch, and Whitechapel. Another wave of industrial action broke out in the late 1760s as the coal heavers, coopers, glass grinders, hatters, sailors, sawyers, tailors, weavers, and watermen fought for higher wages and better working conditions. These demonstrations took place in the midst of high food prices and a government already made nervous by political demonstrations in favor of the radical opposition politician John Wilkes (1725–1797). In particular, the 1769 Spitalfields Riots pitted a community of weavers against the introduction of more efficient engine looms and the new, cheap, and often Irish labor introduced to run them. The more established journeymen were being frozen out of the trade, leading them to form an illegal union and engage in "silk cutting," that is, ripping the work of their opponents. An attempt to arrest the "cutters" at their meeting in September led to fatalities, arrests, and two executions. But, again, the authorities acted on the grievance: the 1773 Spitalfields Act (13 Geo. III, c. 48) empowered JPs to control wages and arbitrate industrial disputes, which stabilized the situation in the short term.

Bread or other food riots were rare in early modern London because the developing food distribution system was fairly efficient and because City authorities watched the price of bread carefully. In the country, such riots often began with women, who were of course especially concerned with the business of putting food on the table, but in the City it might be apprentice boys or servant girls as well as fishwives. In each case, their anger was usually directed against middlemen such as grain sellers, corn factors, and millers. Still, these demonstrations tended to be nonviolent, often involving taking the grain, but leaving whatever sums the rioters thought a fair price. In a show of paternal concern and traditional gender attitudes, the City authorities were reluctant to prosecute women trying to feed their families.

The one serious wave of food rioting in London occurred during the hard years of the mid-1590s. The economy had long been disrupted by war with Spain and high taxes. In 1593 the metropolis was wracked by a deadly plague epidemic, followed by four years of bad harvests and high prices. The price of flour rose 290% between 1593 and 1597; that of food in general rose 46% while real wages fell 23%. The disturbances began in February 1595 with larger than usual Shrove Tuesday riots. In June, a group of apprentices sent to purchase fish at Billingsgate found it all gone. On June 12 and 13, riots broke out over the price of fish and butter. Apprentices spread throughout the city, some taking fish, butter, and eggs, although leaving what they considered to be a fair price. The situation turned ugly on June 29, when a mob of some 1,000 apprentices marched up Tower Hill, determined to seize weapons and "to robbe, steale, pill and spoile the welthy and well disposed inhabitaunts of the saide cytye, and to take the sword of authorytye from the magistrats and governours lawfully aucthorised." Perhaps with this end in view they built a scaffold facing the house of the unpopular lord mayor, Sir John Spencer (d. 1610).[8] This was the high point of the crisis, however. Just one more food riot took place in October at the corner of Milk and Cheapside, without the revolutionary overtones. The City reacted with firmness: the watch was doubled, provost marshals were appointed and given summary powers of execution, and apprentices and journeymen were confined to their masters' homes on Sundays and holidays. Marshal law was imposed for a year, and five apprentice ring-leaders were sentenced to be hanged, drawn, and quartered. But the City also got the message: the next year the authorities began to distribute free bread. Historians still debate whether these events indicate a city on the verge of anarchy or an isolated incident.

In the words of Ian Archer, "the social fabric was highly flammable, but it failed to ignite."[9]

The wars of the seventeenth century saw occasional demonstrations by soldiers, sailors, or their wives demanding their pay from government officials. There were thirteen such disturbances between 1626 and 1640, and they became common again in the mid-1660s. At the height of the Second Dutch War (1664–1668), the Crown found itself running out of money and unable to supply wages, food, or even proper clothing to thousands of seamen who had been pressed into service. Samuel Pepys, besieged in the courtyard of the Navy Office by angry sailors and their wives as clerk of the acts of the Navy, expostulated with some of his fellow officers about "the sad state of our times. And the horrid shame brought on the King's service by the just clamours of the poor seamen."[10] Once again, those in charge agreed that the "just clamours" of protestors indicated a real grievance, but in this case the Restoration regime was too poor and corrupt to do much to satisfy it.

XENOPHOBIC RIOTS

Early modern Londoners have been accused of hating foreigners: certainly the London stage was full of effeminate Frenchmen and gauche Dutchmen, yet as we have seen, throughout the period great numbers of migrants and refugees from abroad found a home and often built a fortune there. Still, in a city in which the labor market was continually flooded by newcomers, economic grievances were often linked to resentment of migrants, especially from foreign lands. The classic example of an anti-alien demonstration, one that haunted respectable citizens' imaginations for decades, took place before the period covered by this book. In the Evil May Day Riot of 1517, hundreds of apprentices, possibly inspired by an anti-alien Paul's Cross sermon by one Dr. Beal or Bell, stormed Newgate and other prisons and St. Martin-le-Grand, a liberty popular with resident aliens north of St. Paul's. Although no one was killed, 278 rioters were arrested. The intervention of Katherine of Aragon saved all but fourteen, and May Day was suppressed for years to come, but Parliament also passed statutes limiting the trading rights of aliens.

Violence against foreigners increased after the Reformation as London took in refugees from the wars of religion. We have already seen that the arrival of Huguenot workers from the 1560s through the 1590s led, even if indirectly, to resentment and riot. Foreigners continued to be targets throughout the period, especially those hailing from whichever country was currently regarded as England's greatest enemy. Thus, on December 7, 1536, the French ambassador's servants were attacked to cries of "Down with French dogs." Under Mary I it was the turn of the Spanish as members of Philip II's entourage were jeered in the streets by small boys. After the hostilities of the Armada War, James I's pro-Spanish foreign policy was similarly unpopular, which helps to explain why, on July 13, 1618, a crowd of some four to five thousand people besieged the Spanish ambassador's house in London after one of his servants accidentally knocked over a child in Chancery Lane. By 1661, popular antagonism had again turned, away from the declining Spanish and back toward the rising French. In that year an international incident occurred in the streets of London when the diplomatic representatives of France and Spain disputed whose coach would go first at the entry of the Swedish ambassador. Pepys records the ensuing battle, the "streets full of people":

> . . . abroad, and in Cheapside hear that the Spaniard hath got the best of it and killed three of the French coach-horses and several men and is gone through the City next to our King's coach. At which, it is strange to see how all the City did rejoice.[11]

London crowds may have had agendas, but they were not monolithic, and their loyalties could change with time. In this case, their behavior put Charles II in a difficult position between rival crowns.

CALENDAR RIOTS

Annually, at the lord mayor's show on October 29, Londoners joined in the street festivities by throwing fireworks and dead cats and dogs, breaking windows, and exacting fees from passing carriages. But the most famous recurrent example of a London calendar festival gotten out of hand traditionally occurred on Shrove Tuesday. From the Jacobean period into the 1670s young men, usually apprentices, attacked the brothels and playhouses concentrated in London's suburbs. Tim Harris, their historian, counted twenty-four such riots in the period from 1606 to 1641. Such demonstrations could be highly ritualized, the rioters destroying specific properties but not generally assaulting persons. They could also be quite large in scale: the 1617 Shrove Tuesday disturbances occurred in three separate locations (Lincoln's Inn Fields, Finsbury Fields, and Wapping), with at times several thousand rioters, many of them apprentices.

They destroyed a new theater in Drury Lane, released the prisoners in Finsbury Prison, and damaged several houses as well as the sheriff and JP who tried to stop them. It is possible to see these riots as expressions of the high spirits of youth, a vestigial example of medieval misrule in which adolescents, supposedly enforced into sexual continence by the terms of their apprenticeships, but who might very well have been customers of the brothels at other times, blew off some steam. That they chose brothels as their target might seem ironic or self-defeating: commenting on a 1668 report that the apprentices "are for pulling down of bawdy-houses, which is one of the great grievances of the nation," Charles II, baffled, replied "why, why do they go to them then?"[12] One reason may be that such targets seemed eminently safe: who would oppose tearing down a bawdy house? Once again, the rioters could claim that they were enforcing righteous community norms. But even bawdy house riots might bring violent suppression if they touched on aristocratic interests. In July 1749, a group of sailors, just home from the War of the Austrian Succession, attacked the Crown, the Star, and the Bunch of Grapes, taverns in the Strand doubling as bawdy houses, to the evident approval of the neighborhood (see Illustration 7.1). The authorities sent in troops, not least because the Bunch of Grapes was owned by Philip, Earl Stanhope (1714–1786).

POLITICAL RIOTS

Londoners had always felt free to demonstrate their political feelings in public. When Katherine of Aragon processed through the streets of London to contest her divorce case at Blackfriars in 1529, the crowd cheered her on; when her replacement wife, Anne Boleyn, was processed through London for her coronation in 1533, the populace was noticeably indifferent. As this indicates, Londoners could make a point with numbers and gestures without resorting to outright riot. For example, crowds gathered to show their support at the executions of the popular Dukes of Buckingham (b. 1478) in 1521 and Somerset in 1552. In the latter case, they dipped their handkerchiefs in his blood, and their coldness toward his ministerial rival, the Duke of Northumberland, presaged their failure to support him and his nominee, Queen Jane, at the change of reign in 1553 (see below). Some Londoners showed similar support for the Marian martyrs and many years later again soaked their handkerchiefs in Protestant blood – that of the Puritan controversialists William Prynne (1600–1669), John Bastwick (?1595–1654), and Henry Burton (1578–1648) – at their ritual mutilations in 1637 (see below). In 1703, they threw flowers at Daniel Defoe, when he was sentenced to the pillory for satirizing Anglican (High Church) attitudes to Dissenters (Puritans). Sometimes, a large crowd spoke volumes by its very presence, as when several thousand gathered in Westminster Palace Yard in 1601 to force Parliament to discuss monopolies.

The London crowd was not consistent because it was not monolithic: groups with differing agendas could form mobs and put pressure on the government. Ordinary Londoners could change their minds. We have seen their alfresco enthusiasm for Elizabeth I, but that did not stop them from protesting her possible French marriage in 1579. When Prince Charles and the Duke of Buckingham considered a Spanish-Catholic match from 1621 to 1623, Londoners wrote libels on the Spanish ambassador, apprentices abused him, bonfires appeared in the streets, and the crowd cheered the duo after the marriage was finally thwarted in 1623. But in the period from 1626 to 1628, after Buckingham persuaded Charles as king to engage in ultimately unsuccessful wars with Spain and France, poorly paid sailors marched on Whitehall for their pay while civilians wrote libels against the Duke, lit bonfires in support of the Petition of Right (1628), assaulted and murdered his astrologer, John Lambe (1545/46–1628), and cheered Buckingham's assassin, John Felton (d. 1628), as he was taken to the Tower. While some of these actions suggest a militantly Protestant worldview, Londoners' support for Mary *and* those she burned, their protests against a Spanish match but *also* against a badly bungled Spanish war remind us once again that London crowds were never entirely predictable.

These were demonstrations and sometimes riots – not acts of rebellion intended to alter drastically the regime or constitution. Londoners had learned to be careful about disloyalty: they did not do more for Somerset in 1552, nor did they rise against Mary I's marriage in 1554 or for the allegedly popular Earl of Essex in 1601 (see below). In the middle of the seventeenth century, however, Londoners began to engage in mass demonstrations that would precipitate rebellion and revolution. To understand why, we have to address London's role in "England's Troubles" from the 1550s on.

REBELLION AND REVOLUTION

Riots were almost never isolated incidents. As we have seen, they took place within complex contexts of factors, some long-standing, like the weavers' grievances against aliens; some immediate, like the economic hardships of 1594 to 1598 or 1708 to 1710. In general, however, it was possible for the authorities to treat riots as isolated incidents; that is, until the Gordon Riots of 1780, individual public demonstrations in London were generally not viewed as a symptom of a much larger problem, or a threat to the fundamental social order. Rebellion was different. As we learned in the Introduction, as London went, so went the nation. Admittedly, it was an open question whether London was truly governable at all, but it could not be ignored. The city's sheer size and wealth; its central role in the dissemination of information; its strategic significance as gateway to the Thames valley and mother to thousands of potential soldiers; and its status as the capital meant that London had to figure in the calculations of anyone plotting to seize or hold the government of England before, during, or after our period. Put simply, a successful rebel had to enlist Londoners in his cause. The failure to do so explains the collapse of the Peasants' Revolt of 1381, and Wyatt's, Essex's, and Venner's Rebellions in 1554, 1601, and 1661, respectively (see later discussion). But the City opened its gates to Jack Cade in 1450; Edward, Duke of York in 1461; Henry, Earl of Richmond in 1485; and William of Orange in 1688. The last three became kings. Even in the seventeenth century, as the British Isles were wracked by Civil Wars on a pan-archipelagic scale, London was the key to the three kingdoms.

All of the rebellions against the Tudors in the previous list failed, not least because they retained London. Having come to power as a result of civil war and rebellion, their guiding principle was to eliminate all possibility of a repetition by increasing their own authority and popularity while containing noble power. For the most part, they succeeded, especially in London, where they maintained good relations with the civic authorities. Moreover, Edward VI's Protestant religious settlement was far more popular in the metropolis than in the remote parts of the country to the west and north. When, therefore, in the spring of 1553, his health began to fail and he and the Duke of Northumberland attempted to divert the succession away from his Catholic elder sister, Mary, to a Protestant relative, Lady Jane Grey, they probably expected London to follow. Upon Edward's death on July 6, the Privy Council in London duly proclaimed Jane queen. But London stayed aloof, eventually rising for Mary. Jane's army disintegrated, the conspirators were imprisoned, and after some months delay, executed. Once again, London went and the nation followed.

London and the nation rallied to Mary I, despite her half-Spanish lineage and Catholic faith, because she was the daughter of Henry VIII. She thought that God, however, and not her people had placed her on the throne expressly to strengthen England's long-standing alliance with Spain and return her people to Roman Catholicism. Both policies tested London's loyalty. First, her decision to marry Prince Philip, the future Philip II of Spain, in 1554 – over the objections of her Privy Council and many of her subjects – led to a rebellion in which London once again held the crucial balance. In January 1554, Sir Thomas Wyatt (?1521–1554) raised a force of 3,000 men in Kent and marched on the city. Their goal was to prevent the Spanish marriage and possibly displace Mary in favor of her Protestant sister Elizabeth. Lacking an army of her own, Mary turned to the citizens of London. She went to the Guildhall and there appealed to the City's allegiance in a speech as eloquent as any her sister would ever give:

> I am your Queen, to whom at my coronation, when I was wedded to the realm and laws of the same (the spousal ring whereof I have on my finger, which never hitherto was, nor hereafter shall be, left off), you promised your allegiance and obedience to me . . . And I say to you, on the word of a Prince, I cannot tell how naturally the mother loveth the child, for I was never the mother of any; but certainly, if a Prince and Governor may as naturally and earnestly love her subjects as the mother doth love the child, then assure yourselves that I, being your lady and mistress, do as earnestly and tenderly love and favour you. And I, thus loving you, cannot but think that ye as heartily and faithfully love me; and then I doubt not but we shall give these rebels a short and speedy overthrow.[13]

It is said that her audience cheered and threw their caps in the air. Mary then rallied the assembled citizenry and the royal guards, who stopped Wyatt at the Southwark end of London Bridge. Retreating, then crossing upriver at Richmond, he got as far as Ludgate, which was also closed to him, and was captured at Temple Bar. After the requisite executions (Jane Grey, Wyatt, and about ninety rebels on twenty gibbets spread throughout the City), the marriage to Philip took place amid spectacular pomp, at Winchester Cathedral – safely away from Protestant London crowds – in July 1554. The Tudor queen, like her predecessors, had her way, mainly because London had stayed loyal. But within a few years, the burnings at Smithfield strained that loyalty, since London crowds seem to have mainly supported the martyrs (see Introduction).

At Mary's death in November 1558, she was succeeded by her sister, Elizabeth. Elizabeth I's relations with London were generally good. For starters, as we have seen, she knew how to charm a city crowd (see Chapter 3). Her chief ministers, William Cecil, Lord Burghley, and Robert Cecil, afterward Earl of Salisbury, cultivated good relations with the City, while her Privy Council worked closely with civic authorities to guarantee the food supply, suppress disorder, and arrange loans. The queen's willingness to turn a blind eye to her privateers' attacks on the Spanish Empire was good for business, and if she was not the sort of reforming Protestant that many London Puritans would have liked, she was certainly no Catholic. Sometimes there was friction: in the 1580s other cities complained of London's privileges, and this decade saw the first royal proclamation against new building. But it was only at the end of the reign that her popularity began to wane, as the war with Spain (1585–1604) and rebellion in Ireland (1594–1603) dragged on, necessitating continued high taxes in the midst of inflation and poor harvests. We have already seen that these conditions helped to produce sporadic riots in London and threatening crowds at Westminster. Because Elizabeth remained unmarried and childless, yet unwilling to name an heir, there was much speculation about the succession.

In early 1601, Robert Devereaux, Earl of Essex (1565–1601), hoping to be kingmaker, attempted to force the issue. On the afternoon of February 7, a group of his supporters sponsored a performance at the Globe Theater of Shakespeare's *Richard II* – which is, of course, about deposing kings. When on the 8th the lord chief justice and three other Privy Councillors arrived at Essex House, the Strand to investigate, Essex detained them in his library. Banking on his popularity in the City, he marched into it with about 300 retainers, shouting:

> For the Queen! For the Queen!
> The crown of England is sold to the Spaniard!
> A Plot is laid for my Life!

In fact, no one seems to have cared. Instead of raising the trained bands on his behalf, the sheriff called for the lord mayor, who trapped Essex by closing Ludgate. The Earl was arrested and executed within the month. London could still depose a king, as we shall see, but it did not back losers. When Queen Elizabeth finally died in March 1603, she was succeeded, peacefully, by James VI of Scotland (reigned there 1568–1625), who reigned in England and Ireland as James I. It could be said that the smooth accession of the Stuarts was the greatest of the Tudors' many achievements.

Histories of the British Isles under the Stuarts (1603–1714) cannot avoid the fact that arguably the most dramatic event in British History – the Civil Wars of the mid-seventeenth century – happened on their watch. Histories of London are not immune, because as we shall see, the metropolis played a crucial role in bringing those wars to fruition, ensuring that Parliament won them, but then ensuring that the Stuarts won the peace. In the words of one anonymous pamphlet:

> If . . . posterity shall ask . . . who would have pulled the crown from the King's head, taken the government off the hinges, dissolved Monarchy, enslaved the laws, and ruined their country; say 'twas the proud, unthankful, schismatical, rebellious, bloody City of London.[14]

Historians used to have no trouble explaining this connection: the British Civil Wars were about the English, Scots, and Irish seeking freedom from Stuart absolutism. London, as the freest place in the British Isles, was bound to spark and support that fight. Unfortunately for this simple interpretation, we now know that nobody in the British Isles necessarily wanted to rebel against the king, let alone depose him. Rather, they wanted the Stuarts to rule as Protestants and within the laws. The authorities in London were especially tied to the monarchy. As we have seen, London's rich City elite, headed by the lord mayor and Court of Aldermen, depended on royal charters to guarantee their own governmental authority as well as the privileges of both livery and trading companies like the Merchant Adventurers, East India, and Levant Companies. Many were Customs farmers or major lenders to the Crown. Tudor and Stuart kings had equal reason to appreciate London, because they depended on the City for loans and for troops – about 10% of nearly every royal land force. As we have also seen, kings and aldermen worried equally and constantly about London's potential for disorder: its size, high rates of disease and crime, and religious diversity all threatened the Stuart ideal of order.

If the Stuarts had issues with London, many Londoners had issues with the Stuarts. As we saw in Chapter 3, neither James I nor his son, Charles I, had the Tudor common touch; both disliked going out among their London subjects. On a more fundamental level, both had a very high notion of their prerogative, and their clashes with Parliament tended to be more prolonged and destructive than Elizabeth's had been. During this period, the Crown resorted to frequent prorogations and dismissals culminating in the Personal Rule of 1629 to 1640; extra-parliamentary taxation such as the impositions (increased Customs rates) on imported goods, forced loans, and the revival of old feudal taxes; and harsh legal action against those who refused to cooperate, including attacks on London's privileges and individual merchants. The forced loans and impositions were an especially sore spot with middling London merchants: the great company merchants, in bed with the Crown, might look the other way, but lesser figures, especially those trading with the American colonies, not only condemned the impositions but also began to call for free trade, that is, an end to the trading companies' privileges. Perhaps more importantly, they began to work with Puritan landowners in Parliament who feared what they saw as absolutist and pro-Catholic policies. It did not help that the Stuarts were spendthrifts, James spending money on his favorites, Charles on his art collection at Whitehall. London's Protestant mercantile community would have preferred that their taxes be spent on an aggressive Protestant foreign policy, including trade war and privateering against Spain in the Thirty Years' War (1618–1648). Instead, Stuart foreign policy was pacifist until 1624. Indeed, in the waning years of James I's life, the Duke of Buckingham was working on a diplomatic marriage between Prince Charles and the Catholic Spanish Infanta that was very unpopular in the City. When those negotiations failed in 1623, Londoners rejoiced with bell ringing and bonfires in the streets. Buckingham's moment of popularity evaporated when, over the next few years, he married Charles to the equally Catholic French Princess Henrietta Maria, while bungling into simultaneous wars with both Spain and France. A distrustful Parliament and City Corporation underfunded the wars, and the government's incompetence in fighting them left many Londoners wondering if the Stuarts were secretly betraying their country to the Catholic powers.

As all of this suggests, religion was another area of tension between many Londoners and the Crown. Most parish priests were nominated by officials in the government or Church, and so were Anglican. But where the vestry or parish could nominate its own clergyman, that parish was often Puritan: for example, St. Anne Blackfriars, All Hallows Bread Street, or St. Stephen Coleman Street. Coleman Street in particular had been a hotbed of dissent since before the Reformation. The city was also studded with Puritan lectureships, namely, preaching positions sponsored by wealthy Puritan merchants. Puritans existed at all social levels of London society, including some aldermen, but they were especially strong among the substantial merchants and small tradesmen, livery, and freemen of Common Council and Common Hall. If the Stuart court looked askance at them for their heterodoxy and social inferiority, they tended to see the

Stuart court as favoring Papists and arbitrary government. More immediately, in the 1630s London Puritans opposed the High Church policies of Archbishop William Laud, who used the Court of High Commission to remove Puritan preachers and replace them with Anglicans who favored elaborate ceremony and church décor (known as *Arminians*). They also feared the policies of Thomas Wentworth, Earl of Strafford (1593–1641), who urged a thorough reform of government and proved ruthless as Lord Deputy of Ireland and later as commander of the king's forces. By the late 1630s, as national tensions grew more strained among King Charles I, his English Parliament, and his three kingdoms, the City's rulers and citizenry began to take sides.

One of the first large demonstrations by ordinary Londoners came in 1637 following the condemnation in Star Chamber of the Puritans Prynne, Bastwick, and Burton for writings critical of the bishops and the queen. Their punishment was to have their ears cropped in Westminster Palace Yard. On the day, a great crowd cheered them to the place of punishment; some threw flowers, and afterward others dipped their handkerchiefs into the "martyrs'" blood. Later that year, the Scots rebelled rather than accept the imposition of an Anglican-style prayer book, leading eventually to the calling of the Long Parliament in 1640. The king's religious and financial policies were by this time so unpopular in the metropolis that even the City mercantile elite, usually loyal, largely balked at sending men and money for the king's armies in Scotland, while at the same time the middling liverymen of Common Hall elected four MPs who would work closely with opposition leaders like John Pym (1584–1643). But it was ordinary Londoners, egged on by Puritan preachers, who turned out to be Pym's most vocal allies. As early as the spring of 1640, city tradesmen and apprentices became restive, marching and petitioning against Archbishop Laud. On May 11, a crowd crossed the river to mount an assault on Lambeth Palace; three days later some attacked a royal prison. When the archbishop was finally ordered to the Tower in March 1641, the apprentice boys jeered at his coach in triumph. As the Long Parliament sat, Londoners of all ages and genders crowded Old Palace Yard, between Westminster Palace and Westminster Hall. Through a series of "monster" petitions, some with thousands of signatures, they demanded redress of grievances, especially the abolition of the bishops "root and branch," and the execution of Strafford. Although this served to bolster the arguments of Pym and the parliamentary radicals, it also put immense pressure on them, pushing them to policies that risked alienating moderates.

The influence of London popular opinion is perhaps most obvious in the case of Strafford. In the spring of 1641, as Parliament agonized over a motion for his attainder for high treason, possibly 20,000 Londoners signed a petition for his execution. On May 4, a crowd armed with swords and staves attacked the House of Lords, threatening any peer voting against Strafford's attainder. Subsequently, their names were posted all around the city. Clearly the control of information and persons implied by the Great Chain of Being was collapsing in London as the public sphere widened. When news broke that the king was considering an "Army Plot" to rescue the earl from the Tower, Parliament demanded control of the fortress and its cache of arms and assumed direction of the London trained bands. When Strafford's attainder was finally brought to Whitehall, the parliamentary delegation was accompanied by a mob that surrounded the palace for a week, shouting for the earl's blood, suggesting that the opposition leaders and the London crowd had coordinated their efforts. They knew that the king was reluctant to condemn a loyal servant who had only done his bidding. With the shouts of the crowd ringing in his ears, however, Charles caved in, conceding control of the Tower to Parliament and signing Strafford's death warrant. The Earl of Strafford was beheaded before a throng of many thousands on Tower Hill on May 12, 1641.

This is not to say that Londoners, or even "the London crowd," were a monolith, thinking in lockstep. As we have seen, there was always more than one London mob. In particular, the king had a party of prosperous aldermen and trading company merchants on his side. During the autumn of 1641, as Pym's program to limit royal power grew more radical, anonymous printed attacks on the parliamentary opposition appeared in the streets. On September 28, a Royalist, Richard Gurney (1578–1647), was elected lord mayor in a hard-fought election. When the king returned from a progress to Scotland on November 25, he was cheered in the streets and feted by the City Corporation. He responded with an Elizabethan graciousness, knighting the loyal Gurney: Charles too had a London constituency, and he seems to have finally learned how to play to it.

But he learned too late. That autumn, the city became the stage for a theater of public power. In early November, London received word, vastly exaggerated, of a rebellion by poor Catholic tenants against their Protestant landlords in Ireland: some 200,000 Protestants were said to have been slaughtered. The actual number was less than a tenth of that, but the city's ability to generate rumor ensured panic that London's Catholics, encouraged by the king, would rise up and murder London's Protestants in their beds. Puritan preachers galvanized opposition London by a sermon campaign linking the Irish rebels to Papists at court and bishops in the House of Lords. On November 29, a crowd armed with swords and staves surrounded Westminster Palace, demanding the abolition of the bishops. Edward, Earl of Dorset (1590–1652), commander of the trained bands guarding Parliament and a Royalist, actually gave the order to fire on the demonstrators, but the London militia refused. Royal authority over the capital was breaking. On December 11, each ward sent four representatives who occupied a total of fifty coaches to present a monster petition with 15,000 signatures against the bishops; on the 23rd another petition with as many as 30,000 apprentice signatures was offered.

In the meantime, on December 21, the citizenry in the wardmotes elected a Puritan/parliamentary majority to Common Council. Thereafter, Common Council began to pressure the more conservative Lord Mayor Gurney and Court of Aldermen to widen the London franchise, and on January 4 named a Committee of Safety to take control of the trained bands. That same day, Charles I stormed into the House of Commons to arrest five of his loudest critics, but, forewarned, they had already fled to Coleman Street. When he went to the Guildhall on the 5th to demand extradition, crowds shouted "Privileges of Parliament!" The mayor and aldermen did not dare cooperate. Instead, City funds for the king dried up, shops closed, citizens began to organize in augmentation of the trained bands, and chains were put across major streets: the capital was preparing to defend itself against its own king. By January 10, Charles I no longer thought his family to be safe in London; they left to the jeers of apprentices. The next day Londoners cheered the five members as they made a triumphant return by barge. That summer, Gurney was impeached, sent to the Tower, and replaced as lord mayor by the radical Puritan Isaac Pennington (c. 1584–1661). From this point, the City authorities threw their weight behind Parliament and, once the war started in August, they threw money as well.

The two sides in the English theater of the British Civil Wars should have been well matched. Most social groups in the country split fairly evenly between the king's supporters (or Cavaliers) and Parliament's supporters (or Roundheads). The crucial difference was London: on balance, London supported Parliament. This gave the Roundheads the apparatus of government, especially taxation; access to the City's vast wealth in taxes and loans; most of the country's manufacturing base, which meant muskets and uniforms; and the trained bands, the closest thing to a professional army in England. Of these advantages, the most important was what Thomas Hobbes called "the great purses of the City of London."[15] Their contents were funneled efficiently into parliamentary coffers by an unpopular weekly assessment. Because the king had all the best generals at first, however, the English Civil Wars, like the American, would be a race to see if those generals could win a decisive blow before London's wealth overwhelmed them. As in previous civil conflicts, capturing London would be such a decisive blow.

As the king's army approached the metropolis in November 1642, the city strengthened the walls, added fortifications at a suburban perimeter, and sent the trained bands out to meet the royal forces, which they did at Turnham Green, five miles to the west. In the event, Charles chose not to press his advantage in cavalry against the untested London militia. Perhaps he thought that withdrawing to winter quarters would be the statesmanlike thing to do, persuading his subjects to return to their senses. After several abortive plots and one more military offensive in the summer of 1643, the king gave up on seizing London by force, and both sides settled into a war of attrition that gave Parliament and its Scottish allies an advantage because of their superior resources in men and material. In May 1646, following the decisive battle of Naseby, Northamptonshire the previous year, the last Royalist army in England surrendered, and Charles was taken prisoner. This did not settle matters; instead the king began to negotiate with Parliament, the Scots, even the New Model Army that had beaten him to return as a constitutional monarch. But he never negotiated in good faith: he was convinced that to give up one shred of his prerogative was a sin against the Crown God gave him. All along, he continually asked to go to London, because if he could play to the crowd and take advantage of the likely pro-Royalist reaction, the new settlement might be more advantageous. Now that the king was in effect a rebel against the victorious parliamentary side, London was his last best hope.

Those hopes grew as the City's support for Parliament began to splinter after 1647. While London contained relatively large numbers of Puritan Independents, Levellers, sectaries, and radicals who wanted to usher in God's republic on Earth, the Court of Aldermen and, increasingly from 1643, even Common Council were dominated by more moderate, or Presbyterian, Puritans who wanted to settle with the king and establish a Presbyterian state church. These men had allies in Parliament and were crucial to the financial health of the new regime. At one point in 1647, after the Parliamentary Presbyterians urged that the Army should be sent, largely unpaid, to settle the situation in Ireland, the soldiers marched toward the capital to demand their pay, halting on the outskirts of the metropolis at Uxbridge. The City responded by raising a cavalry regiment, closing its gates, and preparing to defend itself, this time against a parliamentary army. In late July, the City fathers, accompanied by an angry Presbyterian mob, marched on Parliament, bursting through the doors of both Houses to urge that the City retain control of its trained bands and invite the king to return to his capital. London was launching a counterrevolution. But when the mayor and aldermen subsequently ordered drums beaten to call out all able-bodied Londoners to defend the City, few showed up. Many ordinary Londoners favored the Army, the Independents, and the radical reform of church and state; others might have thought better of pitting their fighting skills against the only truly professional military force in England. The City formally capitulated, and the Army entered London on August 4 with 15,000 men, colors flying. The next day, they escorted back to Parliament the Independent MPs who had fled the city, and then had the Royalist lord mayor, Sir John Gayer (1584–1649), and several aldermen indicted for high treason. For the moment, the radical Independents ruled the City. The Army began the systematic destruction of London's fortifications.

As usual, the nation followed London's lead. Although Charles I attempted to reignite the Civil Wars in 1648, without London his cause was doomed. The king would see his capital but once more, under heavy guard. On December 6, 1648, a detachment of the Army led by Col. Thomas Pride (d. 1658) marched on Parliament and expelled all but the most radical members in what became known as "Pride's Purge." The following month, January 1649, the resulting "Rump" of a Parliament brought Charles I up on a charge of High Treason against the people of England. The dramatic trial took place in Westminster Hall. The verdict of "guilty" being a foregone conclusion, Charles I was executed on a scaffold erected on the street side of the Banqueting House at Whitehall before a London crowd on the frosty morning of January 30, 1649. In the aftermath, the Rump Parliament abolished the monarchy, the court, and the House of Lords. London was now the capital of a republic.

But it would continue to be difficult to rule. First, the execution of the king was a step too far for many. Lord Mayor Abraham Reynardson (1590–1661) refused to proclaim the abolition of the monarchy and was deprived of his office, fined, and sent to the Tower. In fact, London Royalism never died out. Second, the Puritan leadership could not agree among themselves. The Independents who came to power at the end of the 1640s were never able to accomplish their proposed reforms of the livery companies or expansion of the franchise. The Presbyterians soon reasserted themselves, supported by Oliver Cromwell, whom they feasted as lord protector in February 1654 at Grocers' Hall. Still, both the Commonwealth and Cromwellian regimes had to watch London carefully, and frequently there were disputes over whether Parliament or the City Corporation controlled the City militia. London's apprentices also proved restive, protesting attempts to suppress Christmas celebrations and stage plays. Cromwell's death in the autumn of 1658 precipitated another crisis of authority, leading to a succession of regimes over the course of the next year and a half: his son, Richard Cromwell's (1626–1712), then a restored Rump, then the Army, then the Rump again, and so forth. Londoners, angry at high taxes, and fearing a military takeover, took to the streets. In December 1659, a group of apprentices petitioned the Corporation demanding the recall of the full Long Parliament. Later, at the Royal Exchange, they beat off a detachment of the Army sent to suppress them as householders threw stones from their open windows. On the 20th, Common Council declared for a free Parliament; in ward elections the next day, moderate Presbyterians and Royalists made big gains. Once again, the failure to secure London signaled that regime change was imminent.

At this point, General George Monck (1608–1670), the ranking commander in Scotland, began to march south with the only fully paid army in the British Isles. He reached London in February 1660. After some hesitation and pressure by the City authorities (as well as demonstrations by watermen and apprentices), on the 11th he ordered the Rump to call for immediate elections to a new Parliament, thereby dissolving itself. A relieved Corporation lent £60,000 to support the interim regime, and London's citizens, ever enamored of ritual and symbol, celebrated by lighting bonfires and roasting rump steaks in the streets that night. The next few weeks saw jockeying by Anglican Royalists (who wanted a full restoration of the monarchy) and Presbyterians (who wanted a more constitutional arrangement) over the shape of the new regime. In the end, London Royalism reasserted itself decisively. The royal arms reappeared in churches, shops, and livery halls. On April 24, crowds in Hyde Park shouted "God Save the King," and on May Day Anglican rioters attacked Baptist meeting houses. The new Convention Parliament (because it convened itself without royal command) invited Charles I's eldest son, also named Charles, to return as king. On May 29, 1660, coincidentally the anniversary of his birth, Charles II entered London accompanied by Monck, newly created Duke of Albemarle and master of the Horse, as well as a host of aristocratic supporters, both old and new. The words of John Evelyn aptly convey the splendor of this elite demonstration of hierarchy and power, fully worthy of a Tudor royal entry, as well as a palpable sense of relief at the restoration of the Old Order:

> This day came in his Majestie Charles the 2d to London after a sad, & long Exile, and Calamitous Suffering both of the King & Church: being 17 yeares: This was also his Birthday, and with a Triumph of above 20000 horse & foote, brandishing their swords and shouting with unexpressable joy: The wayes straw'd with flowers, the bells ringing, the streetes hung with Tapissry [tapestry], fountaines running with wine: the Major [mayor], Aldermen, all the Companies in their liver[ie]s, Chaines of Gold, banners; Lords & nobles, Cloth of Silver, gold & vellvet every body clad in, the windos & balconies all set with Ladys, Trumpets, Musick, & myriards [myriads] of people flocking the streetes & was as far as Rochester, so as they were 7 houres in passing the Citty, even from 2 in the afternoone 'til nine at night.

Clearly, London remembered how to welcome authority as well as resist it. The Great Chain of Being had not only been restored; it had processed across London Bridge and through Temple Bar. No wonder that Evelyn, a devout member of the Church of England and landed gentleman who had lost much during the preceding revolution, wrote "I stood in the strand, & beheld it, & blessed God."[16]

RESTORATION AND REVOLUTION

The era of good feeling promised by the Restoration did not last. Charles II was willing to work with moderate Presbyterians, but men of Evelyn's background, Anglican and Royalist, saw little difference between moderate Presbyterians and radical Independent Puritans. Seeking to undo the radical experiments of the previous twenty years, they restored not only the Stuarts to their throne but also fellow High Churchmen and Royalists to the pulpits and offices of Church and state. Thus sixty-four Puritan London preachers lost their livings. But the radicals would not go away. In January 1661, a Fifth Monarchist from the meeting house in Swan Alley, Coleman Street named Thomas Venner (1608/09–1661) led an uprising in the streets of the City. His fifty followers, refusing to accept the death of their millinerian dreams, marching under a banner emblazoned "The Lord God and Gideon" and shouting "The Lord Jesus and the [regicides'] heads upon the gates," seized St. Paul's. For the next two days they fought a running battle through the streets of the City, from Cheapside to Aldersgate, Bishopsgate to Leadenhall Street, before being cornered at Wood Street. The Swan Alley meeting house was demolished, and Venner and fourteen rebels were executed within the month.

These events only confirmed in Anglican and Royalist eyes that Puritans were disloyal fanatics. They put an end to any possibility of accommodation between the Restoration regime and even moderate nonconformity. Within a year, a heavily Royalist and Anglican "Cavalier" Parliament passed a series of laws, the Clarendon Code, designed to remove Puritans (i.e., Presbyterians and Independents alike, now lumped together as "Dissenters" because they could no longer claim to be part of the Church of England) from public life. The Corporation Act of 1661 (13 Chas. II, c. 1), in particular, required all holders of municipal office to take oaths of allegiance and supremacy to the king and communion in the Church of England. The only way that a Dissenter could still serve in metropolitan office was by swallowing his scruples and taking Anglican communion, a practice called "Occasional Conformity." A special commission purged Dissenters from City government in 1662–1663. This restored the old tension between a Royalist Court of Aldermen and a Puritan Common Hall and citizenry, who immediately elected Dissenting MPs to the new Parliament in 1661. In 1664, after the Conventicle Act (16 Chas. II, c. 4) outlawed Dissenting meetings, the lord mayor ordered constables to break them up. Finally, as we have seen, the national government sought to regulate the press and the coffeehouse (see Chapter 5).

Clearly, the Restoration honeymoon was over. Londoners grew disillusioned with their king and his brother, James Duke of York, as they began to reveal inclinations toward absolutism and even Catholicism. Worse, at mid-decade London was struck by three major disasters: the Great Plague of 1665, the Great Fire of 1666, and the attack by the Dutch Fleet up the River Medway in 1667. The first two are addressed in greater detail in the next chapter; for now it is important to note that the court (and many Anglican clergy) lost prestige when it fled London to parts west during the plague epidemic, regained some of it when the king and Duke of York took charge of fighting the fire, but lost it again thanks to the Crown's poor performance in the Anglo-Dutch War of 1664 to 1668.

After the Restoration, England's traditional enemies, Spain and France, were still recovering from the effects of the Thirty Years' War. Early in the reign, England's principal trade rival was the independent Netherlands; the Dutch competed with London merchants hoping to dominate trade with the Americas and the Far East. In particular, they hoped to break the Navigation Acts (see Chapter 2) and thus into England's overseas Empire. As a result, by the mid-1660s, the country was, according to Pepys, "mad for war."

The war began well for England with the capture of New Amsterdam, renamed New York, in 1664. It continued with a series of indecisive naval battles in the Channel. To staff the Navy, men were impressed against their will, taken from London pubs and streets without warning. As we have seen, those who survived found themselves poorly paid for their forced service. Worse, the war ended disastrously when, in 1667, Charles II laid up the fleet to save money. This allowed the Dutch fleet under Admiral Michel de Ruyter (1607–1676) to land marines in Essex and Kent; bombard the royal fort at Sheerness; and then sail up the Thames and Medway unopposed to raid the Royal Navy's home base at Chatham between June 10 and 14. There, they sank the ships of the line *Royal James*, *Royal Oak*, and *Loyal London*. In a final mortification, they towed away the *Royal Charles*, flagship of the Royal Navy; part of its stern section is still displayed proudly in the National Museum in Amsterdam. The king was rumored to be spending the evening with his mistress, Lady Castlemaine, while panicked Londoners fled en masse.

Although the Dutch withdrew as quickly as they had come, the disastrous war combined with the economic fallout from the previous year's plague and fire sent government revenues plummeting just as debt was skyrocketing. The metropolis was full of poorly paid demobilized soldiers and sailors, while Puritan preachers thundered that London and the Restoration court were being punished for their sins, for persecuting Dissenters, and for turning away from godliness at the Restoration. All of this helps to explain why the Bawdy House Riots of 1668 turned political. That year's riots were unusually large, involving "many thousands" (one estimate gives 40,000) over five days (March 23 to 27) around Easter, not Shrove Tuesday. The rioters pulled down brothels in Poplar, Moorfields, East Smithfield, St. Leonard Shoreditch, and St. Andrew Holborn. They were also very well organized, with captains and regiments distinguished by green ribbons (the Leveller color) and armed with "iron bars, polaxes, long staves, and other weapons" for tearing down houses. After some of the ringleaders were arrested on March 24, the rioters stormed Finsbury Gaol and the New Prison at Clerkenwell to free them. Perhaps the most alarming aspect to these riots for the national and city elite were the rioters' slogans, which articulated grievances well beyond the proliferation of brothels: "Down with the Red Coats;" that they (the rioters) "would come and pull Whitehall down;" "[I]f the king did not give them liberty of conscience, that May-day must be a bloody day;" and perhaps most comprehensive and frightening of all, "[W]e have been servants, but we will be masters now."

But the regime of Charles II was seen not only as intolerant and authoritarian; the disaster of the Dutch war had proved that it was corrupt and incompetent as well. Many blamed the king's Catholic sympathies and the distractions of his virtual stable of mistresses. Anonymous pamphlets from the London press caught the mood and undoubtedly fanned the flames. One, *The Poor-Whores petition. To the most splendid, illustrious, serene and eminent lady of Pleasure, the Countess of Castelmayne*, identifies the king's favorite (and Catholic) mistress as the patroness and chief examplar of the "undone company of poor distressed whores, bawds, pimps and panders," and associates her with other Catholics at court. There followed two satirical replies in which Castlemaine is made to acknowledge her role as head whore and advocate of Popery at Whitehall. Thus, London's pamphleteers and rioting apprentices anticipated the strategy of Gay and Fielding in linking sin in high places and low, equating the corruption of the court, the advance of Popery, and the lack of toleration for Dissenters with prostitution. The regime took the threat seriously enough to prosecute fifteen of the ringleaders on charges of high treason and levying war against the king. Yet, in keeping with tradition, just four were hanged, drawn, and quartered.[17]

By the late 1670s, the issue of the succession loomed. Although Charles II's mistresses had produced over a dozen children, he had not managed to conceive a legitimate heir with his legal consort, Catherine of Braganza. That meant that the next in line for the throne was the king's brother, James, Duke of York – from 1672 a professed Roman Catholic. By this time, Roman Catholicism was associated in the English mind with the fires of Smithfield under Bloody Mary; the attempt of the Spanish Armada under Elizabeth; the failed Gunpowder Plot under James I; the Irish Rebellion under Charles I; the Great Fire under Charles II (see Chapter 8); and absolutism, tyranny, and persecution in general. The royal family's sympathy for Catholics, pro-French foreign policy, and extravagance provoked the rise of an opposition in Parliament under Anthony Ashley Cooper, Earl of Shaftesbury. That opposition found wealthy allies among Dissenters in Common Council seeking liberty of conscience, that is, an end to persecution. Their position gained traction in late 1678 when allegations surfaced of a "Popish Plot" to kill the king and place James on the throne with French help. These allegations were false but enabled Shaftesbury to mold the opposition into England's first political party, called "Whigs" by their detractors, using a slang term for Scottish Presbyterian rebels. The Whigs swept three successive elections from 1679 to 1681 on a platform of excluding the Duke of York from the throne by parliamentary statute. In his place, Parliament would name as the king's successor his eldest, illegitimate but Protestant son, James Scott, Duke of Monmouth (1649–1685). Clearly, on the question of sovereignty, the Whigs favored the rights of Parliament over those of the king. Consequently, they opposed a standing army and attacked the court's extravagance. They favored liberty of conscience for Dissenters but harsh persecution of Catholics. Because Catholicism was an international movement, they favored a pro-Dutch, anti-French foreign policy. Although popular with the London mercantile community (where Dissent was strong), they claimed to represent "country" values. In short, Whigs stood firm against what they perceived as an international conspiracy to render England an absolutist, Catholic state.

To win the elections noted earlier, Shaftesbury and the Whigs, like John Pym and his circle before them, exploited the capital's peculiar features – the press, the coffeehouses, the crowd, and in particular, a cohesive Dissenting community toughened by persecution – to pioneer many of the techniques of modern party politics. They founded political dining societies, which met at London taverns to plan strategy. They capitalized on the temporary expiration of the Licensing Act by commissioning pamphlets, poems, and other propaganda from London presses. Because monster petitions were now against the law, they found other ways to harness and display popular opinion. Like the parliamentary radicals of 1640 to 1642, they turned the streets of London into a Protestant carnival, using massive processions on national holidays like Gunpowder Treason Day (November 5) and Queen Elizabeth's Accession Day (November 17) as cover to make their points. For example, on November 17, 1679 it was said that 150,000 people – if true, perhaps one-third of the population of greater London – marched from Moorfields to Chancery Lane to commemorate Queen Elizabeth's Accession Day. On these occasions, the pope and assorted cardinals and Jesuits were burned in effigy to the cheers of the masses. The Crown, feeling the pressure, began to harass Catholics and ease the persecution of Dissenters. This resulted in full meeting houses in the City, where Puritan clergymen urged their flocks to take a stand against Popery. Charles II cultivated City leaders by attending lord mayor's feasts. But what the protestors and preachers really wanted was the summoning of Parliament, because the king had refused to call it from May 1679 to October 1680. As a result, the Whigs argued, the people had no way of making their voices heard by the king. Whig London next organized a massive petitioning campaign that was technically illegal, but the *mobile vulgaris* could not be stopped.

The king could refuse the petitions coldly, but there was not much he could do to restrain the City electorate. In 1679 the citizenry returned Dissenting MPs like Thomas Pilkington (1628–1691) and Sir Thomas Player (d. 1686) who were early advocates of Exclusion. In the July 1680 shrieval elections, Common Hall rejected "three persons of more moderate tempers"[18] in favor of two radical nonconformist parliamentarians, Slingsby Bethel (1617–1697) and Henry Cornish (d. 1685), over royal objections. The following year they elected Pilkington and the equally radical Samuel Shute (d. 1685), to whom Charles II refused the customary knighthood. These elections were crucial. First, they split the government of London between a Tory lord mayor (Sir John Moore: lived 1620–1702) and recorder (Sir George Jeffreys: lived 1645–1689) and two Whig sheriffs. Whereas some City officials thus promoted petitions for a Parliament and Exclusion, others, like Jeffreys, attempted to thwart them: this led Pilkington to call him "a common enemy of mankind."[19]

More to the point, sheriffs impaneled juries: radical Whig sheriffs preferred radical Whig, and therefore Catholic-hating, jurors. As a result, many Catholics went to the block unjustly in 1679 and 1680 for their supposed role in the Popish Plot. In contrast, when in the summer of 1681 Charles II had Shaftesbury arrested on a charge of high treason, a Whig jury quashed the prosecution with a verdict of ignoramus. Charles's response upped the ante: he ordered the lord mayor to suppress conventicles and issued *quo warranto* proceedings against the City's charter. *Quo warranto* means "by what warrant?"; this amounted to the king's demand for the charter, which once surrendered he could change according to his lights. London's ancient privileges at stake, Sheriff Pilkington fought the request vigorously: one Royalist observed "His tongue speaks naked swords."[20] Pilkington organized a series of feasts in 1682 paying tribute to Shaftesbury, the Duke of Monmouth, and other Whig leaders, while loyalists had their own feasts in honor of the Duke of York. These dinners, usually held in a guild hall, featured lots of political theater as liverymen, freemen, and the ever active apprentices displayed their allegiance in skits, banners, and loyal toasts. In other words, Londoners could show their colors in many ways: petitioning, deliberating on juries, rioting, and even eating.

By 1681, however, a reaction was developing in the City and the country at large. As in 1640 to 1642, the radical appeal to the rights of Parliament, the press, and the people produced a conservative response. Loyalist citizens who opposed Exclusion and any diminishment of royal power abhorred the constant round of petitions and feasts. These abhorers joined courtiers and old Royalists to form their own political party. Because they were therefore perceived as being soft on Catholics, they were dubbed "Tories" (slang for Irish-Catholic bandits) by *their* detractors. Tories ran on a platform of safeguarding the hereditary succession in the person of James, Duke of York, whatever his religion. As this implies, they favored the rights of the king over those of Parliament. Although Tories conceded the necessity of Parliaments, they thought that the lesson of the Civil Wars was that only a strong king could guarantee order. Because kings were chosen by God and Parliaments were subordinate to kings, no one could tamper with the hereditary succession, nor would they deny the king funds. They wanted the Anglican Church to remain the only legal religious establishment in England. Although they had little love for Catholics, they saw the real danger to English life coming from radical Dissenters (who, they would point out, had actually killed the last king). They therefore wanted to maintain and strengthen the Clarendon Code. They had no particular quarrel with Louis XIV and saw the Dutch as trading rivals. They therefore favored a pro-French, anti-Dutch foreign policy. Their values were those of the court and the Great Chain of Being.

Although the Tories accused the Whigs of undermining the constitution and social order by courting popularity and exploiting the London mob, they were not above copying and extending Whig techniques. In London, they organized Tory clubs, Tory printed propaganda, Tory "loyal addresses," Tory feasts, at which the king and Duke of York were toasted, and Tory demonstrations, at which effigies of "Jack Presbyter" or Shaftesbury himself might be burned. Once again, there never was a single London mob but Whig and Tory variations thereof. Although the Tories abhorred appealing to the masses, they used the Anglican pulpit as well to argue that all authority came from God and that it could be revoked only by Him. Therefore, rebellion was never justified; instead, even a bad king was to be endured patiently, obeyed passively, resisted not at all, because as the Civil Wars proved, the alternative was far worse.

By 1682 the country was beginning to suspect that there was no Popish Plot. Charles II played his cards well, flattering loyal City companies by attending their banquets. A City constitutional crisis developed over the next shrieval election. Pilkington and the Whigs claimed that Common Hall had the right to elect both sheriffs, whereas Charles II and the Tories claimed that it was the lord mayor's customary right to name one: conveniently for them, the current lord mayor, Sir John Moore, was a Tory. The result was deadlocked meetings of Common Council and Common Hall, and abortive elections in June, July, and September. City government was paralyzed, "pulpits rattle[d] . . . like kettle drums,"[21] and the streets buzzed with talk of rebellion when the king, exasperated, threw Pilkington and Shute, whose job it was to organize the election, into the Tower. Then, after a series of hotly disputed polls, in a move of pure political muscle, Moore simply recognized two Tories, Dudley North (1641–1691) and Peter Rich (?1630–1692), despite an obvious Whig majority in the votes. This led Pilkington to attack Charles II to his face in Council.

The Tory "victory" in the shrieval elections of 1682 turned the tide of London politics. The City's new, uniformly Tory administration steered City loans into royal coffers. That, combined with increased Customs revenues thanks to the Commercial Revolution and a secret subsidy from Louis XIV, meant that Charles II had enough money – if he economized – to rule without Parliament. To neutralize Shaftesbury's London organization and its attendant Whig mob, the king convened his last, short-lived Parliament in 1681 at Oxford, the most safely Royalist city in England. Finally, in June 1683 the courts settled the quo warranto case in his favor, declaring the City's charter forfeit to the Crown. From this point, the lord mayor and Court of Aldermen were royal appointees, Common Council was effectively stripped of its powers, and the electorate was gerrymandered to produce a Tory majority. Pilkington and other Whig aldermen were accused of *scandalum magnatum* (libeling peers of the realm) and fined crushing amounts, although the Crown later relented. Whig party leaders were reduced to half-hearted plotting. Thus, Charles II succeeded where his father had failed, besting the City. For once the king, not his capital, had won.

Unfortunately for the cause of Stuart absolutism, Charles II was succeeded by his much less *politique* brother James, who gradually but steadily alarmed and alienated his Tory "base" by threatening the privileged position of the Anglican Church and seeking the toleration of both Catholicism and Dissent (see Introduction). In 1686/87 he used the Crown's new power over the Corporation to restore some Dissenting Whigs to office in the hope that they would support his plans. This offended Anglican Tories without winning over many Dissenting Whigs, who feared Popery more than they wanted their own freedom. As always, Londoners voted with their feet and with their throats. When the court announced the birth of an heir, James, Prince of Wales, on June 10, 1688, the bell ringing was desultory and few bonfires were lit. But when, a few weeks earlier, seven Anglican bishops were sent to the Tower for questioning the king's right to suspend the laws against Catholics and Dissenters, they were supported by massive crowds lining the Thames. John Evelyn wrote: "Wonderfull was the concerne of the people for them, infinite crowds of people on their knees, beging their blessing & praying for them as they passed out of the Barge; along the Tower wharfe &c:" When the seven bishops were acquitted a few days later, pandemonium broke out as enthusiastic Londoners rang church bells, lit bonfires, and illuminated their houses. According to Evelyn, this "was taken very ill at court." And yet, this demonstration was not inconsistent with order and hierarchy: "There was a lane of people from the King's Bench to the water-side, upon their knees as the Bishops passed & repassed, to beg their blessing."[22] Even the Civil War and Exclusion demonstrations had, for the most part, been organized by members of the elite and although possibly rebellious, they were rarely riotous. In 1688, however, the London mob went out of control, beginning a century of crowd initiative.

The birth of a Catholic heir in June 1688 sparked a revolution. A few days before, seven important noblemen had asked William of Orange to invade to save the Protestant religion and the English constitution. He decided to do so mostly to protect his wife's claim to the throne and to bring the power of the British kingdoms into his fight with Louis XIV. The summer and fall of 1688 saw a breakdown in the authority that Charles II had done so much to establish over the City. With William's forces poised for invasion, a panicked James restored London's charter and several Whig aldermen on October 16. Censorship virtually disappeared. When the invaders finally landed on the south coast on November 5, anti-Catholic riots in London delayed the march of James's army. Meanwhile, after some hesitation, English peers and gentlemen began to flock to William's side. On December 11 the king fled his capital. In the wake of this event, the Tory lord mayor suffered a fatal stroke, Whigs began to flood back into City government, and London's recorder, Sir George Treby (1644–1700) invited the Prince of Orange to enter London "in the name of this Capitall City." Some kind of authority was needed, for rumors flew that James's disbanded army, full of Irish Catholics, was running amok in London. According to Roger Morrice (1629–1702), there was "a universall terrible alarme . . . all over London and Westminster . . . that they should have their throats cut by the French and by the Papists; insomuch that almost all, but soldiers and footmen, kept in their houses, locked and bolted their doors."[23] In fact, the only people running amok in London during the "Irish nights" of December 11 to 15, 1688 were anti-Catholic mobs of apprentices, thieves, and looters who attacked Catholic houses and chapels, foreign embassies, and government officials.

It might be fear of the breakdown of authority that explains why other Londoners cheered James's temporary return on the 16th after he had been stopped at the coast. As related by the staunchly Tory Thomas, Earl of Ailesbury (1656–1741), Royalist London turned out in force, recalling the frenzied celebrations of Charles II's restoration a generation before.

> [V]ast numbers of persons out of the City and suburbs came out on horseback, and the road filled with spectators on foot with faces of joy, Blackheath was covered with gentlemen and citizens on horseback, and two eminent merchants came to the coach-side to beg of me to beseech the King to pass through the City and that he would be witness of the joyful acclamations of his subjects. . . . from St. George's Southwark to Whitehall: a long march, there was scarce room for the coaches to pass through, and the balconies and windows besides were thronged, with laud acclamations beyond whatever was heard of. . . . In fine, the joy was so great and general . . . and this I was an eye and ear witness of.[24]

It should be noted, however, that James's southerly route avoided the heavy concentrations of Dissenters in the City.

Both James's homecoming and popularity were short-lived. The next evening William sent a delegation of English peers to demand that the king agree to leave Whitehall. Those demands were backed by the Prince's Dutch guards, massed in St. James's Park, rifles primed and loaded. Had

James resisted, his forces might have rallied, as did Mary Tudor's over a century before, and fought a pitched battle for control of the capital in palace and park. Instead, the king folded, ordering his guards to stand down and agreeing to be escorted by William's guards to Rochester, on the east coast. He departed the next day, the 18th, in a pouring rain and by water so as to avoid the London crowds, "for they feared an insurrection in behalfe of the king who was so joyfully received but the Sunday evening before."[25] A few hours after James left London by barge headed east, William entered by carriage from the west "to the loud acclamations of a vast number of people of all sorts and ranks, the bells everywhere ringing."[26] As William's troops fanned out into the city, crowds, many of them brandishing oranges on pikes, braved the rain to greet them, women in Fleet Street shaking the Dutch soldiers by the hand and shouting "welcome, welcome. God bless you, you come to redeeme our religion, lawes, liberties, and lives. God reward you."[27] Clearly this was a different set of Londoners from the one that had cheered James's return a few days before. All this time William courted the City administration by promising a confirmation of its charter. The lord mayor and aldermen responded by offering £200,000 for "carrying on the government." After much debate, closely followed by the crowds in Westminster Palace Yard, Parliament asked the Prince and Princess of Orange to take the Crown as William III and Mary II at Whitehall on February 13, 1689.

Like all Revolutions, this was a moment of possibility: the 1689 elections saw the return of a Whig lord mayor, sheriffs, MPs, and a majority of Common Council. Restored Whig aldermen considered a radical undoing not only of Charles II's reforms, but of the City's ancient constitutional arrangements, proposing that from henceforward the lord mayor and sheriffs be elected by the freemen of Common Hall and the aldermen elected by the freemen of their wards, a much wider franchise than heretofore. They also proposed to enhance Common Council's power vis-à-vis the Court of Aldermen. In the spring of 1690, however, a Tory Parliament rejected the new proposed City constitution. Soon after, Tories mounted a successful takeover of Common Council, gaining strength among humble craftsmen and shopkeepers in extramural and riverside wards who resented Dissenting influence and wartime taxation. No Whig alderman would want to increase *their* authority. Rather, the once-radical and anti-Royalist Whig oligarchy was now happy to keep the franchise narrow and concentrate on supporting the Crown of William and Mary in return for lucrative financial deals and war contracts. Over the next twenty years, power shifted back and forth, but from about 1707 the lord mayor, most of the aldermen and many directors of companies tended to be Whig Dissenters, whereas Common Council was dominated by Tories. Because the national government was also Whig from 1714 to 1760, Daniel Defoe could write in the 1720s of the "perfect good understanding between the Court and city."[28] Tories became the party of City opposition and democracy, representing small shopkeepers and tradesmen who felt left out. In the words of its historian, Gary De Krey, the City had become "a fractured society."

POLITICAL RIOTS II

This shift explains perhaps the greatest overtly political riot of the period. It occurred in 1710 over the prosecution of Rev. Henry Sacheverell, but politics was one among many factors. As with Evil May Day, all of the trouble began with a fiery sermon. Traditionally, English churches commemorated the four great anniversaries of the Stuart political calendar – Royal Martyr Day on January 30, Restoration Day on May 29, Gunpowder Treason Day on November 5, and Queen Elizabeth's Accession on November 17 – with services that included a sermon tailored for the occasion. That is, these sermons tended to be highly political and partisan. The November 5 sermon for 1709 took place after six and a half years of a bitter and expensive war against France, Britain's second in defense of the Glorious Revolution since 1688, the War of the Spanish Succession. The military conflict had mostly gone well for the British, with the Duke of Marlborough winning decisive victories against the French at Blenheim (1704), Ramillies (1706), and Oudenarde (1708), but Allied forces had been defeated in Spain at Almanza (1707) and Brihuega (1710). Moreover, the raids of French privateers were taking a toll on English trade. Whereas the Whig government, associated with the toleration of Dissenters at home and support for the Germans and Dutch abroad, was determined to fight on until Louis XIV was completely defeated, Tories wondered why, given Marlborough's victories, the war dragged on. Some accused the London financial community – rich financiers and prosperous government contractors, mostly Dissenters and Whigs – of prolonging it for the profits. Londoners also complained about an influx of war refugees, the Poor Palatines, who were perceived as taking advantage of Whig government handouts and taking work away from native Englishmen. Thus, the motivation for the riots combined elements of calendar ritual, xenophobia, religious difference, and political and economic grievances.

It was in this climate that a fiery Tory preacher, Dr. Henry Sacheverell, preached an incendiary sermon on November 5, 1709 on the text "the perils of false brethren" (2 Cor. xi. 26). Although his subject was ostensibly the anniversary of the Catholic attempt to blow up the king and Parliament in 1605, he connected these events with William III's landing at Torbay on the same date in 1688, the ensuing Revolution, and the current Whig regime in England. In fact, the sermon was an explicit attack on the Revolution of 1688/89 and, by extension, the whole course of English history over the last twenty years. Sacheverell decried the current ministry, Whigs, Low Church Anglicans, and the toleration of occasionally conforming Dissenters in government and finance, all of whom he called "this Brood of Vipers. . . . Miscreants, Begot in Rebellion, Born in Sedition, and Nurs'd up in Faction."[29] The message might have been old, but the medium was new: this rant was printed, reaching 100,000 copies and sparking a partisan religious debate carried on in 600 additional titles within a year. In December, the Whig government decided to prosecute Sacheverell on a charge of seditious libel.

The trial took place during a hard winter, when food prices were high and London trade depressed. On the evening of its third day, March 1, 1710, rioting broke out in the West End. Encouraged by Tory gentlemen with cash, a mob of between 2,000 and 5,000 Londoners armed with swords and clubs, crying "High Church and Dr. Sacheverell," attacked the houses of prominent Whigs and the Dissenting meeting houses where they worshiped: six of the latter were destroyed. They also threatened the Bank of England in Grocers' Hall. These were specific targets, and there was an element of organization and ritual to the attacks. Indeed, as so often in the past, many rioters were acting under the impression that they were defending traditional values: the Anglican Church, a poor persecuted clergyman, and Queen Anne herself, who was widely believed to be sick of the war and her Whig government. Perhaps they were not wrong: although the Whigs pursued the ringleaders aggressively, when the government fell later in the year the new Tory administration reversed some of the sentences.

In fact, the Sacheverell riots were only the first of many demonstrations by partisan London crowds over the next decade. During Anne's final years, Whig and Tory mobs found ample excuse to take to the streets on political anniversaries (e.g.,Gunpowder Treason; Elizabeth's accession); royal birthdays (e.g., Anne's, William's, the Hanoverians, the exiled Stuarts), and legislative victories or defeats (e.g., the Commercial Treaty and the Peace, both in 1713). The death of the English, Anglican, and Tory-leaning Queen Anne on August 1, 1714, and the accession of the German, Lutheran, and Whig-inclined George I according to the terms of the Act of Settlement (1701) was a watershed in English history. This accession dashed the hopes of the Jacobite wing of the Tory party and initiated a half-century of Whig dominance of the central government (see Introduction). But no one could have known that in 1714: the new regime had not yet established itself; France remained powerful; the Pretender might yet invade; and Tories could hope that, failing another restoration, if they played their cards right, the Hanoverians might give them office.

In this climate, neither Whig nor Tory crowds were willing to concede the streets of London to the other side. Their historian, Nicholas Rogers, has found little evidence of upper-class manipulation of rioters in this period; rather, by this time, the London crowd was proficient at deploying the signs and symbols of political allegiance on its own. First, each side exploited xenophobia: George I was a foreigner, and the Pretender was a pensioner of a foreign government. Second, demonstrations tended to be staged on anniversaries favorable to each side: for Whigs, the new king's birthday on May 28, his accession day on August 1, and Gunpowder Treason on November 5. Tories celebrated Anne's birthday on February 6, her coronation day on April 23, Restoration Day on May 29, and the Pretender's Birthday on June 10. As noted when we discussed the political calendar (in Chapter 5), apart from George I's birthday, Tories thus owned the streets in the spring and Whigs in the autumn. Both sides employed slogans ("God Bless the Queen and Church"; "No Presbyterian Government"; "No Jacobites; No Wooden Shoes"); they carried pictures, made toasts, lit bonfires, burned figures in effigy, and demanded the illumination of houses. Whig mobs (or "Mugs") organized in large-scale alehouses, known as *mug houses* because regular customers had their own beer mugs. Mobs of Tories, or "Jacks" (for Jacobite), responded by attacking the mug houses. The most famous such attack was the wrecking of Read's Mug House, Salisbury Court, in the summer of 1716, which resulted in five hangings. Tory-Jacobite crowds persisted throughout the early Hanoverian period, cheering the Jacobite rebels of 1715 to their executions.

It was in the midst of this "war for the streets" that a Whig Parliament passed the Riot Act (1715). As we have seen, the Riot Act famously declared that any twelve people unlawfully assembled constituted a riot. It further enacted that it was a felony, not excusable by benefit of clergy, to cause damage to places of worship, houses, barns, or stables. Clearly, this was a delayed Whig reaction to the Sacheverell Riots. The most famous provision of the act was the requirement that it actually be *read* in the presence of the rioters; that is, once the Riot Act had been read (hence the modern phrase), the rioters became accused felons, and law enforcement officials were indemnified for any violence that they might commit on the rioters. To "read the Riot Act" was to declare to the crowd that, whatever they might claim, they were a mob engaged in an illegal act, not respectful petitioners for redress, and that there were new consequences for such engagement. This legislation can be seen as part of a series of Whig moves (including the Septennial Act: 1 Geo. I, c. 38) to consolidate their grip on power, but it also marks a rejection of the traditional idea that riot was a legitimate and tolerable form of political communication, even communal law enforcement, to be punished leniently by the authorities. Instead, the Riot Act reserved the right of assembly to the elite itself and took part of the right to enforce community standards away from ordinary people and gave it to the state. In this, too, modernity was being forged on the streets of London.

But ordinary Londoners could still push back. In the late 1730s and early 1740s, the mayoralty and Court of Aldermen gradually came to be dominated by opposition politicians, partly because, after two decades of Walpole's peace policy, City merchants wanted aggressive trade war and more colonies. When Sir Robert proposed an unpopular increase in the Excise in 1733, a mob surrounded the House of Commons, jostled the prime minister, and responded to the reading of the Riot Act with: "Damn your laws and proclamations." Once again, they got what they wanted, as Walpole backed down. By the second great Jacobite rebellion of 1745, however, Tory crowd activity was largely ancient history: although ninety-seven Londoners were arrested, it was mostly for muttering something about the Pretender while in their cups. It might be argued that the London mobs grew less politically active by 1750 because the liberties for which they had marched in the seventeenth century were now more secure. Certainly, as under the Tudors, Londoners could just as often find reason to cheer their government out of doors, as in Queen Anne's frequent processions to St. Paul's to celebrate Marlborough's military victories, or the incendiary festivities in Green Park to celebrate the Treaty of Aix-le-Chappelle in 1749.

But they would never accept that they did not have a right to demonstrate. The streets of London grew more volatile again in the half-century after our period. As we have seen, weavers and other workers broke machines and attacked competitors throughout the 1760s. London crowds were active in the "Wilkes and Liberty" agitation of 1768/69 and produced "The greatest outburst of civil disorder in modern British history"[30] in the anti-Catholic Gordon Riots of 1780. Ten thousand troops were called out and fired on the rioters; 285 were killed; 450 were arrested; 59 sentenced to death; and 26 actually did hang – far more than for any riot in our period. In their wake, the public cavalcade of the condemned to Tyburn was done away with in 1783. Clearly, the Gordon Riots marked the end of elite tolerance for riot. Nevertheless, Londoners marched for Reform in the early 1830s, for a National Charter in the 1840s, for women's suffrage in the 1910s, and against nuclear weapons in the 1960s. They rioted in the East End in the 1930s, Brixton in the 1980s, and across Greater London in 2011. They gave the Thatcher government its final push via the Poll Tax Riots of 1990. Still, if the Crown has sometimes lost London, early modern City authorities, for all their fears, never really did so. This is just as well, for riot and even rebellion were not to be the greatest challenges facing their city.

8 . Plague and Fire

*W*e have seen how early modern Londoners handled chronic, man-made urban problems: poverty, crime, riot, and political upheaval. Challenging as they were, none of these afflictions, not even the rebellions of the sixteenth and seventeenth centuries, fundamentally threatened London's livelihood, the viability of its population, or its very existence. We must now examine London in extremis. Between the spring of 1665 and the autumn of 1666, two catastrophes befell the city: the Great Plague (although there is some debate whether it really was the greatest plague) and the Great Fire. In fact, neither was unprecedented, except in size. What was Londoners' experience of these disasters? How did they cope? Perhaps more important, how did they recover?

As we have seen, the 1660s were the decade of Restoration. Historians used to view the period as one of optimism and rational advance from the dark days of Civil War sectarian violence. It is true that these years saw an explosion of scientific progress, both symbolized and sustained by the foundation of the Royal Society, headquartered at Gresham College, in 1663. In addition, the English economy began a long-term recovery during this decade. National population growth began to slow down, and with it, the crippling inflation of the previous hundred years. The renewal of the Navigation Acts and the acquisition of New York in 1664 laid the groundwork for the Commercial Revolution that would make London the greatest port in Europe by the end of the century. Admittedly, only the most prescient could have anticipated the future benefits from these developments in the midst of a losing war, political tensions, and the natural disasters that characterized the middle of the decade, but a few scientists and statisticians, like John Graunt, Isaac Newton, and Sir William Petty, did try.

In fact, if Londoners were optimistic following the Restoration, it was less out of anticipation of the new than nostalgia for the old. Cromwell, Puritanism, and the austerity regime of the major generals had been repudiated in favor of Merrie Olde England. The Stuarts, the Church of England, and their ceremonial trappings had been reborn in springtime. The court was back in session, and fun was back in style. The public theaters and pleasure gardens reopened; Christmas celebrations and may-pole dancing were legal again. But, as Venner's Rebellion suggests, the Puritans did not go quietly. Puritan preachers rejected the new dispensation and thundered that England – and its Sin City capital – were ripe for God's punishment. It came in 1665.

THE GREAT PLAGUE OF 1665

Sometime after Christmas, 1664, Dr. Nathaniel Hodges (1629–1688) "was called to a young man in a Fever, who after two days course of alexiterial medicines, had two Risings about the bigness of a Nytmeg broke out, one on each Thigh."[1] The young man survived, but he was the first harbinger of London's last and most notorious outbreak of the plague. Plague was a constant worry in early modern London, but the winter of 1664/65 was one of the hardest in years, and it was thought that this would keep the scourge at bay. May and June 1665 were, however, unusually warm, and the parish clerks who compiled the Bills of Mortality began to notice that they were recording more burials, and that most of those were from plague. For example, in the parish of St. Giles-in-the-Fields, the tallies rose as follows:

Week ending:	Plague Deaths:
May 30:	9
June 6:	31
June 13:	68
June 20:	101
June 27:	143

The statistical impulse is a modern one, but these figures are not entirely reliable. As Samuel Pepys noted, the poor were underreported, and Dissenters often lived outside the parish structure in a variety of ways. For example, Quakers would not toll a bell for the dead. Later, at the height of the epidemic, parish clerks tried to avoid mass panic by reporting plague deaths as being from "dropsy" or French pox, griping of the guts, "frighted," or lethargy. Thus, the clerk at St. Olave Hart Street admitted to Pepys that "there died nine this week though I have returned only six."[2] In any case, the diarist knew that something was amiss by early June:

> This day, much against my Will, I did in Drury-lane see two or three houses marked with a red cross upon the doors, and "Lord have mercy upon us" writ there – which was a sad sight to me, being the first of that kind that to my remembrance I ever saw. It put me into an ill conception of myself and my smell, so that I was forced to buy some roll-tobacco to smell to and chaw – which took away the apprehension.[3]

People who remembered the epidemics of 1636 and 1647 began to remove their families from London. What were they so afraid of?

It is generally agreed, although not without dissent, that from 1347 through the 1720s Europe was subjected to repeated visitations of the same disease. Although medieval Europeans called it "the Black Death" (not the "Black Plague" as careless students sometimes do), by the seventeenth century they referred to it simply as "the plague." There are two types of plague, bubonic and pneumonic, both caused by enterobacteria. Pneumonic plague, passed through the air, is the less common. Bubonic plague is contracted from the bite of a flea carried on the European black rat (*Rattus rattus*); the fleas carry *Yersinia pestis*, the bacteria responsible for the infection. Most contemporaries missed this connection completely, leading to a great many mistaken strategies to combat the disease, such as the setting of fires to purge the air of supposed plague "effluvia."

One of the most frightening aspects of the plague was its suddenness. If a person were breathed on or bitten, symptoms appeared in 3 to 7 days, but their onset could be abrupt. You could be fine one minute, dying the next, as happened to Samuel Pepys's coachman on June 17, 1665:

> It stroke me very deep this afternoon, going with a Hackny-coach from my Lord Treasurer's down Holborne – the coachman I found to drive easily and easily; at last stood still, and came down hardly able to stand; and told me that he was suddenly stroke very sick and almost blind, he could not see. So I light and went into another coach with a sad heart for the poor man and trouble for myself, lest he should have been stroke with the plague, being at that end of town that I took him up. But God have mercy upon us all.[4]

Typically, the victim experienced fever, then diarrhea, headaches, swelling of the armpits and groin (infected lymph nodes), and finally rampaging internal bleeding. It was the resulting pooling of blood under the skin that produced the characteristic black blotches, or "buboes," that inspired the name *Black Death*. Once you were infected, your chances of dying were high: the death rate varied in London's past plague epidemics from 30% to 70%. This was partly because there was little that you could do: popular remedies were rosemary (sold for 8 shillings a handful in 1603), cakes of arsenic under the armpits, charms, amulets, and the maintaining of open fires to "burn" the plague out of the air as noted previously. Dr. Hodges, who stayed at his post throughout the epidemic, drank sack "to dissipate any Lodgment of the Infection."[5] It worked: Hodges survived. Dr. William Boghurst (?1631–1682), who also remained in London, recalled what little else a medical professional could do, the risk in doing it, and the poignancy of many last moments:

> I commonly drest forty soares in a day, held their pulse sweating in the bed half a quarter of an hour together to give judgment and informe myself in the various tricks of it. I lett one blood, gave glisters though but to a few, held them up in their bedds to keepe them from strangling and choking half an houre together, commonly suffered their breathing in my face severall tymes when they were dying, eate and dranke with them, especially those that had soares; sate downe by their bedd sides and upon their bedds discoursing with them an houre together if I had tyme, and stayd by them to see the manner of their death, and closed up their mouth and eyes (for they dyed with their mouth and eyes very much open and stareing); then if people had noe body to helpe them (for helpe was scarce at such tyme and place) I helpt to lay them forth out of the bedd and afterwards into the coffin, and last of all, accompanying them to the grave.[6]

Somehow, despite such close attendance, Boghurst also survived. Contemporaries thought that survival guaranteed immunity, but sadly this had been disproved by London physicians in the sixteenth century.

Londoners were no strangers to plague. The first known plague epidemic in London was recorded by Bede for the year 664. The plague returned in 1258 and then most infamously in 1348/49, when perhaps 15,000 people died, of a total population of about 45,000. Medieval London was scourged again in 1361/62, 1368/69, 1405–07 (when 30,000 were said to have died), 1426, 1433/34, 1437, 1439, 1450, 1452, 1454, 1474,

1499/1500 (when 20,000 died), 1517–1521, 1531, and 1535. The worst early modern visitations are recorded (or, more likely, under-recorded) here:

	Year	Deaths	Population	% of Population
a.	1563	17,404	85,000	20.5
b.	1593	10,675	125,000	8.5
c.	1603	25,045	141,000	17.7
d.	1625	26,350	206,000	12.8
e.	1636	10,400	313,000	3.3
f.	1665	55,797	459,000	12.1[7]

So, when was the Great Plague? In *absolute* terms, 1665 killed more people, a devastating 56,000 or more than 12% of London's population. If one includes the suburbs and outlying areas, the estimate rises to between 70,000 and 100,000. As a percentage of the city's population, however, 1348/49 was far worse, killing 33%. The years 1563, 1603, and 1625 were also bad: in each case London lost one-tenth to one-fifth of its people within a few short months. The worst months were in the summer: in contrast to modern urban dwellers, who tend to dread winter, early modern people hated summer because disease seemed to thrive in the warmer months. By July 1665, 1,000 were dying per week. The previous weekly record had been set in 1603, when 2,795 died in one week, but in the third week of September 1665, the Bills of Mortality report 8,297 dead, and the French ambassador thought the real figure was 14,000.

It is worth pausing to reflect on the fact that between 1563 and 1665, on average every 25 years or so, London saw about a tenth or more of its population simply wiped out. What was the impact of these successive disasters? Demographically and economically, plague epidemics had little *long-term* significance: London continued to grow through them; indeed, one wonders how the metropolis would have coped if these people had *not* died. In the *short term*, the loss was devastating at every level. That summer, Samuel Pepys faithfully recorded the rising death toll as well as his own personal losses: August 8 " . . . And poor Will that used to sell us ale at the Hall-door – his wife and three children dead, all I think in a day."[8] By mid-August, the city streets were deserted, and London began to take on the atmosphere of a city abandoned, as in a postapocalyptic science fiction epic:

> But Lord, how sad a sight it is to see the streets empty of people, and very few upon the Change – jealous of every door that one sees shut

up, lest it should be the plague – and about us, two shops in three, if not more, generally shut up.[9]

Indeed, when plague hit, economic London ground to a halt (see Illustration 8.1). Shops closed, the Royal Exchange grew quiet, and long-distance trade became impossible: foreign merchant vessels were stopped or quarantined, and no one wanted anything that had passed through the city. Although contemporaries did not understand about the fleas, they knew that objects could carry disease. Thus, Pepys wondered what would happen to "the fashion after the plague is done as to periwigs, for nobody will dare to buy any haire for fear of the infection – that it had been cut off of the heads of people dead of the plague."[10] London's entertainment industry also shut down, because people avoided taverns and theaters. On July 22, 1665 Pepys records, "I to Fox-hall, where to the Spring-garden, but I do not see one guest there – the town being so empty of anybody to come thither."[11] The political world also came to a standstill during plague epidemics: both James I and Charles I postponed their coronations because of the 1603 and 1625 outbreaks, respectively. In 1665, Charles II and his court fled London for parts west, abandoning the capital to the care of the City authorities. Pepys, a central government official, complained at the end of the year that "all goes to wrack as to public matters, they at this distance not thinking of it."[12] Although this is what rich people did, Charles II's flight in 1665 was viewed by many as ignominious.

In contrast and in keeping with tradition, Lord Mayor Sir John Lawrence (d. 1692) and the Court of Aldermen stayed at their posts to frame the civic response to the plague. The City had issued its first Book of Plague Orders in 1583. This and subsequent measures were a mixture of the practical and what we now know to be fanciful. For example, directives to stop foreign vessels from entering the Thames, close schools, and restrict begging and attendance at inns, taverns, coffeehouses, and funerals made sense by limiting exposure to, and propagation of, the disease. But orders to expel vagrants and clear the streets of dogs and cats must have made things worse: the former would have tended to spread the disease to the countryside; the latter eliminated the one major predator for the rats carrying the fleas that infected the people. Each dog or cat destroyed was worth a tuppence reward: a day's wage for a laborer. The result was more corpses, often left in the streets to rot. The restriction on alehouse attendance, combined with a ban on ballad singers and hawkers, was ostensibly to prevent gatherings of people in close quarters and on the streets, but this was also a convenient way for the authorities to stick it to a counter-culture that they hated. Finally, the City started its first pest house or plague hospital in St. Giles Cripplegate in 1594; subsequently it added new pest houses beyond the walls in Marylebone, Soho, and Stepney, to which the homeless were ordered. In 1665, these and the other municipal hospitals were soon overwhelmed: it was said that medical personnel could not walk around the rickety pallet beds on which victims lay; they had to walk *on* them.

In any case, the real war against the plague was fought in the parishes. From the late sixteenth century, City authorities required parish clerks to examine the Bills of Mortality for any uptick in plague deaths. From 1581, each parish was to nominate "two discreet matrons" as paid searchers to inquire in neighborhoods as to who was sick. Any house in which plague was reported was marked with a red cross and quarantined for 40 days. These measures were controversial: first, they violated the Christian duty to care for the sick. Second, the confinement of healthy and infected members of a household together was a virtual death sentence. No wonder that one physician reported seeing the confined "crying and roaring at their windows."[13] To enforce the quarantine, guards with sharpened halberds were positioned at front doors.

As this implies, because local government normally relied on ordinary citizens who were now dead, dying, or afraid of their own neighbors, order and community, paternalism and neighborliness threatened to break down at the parish level. Masters turned out apprentices, pastors abandoned their flocks, doctors their patients, and parish authorities might pay to remove the infected beyond the bounds. Some ratepayers refused to pay the special plague rate; fortunately, in 1625 and 1665 supplementary collections were taken up throughout England. In theory, the parish brought food to the quarantined and left it, but in reality families suffered in terrible isolation or worse. For example, when in 1603 one of the servants of the physician and astrologer Simon Forman (1552–1611) became infected, his whole family was shut up. Instead of sympathy from their fellow parishioners, they received abuse: "They would say to me that it was better that I and my household should starve and die than any of them should be put in danger."[14] Some victims refused to stay put and die: for example, in 1630 a distraught widow escaped quarantine and marched into Westminster Abbey, bewailing her fate. By late summer 1665, people began to attack their guards, throw themselves from upper-story windows, or run into the streets naked and delirious, foaming at the mouth. One contemporary hinted at the psychological, governmental, and social fallout:

> Death is now become so familiar and the people so insensible of danger, that they look upon such as provide for the public safety as tyrants and oppressors; whilst neither the richer sort will be brought to contribute, nor the meaner to submit, though to their own apparent good and preservation.[15]

London's responsibility to its inhabitants did not end with death. The City hired servants abandoned by their masters to drive the notorious "dead carts." There was perhaps no more melancholy sight in the diseased metropolis than the stacks of bodies being trundled through otherwise empty streets, grass growing through cobblestones, dead animals littering the roadway. The stench of rot, mingled with the soot and smoke from the perpetually burning "purging" fires, must have made London seem like the antechamber to hell. The carts carried the dead out to mass graves or "plague pits" just beyond the City walls. Because of the sheer volume of corpses, bodies were stacked nearly up to the surface, then covered over with a few inches of dirt and quicklime by shifts of gravediggers who worked around the clock, drinking profusely to get through their work. By late summer, the cart drivers and gravediggers themselves began to be infected: "Some died at the reins of their carts which, stacked with corpses, moved on aimlessly at the whim of the horses."[16] As Pepys noted on August 22, 1665, even this last City service began to be neglected:

> I went away and walked to Greenwich, in my way seeing a coffin with a dead body therein, dead of the plague, lying in an open close belonging to Coome farme, which was carried out last night and the parish hath not appointed anybody to bury it – but only set a watch there day and night, that nobody should go thither or come thence, which is a most cruel thing – this disease making us more cruel to one another then we are [to] dogs.[17]

Still, some Londoners continued to attend the funerals of loved ones in violation of the City Plague Orders.

The greatest impact of London's plague epidemics may have been psychological. Perhaps the first reaction to the plague was alarm at the news of death, still distant: "30 [April 1665] . . . Great fears of the Sickenesse here in the City, it being said that two or three houses are already shut up. God preserve us all."[18] Then came the dreadful first encounter with the red-crossed doors and uncertainty about your own health, hence Pepys's worry about his "smell," quoted earlier. Soon you would be affected by the deaths of your neighbors, as Pepys was by that of "poor Will . . . his wife and three children." In 1665, Samuel Pepys experienced two more psychological effects of the plague, a sense of isolation as the city became a ghost town, as well as widespread obsession with the fundamental fact of relentless death:

> But Lord, how empty the streets are, and melancholy, so many poor sick people in the streets, full of sores, and so many sad stories overheard as I walk, everybody talking of this dead, and that man sick, and so many in this place, and so many in that. And they tell me that in Westminster there is never a physitian, and but one apothecary left, all being dead – but that there are great hopes of a great decrease this week. God send it.[19]

Of course, he was an eyewitness to much grief as well: "But in the street did overtake and almost run upon two women, crying and carrying a man's Coffin between them: I suppose the husband of one of them, which methinks is a sad thing."[20] Dr. Thomas Lodge (1558–1625), writing at the time of the 1603 epidemic, worried about the utter despair and isolation of patients in pest houses.

Some reactions might strike us as perverse but are all too familiar from modern disasters. For example, wild rumors flew of people infecting each other deliberately, "And in spite to well people, would breathe in the faces (out of their windows) of well people going by."[21] Others fell into a fatalistic despair of eat, drink, and be merry, or busied themselves by looting abandoned shops or waylaying passersby. Some became disoriented: "But now, how few people I see, and those walking like people that had taken leave of the world."[22] Perhaps finally came resignation:

> Thence to the office; and after writing letters, home to draw over anew my Will, which I had bound myself by oath to despatch by tomorrow night, the town growing so unhealthy that a man cannot depend upon living two days to an end.[23]

Sixty years later, Daniel Defoe, who was a small boy during the 1665 epidemic, captured all of these reactions in one of the greatest psychological novels in the English language, *Journal of the Plague Year* (1722).

None of this is to imply that all Londoners suffered equally. In 1563 the City was still fairly compact, and it was the center parishes that had the highest rates of mortality. But as London expanded, it was the out parishes that did worse in 1665, especially to the south and northeast. Why? These were the areas where newcomers and the poor settled; as a result, they were already overcrowded and unhealthy. Those who lived in the better areas might not have been present to fall ill, because the rich could, as we saw in the case of the court, get away. But as the summer epidemic raged on, country towns began to lock their gates against London refugees; some were met by thrown stones and manure. The best survival rates were among the 10,000 Londoners who moved to boats on the river. Among those who did not take to the roads or river, Boghurst and Hodges; the Duke of Albemarle, delegated by the king to watch things while he was gone; Lord Mayor Lawrence and his fellow aldermen; and Pepys himself stayed at their posts and in their various ways kept the city running.

London did not get a reprieve until late autumn 1665: casualties fell by half in the last week of September, and to 900 by the last week of November. Plague deaths continued into the spring of 1666, and the stench remained in the city for weeks. Still, Londoners began to drift back and reclaim their boarded-up properties. The city sprang again to life with remarkable quickness. Writing in January 1666, Samuel Pepys found it

> ... a delightful thing ... to see the town so full of people again, as now it is, and shops begin to open, though in many places, seven or eight together, and more, all shut; but yet the town is full compared with what it used to be – I mean the City-end, for Covent Gu[a]rden and Westminster are yet very empty of people, no Court nor gentry being there.[24]

The court finally returned on February 1 to the peal of church bells. With it came the elite and a revival of business for local merchants.

The 1665/66 visitation was the last major plague epidemic in London's history. There was to be one more significant scare in 1720–1722, when an outbreak in Marseille threw the metropolis into a panic. The plague regulations were debated again, and Defoe wrote the *Journal of the Plague Year* as part of that debate. The quarantine of French trade worked, however, and London's Dreadful Visitation did not return. Why not? Contemporaries thought that the fire of 1666 "burned it out," but this is nonsense. Later, historians argued that the brown rat (*Rattus norvegicus*) drove out the black rat (*Rattus rattus*), but this did not happen until the eighteenth century. It is possible that the rats themselves acquired immunity. In any case, the Commercial Revolution of the late seventeenth and early eighteenth centuries should have left London wide open to a relapse, yet the plague did not return.

Still, London's *anni horribili* continued.

THE GREAT FIRE OF 1666

The summer of 1666 was hot and dry. Most people were grateful for this, because they thought that the heat would kill the plague. What it certainly did was render London more combustible. The Great Fire that began in the early hours of September 2 was unusual only in its size, because London was always burning. The first recorded fire in London history took place nearly at the founding, in conjunction with Boudicca's massacre of 60 CE. Another fire in about 125 so devastated Londinium that it took a decade to rebuild and recover. In about 675 the first St. Paul's Cathedral burned down, the second in 961, and the third in 1087. A series of fires from 1132 to 1135 destroyed property from London Bridge north to, once again, St. Paul's Cathedral. In 1212, Southwark burned, destroying St. Mary's church and houses on London Bridge; according to Stow, 3,000 died. The houses on the bridge burned again in 1633. Nor would 1666 be London's last major fire: in 1675, 624 houses went up in Southwark. Whitehall burned twice: partially in 1691 and fatally in 1698.

Why was London so combustible? Prior to 1666 especially, the old medieval City was a tangled web of narrow streets, a "wooden, northern, and inartificiall [unplanned] congestion of Houses" in the words of John Evelyn. Apart from the churches, palaces and guild halls, most of the building stock was made of wood and plaster, lit by candles, heated by flaming hearths, its floors strewn with straw, with some of its roofs made of thatch. Daniel Defoe recalled the Old London of his childhood from the distance of a half-century later: "the buildings look'd as if they had been form'd to make one general bonfire, whenever any wicked party of incendiaries should think fit."[25] Charles II tried to ban this sort of construction in 1661 and 1665, but London was growing so fast that its development was impossible to police. Finally, even the city's vibrant economic life was combustible. The docks and shipyards were piled with wood, barrels of tar, bales of fabric, and other materials ripe for burning. In addition, the city was full of open forges, blacksmith's shops, cookshops, and private kitchens, all of which required open flame. It was precisely such a flame that caused the Great Fire.

The fire began on the morning of September 2, just after midnight in the house and bakery of Thomas Farriner (1616–1670), a groom of the king's Bakehouse, in Pudding Lane, just north of the City end of London Bridge. He had probably failed to damp the fire properly. The family, trapped upstairs, escaped by climbing through a window into an adjoining house – all but one maid who, paralyzed with fear, became the first victim of the fire. Farriner's neighbors tried to fight the flames, but early modern Londoners had few tools with which to do so: buckets and hand-squirts if a fountain were nearby, ladders to rescue those on upper floors, and staves with which to pull houses down to form firebreaks. The last was by far the most effective method. Unfortunately, London's dryness and high winds overwhelmed their efforts.

It took some time for the City authorities to become aware of the situation, and in contrast to their handling of the plague, they did not react well. The parish constables arrived about 1 AM and immediately suggested pulling down houses as a firebreak. But to do this they needed permission from a higher authority. The lord mayor, Sir Thomas Bludworth (1620–1682), a Levant merchant of Royalist sympathies, was awakened, brought to the scene, and told what needed to be done. Bludworth was reluctant: this area contained a great deal of rich mercantile property, and the City was still recovering from the plague. He therefore uttered some of the most famous last words in London history, exclaiming with impeccable sexism, "Pish! A woman might piss it out!" In other words, those close to the situation "got it"; those inhabiting the highest levels at the Guildhall did not, even when on site. Within hours the flames had hopped from Pudding Lane to Fish Street and down to the northern end of London Bridge. From there it was a short leap to the docks off Thames Street, in the words of Edmund Waterhouse

> the lodge of all combustibles, oil, hemp, flax, pitch, tar, cordage, hops, wines, brandies and other materials favourable to fire, all heavy goods being warehoused there near the waterside, and all the wharfs for coal, timber, wood etc. being in line consumed by it.

As with the plague, London's commercial reach, "the very heart of the trade and wealth of the City," was fueling its destruction.[26]

That night, the maids in the Pepys household in Seething Lane were up late preparing food for Sunday dinner the next day. At 3 AM they awakened their master and mistress "to tell us of a great fire they saw in the City," but Pepys, like his mayor, dismissed it: "being unused to such fires as fallowed, I thought it far enough off, and so went to bed again and to sleep." At seven he rose and headed the short distance up Tower Hill to get a view. What he saw appalled him: "So I . . . walked to the Tower and there got up upon one of the high places . . . and there I did see the houses at that end of the bridge all on fire, and an infinite great fire on this and the other side the end of the bridge. . . . So down, with my heart full of trouble."[27] At first, people stood their ground and tried to put out the flames, but by mid-morning they were starting to give up on their houses in favor of trying to save their belongings. Pepys saw "Everybody endeavouring to remove their goods, and flinging into the River or bringing them into lighters that lay off. Poor people staying in their houses as long as till the very fire touched them, and then running into boats or clambering from one pair of stair by the water-side to another." Some shipped their possessions across the river or deposited them with goldsmiths, who had secure vaults. Others took their belongings to the crypt of St. Paul's, which was thought safe because it was made of stone. West End cart loaders and drivers turned up, offering to transport goods for exorbitant fees. On Saturday, a cart cost a few shillings to rent in London; on Monday, £40.

Having satisfied himself of the seriousness of the situation, Pepys shot off to Whitehall to break the news to the sovereign. He found Charles II in his closet at chapel "where people came about me and I did give them an account dismayed them all." Recall that the king and court had been much criticized for fleeing the plague; they were determined not to make the same mistake twice. Charles ordered Pepys to tell the lord mayor to begin pulling down houses, and the duke volunteered soldiers to help. Pepys tried to return by coach but found the streets clogged with carts and refugees: "every creature coming away loaden with goods to save – and here and there sick people carried away in beds. Extraordinary good goods carried in carts and on backs." We might wonder about Londoners' obsession with their goods, but it becomes more understandable if we recall that the household was the basic unit of economic production, and that insurance companies in the modern sense did not yet exist. Families were trying to save the tools and materials essential to their livelihoods. To lose your home *and* its contents was to lose everything with appalling finality.

Alighting near St. Paul's, Pepys found Bludworth at Canning Street "like a man spent, with a handkercher about his neck . . . like a fainting woman," whining "Lord, what can I do? I am spent! People will not obey me. I have been pull[ing] down houses. But the fire overtakes us faster then we can do it."[28] When later that afternoon the king arrived at the scene by barge and found few houses had been pulled down, he ordered in the Coldstream Guards to do it. According to the Earl of Clarendon (1609-1674), over the next few days he and his brother stepped into the leadership vacuum:

> The King and Duke, . . . rode from one place to another, and put themselves into great dangers among the burning and falling houses, to give advice and direction what was to be done, underwent as much fatigue as the meanest, and had as little sleep or rest; and the faces of all men appeared ghastly and in the highest confusion.

Henry Griffith has the royal brothers "handling the water in buckets when they stood up to the ankles in water and playing the engine [pumps] for many hours together."[29] Whatever the truth of these encomia, it is clear that the king and duke did what leaders are supposed to do in a crisis: they showed firmness and resolve, gave direction, and stood their ground while others fled. The duke organized command posts headed by courtiers who gave orders to constables and soldiers. Able-bodied men were dragooned into teams to pull down houses. Thus, the governmental reaction to the fire stood in contrast to that toward the plague: this time it was the court that rose to the occasion while the City stood paralyzed.

By the afternoon of the 2nd, a firestorm developed, created by the high winds and chimney effect, as the heat rose in the narrow areas between buildings. In the evening, Pepys and his friends secured a boat to get close, coming "So near the fire as we could for smoke; and all over the Thames, with one's face in the wind, you were almost burned with a shower of Firedrops." So they abandoned this vantage point for an alehouse on the south bank from which they

> saw the fire grow; and as it grow darker, appeared more and more, and in Corners and upon steeples and between churches and houses, as far as we could see up the hill of the City, in a most horrid malicious bloody flame . . . till . . . we saw the fire as only one entire arch of fire from this to the other side of the bridge, and in a bow up the hill, for an arch of above a mile long. It made me weep to see it.

Some idea of this horrific vision is conveyed in contemporary paintings (see Illustration 8.2). That morning at 4 AM, Pepys, in his nightshirt, moved his valuables to a colleague's house in Bethnal Green in the East

End; later he would bury his wine and a large Parmesan cheese in his back garden.[30]

On Monday, September 3, the flames pushed outward, north, west, and south. To the south they were stopped by the river but threatened to cross London Bridge. To the north, the Royal Exchange, the General Letter Office in Threadneedle Street, and London's great shopping district in Cheapside – the very heart of the City – went up, the latter "with such a dazzling light and burning heat and roaring noise by the fall of so many houses together that was very amazing."[31] At this point John Evelyn came to town and saw

> . . . the whole Citty in dreadfull flames neere the Water side; & had now consumed all the houses from the bridge all Thames Streete, & up-wards towards Cheape side, down to the three Cranes. . . .

That evening, he found himself among vast crowds trying to make their way out of the City on barges or through the gates that acted as massive bottlenecks. Imagine the panic and frustration of being in that crowd, the air thick with smoke, the heat of the fire at your back, the wind blowing sparks everywhere, the "crying out & lamentation" of despair in your ears. At one point the magistrates actually ordered the gates shut to persuade people to return and fight the fire. Londoners were not to be contained, and the order was rescinded the next day. Evelyn followed the crowd to open fields beyond the wall "which for many miles were strewed with moveables of all sorts, & Tents erecting to shelter both people & what goods they could get away. O, the miserable & calamitous speectacle!"[32] By this time, London was lethargic, demoralized, fearful – and paranoid.

It is a characteristic human reaction that few could conceive of such an epic disaster as having begun with a baker's error. Rumors spread of foul play: remember that in 1666 England was at war with the Dutch, the Restoration was new, and the Civil Wars were a recent memory. Everybody was afraid of somebody: Anglicans feared Dissenters and Catholics, Dissenters feared Catholics even more, and Catholics feared everybody. Because the high winds carried sparks, houses seemingly far away from the fire would combust, which led to rumors of Dutch or French spies throwing fireballs. In particular, French shops – normally quite popular – and French nationals were openly attacked in the streets. A Westminster schoolboy, William Taswell, remembered seeing a Frenchman clubbed in the head with an iron bar; his brother saw another torn almost limb from limb. The Duke of York rode up and down with the Life Guards to rescue foreigners and Catholics and take them into protective custody. By this point the City government was out of commission, the lord mayor having apparently fled.

Tuesday, September 4 saw the worst destruction. Fire consumed Bridewell and the City's grain stores, then leaped over firebreaks at the Fleet River and Cheapside. The flames threatened St. Paul's and the Guildhall to the north, Whitehall Palace to the west, and the Tower of London – with its gunpowder stores – to the east. To prevent disaster, the Navy was ordered in the next day to save the Tower by bombarding houses in Tower Street to form a firebreak. St. Paul's received no such reprieve. The cathedral never had a chance: although it was made of stone, its crypt was stuffed with furniture and books from the nearby bookstalls, its walls framed by wooden scaffolding from the recent renovations (see Chapter 1). The lead roof started to melt, molten metal running down the walls into the crypt. The sight, as recorded by John Evelyn, was hellish: "the stones of Paules flew like granados, the Lead mealting downe the streetes in a streame, & the very pavements of them glowing with fiery rednesse, so as nor horse nor man was able to tread on them."[33] Although no one could know it at that dark moment, the burning of St. Paul's was the crescendo of the Great Fire.

On Wednesday, September 5, Samuel Pepys awoke at 2 AM to cries that the flames had reached All Hallows, Barking, at the end of his lane. After securing his wife safely at Woolwich, he returned at 7 AM: "But going to the fire, I find, by the blowing up of houses and the great help given by the workmen out of the King's yards, sent up by Sir W. Penn, there is a good stop given to it, as well at Marke-lane end as ours – it having only burned the Dyall of Barkeing Church, and part of the porch, and was there quenched."[34] At Leadenhall, an alderman with a "hatful of money" secured similar cooperation.[35] The winds had died down, and the firebreaks ordered by the king and duke began to work. Still, going up the steeple of All Hallows to survey the damage, Pepys "saw the saddest sight of desolation that I ever saw. Everywhere great fires. Oyle-cellars and brimstone and other things burning."[36] The greatest conflagration in London's history was beginning to burn itself out, but that process would take a very long time: eyewitnesses reported smoldering embers and hot spots for months. Because the Fire began in Pudding Lane and ended at Pye Corner, some wits opined that it was God's punishment for the sin of gluttony. More seriously, that afternoon, both Pepys and Evelyn witnessed the refugees in Moorfields, fields adjacent to Southwark, and elsewhere "as far as higate, & severall miles in Circle, Some under tents, others under miserab[l]e Hutts and Hovells, without a rag, or any necessary utinsils, bed or board . . . reduc'd to extreamest misery & poverty."[37] The king also rode out to see them, promising provisions and reassurance that there was no foreign plot. Still, the next few days saw continued panics as Londoners expected the imminent arrival of French or Dutch armies. Just the appearance of a Frenchman or Dutchman on the streets led to rioting, which had to be suppressed by the Life Guards and trained bands.

Londoners could now begin to take the toll: 436 acres had burned; 13,200 houses, 87 parish churches, 44 livery halls, and nearly all of the old City were destroyed (see Illustration 8.3). Among major public buildings lost were the interior of the Guildhall, the Royal Exchange, Newgate, the Old Bailey, the Custom House, and St. Paul's Cathedral. The direct financial cost was £10,000,000. There is evidence of very few deaths, although, as with the plague, poor people and vagrants probably went unreported, and the chances of their remains being found were few. After all, the Great Fire was hot enough to melt imported steel at the docks, suggesting temperatures between 1,200°F and 3,000°F. That would have melted not only flesh, but bone as well. Teeth might survive, but poor people of any age probably had few of those. Hundreds more might have died that winter from poor nutrition and exposure. The Great Fire rendered some 70,000 homeless out of a population of perhaps 460,000 (15%). Although some fled to the country or to America, others set up shanties on the sites of their former homes, or camped out in tents on Moorfields and other open spaces. Of course, all this came after losing 70,000 to 100,000 Londoners to disease just a year before.

In the aftermath of the Fire, the survivors sought scapegoats. Enter Robert Hubert (c. 1640–1666), a French immigrant who confessed to setting the fire in Pudding Lane. Although his story was riddled with inconsistencies, he was hanged on September 28, 1666, making him the ninth known victim of the Fire. Later, it was discovered that he had not even set foot in London until September 4! Subsequently, a Parliamentary commission assembled a vast amount of rumor and hearsay in favor of a plot, but the Privy Council concluded, more judiciously, that the Fire occurred by "the hand of God upon us, a great wind, and the season so very dry."[38] Nevertheless, the idea that Catholics (i.e., the French, the Jesuits) set the Fire would not go away. It fit current expectation and national memory, which included the surprise St. Bartholomew's Day Massacre in Paris in 1572, the numerous failed plots under Elizabeth, the failed Gunpowder Plot of 1605, and the Irish Rebellion of 1641, the atrocities of which, exaggerated in the telling, still lived vividly in London consciousness, kept alive by annual sermons. Basically, if there were a plot against London, Catholics were the obvious suspects.

This notion would be enshrined in the Monument, designed by Christopher Wren and erected 1671–1677 by Act of Parliament (18–19 Chas. II, c. 8) "in perpetual Remembrance" at the corner of what is now Monument and Fish Streets (see Illustration 8.4).[39] The Monument is a Doric Column surmounted by flames of gilt bronze, standing 202 feet tall, the exact distance from its base to the location of Farriner's ill-fated bakeshop. Daniel Defoe thought it "out does all the obelisks and pillars of the ancients," although he qualified that assertion with the doubt-inducing phrase "at least that I have seen."[40] (One wonders how many such monuments a Dissenting journalist from London *had* ever seen.) Ned Ward claimed, more waggishly, that "it's [sic] very height was the first thing that ever occasioned wry Necks in *England*, by the Peoples staring at the Top on't."[41] Visitors can still climb the 311 steps to the top to get a panoramic view of the city as James Boswell did in April 1763: he found the building "most amazing" but the experience "horrid to find myself so monstrous a way up in the air, so far above London and all its spires. I durst not look round me."[42] Safely back on the ground, he may have noticed the bas relief on the west side of the base depicting Charles and James ordering the reconstruction of London by Architecture, Nature, and Science. The other three sides contain inscriptions describing the Fire, the reconstruction, and a list of mayors who supervised the erection of the Monument. In 1681, at the height of the Exclusion Crisis, Whig aldermen added a concluding line to the north panel "But Popish frenzy, which wrought such horrors, is not yet quenched." This later inspired the following couplet from the Catholic Alexander Pope:

> *Where London's column pointing at the skies,*
> *Like a tall bully, lifts its head, and lies.*[43]

The offending line, an embarrassing relic of ancient prejudice, was chiseled out only on the eve of Catholic Emancipation in 1831.

The Act of Parliament that authorized the Monument also directed the rebuilding of the city. Talk of rebuilding began almost immediately after the flames died out, and within a week Wren had submitted a plan (see Illustration 8.5), closely followed by John Evelyn (see Illustration 8.6), Richard Newcourt (c. 1610–1679), and Valentine Knight (fl. 1666), among others. These men saw the Fire as a tremendous calamity, of course, but also a great opportunity to fix everything that was wrong with London before the conflagration. They envisaged redrawing the street plan of the City, creating a logical grid overlaid with wide boulevards radiating from central plazas or squares. Knight even came up with the novel idea of encircling the City with a canal. Unfortunately, none of these plans was practical given the realities of London land ownership: the lots had been irregular for centuries, and to require or persuade their many owners to exchange portions so as to create neat squares and rectangles would have been to court chaos. London might never be rebuilt. The only alternative would have been for the Crown to use its authority to simply confiscate property, clear the rubble, and build on the massive scale of Paris during the Second Empire. But neither English property law nor English property holders would ever allow it. So the Commission for Rebuilding, established in October, therefore decided to erect the new City on the old medieval street plan, thus preserving much of the irrationality and charm, but also some of the hazard, of old London.

Still, if the resurgent City could not be made rational, spacious, and airy, it might be made fire safe and a bit less claustrophobic. As early as September 13, the king issued a proclamation calling for wider streets and that buildings be made of brick. This became the basis for the momentous Act for Rebuilding the City of London (18–19 Chas. II, c. 8) of 1667, which specified that houses built in by-lanes could not exceed two stories, three along the river, and four along high streets "for citizens of extraordinary quality." The act also regulated party walls, windows, and other details, while mandating wider streets, that the docks be clear of houses, and above all, that London be rebuilt in brick and stone. The ultimate responsibility for administering the act and rebuilding public areas was given to the lord mayor and aldermen, their expenses to be supplied by a tax on coal of one shilling per ton. Private dwellings were to be rebuilt by the lease-holding tenants; if they could not do so within three years and nine months, they were to be compensated by the City for losing their leases out of the Coal Tax. To settle disputes, a Fire Court was established that quickly achieved a reputation for fairness.

The chance to rebuild proved a field day for landlords, speculators, and housebuilders like Nicholas Barbon, who recreated the City on mountains of paper by means of a series of precarious speculations (see Chapter 4). Barbon is often credited with helping to invent what became the classic London row house: a rational, unassuming, narrow flat-fronted brick building of two, three and four stories plus cellar and garret, as specified in the statute. Within the ancient City walls, such houses had to be crammed into narrow courts and alleyways, but in the developing West End, speculators like Barbon and the Russells could lay them out in squares, giving the court end of town something of the rational and spacious character that Wren and Evelyn had envisioned for the City (see Conclusion).

Perhaps the individual most associated with London's physical resurrection is Christopher (from November 1673, Sir Christopher) Wren. He was named to the Commission for Rebuilding and was given the task of reconstructing one of the first big structures to go up, the new Custom House by the river: the Crown could not do without London's Customs revenue, and the new building was completed by 1671. In May 1670, Wren was put in charge of an office under the Commission for the Rebuilding of Churches to replace the eighty-seven houses of worship destroyed in the Great Fire. That office became a training ground for a new generation of distinguished architects like Nicholas Hawksmoor (?1662–1736), William Dickinson (c. 1671–1725), and above all the polymath Robert Hooke (1635–1703). In a remarkable tour de force of energy, creativity, and sheer variety, Wren and his associates supervised the design and rebuilding of about fifty London churches. (The total is inexact because some churches needed only to be repaired and others, like St. James Piccadilly, were entirely new parishes.) If Wren were denied the chance to rationalize London with a new street plan, his fifty new churches brought metropolitan church architecture into the seventeenth century and in line with both the Reformation and the Age of Reason. A good example can be seen at St. James Piccadilly (see Illustration 8.7). Whereas Prayer Book services before the Great Fire had been conducted in old, musty Gothic structures divided into numerous add-on bays and alcoves, the congregation's view of the altar shadowed by hulking arches, blocked by massive columns, and often still darkened by stained glass (see Chapter 1, St. Olave Hart Street), Wren's new churches featured wide-open spaces, clear sight lines, and lots of light flooding in from windows set with clear glass. Upper galleries provided more seating. In this setting, the pulpit and the Word became as much a focus as the altar and the Eucharist. Admittedly, accommodation had to be made for the odd lots on which these churches sat: many had to follow the outlines of their medieval predecessors. St. Benet Fink was polygonal with a dome; St. Martin Ludgate took the shape of a Greek cross. Where Wren really showed his originality was in the spires he designed for each church: no two are alike. Wren's churches were mostly completed by 1690, the spires added later, after the renewal of the Coal Tax in 1697. They are among London's glories. The loss of about half of them to Nazi bombs and modern development is therefore as much a tragedy, albeit a slower-going one, as was that of their predecessors over four days in September 1666.

Wren's greatest achievement was to rebuild London's cathedral in a style completely different from its predecessor, yet sufficiently magnificent to resume its place in Londoners' hearts. He had been consulted about repairs to Old St. Paul's before the Great Fire and had proposed replacing the dilapidated tower with a dome just days before the cathedral burned down. The Bishop of London still hoped to save the building, for much of the choir remained standing. By July 1668, however, it became clear that the old edifice was not salvageable because more of the choir had collapsed, and so demolition began. At first Wren used gunpowder, but the resultant explosions, coming so soon after the shock of plague, fire, and war, traumatized the inhabitants of Ludgate Hill, and so he opted for a battering ram.

Still, the project stalled waiting for rubble to be cleared, funding, and a plan. The first proceeded slowly; the second arrived with an augmentation of the Coal Tax voted in 1670 (3 shillings per ton, of which half would go to the rebuilding of St. Paul's). The third took seven years while Wren submitted three models. The second, the "Great Model" was approved by the king but rejected by the dean and chapter as too reminiscent of continental Catholic Baroque, at which it is said Wren wept. The king and clergy finally settled on the compromise "Warrant Design" of a conventional cross, with a dome at the crux. Wren's warrant of commission included a fortunate loophole allowing him "to make some variations rather ornamental than essential, as from time to time he should see proper."[44] During this period Wren was knighted and became official surveyor for the reconstruction of the cathedral. In the summer of 1673, he went to the site to mark the spot for the center of the dome. According to legend, he asked a workman to fetch a stone from amid the sea of still uncleared rubble to hold down his plans. The worker returned with a piece of masonry from the old cathedral that had carved on it the Latin word *"resurgam"* – "I shall rise." Wren instantly decreed that this would be the motto of the new cathedral; later he commissioned the distinguished sculptor Caius Gabriel Cibber to carve this inscription beneath a phoenix rising from the ashes over the south door.

St. Paul's did rise, to more than 365 feet above the pavement, but slowly, over the next 35 years (see Illustration 8.8). The nave finally opened, amid great rejoicing, in 1697. Wren was nearly eighty when he delegated his son to be lifted to the top of the dome by a crane to place its capstone on October 26, 1708. He continued tinkering with the design until his death in 1718, which came after contracting a cold on a walk to inspect the cathedral. Thus St. Paul's occupied England's greatest architect for most of his professional life. Although decorated by the most notable artists of the day – Cibber, the history painter Sir James Thornhill (whose scenes from the life of St. Paul adorn the interior of the dome), the ironworker Jean Tijou ([fl. 1689–1711], gates to the chancel aisles), the carver Grinling Gibbons (quire screens and choir stalls), and the sculptor Francis Bird ([1667–1731], the statue of Queen Anne before the west front) – the triumph is Wren's. His grave can be found in the crypt, marked with what is arguably the most apt epitaph ever penned in an age known for pith and wit: *"Lector, si monumentum requiris, circumspice"*: "Reader, if you require his monument, look about you." In fact, St. Paul's has assumed the status of a national monument, and its stalwart neoclassical facade and great dome have become enduring symbols of London.

Other buildings were thrown up much more quickly: by 1669, 8 livery halls and 1,600 houses had been rebuilt; by 1672, Newgate, the Royal Exchange, and nearly all of the housing was completed. In the end, some streets were widened, and only about 8,000 of the destroyed 13,200 houses were replaced, thus easing some of the City's congestion. In 1724, Defoe found much to commend in the fact that "the buildings of this great city are chiefly of brick, as many ways found to be the safest, the cheapest, and the most commodious of all other materials; by safe, I mean from fire." He went on to argue that "no where in the world is so good care taken to quench fires as in London," (1) because of the proximity of the river and a system of pipes bringing it to hydrants all over the City; (2) the multitude of "admirable engines," that is, mobile pumps bought by individual parishes to pour water onto the flames; and (3) the rise of insurance offices.[45] In fact, the Fire catalyzed the development of the insurance business: Nicholas Barbon began to offer insurance by 1667, establishing a Fire Office in 1680. Others followed soon after, the greatest being the Sun Fire Office (1710), its descendant company still in business today. To reduce their liability, the insurance companies actually maintained firemen. Eighteenth-century London was still not fireproof, however: major fires broke out in Wapping in 1716 and 1725, and in Exchange Alley (destroying Jonathan's) in 1748.

Nor, as we have seen, were the city's immediate trials over in 1666, because the scourges of plague and fire were followed by the disasters of the Second Dutch War (see Chapter 7).

And yet, London neither folded nor dropped to its knees in supplication of forgiveness. Londoners did not cave; they coped, rebuilding their city to be far bigger and more opulent than before. During the last 90 years covered by this book, their metropolis doubled in size (again!) and emerged as the greatest city in the Western world. Wren's motto for St. Paul's might just as well serve for the city as a whole: *resurgam*. To some extent, this was part of the Restoration rejection of the Puritan theocracy. We would argue that the essential attributes of the Restoration period are not perhaps reason and frivolity, but practicality and irrepressibility. Add to these the essential attributes of Londoners, toughness and good humor. These characteristics determined that, despite the devastating blows of the 1660s, London would not be stopped. Like New York, Tokyo, or Los Angeles today (all cities that have survived disasters), London was not about to look back. Instead of waiting for the next catastrophe, Londoners, as Daniel Defoe noted above, developed better fire-fighting methods and insurance companies. Fire departments are at least as old as Rome, but insurance companies are an essentially modern development, requiring a modern mind-set: to purchase an insurance policy is to refuse to accept "Acts of God" as irrevocable. Rather, policyholders pay their money so that, in the event of disaster, they nevertheless can resume the upward trajectory of their lives, rebuild them, or in the case of life insurance, sustain their material worth beyond even death. Instead of risk and loss being matters of personal honor and fortune, as was traditional, they are shared, amortized, and minimized. Defoe caught the spirit of the rebuilt city when he wrote, "and how much farther it may spread, who knows? New squares, and new streets rising up every day to such a prodigy of buildings, that nothing in the world does, or ever did, equal it, except old Rome in Trajan's time. . . ."[46] Let us revisit the streets of London, this time as rebuilt and replenished after plague, fire, war, rebellion, and revolution.

$\mathscr{C}$ONCLUSION: London in 1750

THE VIEW FROM HIGHGATE

$\mathscr{P}$eople came to London in 1750 much as they did in 1550: by ship, in carriages, on horseback, on the back of a cart, or on foot, more or less along the same waterway and roads as before. Admittedly, travel had improved considerably for those at the upper end of society: ships were bigger, with better accommodation for well-paying passengers, and coach service between capital and countryside was now a standard amenity. But whether we are arriving by coach and six or hoofing it ourselves, our first sight of London would be just as startling as before. If, as in 1550, we came down Highgate Hill from the north, we would again see the metropolis laid out before us along the still silver thread of the Thames (see Illustration c.1). The city fills more of our peripheral vision now: its population having grown from 120,000 to nearly 700,000, London has advanced in all directions well beyond its three great bookends. To our left, the docks and maritime conurbation of the East End have crept past the bend in the river at the Isle of Dogs to Blackwall Reach. To our right, the Strand is now obscured by building, and the West End has been filled in to Hyde Park. Looking still farther west, we see that Notting Hill and Knightsbridge remain rural and green. Toward the horizon, the south bank has also filled in, but shallowly, greater London extending only about half a mile into Surrey at its deepest point. In the foreground, northern London has grown up to Tottenham Court, Lambe's Conduit Fields, and Shoreditch, a parish of 10,000 people anchored by George Dance's (c. 1694–1768) St. Leonard's church. From our elevated vantage point, we are instantly aware of the growth of suburbs and satellite communities like Newington, Mile End, Hackney, Shadwell, and Islington, tied to the capital by roads well maintained by the wealthy taxpayers of Middlesex, Essex, Kent, and Surrey. It was now possible for a successful merchant or a nobleman with London connections to do his business in the city, do his living in the country, and commute between the two by coach. The London season was, in 1750, porous and, if one preferred, a daily affair.

It is the aggregation at the center of our vision that still draws our eye most emphatically, for it has changed a great deal since 1550. First, of the three great landmarks that we noticed then, only the Tower of London, guarding the eastern approach to the city, remains more or less unchanged. The Westminster complex that formed the western boundary of our view still stands, and somewhat more imposingly in 1750 because of the addition, five years before, of Nicholas Hawksmoor's towers to the Abbey. But Whitehall burned down in 1698, leaving a hodgepodge of houses and government offices to fill in the valuable real estate between the Strand and Westminster. In the very center of our view, rising from a city of trim Augustan and Georgian brick, the Gothic pile of Old St. Paul's has been replaced by the imposing dome of Wren's cathedral, looming in the sunlight.

That is, if there is sunlight today. More likely, a pall of smoke sits over the city. London's growth has meant more chimneys, perhaps a million of them, belching soot from coal fires. Modern cities have modern problems, and by 1700, smog was one of London's. Pierre Jean Grosley (1718–1785), first writing in 1765, complained:

> This smoke, being loaded with terrestrial particles, and rolling in a thick, heavy atmosphere, forms a cloud, which envelopes London like a mantle; a cloud which the sun pervades but rarely, a cloud which, recoiling back upon itself, suffers the sun to break out only now and then, which casual appearances procures the Londoners a few of what they call GLORIOUS DAYS.

If there is a breeze we can actually see the smog being dragged east by the prevailing winds, thus illustrating for us one reason why the West End is the smart end of town. The other is of course the Thames's eastward current: both smoke and sewage still flow west to east, but there is now much more of both, and so it is all the more desirable to live at the former end.

Grosley observed that "Even the buildings themselves feel the effects of the smoke," and indeed if it parts, we see that St. Paul's and the rebuilt City are just beginning to take on a gloomy patina of black, so that they seem "to be built with coal," that would mark them into the late twentieth century.[1] Looking past that dingy veneer, we might reflect on the aesthetic contrast between Wren's church and its predecessor: London in 1550 was still emerging from the Middle Ages, a city gripped by the first flush of the Reformation. The sober-sided angularity of Old St. Paul's, a dilapidated Gothic hulk, bereft of its spire after 1561 and stripped of its decorative accoutrements, fit the jury-rigged Church emerging under the Tudors. Wren's sleek masterpiece suited an imperial city and a church that had rejected Puritanical enthusiasm for a more reasoned and urbane faith. The new St. Paul's was everything that the rebuilt, modern city needed in its parish church.

THE APPROACH FROM THE RIVER

As in 1550, we will not make our approach from the north. This time, to get the maritime and commercial flavor of London in 1750, we arrive from the east, by water (see Map 1). Whether a passenger on a packet boat from France or a crew member on a Newcastle collier, a West Indian slaver, or an East Indiaman, we enter the Thames at its mouth, the Nore. Gliding slowly west past open fields and isolated riverside communities like Gravesend and Tilbury with its imposing fort, we are part of a constant stream of river traffic and, once past Woolwich, a good six miles out from London Bridge, we see many more ships than in 1550. Their numbers increase as we advance up the Thames estuary so that by the time we reach Deptford, about three miles out, our eyes are greeted by a forest of masts, all propelling the world's trade to the great city. Daniel Defoe counted 2,000 ocean-going vessels in the Thames in the 1720s, ignoring a further 3,500 barges and lighters necessary to unload the big ships and get their cargoes to shore. Precisely because the river was growing so crowded and ships were getting bigger and drafting deeper with the expansion of London's overseas and coastal trade, the old system of seventeen legal docks between the Bridge and the Tower of London no longer sufficed. Goods paying Customs duties still had to pass through there, but to unload them from the ships a further 1,200 "sufferance docks," stretching from here to the Tower, now handled the bulk of London's sea-going commerce. Still, there were not enough quays and warehouses in 1750 to handle its ever-increasing volume, which meant long delays and sometimes spoiled or rotted cargoes.

As we make our way slowly through this obstacle course of watercraft, the ships get smaller. On either bank we see the subaltern downriver communities that service them and form the entry point for many immigrants: in order, east to west, they are Blackwall, Limehouse, Shadwell, and Wapping on the north bank; Deptford, Rotherhithe (pronounced Redriff), and Bermondsey on the south. In the nineteenth century, the north bank communities would come to be known, collectively, as the East End, with connotations of the most abject poverty and brutal crime. South London's reputation was little better, if more industrious. In 1750, however, these neighborhoods were booming thanks to London's domination of overseas trade and the growth of shipping and related industries. Although their work was never easy, the watermen, lightermen, longshoremen, coal heavers, porters, warehouse workers, shipbuilders, carpenters, founders, smiths, sailmakers, victuallers, and of course, seamen who populated both banks generally had plenty of it, and the result was busy and prosperous, if by no means elegant.

As we get closer to the city, our noses, already assaulted by the smog, become aware of the sewage. The Thames is still London's open sewer. The stench grows more nauseating the closer we get and is more pronounced than it would have been in 1550 because of the expanding population. London had Commissioners of Sewers from 1427, but they concentrated on surface drainage, not the miles of cesspits on which London rested. That is, by the mid-seventeenth century, while the poorest stretches of London still relied on a bucket and the open street for waste disposal, many houses had their own basement cesspits. Pepys records how, in 1660, his neighbor's retaining wall collapsed, giving him an unpleasant surprise: "going down into my cellar to look, I put my foot into a great heap of turds, by which I find that Mr. Turner's house of office is full and comes into my cellar, which doth trouble me, but I will have it helped."[2] When your cesspit filled up and the stench became unbearable, you called in the night-soil men, jocularly known as "goldfinders" – basically, guys with shovels – to empty it. This was surely the dirtiest job in London. They carted the waste into the country to sell as fertilizer, or deposited it in laystalls down by the river, into which it usually was dumped.

Out of doors, there were no public lavatories, and if one were caught in need, any dark corner down a courtyard or on the street would do. Thus, Pepys records his wife stooping in the street to "do her business." Add to this the lack of refuse collection generally, and it is little wonder that as late as 1741, John Brownlow, Lord Tyrconnell (1690–1754), thundered in the House of Lords of "the streets of London, a city famous for wealth, commerce, and plenty, and for every other kind of civility and politeness;

but which abounds with such heaps of filth, as a savage would look on with amazement."[3] Although individual parishes appointed sweepers and refuse collectors, the only truly effective street cleaning came when it rained, producing a deluge of muck rolling down to the river, as recorded by Jonathan Swift:

> *Sweepings from butchers' stalls, dung, guts, and blood,*
> *Drowned puppies, stinking sprats, all drenched in mud,*
> *Dead cats, and turnip tops, come tumbling down the flood.*[4]

No wonder that Londoners, famously, would not drink the water, relying on ale, porter, and spirits instead. They still needed it for cooking, brewing, washing, and manufacturing, however, the last three of which added their own pollutants to the noxious mix.

So long as London's population remained under a half a million, settled only sparsely downriver, and got its water from northern springs instead of from the Thames, the system remained relatively sanitary. But by 1750, as we have seen, that population had exceeded half a million, the eastern suburbs were thriving, and the metropolis had long outgrown the conduit system, not least because as it expanded northward, natural springs and wells were built over. As early as the reign of James I, newly formed water companies began to pipe Thames water to outdoor fountains and standpipes and into wealthy private homes. What was left of the conduit system was gradually leased to the companies. The Chelsea Waterworks Company, established in 1723, used a series of canals, sluices, and a waterwheel to pump Thames water. By 1767 the company was pumping 1,750 tons of water daily into London homes, but there was no attempt to purify that water. Later, Victorian Londoners were subject to several deadly cholera epidemics; first, because overseas trade brought it from the East Indies; second, because London's population – around a million in 1801, 2.7 million in 1851 – began to overwhelm the river's ability to absorb its sewage. The problem would not be solved until the construction of a modern underground sewer system by the Metropolitan Board of Works, completed in 1875.

THE TOWER AND CHEAPSIDE

In 1750, perhaps a bit queasy but still healthy, we alight just east of the Tower at St. Catherine's Stairs (as it is now spelled); just as in 1550, we have to be careful of the mud. Once we reach St. Catherine's Street (see

Map 4 for our route), parallel to the river, we are relieved to find it cobbled and lit with oil lamps. If we choose, we can order a hackney coach or a sedan chair, but being poor and inquisitive scholars, we walk, wending our way through the tightly packed courts of the Tower Hamlets up to the Tower itself, much as we would have done in 1550, but perhaps assisted by a pocket map or guidebook, like William Stow's *Remarks on London* (1722), generated by London's popular press. Because this area was left untouched by the Great Fire, it contains several buildings that we might recognize from that time, and it is certainly just as crowded, noisy, and ramshackle as ever. As before, this is dockland, and the sounds of London's commerce are much the same as they were in Tudor times: the barking of orders, the shouts of longshoremen, the whir and clack of block and tackle, the satisfying ping of hammer on nail, and the common foreign voice – French or Dutch, or now, African or West Indian – as all the world serves in British merchant vessels. No wonder that Sir John Fielding thought "a man would be apt to suspect himself in another country" walking through London's docklands.[5]

As we make our way up the back side of Tower Hill, the high walls and four impressive turrets of the Tower loom over us. Our sense of foreboding is appropriate, for in 1750 state prisoners are still held here. As recently as 1747 the Tower had played host to the most prominent Jacobite rebels of the '45 prior to their trials and executions. The last public beheading in British history took place here on April 9, 1747, when the 80-year-old Jacobite conspirator Simon Fraser, Lord Lovat (1668–1747) met his end before a large crowd on Tower Hill. Thereafter England's growing political stability and rising public distaste put an end to such spectacles. Another sign of that stability becomes clear to us as we round the north side of the Tower: it no longer anchors a continuous wall around the City as it did in 1550. Although the wall was prepared for defense as recently as the Civil Wars, by the mid-eighteenth century discrete sections were falling to London's building boom. The City gates, notorious choke points for traffic, will be mostly demolished in the 1760s. Thus London's Wall finally fell, not at the hands of a foreign conqueror but before the commercial needs of the City that it had once defended.

From the Tower we head west, descending Tower Street toward Eastcheap and the City. This area was gutted by the Fire. Although there are no remaining scars in 1750, there is plenty of evidence, for we begin to encounter London's new look. The streets of the old City remain a tangled web of narrow, twisting lanes and sunless courts, relieved by occasional broad avenues, like Cheapside or Bishopsgate, but the two- to four-story houses that make up those lanes and courts are more regular and rational than their tumbledown Tudor predecessors. They now present a narrow, flat, and upright front right up to the pavement, punctuated by a doorway and sash windows (see Illustration c.2). Above all, they are made of brick, not wood frame and plaster. This will be the basic London house into the twentieth century. It burns less easily than its antecedent and it rarely falls down, although London's air pollution will render it increasingly dreary in appearance.

Turning north at the corner of Eastcheap and Gracechurch Street as we did in 1550, we once again ascend Cornhill, the heart of London's financial and mercantile district. Turning left down Cornhill street, we encounter the second Royal Exchange, a neoclassical building with a tall tower, designed by Edward Jarman (c. 1606–1668) and built between 1667 and 1669 to replace the original, which had gone up in the Fire. But Sir Thomas Gresham's vision survives: here in the courtyard, observed by statues of every English monarch from Charles I to George II, London's merchants strike deals and trade commodities while expensive shops display the goods of the world. But London's commerce has diversified since Gresham's day, and many of the business deals that used to be struck along these colonnades are now worked out in nearby coffeehouses like Lloyd's in Lombard Street (for shipping), Jonathan's (for stock-jobbing), and Garraway's (for auctions), the latter two in Exchange Alley, a narrow and winding passageway connecting Cornhill and Lombard. As a result, the shops of the Royal Exchange sometimes lie empty. Basement vaults might be rented to bankers or to the East India Company to store pepper. In other words, the Exchange survives, like many Londoners, on sheer versatility and opportunism.

Exiting the Royal Exchange on Threadneedle Street, we encounter an even more stately edifice to our right: the Bank of England. Established as the government's banker in 1694, it had moved about during the first few years of its existence, finding space in various livery halls. In 1734 it settled into the building before us, a magnificent purpose-built structure designed by George Sampson (d. 1759). We pass through the doors of this neoclassical monument to finance and find ourselves in a vast pay hall (see Illustration c.3): the eighteenth-century bank of England also serviced private accounts, and according to Daniel Defoe, "No place in the world has so much business done with so much ease."[6] That notwithstanding, we note that some account holders mistake the giant coal-burning heater for a teller's window – with disastrous results for their finances! The year after Defoe's encomium was written, in 1725, the Bank issued its first notes in fixed denominations of £20, £30, £40, £50, and £100. Frequently added to and renovated after 1750, the Old Lady of Threadneedle Street looks much different today.

Instead of retracing our 1550 route into Cheapside, we head east back up Cornhill to Leadenhall Street, crossing Bishopsgate Street for a moment to take note of two other bastions of London trade: on our right, East India House and Africa House, headquarters of two of the most powerful trading companies. In 1750, few Londoners were prepared to confront the moral implications of their activities. Retracing our steps to Bishopsgate, we head north to the gate itself. It would stand until 1760, when its stones were cannibalized to reinforce London Bridge. To our left we see another monument of Sir Thomas Gresham's vision for his city, the back garden of Gresham College, endowed to provide free annual lectures in astronomy, divinity, geometry, law, medicine, music, and rhetoric to his fellow Londoners. In 1750 this is the headquarters of the Royal Society, chartered by Charles II in 1663 and the premiere example of London's ability to bring together men of genius. The Scottish tourist Rev. Robert Kirk's description from 1690 gives a flavor of the Society's eclectic interests during its first century:

> . . . the Hall for containing the curious rarities is not large, but full of varieties, above 2,000. Among which the main that I remarked and remembered were 3 manacodiatas with plain bills, long wings and tails, walking feet. I took a feather out of the wing of one of them and out of the tail of the ostrich's skin . . . A Hudson's bay partridge . . . A serpent of East India 7 yards in length, a small head and body as big as my leg at the ankles. . . . The black and white pigritia [sloth], in shape like a man, a big body and slender legs. . . . A crocodile. An embalmed princely body above 3,000 years old. . . . The rattling serpent, the most deadly. The star fish. A microscope. . . . A calf with two heads etc. This is the best show in Christendom. The Society meets once a week and have experiments and Latin and English lectures. Besides I saw the Antelope like a goat, a small round body. An Unicorn horn, white and wreathed, straight and small at top, hard as elephant's tooth. It stuck 22 inches in a ship's keel; 'tis 2 yards and a half long. A sea beast. A camel.[7]

Having digested the wonders of Bishopsgate, we turn left and follow Wormwood Street west, which broadens out into London Wall. Along our right is an impressive edifice and one of London's major tourist attractions in 1750. The first of two hospitals we will visit, one dark, one light, this is New Bethlehem Hospital, or Bedlam. A version of Bedlam has served as London's lunatic asylum since the Middle Ages, but it became a fashionable tourist attraction only at the beginning of the seventeenth century. In 1675/76 the hospital moved to palatial new buildings designed by Robert Hooke: Ned Ward thought "they were mad that Built so costly a Colledge for such a Crack-brain'd Society." We enter through an arched doorway framed by Cibber's two striking carved figures of *Madness* and *Melancholy*, rendered all the more ominous by the fact that they were modeled from actual inmates, and painted to reflect life. The sight before us is well described by Kirk and portrayed at the end of Hogarth's *Rake's Progress*: patients, "some dumb, others talkative, some furious" chained in their chambers, arranged along galleries to facilitate their viewing – an exhibition of human misery (see Illustration c.4). The fees extracted from visitors paid for the care and feeding of the inmates until 1770, when it was determined that the former " . . . tended to disturb the tranquility of the patients . . . [by] . . . making sport and diversion of the miserable inhabitants."[8]

Emerging with relief back into the street, we turn right at the gate and resume our westward route along London Wall. Just past the facade of Bedlam to our right is the entrance to Moorfields, a vast public park that was a swamp until drained in 1527. It was here that displaced Londoners camped after the Great Fire. Continuing west, we rejoin our 1550 route by turning left, down Basinghall Street, to see several livery halls, including the Guildhall on our right. The Guildhall was severely damaged by the Fire, burning from the inside out like "a bright, shining coal as if it had been a palace of gold or a great building of burnished brass" because of its oaken interiors.[9] London's city hall was rebuilt by Wren, adding a story to its height, by 1671. We emerge by Ironmonger Lane into Cheapside, still a wide and vibrant thoroughfare, still lined with shops, still filled with the cries of London's street vendors. By 1750, however, the wealthy have moved west, and the smartest shops are to be found in Mayfair or Pall Mall. These days, the City was less about retail than wholesale and finance.

At the western end of Cheapside we come to a fork in the road. As it is by now lunchtime, we might be tempted to take the left fork, down Pater-Noster Row, to drop by Dolly's Steak-house, Boswell's favorite. But to continue our tour we have to go right, heading west up Newgate Street, past the grounds of Christ's Hospital for orphans, through Newgate itself.

The prison, rebuilt after the Fire, still flanks the street adjacent to the Old Bailey. Accosted by the smells and hearing the cries of the poor prisoners through a grate, we might pass them some bread or coins to purchase beer. If this is a "hanging match" Monday, we encounter the crowds gathering to cheer London's next entries on the Bills of Mortality: the condemned. We join the cavalcade west down Hart-Row Street and Snow Hill to Holborn Bridge, where we break off, having already experienced the sordid pleasures of a public hanging earlier, in Chapter 6. Instead, we turn south down Fleet Market. This used to be the smelly Fleet Ditch, which was boarded over by Act of Parliament in 1733 to provide space for a meat market: thus, the area remains "fragrant." In fact, reminded by the clock tower in the center that it is midday, and by our stomachs that we have not eaten, the opportune cry "One a penny, A slice, Hot" persuades us to patronize a local character, James Sharp, the "Flying Pie Man" (fl. 1750s).[10] While munching our pie, we examine the many new shops built under a covered walkway with skylights.

LUDGATE HILL, FLEET STREET, THE STRAND

At the bottom of the market we come to the juncture of Fleet Street and Ludgate Hill. For the second time today, we backtrack and turn east. We have taken this roundabout route to approach London's greatest building from the west, for as we walk up Ludgate Hill, St. Paul's Cathedral rises majestically, like a great ship, from the ocean of buildings. St. Paul's represents London's most stunning architectural achievement since the Fire. (We addressed its construction in Chapter 8.) Now, climbing the stairs of the west entrance, passing Bird's statue of Queen Anne, and under a portico supported by twelve massive columns, itself supporting another portico on top of which are statues of Saints Paul, Peter, and James, we enter London's parish church (see Illustration c.5). Where Old St. Paul's was dark and dank, the new cathedral, although not flooded with light, gives an impression of greater space because of the wide central aisle and distantly spaced piers. St. Paul's is also airier than Westminster Abbey, not least because it has few monuments in 1750. Our eyes and our steps are drawn, not so much to the magnificent choir, the stalls carved by Gibbons, but to the space under the dome, which rises above us to 300 feet. We gaze up at Thornhill's frescoes of scenes from the life of St. Paul, not realizing that we are looking at the brick inner dome. This resides within a brick cone and an outer shell made of timber and covered with lead, rising another 60 feet. This architectural trick allowed Wren to achieve proportions pleasing to the eye both within and without the cathedral. According to legend, while working on the paintings Thornhill stood back to examine his work, coming dangerously close to the edge of the scaffolding and a fatal plunge. His assistant, fearful that he might startle Sir James if he called out a warning, instead did the one thing guaranteed to get him to step forward: he began to smear the paint on the fresco that Thornhill was assessing! It worked, and both Thornhill and the fresco were saved.

Anxious to see the frescoes up close, we begin to climb an interior stair, bounding up the 259 steps to the whispering gallery that rings the dome 100 feet up: conversations can clearly be heard at the opposite side, over 100 feet away. Not yet exhausted, we trudge another 99 steps up to the Stone Gallery, giving a fine view of London; the more adventurous plod another 152 steps higher to the Inner Golden Gallery at the top of the dome; and finally, the most persistent slog a few more steps to the Outer Golden Gallery at the top of the lantern. This is the highest point in London; from it we can survey the whole of the metropolis. Below us to the south, the bustling river, and if we look up, London Bridge and the shallow development of the South Bank; to the east, the crowded square mile of the City, the Tower, and the ribbon of communities growing along the banks of the Thames; to the north, some development but beyond it open fields; and finally, to the west, the congestion of Fleet Street and the Strand. Beyond that, the ancient Gothic palaces of Westminster contrast with the perfectly Georgian squares of the West End, bordered by Hyde Park. Eighteenth-century people tended to not like heights, and our precarious position becomes alarming on the hour when the giant bell in the southwest tower, Old Tom, strikes with its earth-shaking bass note. This bell also tolls the deaths of members of the royal family, Bishops of London, Deans of St. Paul's, and lord mayors who die in office.

St. Paul's has continued to have a distinguished career as both a national and a London church. It was the site of thanksgivings for military victories under Queen Anne and in the Napoleonic wars, for royal weddings (most famously that of Prince Charles [b. 1948] and Lady Diana Spenser [1961–1997] in 1981), and for state funerals, such as that of Lord Nelson (1758–1805) in 1806 and the Duke of Wellington (1769–1852) in 1852. Perhaps the most iconic image of the cathedral, the one that cemented it in the public imagination as a symbol of London itself, was a series of photographs taken during the Blitz of 1940/41. While the Luftwaffe went after the East End docks and did not specifically target St. Paul's, its sheer size and proximity to their intended target put it in danger. On several occasions bombs did penetrate the roof, and once the crypt. But "Paul's," like London, survived, the image of its dome standing stalwartly against the flames and smoke a symbol of the resolve of the city and its inhabitants.

Exiting where we came in, we head down the west steps, catching another view of commercial London, this one down Fleet Street and the Strand. In 1750, Fleet Street's criminal reputation had faded a bit, and we are fairly safe in daytime. But it continued to be associated with slightly shady activity, such as irregular and cheap Fleet marriages. In the seventeenth century, poor clergymen incarcerated for debt in the Fleet Prison (to our right) made a few shillings by marrying inmates, no questions asked. Eventually, they were happy do so for visitors to the prison. By the 1690s they had set up clandestine "wedding houses" in the Fleet Liberty, sometimes offering package deals with local innkeepers à l Reno or Las Vegas today. The practice was outlawed in 1754 by Hardwicke's Marriage Act (26 Geo. II, c. 33). Fleet Street remained a center of publishing and the press throughout the period and beyond. For example, Jacob Tonson, the most important publisher of the Augustan Age, started his first bookshop at the Fleet Street end of Chancery Lane in 1678. The *Daily Courant*, the world's first daily newspaper, began publication "next door to the King's Arms Tavern at Fleet-Bridge," on March 11, 1702. As pointed out in Chapter 1, the street's name operates as shorthand for the London press to this day.

Just off the street are innumerable little lanes and courts. Several of them (e.g., Hind's Court, Bolt Court, or Johnson's Court) on our right will lead us to Gough Square, a small development named for the London mercantile family who owned it in the eighteenth century. On the western side of the little square is a fine early eighteenth-century house, 17 Gough Square, inhabited between 1746 and 1759 by one of the most famous Londoners of the day, the writer Samuel Johnson. In the garret of this house, Dr. Johnson and several assistants compiled the first comprehensive dictionary of the English language (1755), which made him something of a national hero and local monument. Downstairs, the convivial Johnson entertained scores of writers and artists, including the painter Joshua Reynolds and the music historian Charles Burney (1726–1814). If a dinner invitation proves not to be forthcoming, we might encounter the great man at any number of coffeehouses and taverns in the area because, like all scholars, he required constant refreshment from his labors. Johnson's large frame, scrofulous face, and unkempt appearance renders him one of London's sights, and so we will know him when we see him.

Moving farther down Fleet Street we pass the church of St. Dunstan-in-the-West, looking a little more run-down than it was in 1550. St. Dunstan's was one of the few churches in central London to survive the Fire, it is said because the Dean of Westminster drafted the boys of Westminster School to form a bucket brigade. In gratitude, the parishioners endowed a great clock in 1671, which projects over the street. A few steps west bring us to the official boundary between the City of London and Westminster: Temple Bar. The old gatehouse survived the Fire, but in the 1670s it was redesigned by Wren. It now consists of a large central arch over the street, with two flanking arches for pedestrians, topped by a new gatehouse sporting statues of James I, Anne of Denmark, Charles I, and Charles II, and above them, the obligatory heads of executed malefactors (see Illustration c.6). The heads were a hit with tourists, who could rent sidewalk telescopes to have a better view of them. In 1750 we might just catch site of the last such traitorous head, that of Francis Towneley (1709–1746), a Jacobite rebel executed in 1746. The heads looked down on horrendous traffic, which Temple Bar's elegant arches only made worse. As a result, it was taken down in 1878. For a while it lay disassembled in a yard at Faringdon Road until Sir Henry Bruce Meux (1856–1900) re-erected it, incongruously, in Theobald's Park north of the city in rural Hertfordshire. There it remained until 2004 when it was erected once again in the churchyard of St. Paul's Cathedral, thus uniting Wren's masterpiece with its larger brother.

After much jostling, we emerge from this bottleneck into the Strand. Perhaps nowhere else is the contrast with 1550 so pronounced as here. Before, the Strand was a muddy track with a few tradesmen's shops on one side and magnificent bishop's palaces on the other. Now the commercial side of the street thrives whereas only two of the great palaces survive, Somerset House halfway down the street, and Northumberland House, built circa 1605 for Henry Howard, Earl of Northampton (1540–1614), at Charing Cross. York House has been subdivided as York Buildings, housing one of London's major concert halls as well as an important waterworks. The rest is taken up with shop windows, gaudy wooden signs, hawker's calls, coffeehouses, taverns, houses, and above all, traffic. Grosley in 1765 found the shops in Cheapside, Fleet Street, and the Strand

> Brilliant and gay, as well on account of the things sold in them, as the exact order in which they are kept; so they make a most splendid show, greatly superior to any thing of the kind in Paris.[11]

Amid all this commerce, indeed situated on islands right in the middle of the Strand, and so no help either to traffic or business, we find two new churches: St. Clement Danes, and an eighth of a mile farther, St. Mary-le-Strand. Nobody knows why the parish of St. Clement's was associated with the Danes, although one tradition is that after Alfred drove the Vikings out of London in the ninth century, those who had married Englishwomen were allowed to settle between Westminster and Ludgate. The medieval St. Clement Danes church survived the fire but was condemned as unsafe in 1679, and so Wren designed a new church in the Baroque style, to which an ornate steeple was added by James Gibbs. If this is a Sunday, we might catch a glimpse of Dr. Johnson at his devotions in seat No. 18, north gallery, because this was his preferred parish church.

Just a few hundred yards down the street we encounter the second church in the road, St. Mary-le-Strand, designed by Gibbs and erected from 1714 to 1717, the first of fifty churches that Queen Anne planned to build to accommodate London's growing population. In the end, only about a dozen were completed, but Gibbs's work on this charming church launched his career. He had studied in Italy, and therefore the building combines the influence of Wren with that of the Catholic Renaissance and Baroque. If we time our visit just right, we might witness a remarkable historical event. It was probably in this church, between September 17 and 22, 1750, that the Young Pretender, Charles Edward Stuart (1720–1788), also know as Bonnie Prince Charlie, grandson of James II and Jacobite heir apparent to the British thrones, on an incognito visit to London tried to revive his flagging English support by being received into the Church of England. Both St. Clement Danes and St. Mary-le-Strand exacerbated the traffic situation in the Strand, and by the 1970s the traffic was striking back: a combination of German bombs and the vibration of heavy London buses and lorries had so weakened the spire of St. Mary's that it was threatened with demolition for safety's sake. Donations poured in to save the steeple, although not before demolition actually got under way. Today, these two churches continue their stately progress in the Strand, like two advance escorts in whose wake sails the larger vessel of St. Paul's.

The West End

At this point in 1550 we carried on down the Strand to Charing Cross, gaping at the nobles' and bishop's palaces to the south, partly because of their inherent interest, and partly because there was so little to see on the north side of the street and beyond. By 1750 that had all changed: the area north of the Strand had been filled in by the explosion of growth in the West End (see Illustration c.7), beginning with the building of Covent Garden in the 1630s. For example, just west of Covent Garden, up St. Martin's Lane, is the parish of St. Martin-in-the-Fields. In 1550 its name described its situation, with a population of just 1,400, but this had risen to 18,500 by 1640, to 69,000 by 1685, and to more than 100,000, now split into a total of four parishes (St. Martin's, St. Paul Covent Garden, St. James Piccadilly, and St. Anne Soho) by the 1720s – larger than any other city in Britain! This growth was part of the ongoing expansion of London's population in all directions beyond the lord mayor's jurisdiction; by 1750, only about one-quarter of the metropolitan population lived within the old City.

As more squares were added to the West End, and more City tradesmen moved into Covent Garden, it ceased to be at the cutting edge of fashion. In fact, by 1750 London's first swanky square had become rather seedy, forming the southern tip of a swath running up through Drury Lane dedicated to the pursuit of less respectable and even illicit pleasures. It could be argued that Covent Garden began its decline from exclusivity about 1656 with the establishment of the market. At first, Covent Garden Market was a small-scale operation out of the gardens of Bedford House, serving the residents of the square. But when the Fire dislocated markets in central London, Covent Garden to the west became the most important source of fruit, flowers, and herbs in the city. In 1678 one Adam Piggot was granted a license to build twenty-two shops against the garden wall of Bedford House on the south side of the square. Forty-eight more shops were built early in the eighteenth century near the center, and these were made into a permanent complex in 1748. Walking through the stalls, we see not only London's freshest fruit, but exotic produce from foreign lands – dates, currants, oranges – unloaded directly from the river. Grosley found the domestic produce better to look at than to taste, for London's foul atmosphere ruins anything grown nearby.

With the shops came coffeehouses and a theater. We stop in at the Bedford, on the square under the piazza, hoping to see a literary celebrity. At one time or another, this establishment was patronized by Boswell, Fielding, Garrick, Pope, Sheridan, and Horace Walpole. It was convenient for actors and writers because it stood just across the way from the Theater Royal, Covent Garden, built in 1732 and managed by John Rich. The first of three buildings on the site, it would burn down in 1808, its successor in 1856. The third is today the home of the Royal Opera, Covent Garden.

As the center of Covent Garden became more commercial, aristocratic tenants began to move farther west to the more fashionable squares growing up around St. James's, and by the mid-eighteenth century, Mayfair. As early as the reign of Charles II, they were starting to be replaced by professional men, courtiers, and artists like Sir Thomas Killigrew, the dramatist and master of the revels, Sir Peter Lely, principal painter to the king; and his successor Sir Godfrey Kneller. In the early eighteenth century, they were succeeded by Thornhill, whose academy was located here from 1722 to 1734, and theater manager Rich, who lived in the square from 1743 to 1760. He might have regretted his last years there, because by 1750 most of the respectable professional residents were gone, their houses converted into squalid flophouses, gambling dens, and bagnios (ostensibly a Turkish bath, but often a contemporary euphemism for a brothel). The area also had a fair number of molly houses: homosexual brothels unique to London. At night, pimps, prostitutes, pickpockets, and press-gangs patrolled the square. According to Steele, at the dawn shift change "the Purveyors [of fruit] for Covent-Garden, . . . frequently converse with Morning Rakes."[12] Hogarth also notes the traffic of sinners home in "Morning," part of his series *Four Times of the Day* (1736).

Making our way gingerly through this throng, we head east along Russell Street, then north along Drury Lane, past the theater of that name and into the heart of the theater district. It swarms with actors and stage personnel: on May Day 1667 Samuel Pepys was happy to see the comic actress and royal mistress "pretty Nelly" Gwynn "at her lodgings' door in Drury-lane in her smock-sleeves and bodice, looking upon one – she seemed a mighty pretty creature."[13] In the eighteenth century Drury Lane was another haunt for gentlemen and ladies of pleasure: one tourist alleged the existence of 107 "houses of pleasure" in the area, and Hogarth sets part of *A Harlot's Progress* here. A little farther west is the rookery of St. Giles's, a home for Irish immigrants and criminals and the setting of Hogarth's *Gin Lane*. In short, here, at the gateway to the prosperous West End, we are reminded of the social diversity of metropolitan London.

From Drury Lane we turn east along Great Queen Street to have a look at Lincoln's Inn Fields. This is the largest square in London, the second one developed and a sort of transitional space between Covent Garden–Drury Lane and the new West End. It is lined with distinguished houses occupied by some of the leading Londoners of the eighteenth century: Thomas Pelham Holles, the fabulously wealthy Duke of Newcastle, several earls, successive lord chancellors (i.e., Somers, Cowper [1665–1723],

Macclesfield [1667–1732], Hardwicke [1690–1764], Erskine [1750–1823], and Brougham [1778–1868]), future prime ministers William Pitt the Elder (1708–1778) and Spencer Percival (1762–1812), and the legal commentator Sir William Blackstone (1723–80). It is ironic that so many legal figures live here, for at night this broad expanse of green is also dangerous.

Having been appalled by Bedlam and discomposed by Drury Lane, we head for something more edifying. Exiting cautiously to the north, we cross Holborn and walk up Red Lyon Street, named after a famous inn on the corner. At the very top of the street we emerge into Lamb's Conduit Fields, named for an Elizabethan dam of the Fleet River that supplied water for the area. Much of this neighborhood was developed after the Fire by Nicholas Barbon. Proceeding up a tree-lined promenade, we enter the grounds of Thomas Coram's Foundling Hospital. The building, designed by Theodore Jacobsen (d. 1772) and not quite finished in 1750, is U shaped, consisting of two wings, the east for girls, the west for boys, linked by a chapel at the back of a central court (see Illustration c.8). It is not as impressive as Bedlam, but the scene at the gates on reception days is every bit as heartrending, as mothers beg for the chance to save their babies. Beyond those gates are clean accommodations and spacious open fields. Inside, we marvel at the works of art by Hogarth and others, including a magnificent molded Rococo ceiling and a relief of *Charity and Children Engaged in Navigation and Husbandry* by John Michael Rysbrack over the fireplace in the Governor's Court Room. It was fashionable to attend Sunday services with the children, where Handel might play the organ. Above all, the eighteenth-century mind was edified by the rows of neatly dressed youngsters being fed, clothed, and apprenticed. As we have seen, the Foundling Hospital's efforts were a mere drop in the sordid bucket of London's child-welfare problem. To judge from the response of artists and patrons, however, most visitors left with a heartwarming sense that something was being done. Today, the Foundling Hospital is long gone, but the twenty-first century visitor may sample some of the artwork in the reconstructed Picture Gallery and Governor's Court Room or ponder the fates of the children whose tokens are still on display, both at the Foundling Hospital Museum; or he or she may amble about the grounds, now called Coram's Fields – but only, as the sign says, if accompanied by a child.

Having seen London at its most enlightened, we now turn to the metropolis at its showiest. Retracing our steps down Red Lyon Street, we turn west down Great Ormond Street, past several Barbon houses

(Nos. 55 and 57) and the French Embassy at Powis House on our right, into the neighborhood known as Bloomsbury. Bloomsbury is bounded by Holborn to the south, Gray's Inn Lane to the East, Tottenham Court Road to the west, and open fields to the north. As with the Bedford Estate, Bloomsbury was acquired first by the Church, then confiscated by the Crown. In the mid-sixteenth century its open fields were awarded to Thomas Wriothesley (1505–1550), who became Earl of Southampton, in 1547. It was his descendant, the fourth Earl (1608–1667), later lord treasurer of England, who began to develop the manor. In 1657 he pulled down the old manor house, built a London mansion called Southampton House, and then laid out Southampton Square around it. If Covent Garden was the first London square, this one, renamed Bloomsbury in the eighteenth century, was the first with *Square* in its title. In 1665 John Evelyn caught the idea behind this housing arrangement when he called it "a noble square or Piazza – a little towne."[14] Offered long leases of 42, and later 60 or even 99 years, aristocratic tenants flocked to Bloomsbury. Among its great houses, a little farther west down Great Russell Street, was Montagu House, which burned down in 1686. Horace Walpole wrote of the second Montagu House that "What it wants in grace and beauty is compensated by the spaciousness and lofty magnificence of the apartments."[15] That was fortunate, for in 1755 the Montagu family, seeking more modest accommodation, donated the house to the nation to be the first home of the British Museum.

Prior to 1755, the closest thing to a British Library and Museum was the royal library and art collection, spread around various royal palaces. But scholars needed royal permission to examine the king's books and manuscripts; although the art collection was on display to courtiers, the court was not exactly a "public" museum. The idea for the British Museum arose thanks to the will of Sir Hans Sloane (1660–1753), one of London's leading physicians, a resident of Bloomsbury who had spent many years and £50,000 amassing a collection of scientific books, manuscripts, and specimens. At his death in 1753 he offered his collections to the nation at the discount price of £20,000. At the same time, the Foundation Act (23 Geo. II, c. 22) authorized the purchase of the Harleian Collection of manuscripts collected by Robert Harley, Earl of Oxford; the Cottonian Library assembled by Sir Robert Cotton (1571–1631); and the Royal Library presented by George II. These four collections formed the nucleus of the British Museum. Funds for purchase were raised by a public lottery, and the museum opened its doors in 1759. In the beginning, those doors were open only three hours a day by written application to the librarian. Even then, only small groups were admitted for guided tours until well into the nineteenth century. In future years the British Museum would acquire such treasures as the Rosetta Stone (1801), the Elgin Marbles (1816), innumerable Egyptian mummies, botanical collections, state papers, diaries, correspondence, newspapers, and works of literature, history, and science. In the 1840s Montagu House was demolished in favor of the present neoclassical building. In 1973 the British Library became a separate entity and moved to its own building in 1997. Together, these two form one of the world's preeminent national collections, made available to ordinary users of all nationalties.

Because all of this lay in the future in 1750, we inquisitive scholars must move on, turning our attention to the development that made it possible. During the seventeenth century, the Wriothesleys united in marriage with the Russells, who renamed Southampton House "Bedford House" in 1734, having abandoned the old Bedford House in the now seedy Covent Garden in 1705/06. This alliance created a vast estate and an unstoppable development combination. During the later eighteenth century, the surrounding Bedford property filled up with fashionable and exclusive squares centering on iron railed-in gardens and often named for Russell titles: Russell Square, Bedford Square, and Tavistock Square. But the Russells were not alone. If we continue west along Oxford Street (built on the ancient Roman track to Oxford and the west), we encounter a parade of regular squares named for the great aristocratic families that developed them; together, they form the characteristic housing arrangement of the West End. They were built east to west, and so the oldest come first. With much of London still to cover, a few examples, in roughly chronological order, will suffice.

First, to our left down Charles Street, comes Soho Square, named for a hunting call from the time when this area was open fields. The square was developed in the 1680s by Henry Jermyn, Earl of St. Albans (1605-1684), another favored and opportunistic courtier, as King's Square. It centers on a delightful garden, described by Strype as "a very large and open place, enclosed with a high Palisado Pale, the Square within neatly kept, with Walks and Grass-plots, and in the midst is the Effigy of King Charles the Second, neatly cut in Stone to the Life, standing on a Pedestal."[16] The development was immediately fashionable, and by the 1690s it featured a series of splendid aristocratic houses, Monmouth House, Carlisle House, and Fauconberg House being the most notable. This was also a convenient site for the diplomatic missions of Spain, Venice, Russia, and Sweden. Only in the 1770s did the wealthiest clientele leave for newer fashionable areas like Mayfair. By the nineteenth century the residents were largely professional, and by the twenty-first, office blocks were surrounded by an area long known for jazz clubs and sex shops.

Eighteenth-century Oxford Street further delights our senses with the lovely groves at Marybone Place before, darting north along Prince's Street or Holles Street, we encounter Cavendish Square. This was begun for the Harley family in 1717 as a Tory answer to Hanover Square (see later discussion), popular with Whigs. But Cavendish Square was left unfinished for much of the century, partly because of the South Sea Bubble crash and partly because it was at first considered too far from the court to be attractive to aristocrats. In 1721 the Oxford Market was built nearby, specifically to cater to the residents, but this did nothing for its exclusivity. Early in the eighteenth century the bluestocking and promoter of vaccination Lady Mary Wortley Montagu lived here, and later the painter George Romney (1734–1802). In 1736, *A New Critical Review of Public Buildings . . . in and about London and Westminster* observed that the square's uncompleted state demonstrated "the folly of attempting great things, before we are sure we can accomplish little ones."[17]

We are now on the fringes of eighteenth-century London. Farther to the north lie several little villages surrounded by open fields where Tottenham Court Road turns into the toll road to Highgate. Perhaps more intriguing, near the end of Mary-le-Bone Lane is Mary-le-Bone (or Marybone) Gardens, opened here in 1650, just as development was getting started in the West End, as a northern alternative to the south bank pleasure gardens. Like them, it offered dog, cock, and prizefights, bear- and bull-baiting, and bowling greens. The most famous boxer of the early eighteenth century, James Figg (by 1700–1734), mounted exhibitions here between "the most eminent professors, both male and female, of the art of defense."[18] Although Pepys thought the gardens pretty, they came to be associated with card sharps and their wealthy, aristocratic marks. Mary-le-Bone Gardens was one of the fictional Macheath's hangouts in *The Beggar's Opera*, and in real life the celebrated thief Dick Turpin frequented them. In 1738, worried about the clientele and losing their business, the management expanded the gardens but began to charge an entrance fee of 6 pence. The next year a set of assembly rooms for balls and teas was added. In 1750 we pay our sixpence and get to walk along a grand promenade formed by trees that meet at the center, or we might dart into an alcove with latticework for privacy and, between 6 PM and 10 PM, listen to the orchestra.

Resuming our exploration of Oxford Street, to our left down Little Holles Street (named for the family of the Duke of Newcastle) is Hanover Square, built soon after the Hanoverian accession by Richard Lumley, Earl of Scarborough (1650–1721), as the first of three squares (Hanover, Berkeley, and Grosvenor) that form the district of Mayfair. Mayfair is today bounded by Oxford Street on the north, Regent Street on the east, Piccadilly on the south, and Park Lane on the west, but in 1750 some of these streets had not yet been laid out. Mayfair was so-called because it was the site of a fair held during the first two weeks of May to herald the beginning of summer. Aristocratic developers began building here in the 1660s, and the fair had to move from Haymarket to Great Brookfield. It was suppressed altogether in 1764 after the aristocratic residents complained.

The greatest square in Mayfair, and indeed in the whole West End, is Grosvenor Square (see Illustration c.9). In 1677, Sir Thomas Grosvenor (1655–1700), a Cheshire baronet, acquired 500 acres in the West End through a fortunate marriage to the twelve-year-old heiress Mary Davies (1665–1730). Grosvenor Square was built between 1725 and 1731 to an overall plan by the carpenter and master builder Thomas Barlow (c. 1669–1730), not by the Grosvenors themselves, but by the holders at long leases of fifty-five plots. From the first, the square was built on a grand and luxurious scale, with houses up to £7,500 in value. The Grosvenor family kept the rents high, partly to preserve the social prestige of the square. One result was that, until the twentieth century, more than half of the residents were titled nobility, including, in the eighteenth century, prime and cabinet ministers. Another result was that the Grosvenors got very rich: their annual rents in the 1780s from the square alone were £3,000 per annum. Approaching the square in 1750 from any direction, we are struck by its vast size (roughly 200 feet by 150 feet), which gives it an open-air feeling, and the magnificent, if stylistically variable, three- and four-story houses, most of which would survive into the twenty-first century. Residents spent vast sums on their upkeep and renovation, and some of the greatest names in English building – Adam, Chambers, Soane, Wyatville, and Wyatt, for example – worked here. In 1765 Sir Josiah Wedgwood opened his first London showroom in Grosvenor Square.

Grosvenor Square never went into decline like Covent Garden or Soho. One reason was its convenient location close to the court at St. James's, the Parliament at Westminster, and the parks. Second, the developers laid out airy and rational streets with convenient stabling on the borders of the nearby fields: in fact, we notice that the streets are filled with footmen and grooms in livery, as well as other servants necessary to run an aristocratic household. Eventually, Mayfair developed convenient markets for food and shops for luxury items; by the 1720s, these spilled off onto Bond Street, located between Hanover Square and Grosvenor Square. Londoners loved then, as they do now, to window shop while strolling Bond Street. This was also a convenient address for those who could not afford the more fashionable squares, including at various times Jonathan Swift, William Pitt the Elder, the novelist Lawrence Sterne (1713–1768), the historian Edward Gibbon (1737–1794), James Boswell, Lord Nelson, and much later, his lover Lady Hamilton (1765–1815). Finally, we are shocked at the number of beggars who ask for our charity: like the shopkeepers, they follow the money. This reminds us that while Addison and Johnson may have thought of the city as many Londons, "An Aggregate of various Nations, distinguished from each other by their respective Customs, Manners, and Interests,"[19] the truth is that Londoners roam, mix, and mingle, making it possible to encounter men and women of all ranks, hear any cry, and have one's sympathy engaged or one's pocket picked anywhere in the great conurbation.

PARKS AND PALACES

After a long day of rambling the streets of London, we might refresh ourselves in the network of royal but open space comprising Hyde Park, Green Park, and St. James's Park. Walking west from Grosvenor Square, we cross Tyburn Lane (later to be rehabilitated as Park Lane), pass through a double row of trees, and emerge into Hyde Park, the largest of all London parks. At 340 acres, Hyde Park stretches from Tyburn Lane in the east to Kensington Gardens in the west, Bayswater Turnpike in the north to Knightsbridge Turnpike in the south. As this implies, Hyde Park and Kensington Gardens mark not only the western extreme of the West End, but of greater London itself in 1750: beyond Kensington Palace lie more open fields. Like so much of London's green space, this was originally Church land, owned by the monks of Westminster, before confiscation by the Crown in 1536. The Tudors used it as a hunting ground, and deer were still being pursued there in 1750. The park also had military associations: as the largest open space adjacent to London it was a convenient muster point for troops – both professional and citizen soldiers – in times of crisis, such as the execution of the king in 1649, the restoration of his son in 1660, the Jacobite Rebellion in 1715, or the Gordon Riots in 1780.

The early Stuarts opened Hyde Park to the public, and it quickly became a place of fashionable resort. In particular, the elite liked to parade around "the Tour" or "the Ring." This was an area at the western end of the park containing two concentric carriage tracks, separating it from Kensington Gardens. Anybody who thought themselves somebody in the seventeenth century rode on horseback or in their coach to see and be seen. Rival gentlemen sometimes raced their coaches: according to legend, Oliver Cromwell almost lost his life when he was thrown during such a contest. Pepys regarded attendance as a good career move, and Mrs. Pepys insisted on appearing on May Day. For May Day 1663, the diarist bought new gloves, put on his best clothes, and rented a horse, but he proved unable to manage the animal and so missed his chance to impress the king. By 1669, he was a rising man and could afford a coach of his own:

> and thence to Hyde-park, the first time we were there this year, or
> ever in our own coach – where with mighty pride rode up and down;
> and many coaches there, and I thought our horses and coach as pretty
> as any there, and observed so to be by others. Here stayed till night,
> and so home. . . . [20]

Restoration Londoners understood quite well the seemingly modern notion that you are what you drive.

Because William III could not abide London's damp, sooty atmosphere, he purchased Kensington House in the relative fresh air to the west and made it his preferred residence. His route to Whitehall took him along the south side of Hyde Park, which became known as *le route du roy* (route of the king), soon corrupted into "Rotten Row." In part because the park was a notorious hangout for thieves and highwaymen, he ordered 300 lamps hung from trees, thus making the *route du roy* the first lit road in England. By the 1730s, this had replaced the Ring as the favorite upper-class carriage promenade. The park was also a preferred dueling ground, the most famous example being the mutually fatal contest between the Duke of Hamilton (1658–1712) and Lord Mohun in 1712. In the 1730s, Queen Caroline (1683–1737) improved both Hyde Park and Kensington Gardens, adding the Serpentine Lake to the latter. We pass by, attempting to affect a gentle air, noting the two small royal yachts sailing placidly in the water.

Turning east, back toward London along the Knightsbridge Turnpike, we round Hyde Park Corner into Piccadilly. On our right is Green Park, a popular resort for highwaymen and duelists laid out by Charles II. Piccadilly takes us back into the West End. The street with London's most lighthearted-sounding name originated around 1612 when Robert Baker (d. 1623), a Strand-based tailor, decided to build a country house at the eastern end. He had grown wealthy supplying piccadills (stiff laced collars) to the court. The popular name of the street was a jab at his mercantile origins. Building really began after the Restoration, when the court insisted on calling the street "Portugal Street" after Queen Catherine of Braganza, but it was the name "Piccadilly" that stuck with Londoners. The south side of the street was developed by the Earl of St. Albans in the 1660s and 1670s. Part of the north side was awarded by Charles II to the Earl of Clarendon, who sold lots for a series of great aristocratic houses: Clarendon House, torn down in 1683; Berkeley House, burned down in 1733; and Burlington House, still standing in the early twenty-first century. The rest of the area was developed to Hyde Park by 1750. Many of the new buildings were shops and workshops; they would be replaced by a second wave of aristocratic development after 1760.

Strolling up the broad boulevard, we come to Burlington House on our left, just past Old Bond Street. Begun by the courtier Sir John Denham (1615–1669) for his own use, it was completed by the court architect Hugh May (1621–1684) for Richard Boyle, first Earl of Burlington. In 1714/15, Richard Boyle, the third earl (1694–1753), fresh from a trip to Italy, commissioned Sir James Gibbs to add the distinctive curved colonnade that we see in the forecourt and Sebastiano Ricci (1659–1734) to do a series of mythological ceiling paintings. In 1717–20, Colen Campbell (1676–1729) was charged with remodeling the whole house to more resemble the Palazzo Porto at Vicenza. The result is one of the great examples of Palladian architecture in Britain, of which John Gay said "Beauty within, without Proportion reigns."[21] Desiring to see what Gay meant, we bribe the porter, enter Campbell's impressive gateway, and make our way across the court to the house. Inside we marvel at the ceiling paintings, such as Ricci's *Cupid before Jupiter* over what was then the main staircase, and William Kent's (1686–1748) *The Banquet of the Gods* in the Great Room or Saloon. Bought by the British government in 1854, Burlington House is today the last great seventeenth-century aristocratic palace in London. It has provided a home, at various times, for the Royal Society, the Royal Academy, the Royal Astronomical Society, the Society of

Antiquaries, the Linnean Society, the Chemical Society, and the Geological Society.

Carrying on down Piccadilly we encounter on our right one of Wren's masterpieces, St. James Piccadilly, built as part of the St. Albans development between 1676 and 1684. Designed to allow all 2,000 congregants a clear view of the pulpit, its barrel vaulting yields acoustics that enable them all to *hear* the sermon as well – a necessity in a Protestant church. Grinling Gibbons carved the reredos, the organ casing, and the baptismal font, which served the christenings of both William Pitt the Elder and the poet William Blake (1757–1827). The organ, on which Blow and Purcell played, started life in James II's Catholic Chapel and was removed here on the chapel's demolition in 1691.

St. James Piccadilly was always one of the smartest churches in London: it is the parish church of Lord Foppington in Vanbrugh's *The Relapse*, because "there's much the best company!" The principal reason for that is its proximity not only to the mansions of Piccadilly but also, just to the south down York Street, our last square of the day, St. James's Square. Sitting at the heart of the St. Albans development and a few yards north of the gates of St. James's Palace, this was one of the first squares to have been developed after the Restoration. For its first fifty years, it was, with Soho Square, London's most fashionable address, but by 1750 it had yielded that position to the squares in Mayfair – another sign of the court's relative social decline. Still, this neighborhood was convenient for peers with duties in the royal household, and as late as the 1720s six dukes and seven earls lived there. Some idea of the political significance of the square is that during the first half of the eighteenth century it was home to both Ozinda's Chocolate House (est. 1694), a leading Tory hangout, and the St. James's (est. 1705), which catered to Whigs. On entering the square we note that, unlike those in say, Grosvenor Square, the houses themselves are neat, red-brick structures, not particularly opulent. According to one observer writing in 1776:

> Although the Appearance of the Square hath an Air of Grandeur, yet that by no Means resulteth from the Pomp and Greatness of the Structures about it; but rather from a Prevailing Regularity throughout, joined to the neatness of the Pavement.[22]

The area was also popular with ambassadors, but gradually it came to be filled with aristocratic clubs and shops.

We emerge from the south side of St. James's Square into Pall Mall, the broad street that borders St. James's Park. Pall Mall might be the only street in London named after a game, similar to croquet, that was imported from the continent and became very popular at the court of Charles II. It was he who laid out the street, banning carriage and chair traffic in 1661. From the first it was fashionable, which helps to explain why the king ensconced Nell Gwyn here once she had moved up in the world. By the end of the seventeenth century, as elsewhere in the West End, shopkeepers had followed the aristocrats. It was at the bookshop of Robert Dosley, No. 52, that the proprietor encouraged Samuel Johnson to compile his dictionary. As this implies, the area was popular with artistic and literary figures: Sterne, Gibbon, and the painter Thomas Gainsborough all lived here at one time or another. They liked to visit popular local coffeehouses like the Smyrna. Later in the eighteenth century, as some coffeehouses began to limit their clientele by becoming clubs, many of them established themselves in Pall Mall, such as Almack's, Brookes's, Boodle's, the Carlton Club, and the Macaroni Club.

From this point, our choice of route is easy. At the eastern end of Pall Mall is the Haymarket, home of London's largest theater; beyond it is the Royal Mews. The Mews, or stables, are surrounded by run-down shops and tenements. They will all be cleared away at the beginning of the nineteenth century, to be replaced by Trafalgar Square and the National Gallery. But in 1750, this is a hole in the center of west London. So, instead, we double back west down Pall Mall to St. James's Palace, whose impressive Tudor gate is all covered with soot, rendering it old, ominous, even forbidding in the context of so much eighteenth-century elegance (see Illustration c.10). It stands in sharp contrast to Marlborough House (1709–1711) next door, designed for the Duchess of Marlborough by Sir Christopher Wren to be "strong plain and convenient."[23] St. James's was built by Henry VIII as a hunting lodge and served as the headquarters for various ancillary members of the royal family until 1698, when Whitehall burned down. From that point it became the official home of the British monarch, as it remains to this day. Never very large, it was immediately viewed as cramped and unsuitable: Queen Anne and her successors tried to remodel it, but it was never big enough to house the entire court, and a fire in 1809 reduced its size still further. Nor was it ever considered elegant or grand: Daniel Defoe called it "mean," and foreign visitors were shocked that the most powerful monarch in Europe lived in such an unimpressive structure. As we have seen, he or she tried to spend as much time away from it as possible: William III preferred Kensington and Hampton Court; Anne, Kensington and Windsor; George II, Hampton Court; and George III, Windsor and Kew. Only George I, with his preference for quiet living out of the public eye, seems to have been comfortable here.

The fact that in 1750 the British sovereign does not have a splendid city palace but must instead inhabit this run-down pile reminds us that he is a constitutional monarch. Unlike Louis XIV, he cannot build a Versailles without securing the funds from Parliament, which tended to want to spend national treasure on more practical matters like war and empire. In this, too, London, although a royal city, points toward a future in which rulers are servants of the people, not gods. In the meantime, the situation would become acute under George III (1760–1820), whose burgeoning family could not be housed in the old palace. In 1761, the mansion just south of St. James's and Green Park, Buckingham House, was purchased for Queen Charlotte (1744–1818). This remained yet another small country palace until the 1820s when, following the designs of John Nash (1752–1835), it became the nucleus for a house worthy of the pretensions of the British monarchy, Buckingham Palace.

Unaware of these future plans, we make our way across St. James's Park toward Westminster. When last we visited the park in 1550, it was mainly a Tudor hunting ground. After a period of neglect under the Commonwealth, Charles II laid out the canal, planted fruit trees, restocked the deer, built the Mall (south of Pall Mall), and opened the grounds to the public. During his reign (1660–1685), the king held court at Whitehall and his brother, the Duke of York, at St. James's Palace, and so there was a constant flow of elite traffic across the park. As we have seen, the king could be seen and approached while sauntering with his courtiers, feeding the ducks, and playing pall mall. The park began to decline after the death of Charles II in 1685, and by Anne's reign it was overrun by thieves, prostitutes, and, according to common report, the gangs of "Mohocks" whom we met in Chapter 6. In theory, the park gates were locked at night, but some 6,500 people were authorized to have keys! Although always fashionable for daylight promenaders, it was not until 1751, with the appointment of Thomas Fermor, Earl of Pomfret (?1698–1753) as ranger, that the Park began to be cleaned up (see Illustration c.11).

WESTMINSTER

Crossing the park at dusk, we see the twin towers of Westminster Abbey rise before us. Apart from those towers, erected in 1745 from designs by

Nicholas Hawksmoor, the exterior of the Westminster complex is little altered from what it was in 1550. Inside, the Abbey retains its medieval grandeur, but there are many more monuments and plaques to distinguished Britons than before. This is a sign of both a growing sense of nationalism and of the increasing value for nonroyal achievement. In fact, the one group beginning to be frozen out of the Abbey in 1750 is royal: the Henry VII Chapel is nearly full, and it would receive its last royal corpse with the death of George II in 1760. Westminster Hall across the street still houses the law courts and bookstalls and provides a convenient place of promenade when it rains in St. James's Park. The booksellers would leave in the reign of George III, the law courts at the end of the nineteenth century. Westminster Palace continues in 1750 as an inadequate space for the oldest continuously sitting legislature in the world, which began to meet annually from 1689. Under Anne, Wren built galleries in St. Stephen's Chapel to accommodate the Scottish MPs who came to London after the Act of Union of 1707 (6 Anne, c. 11), but if every member turned up, some could not be seated. The palace would meet its end on October 16, 1834 when, in a fit of reformist zeal, the government decided to burn so many old financial records in its furnace that it became overwhelmed. This gave the nation the chance to build the present, larger, more elegant and seemingly more medieval-looking Palace of Westminster, to designs by Sir Charles Barry (1795–1860) and Augustus Pugin (1812–1852). The nineteenth-century palace, with its distinctive Clock Tower and Big Ben's famous chime, has become a symbol of London, of Parliament, and of the nation, even more famous than St. Paul's.

In 1750, Westminster remains a western outpost of the metropolis, since Tothill Fields to the south is still undeveloped. Nevertheless, there are two hugely important changes to the topography and traffic pattern of this area: one a loss, the other a gain. The loss took place in 1698 when most of Whitehall Palace burned down. The palace used to bestride the street of the same name and its continuation as King Street, between the mews at Charing Cross and the Westminster complex. In 1750 there remains only the magnificent Banqueting House, used as a royal chapel, and the Holbein Gate. In place of the ramshackle palace has grown an even less rational hodgepodge of government offices and private homes, the most important of which combines features of both: No. 10 Downing Street (see Chapter 3). Parallel to King Street, Parliament Street has just been carved through the old palace's Privy Garden to connect Whitehall with Westminster Palace: it is symbolic of constitutional change that it is wider than King Street. In 1759, to relieve traffic, Holbein Gate would come down, eliminating one more reminder of Henry VIII's principal London residence. Already by 1750, "Whitehall" means the street, not the palace; by the early nineteenth century, it would come to mean the government.

The crucial addition to Westminster in 1750 is a second bridge across the Thames, Westminster Bridge, linking Westminster on the north bank with Lambeth on the south. As we saw in 1550, London Bridge was a notorious choke point for north–south traffic on the bridge itself, and east–west traffic on the Thames below. Between 1758 and 1762, the houses would be cleared and a wider navigation arch built, easing congestion somewhat. The bridge would be replaced with a more commodious structure from 1828 to 1831 and again from 1967 to 1972, the second bridge being removed to Lake Havasu City, Arizona. Still, the location of London Bridge was inconvenient for the burgeoning West End; the most populous city in Europe needed a second river crossing. The idea for a new bridge was first proposed at the Restoration, but it was opposed by the City authorities and the Thames watermen, both of whom feared a loss of business. The lord mayor was quoted as saying of an alternative upriver crossing, "if carts went over Putney Bridge the City of London would be irretrievably ruined."[24] The new span was begun over similar objections in 1738 and just completed in time for our crossing it in November 1750. It represented a radical change to London's traffic patterns and a recognition that Westminster was every bit as important to the metropolis as the City. Although tired from our trek through London, we hurry across the bridge, barely acknowledging the magnificent view of the City it affords as the sun sets behind us, because we have another stop to make: the pleasure garden at Vauxhall.

THE SOUTH BANK

We have so far neglected the south bank. It cannot be said that its growth kept pace with that of the north bank. While the marshy area between Lambeth and Southwark has filled in along the river by the end of our period, it does not project very far into Surrey. In 1750 London has only two real uses for this area: necessary but unpleasant industry and amusement. This is a convenient location for breweries and tanneries that need lots of water, but the smells and waste of which would be most unwelcome on the north bank; as a result, Bankside has declined into "a filthy and down-at-heel industrial slum" with indicative street names like Dirty Lane and Foul Lane.[25] As for amusement, the bear gardens and open-air theaters were long gone by 1750, but Vauxhall Pleasure Garden remains. Vauxhall, officially known as the New Spring Garden until 1785, was the successor to the Paris Garden noted in Chapter 1, albeit farther south along the bank. Because admission was free until 1732, up to that date ordinary Londoners could, as they had 150 years earlier at the Rose and Globe, enjoy its pleasures along with the elite:

Now the summer months come round,
Fun and pleasure will abound,
High and low and great and small,
Run in droves to view Vauxhall.
See the motley crew advance,
Led by Folly in the dance,
English, Irish, Spanish, Gaul,
Drive like mad to dear Vauxhall.

Each profession, ev'ry trade
Here enjoy refreshing shade,
Empty is the cobbler's stall,
He's gone with tinker to Vauxhall,
Here they drink, and there they cram
Chicken, pasty, beef and ham
Women sqeak and men drunk fall
Sweet enjoyment of Vauxhall.[26]

As we have seen, the pleasure garden was the closest thing to an amusement park – for adults – in eighteenth-century London. In 1750, for one shilling we can promenade along Vauxhall's 900 foot Grand Walk and several side- and crosswalks, stroll beautifully manicured gardens, or if we are able to pay more, retreat to a secluded booth for dinner and drinks, accompanied by the latest music, amid trees and bushes lighted by small lamps to give the twilight a magical cast. A character like Boswell might plan an amorous intrigue: the word *sqeak* in the above ballad was an eighteenth-century euphemism for a female orgasm. Between 1728 and 1761, Vauxhall's manager, Jonathan Tyers, added statues, a waterfall, a music room, a Chinese pavilion, paintings by Francis Hayman (1708–1776) in the supper boxes, and picturesque arches and fake ruins that were all in vogue at the time. It was to pay for these new attractions that management began to charge the aforementioned one shilling admission in 1732, thus drawing the same line that so many other London establishments did in the eighteenth century between the elite and respectable on one side and the hoi polloi on the other.

Part of the reason for these improvements was the competition coming from across the river at Chelsea: Ranelagh Gardens. Chelsea, just south of Kensington, had long been a fashionable suburb: Tudor nobles had palaces there, and Sir Thomas More was a famous inhabitant. Ranelagh Gardens, which we can reach by barge, was laid out on the Ranelagh estate in Chelsea in 1741/42. What Ranelagh had to distinguish it from Vauxhall was a massive music rotunda, 150 feet in diameter, designed by William Jones (d. 1757), to which "[E]verybody that loves eating, drinking, staring, or crowding" was admitted for just 12 pence (see Illustration c.12). Admission on fireworks nights was 5 shillings. As described by Tobias Smollett in *Humphry Clinker* (1771), Ranelagh is

> the enchanted palace of genius, adorned with the most exquisite performances of painting, carving and gilding, enlightened with a thousand golden lamps that emulate the noon-day sun; crowded with the great, the rich, the gay, the happy and the fair; glittering with cloth of gold, and silver lace, embroidery and precious stones.

Horace Walpole, writing in 1750, thought that "It has totally beat Vauxhall."[27] But Vauxhall outlasted its rival: Ranelagh closed in 1803, Vauxhall in 1859. In any case, after our exhausting day, and the two centuries of London history preceding it, we seek repose and reflection.

THE VIEW FROM THE BRIDGE

Having enjoyed ourselves at the pleasure garden into the wee hours, we make our way back to Westminster Bridge. As we cross to the middle of the span, we hear voices; looking down, we see barges laden with fruit and vegetables intended for London's growing number of markets. London in 1750 never shuts down: it will be a few hours before the hackney coachmen and prostitutes call it a night. As the moon sets behind the dome of St. Paul's, followed by the rising sun, we contemplate the vast city that we have just traveled. The poet William Wordsworth (1770–1850), standing on this very spot half a century later, thought that "Earth hath not anything to show more fair" than this view. Indeed, this vantage point, looking downriver from Westminster Bridge, perhaps more effectively than the top of the cathedral or the Monument, lays all London – "Ships, towers, domes, theatres, and temples" – before us (see Illustration c.13), assuming, of course, that the soot parts. We reflect that the city has grown mightily since 1550 and has met untold challenges to its demographic, political, social, and cultural health.

In fact, the period from 1550 to 1750 is unique in London's history, unlike the period immediately before or after. Before, London was the greatest city in the kingdom, to be sure, but that kingdom was relatively small and not of the first rank in Europe. Its capital was not unlike other capitals, and indeed, although London was bigger, it was not fundamentally different from other great commercial towns in England or Europe. It was smaller than Venice, Naples, and Paris, in many ways a larger version of York, Norwich, or Bristol. Above all, its culture and mind-set were dominated, as they were in other European countries, by the Church and the court, which had influence on the wider world to be sure, but not as much as they would have liked. It is true that the court and government were headquartered in London and the Church was, for the most part, run from there. In big matters like rebellion, as London went, so went the nation, but in smaller matters of politics and culture, London's influence was intermittent and precarious.

By 1750, all of that had changed. First and foremost, London grew, from 120,000 to 675,000 souls, becoming the greatest city in Europe. It grew in physical extent to include all of the old City, Westminster, Southwark and South London, and extended East and West Ends. For a while, the influx of immigrants threatened to overwhelm the time-honored institutions of City and company, county and parish. To many contemporaries, especially before 1650, early modern London seemed a monster city, out of control, on the brink of chaos or collapse. London appeared to cross that brink with every major plague epidemic, culminating in the three hammer blows of plague, fire, and war, from 1665 to 1667. Commerce ground to a halt, and community disintegrated, but London survived, rebuilt, and grew some more.

Over the course of the next century, metropolitan London grew economically to become Europe's busiest port; its freest, least restrictive trading environment; its greatest banking center; and its most voracious consumer and bountiful distributor of overseas imports and home-finished goods. The wealth generated by London, by first the Commercial and then the Financial Revolutions, won for Britain a series of world wars for empire. These led in turn to the growth of the London-based central administration and the British military, their increasing efficiency, and the resultant acquisition of valuable colonies linked to London by a worldwide network of shipping lanes. These brought sugar, tobacco, silks, spices, fruit, and slaves to the capital for redistribution to Europe and the empire. London became the center of a global web of communication, credit, and exchange, hardly pausing to reflect how that web entangled and exploited foreign lands and native peoples. The resulting wealth was also plowed into London's own development, in particular that of the West End, which led in turn to more investment and consumption. Finally, all of this economic activity surely helped to establish the demand and set the economic, social, and cultural pace for the Industrial Revolution, which would in turn fund Britain's political and economic ascendancy into the twentieth century.

Throughout the period, and simultaneously with the economic development noted earlier, politics and religion split London and the nation, although the city leaned heavily Protestant. These fissures led to constitutional upheaval and eventually to constitutional monarchy by way of two revolutions, the world's first modern political parties, a relatively free political press, and the rise of public opinion as represented by its readership: the London voter and the London crowd(s). In fact, most of these dramatic events were headquartered in London. Nowhere was the franchise wider than in London; nowhere did the opinion of ordinary people matter more. The London press, freed from the most onerous forms of censorship in 1695, was intimately connected with a growing public sphere independent of Church and court, flourishing in the city's inns, taverns, alehouses, coffeehouses, clubs, and pleasure gardens. Old verities like the Great Chain of Being, paternalism, and deference could not survive intact in such a hothouse atmosphere. As this implies, London pioneered many new forms of culture and entertainment and their funding during our period: the court masque and the public masquerade ball, the literary essay magazine, the public theater run by entrepreneurial managers, the public concert hall, literary and musical publication by subscription, and so forth. At the beginning of the seventeenth century, Inigo Jones borrowed from Italy a new national architectural style – Palladian neoclassical – that would be fused with the Baroque by Wren and his students in London's rebuilding. Jones also imported a new way to live in the city for those who wanted privacy and elegance: the Italian *piazza* became the London square.

All of these institutions, styles, and strategies had national, imperial, and international implications. Amphibious aristocrats, gentle tourists, colonial and foreign agents, newsletters, then newspapers, new carriage routes, and better mails disseminated London thought and London fashions into the countryside and beyond. Because of the concentration of publishing houses in London, metropolitan taste – set by essayists like Addison, Defoe, Steele, Swift, and Johnson; painters like Hogarth and Reynolds; musicians like Purcell and Handel; and the academies and societies that they founded – dictated what was fashionable throughout Britain. The London-based Royal Society became the arbiter of Enlightenment science, far surpassing what contemporary Oxford and Cambridge were doing.

These developments also brought immense social and cultural dislocation, especially for those at the bottom rungs of the social ladder. The very act of migrating to London made you – if you had not already arranged a place for yourself – a vagrant until you landed a job. For many, the act of coming to London led not to wealth and fame, but to poverty, homelessness, disease, and death; or possibly crime, arrest, imprisonment, and execution. To some extent, London's problems were age-old – what city does not have poverty, crime, and high death rates? But London's sheer size, phenomenal growth, and rapidly changing environment were unprecedented and they led to modern variations: the Gin Craze, the rewards system of thief-taking, *anomie*. At the same time, Londoners also pioneered modern solutions: the government-initiated but parish-run Poor Law, the newspaper as community bulletin board, the conditional and often harsh charity of Bridewell, the entrepreneurial charity of Coram's Foundling Hospital. Above all, the pressure cooker of living and dying, getting and spending, talking, reading, fighting, and entertaining in the great metropolis fostered new attitudes – practical, rational, secular, cosmopolitan, none too scrupulous, a tendency toward equality, democracy, social fluidity, acceptance of diversity, suspicion of authority, more casual and mutable relationships, looser gender roles – all of which will seem natural to the modern reader.

London's growth and London's leadership continued after 1750. Greater London's population expanded further, reaching about a million by 1801, 6.5 million by 1901, and just over 7 million in 2001. London's economic growth continued from the establishment of the first official stock exchange in 1773 through the Big Bang of financial market deregulation in 1986 and beyond. But for all of London's influence on the first Industrial Revolution, London did not participate directly in it. The first great factories were built far from London, near the coal deposits and water sources of the Midlands, Wales, and Scotland. Although largely bankrolled from the capital, the great shock cities of the Industrial Age were

Birmingham, Leeds, Sheffield, Preston, and above all, Manchester. Beginning in the eighteenth century and expanding in the nineteenth, even London's preeminent financial role was eroded somewhat by regional banks. As America grew into an industrial power and alternative population safety valve for poor people from England, Scotland, and Ireland, western ports like Bristol, Liverpool, and Glasgow began to steal some of London's trade in goods and people; that is, although the metropolis remained the leading economic engine of the nation, its lead was shortened as other regional centers found that they did not need London.

So too in the arts. London remained the national center of publishing, fashion, and the decorative and performing arts. In 1768 the Royal Academy of Arts was founded, and in later years, the Royal and English National Operas, the National Gallery of Art, the National Portrait Gallery, the Tate Gallery for British art, the Victoria and Albert Museum, half a dozen internationally known orchestras, innumerable theaters (including a reconstructed Globe), and many smaller cultural institutions, all based in London. Even before 1750, however, London ceased to be the *exclusive* leader in these areas. After 1650, it faced competition for the leisure and purchasing power of the elite. England's spas – most notably Bath, Tunbridge Wells, and Epsom – all offered genteel society an increasing range of social and cultural entertainments, many modeled on London initiatives. For example, Bath had its own theater company from 1705. Elsewhere in the countryside, local aristocrats, home for the summer from London or the spa, began to demand similar amenities in Yorkshire or Devonshire. County towns built assembly rooms for balls and teas. Regional music festivals grew up, most notably the Three Choirs Festival, showcasing the talents of the Hereford, Gloucester, and Worcester cathedral choirs, from around 1713. During the eighteenth century, provincial newspapers published the same news offered in London, but with a local slant: there were twenty-five such papers in 1735, thirty-five in 1760. Local county culture now had a focus, and it was not London. This is not to say that London did not continue to influence that culture, or that its mavens did not occasionally seek refreshment in the capital, but they had a reasonable if smaller-scale substitute closer to home.

Above all, from the mid-eighteenth century onward, Scotland began to experience its own Enlightenment. In the seventeenth and early eighteenth centuries, prominent Scottish intellectuals like John Arbuthnot and Gilbert Burnet (1643–1715) had to come to London to make their fortunes. In 1776, however, Adam Smith, a professor at the University of Glasgow, published *The Wealth of Nations*, albeit in London and Dublin. David Hume (1711–1776) produced great works of philosophy from a base in and around Edinburgh. The Scottish capital developed its own salon society, and the University of Edinburgh became the greatest medical school in Britain. Admittedly, the economic and social problems that we have detected in London also manifested themselves in these other places, but rarely on the same scale.

So London continued to be the greatest city in the three kingdoms, and indeed in the Empire, Europe, and arguably the world. But by 1750 it was no longer unique. The rest of the Anglophone world was catching up. London now had competitors in wealth and culture, and for the time and attention of the British governing classes. For the working classes, too, other cities would, over the next hundred years, provide even more – if not necessarily more attractive – opportunity. For two hundred years, London had shown the world the frenetic face and the dark underbelly of modern city life. Along the way, it produced a model for urban living that would be embraced by much of the world over the next two centuries. But it also produced something else, arguably just as important. London's economic opportunities, its possibilities for self-fashioning and re-fashioning, its enforced opportunism, practicality, and resilience, its watering holes, its print culture, public sphere, and overriding sense of something happening would produce, in turn, the Londoner: tough, smart, entrepreneurial, opinionated, humorous in every sense of the word, fully the "glory, jest and riddle of the world" that Pope thought all humanity.

Notes

Place of publication is London unless noted otherwise.

Introduction: London's Importance

1. For a fuller discussion of non-London life in early modern England, *see* R. Bucholz and N. Key, *Early Modern England 1485–1714: a Narrative History* (2nd ed., Chichester, 2009), Introduction and chapter 6.
2. Speech in Star Chamber, 20 June 1616, quoted in L. Manley, *Literature and Culture in Early Modern London* (Cambridge, 1995), p. 133.
3. John Carpenter (fl. 1417–1442), quoted in *London in the Age of Shakespeare: an Anthology*, ed. L. Manley (1986), p. 29.
4. Quoted in R. Gray, *A History of London* (New York, 1979), p. 61. *Wic* means a trading town in Anglo-Saxon.
5. As in the reigns of William I (1066–1087), William II (1087–1100), Henry I (1100–1135), Henry II (1154–1189), Edward I (1272–1307), Edward III (1327–1377), Henry V (1413–1422), Edward IV (1461–1483), Henry VII (1485–1509), or Henry VIII (1509–1547).
6. As was the case under Stephen (1135–1154), John (1199–1216), Henry III (1216–1272), Edward II (1307–1327), Richard II (1377–1399), Henry IV (1399–1413), Henry VI (1422–1461), Richard III (1483–1485), and, arguably, Edward VI (1547–1553).
7. William Fitzstephen (fl. 1162–1174), quoted in S. Inwood, *A History of London* (1998), p. 121.
8. For example, Bucholz and Key, cited above, *passim*.
9. Edmund Grindal (by 1520–83), quoted in S. Brigden, *London and the Reformation* (Oxford, 1989), p. 129.
10. R. Seymour, *A Survey of the Cities of London and Westminster, Borough of Southwark, and Parts Adjacent* (1734), p. 3.
11. T. Addison, *The Spectator* No. 403: 12 June 1712.
12. J. Boswell, *Boswell's Life of Johnson* (Oxford, 1904) I, 282.

1: London in 1550

1. The following depends utterly on the wealth of information contained in B. Weinreb, C. Hibbert, J. Keay, and J. Keay, *The London Encyclopaedia*, 3rd ed. (2008; hereafter, *LE*), to which the authors wish to pay full acknowledgment. The words *today* and *modern* refer to conditions in the twenty-first century. All other present tense descriptions are of London in 1550.

2. Quoted in J. Boulton, *Neighborhood and Society: A London Suburb in the Seventeenth Century* (Cambridge, 1987), p. 64.
3. Quoted in *LE*, p. 818.
4. Quoted in Manley, *London in the Age of Shakespeare*, p. 38.
5. Quoted in Manley, *London in the Age of Shakespeare*, p. 35.
6. J. Stow, *A Survey of London Reprinted from the Text of 1603* (Oxford, 1971) I, 206.
7. Stow I, p. 127.
8. Stow I, p. 124.
9. *LE*, p. 803.
10. Fynes Moryson (1566–1630), quoted in Manley, *London in the Age of Shakespeare*, p. 43, order rearranged.
11. For Stow's account of how some of the following locations would change by 1598, see Manley, *London in the Age of Shakespeare*, p. 37.
12. Paul Hentzner (1558–1623), quoted in Manley, *London in the Age of Shakespeare*, p. 41.
13. John Chamberlaine, quoted in P. Griffiths, "Politics Made Visible: Order, Residence and Uniformity in Cheapside, 1600–45" in *Londinopolis: Essays in the Cultural and Social History of Early Modern London*, ed. P. Griffiths and M. S. R. Jenner (Manchester, 2000), p. 177.
14. S. Pepys, *The Diary of Samuel Pepys*, ed. R. Latham and W. Matthews (Berkeley, 1971–1983; hereafter *PD*) I, 236: 1 Sept. 1660.
15. Quoted in *LE*, p. 808.
16. *Henry IV Part 2* I, ii. l.50.
17. Quoted in *LE*, p. 808.
18. Quoted in J. F. Merritt, "The Reshaping of Stow's *Survey*: Munday, Strype, and the Protestant City" in *Imagining Early Modern London: Perceptions and Portrayals of the City from Stow to Strype 1598–1720*, ed. J. F. Merritt (Cambridge, 2001), p. 68.
19. Frederick, Duke of Wirtemberg, writing c. 1600: quoted in Manley, *London in the Age of Shakespeare*, p. 36.
20. Quoted in *LE*, p. 883.
21. Quoted in Manley, *London in the Age of Shakespeare*, p. 30.
22. Inwood, p. 194.
23. *PD* IV, 119: 1 May 1663.
24. *LE*, p. 1008.
25. *LE*, p. 1006.

2: The Socioeconomic Base

1. Population figures are taken from R. Finlay and B. Shearer, "Population Growth and Suburban Expansion" in *London 1500–1700: The Making of the Metropolis*, ed. A. L. Beier and R. Finlay (Harlow, 1986), pp. 37–59, esp. Tables 2 and 5. See the critique of these figures in V. Harding, "The Population of London 1550–1700: a Review of the Published Evidence," *London Journal* XV (1990). The following paragraphs are based on E. A. Wrigley, "A Simple Model of London's Importance in Changing English Society and Economy 1650–1750," *Past and Present* 37 (1967), pp. 44–70; amplified by the discussion in Inwood, pp. 157–61; and P. Williams, *The Later Tudors: England 1547–1603* (Oxford, 1995), p. 164. Although Wrigley's article is principally

concerned with the period after 1650, many of the phenomena it describes clearly began in or applied to the previous century.

2. Quotes from P. Thorold, *The London Rich: The Creation of a Great City from 1666 to the Present* (1999), p. 7; Royal Proclamation 7 July 1580, printed in Manley, *London in the Age of Shakespeare*, p. 185.

3. Quoted in Inwood, p. 252.

4. Quoted in Thorold, p. 21.

5. J. Graunt, *Observations on the Bills of Mortality* (1662).

6. J. Lempriere, *Universal Biography Containing a Copious Account, Critical and Historical, of the Life and Character, Labours and Actions of Eminent Persons, in all Ages and Countries, Conditions and Professions* (1810) II, sub "Heidegger, John James."

7. P. Linebaugh, *The London Hanged: Crime and Civil Society in the Eighteenth Century* (Cambridge, 1992), p. 70.

8. Quoted in Inwood, p. 204.

9. Sir William Cavendish (1590–1628), quoted in Manley, *Literature and Culture*, p. 489.

10. John Evelyn, quoted in Manley, *Literature and Culture*, p. 488.

11. *The Journal of John Harrower, An Indentured Servant in the Colony of Virginia, 1773–1776*, ed. E. M. Riley (Williamsburg, Virginia, 1963), p. 3, quoted in T. Hitchcock, *Down and Out in Eighteenth-Century London* (2004), p. 23; and R. B. Shoemaker, *Persecution and Punishment: Petty Crime and the Law in Middlesex, c. 1660–1725* (Cambridge, 1991), p. 184.

12. R. Kirk, "London in 1689–90," *Transactions of the London and Middlesex Archaeological Society* n.s. 6 (1927–31), p. 333.

13. Kirk, "London in 1689–90," p. 335.

14. J. Boswell, *Boswell's London Journal*, ed. F. A. Pottle (New York, 1950), p. 227.

15. D. Defoe, *A Tour of England and Wales* (Everyman, 1927) I, 43.

16. *Spectator*, No. 69: 19 May 1711.

17. Quoted in G. Williams and J. Ramsden, *Ruling Britannia: A Political History of Britain, 1688–1988* (1990), p. 32.

18. Quoted in G. Holmes, *British Politics in the Age of Anne* (1967), p. 177.

19. J. Swift, *Examiner*, No. 13: 2 Nov. 1710.

20. *Spectator*, No. 3: 3 Mar. 1711.

21. Quoted in Inwood, p. 328.

3: Royal and Civic London

1. Defoe, *Tour* I, 335.

2. Quoted in Thorold, p. 37.

3. The full names and dates of the individuals named before were William Cecil, Lord Burghley (1520/21–1598); Robert Dudley, Earl of Leicester (1532/33–1588); Robert Cecil, later Earl of Salisbury (1563–1612); Robert Devereaux, Earl of Essex (1565–1601); Sir Philip Sidney (1554–1586); William Shakespeare (1564–1616); William Byrd (by 1543–1623); John Dowland (?1523–1626); Edward Hyde, Earl of Clarendon (1609–74); Thomas Osborne, Earl of Danby (1632–1712); Sir Isaac Newton (1642–1727); Sir Christopher Wren (1642–1723); John Dryden (1631–1700); John Wilmot, Earl of Rochester (1647–1680); Henry Purcell (1659–95); Sir Peter Lely (1618–1680); Barbara

Villiers née Palmer, Countess of Castlemaine, later Duchess of Cleveland (1640–1709); Louise de Kéroualle, Duchess of Portsmouth (1649–1734); John Evelyn (1620–1706); and Samuel Pepys (1633–1703).

4. Quoted in J. Beattie, *The English Court in the Reign of George I* (Cambridge, 1967), p. 106.

5. T. Dekker, *The Magnificent Entertainment: Given to King Iames . . . Vpon the Day of his Maiesties Tryumphant Passage . . . Through his Honourable Citie (and Chamber) of London* (1604), quoted in Manley, *Literature and Culture*, p. 241.

6. J. Hayward, *Annals, or the First Four Years of the Reign of Queen Elizabeth*, ed. J. Bruce (1840), pp. 15–18.

7. Venetian ambassadors' report, quoted in D. M. Bergeron, *English Civic Pageantry 1558–1642* (Columbia, South Carolina, 1971), p. 108.

8. *PD* IX, 415: 15 Jan. 1669.

9. TNA LS 13/173, pp. 106–07.

10. *PD* III, 87: 21 May 1662.

11. *HMC Fifteenth Report* App. IV, 657: [Edward Harley] to Abigail Harley at Eywood, 6 Feb. 1710/11.

12. *PD* VII, 371–72: 15 Nov. 1666.

13. Beattie, *English* Court, p. 16.

14. *PD* III, 239: 27 Oct. 1662; IX, 351: 5 Nov. 1668, 516: 12 Apr. 1669.

15. The following discussion depends greatly on the pioneering work of S. Thurley, *Whitehall Palace: An Architectural History of the Royal Apartments, 1240–1698* (New Haven, 1999), chap. 7; and A. Keay, *The Magnificent Monarch: Charles II and the Ceremonies of Power* (2008), esp. chap. 7.

16. Kirk, "London in 1689," p. 326.

17. *ED* IV, 537: 30 Jan. 1687.

18. *PD* VIII, 588: 24 Dec. 1667.

19. *ED* III, 490–91: 7 Aug. 1667, 513: 19 Aug. 1668; *A Collection of Ordinances and Regulations for the Government of the Royal Household . . . from King Edward III to King William and Queen Mary* (1790), p. 354; *The Journal of Willem Schellinks' Travels in England, 1661–1663*, ed. M. Exwood and H. L. Lehmann (1993), p. 90; TNA LC 5/201, pp. 259–60.

20. F. Burney, *Journals and Letters*, ed. P. Sabor and L. E. Troide (Harmondsworth, 2001), p. 230.

21. *HMC Seventh Report* App., p. 351: Henry Savile to Lord Preston, London, 10 May 1682.

22. G. De Krey, *A Fractured Society: The Politics of London in the First Age of Party, 1688–1715* (Oxford, 1985), p. 40.

23. Quoted in G. Rudé, *Hanoverian London 1714–1808* (Berkeley, 1971), p. 131.

24. Rudé, p. 132.

25. Quoted in Rudé, p. 129.

26. Quoted in P. Griffiths, *Lost Londons: Change, Crime, and Control in the Capital City, 1550–1660* (Cambridge, 2008), p. 337.

4: Fine and Performed Arts

1. *PD* III, 47: 16 Mar. 1662.

2. Quoted in Inwood, p. 207.

3. Quoted in Griffiths, *Lost Londons*, p. 48.
4. Quoted in J. P. Ward, *Metropolitan Communities: Trade Guilds, Identity and Change in Early Modern London* (Stanford, 1997), pp. 11–12.
5. *LE*, p. 326.
6. Quoted in Inwood, p. 212.
7. A. Gurr, *Playgoing in Shakespeare's London*, 2nd ed. (Cambridge, 1996), p. 118.
8. E. Guilpin, "Satire V," *Skialetheia* (1598), ll. 66–68, quoted in Manley, *London in the Age of Shakespeare*, p. 165.
9. *ED* IV, 6: 24 Mar. 1673.
10. Gaston Jean Baptiste, Comte de Cominges to Louis XIV, 25 Jan. 1663 quoted in J. J. Jusserand, *A French Ambassador at the Court of Charles II* (1892), p. 91.
11. H.M.C. *Heathcote MSS.*, p. 78: Samuel Boothhouse to Sir Richard Fanshaw, Whitehall, 12 April 1663.
12. W. Bagehot, *The English Constitution* (Oxford World's Classics Edition, 1928), p. 45.
13. *DC* No. 4913: 19 July 1717.
14. Quoted in M. Foss, *The Age of Patronage: the Arts in England 1660–1750* (Ithaca, 1972), p. 78.
15. Anon., *Hell Upon Earth* (1729).
16. *Spectator* No. 454: 11 Aug. 1712.
17. N. Ward, "To the Reader" in *The London Spy in Eighteen Parts* (1700), Pt. II.
18. *A Trip Through the Town: Containing Observations on the Humours and Manners of the Age*, 4th ed., (1735), pp. 1–2.
19. *PD* VIII, 339–40: 14 July 1667.

5: The Public Sphere and Popular Culture

1. *PD* I, 19: 16 Jan. 1660.
2. According to the act, lawbooks were to be licensed by the lord chancellor; history or political books by the secretaries of state; and religious, philosophical, or scientific books by the archbishops of Canterbury or York, the bishop of London, or the vice chancellors of Oxford or Cambridge Universities.
3. R. L'Estrange, *The Observator*, 21 Mar. 1684.
4. *LG* No. 1: 7 Nov. 1665.
5. F. M. Misson, *Memoirs and Observations in his Travels over England* (1719), pp. 203–04.
6. T. B. Macaulay, *The History of England from the Accession of James II* (Longman's Popular Edition, 1895) II, 503.
7. Quoted in Inwood, p. 295.
8. *Post Boy*, 28–31 Mar. 1713; *Flying Post*, 28–31 Mar. 1713, quoted in W. B. Ewald, *The Newsmen of Queen Anne* (Oxford, 1956), p. 77. St. Mary Overie and St. Saviour's were different names for Southwark Cathedral.
9. *DC*, 6 Jan. 1714, quoted in Ewald, p. 167.
10. *DC* No. 2557: 3 Jan. 1710.
11. *Post Boy*, 26–29 Dec. 1713, quoted in Ewald, p. 97.
12. *Flying Post* 31 May-2 June 1705, quoted in Ewald, p. 96.
13. J. Dunton, *The Life and Errors of John Dunton, Citizen of London... Written by Himself* (1818) I, 188.

14. *Athenian Mercury* IX, No. 21: 21 Feb. 1693.
15. *Flying Post* 22–24 May 1712, quoted in Ewald, p. 94.
16. Kirk, "London in 1689–90," p. 333. He doubted the infant press's reach: "which come not to every man's notice."
17. *Spectator* No. 10: 12 Mar. 1711.
18. *Spectator* No. 2: 2 Mar. 1711.
19. *Spectator* No. 102: 27 June 1711.
20. *Spectator* No. 5: 6 Mar. 1711.
21. *Spectator* No. 8: 9 Mar. 1711.
22. *Spectator* No. 10: 12 Mar. 1711.
23. Boswell, *Life of Johnson* I, 577.
24. *PD* II, 61: 27 Mar. 1661.
25. Boswell, *Life of Johnson* I, 661.
26. *Boswell's London Journal*, pp. 86–87.
27. Quoted in P. Clark, "The Alehouse and the Alternative Society" in *Puritans and Revolutionaries*, ed. D. Pennington and K. Thomas (Oxford, 1978), p. 47.
28. Quoted in *LE*, p. 556.
29. Quoted in B. Cowan, "Pasqua Rosée," *NDNB*.
30. Misson, *Memoirs and Observations*, pp. 39–40.
31. C. de Saussure, *A Foreign View of England in the Reigns of George I and George II*, trans. M. van Muyden (1902), p. 162.
32. *PD* X (Companion), p. 71. The discussion of coffeehouses relies heavily on this source.
33. "Memorial to the Princess Sophia," attrib. Tallard, quoted in A. S. Turberville, *The House of Lords in the Reign of William III* (Oxford, 1913), p. 44 n. 1.
34. *PD* V, 37: 3 Feb. 1664.
35. *The Guardian* No. 114: 22 July 1713.
36. Quoted in Inwood, p. 313.
37. *PD* VIII, 240: 28 May 1667.
38. Quoted in *LE*, p. 863.
39. Quoted in *LE*, p. 969.
40. Horace Walpole, quoted in Inwood, p. 314.
41. Quoted in M. Holmes, *Elizabethan London* (New York, 1969), p. 50.
42. *PD* IV, 427–28: 21 Dec. 1663.
43. Quoted in Archer, *Pursuit of Stability*, p. 231.
44. Quoted in Archer, *Pursuit of Stability*, pp. 233–34.
45. Quoted in F. Dabhoiwala, "The Pattern of Sexual Immorality in Seventeenth- and Eighteenth-century London" in *Londinopolis*, ed. Griffiths and Jenner, p. 96. The examples cited and statements in this and the previous paragraph come from pp. 95–97 of this article.
46. Quoted in D. Cressy, *Bonfires and Bells: National Memory and the Protestant Calendar in Elizabethan and Stuart England* (1989), p. 18. The present account of the traditional calendar is utterly dependent on this source, chapters 1 and 2, as well as R. Hutton, *The Rise and Fall of Merry England: The Ritual Year 1400–1700* (Oxford, 1994), chap. 1.
47. Cressy, *Bonfires and Bells*, p. 23.
48. Quoted in M. Berlin, "Reordering Rituals: Ceremony and the Parish, 1520–1640" in *Londinopolis*, ed. Griffiths and Jenner, p. 51.

49. *PD* II, 36: 14 Feb. 1661.
50. *LE*, p. 537.

6: The People on the Margins

1. Quoted in Inwood, p. 156.
2. Quoted in Inwood, p. 165.
3. Quoted in Inwood, p. 163; and V. Harding, *The Dead and the Living in Paris and London, 1500–1670* (Cambridge, 2002), p. 22.
4. Quoted in S. Rappaport, *Worlds Within Worlds: Structures of Life in Sixteenth-Century London* (Cambridge, 1989), p. 65.
5. Quoted in Griffiths, *Lost Londons*, p. 105.
6. Quoted in Griffiths, *Lost Londons*, p. 51.
7. *Boswell's London Journal*, p. 119.
8. Old Bailey Proceedings, 7 Sept. 1722, quoted in T. Hitchcock, *Down and Out in Eighteenth-Century London* (2004), p. 66.
9. Quoted and statistics from V. Harding, "City, Capital, and Metropolis: The Changing Shape of Seventeenth-Century London" in *Imagining Early Modern London*, ed. Merritt, p. 132.
10. *PD* II, 60: 25 Mar. 1661.
11. J. Gee, *The Trade and Navigation of Great Britain Considered* (1729), pp. 38–39.
12. MD., *A Present Remedy for the Poor* [1700], p. 6.
13. *Boswell's London Journal*, p. 119; see also p. 123 for his further efforts for Cholmondeley.
14. *Boswell's London Journal*, pp. 127–28.
15. The following paragraph follows closely C. Roberts and D. Roberts, *A History of England: Prehistory to 1714*, 2nd ed. (Englewood Cliffs, New Jersey, 1985), p. 304.
16. Quoted in Boulton, p. 263.
17. Quoted in Griffiths, *Lost Londons*, p. 280.
18. Quoted in R. Porter, *London: A Social History* (Cambridge, Massachusetts, 1995), p. 149.
19. Quoted in *LE*, p. 760. The following discussion of London's hospitals relies heavily on their respective articles in ibid.
20. Quoted in *LE*, p. 818.
21. Quoted in *LE*, p. 825.
22. M. Saxby, *Memoirs of a Female Vagrant, Written by Herself* (1806), pp. 5–6, quoted in Hitchcock, *Down and Out in Eighteenth-Century London*, p. 33.
23. *Flying Post*, No. 1666: 3–5 Jan. 1706.
24. See J. A. Sharpe, *Crime in Early Modern England, 1550–1750*, 2nd ed. (1999), chap. 3, sub. "Fluctuations in the Prosecution of Felony"; and J. M. Beattie, *Policing and Punishment in London 1660–1750: Urban Crime and the Limits of Terror* (Oxford, 2001), chap. 1, sub. "Patterns of Prosecution."
25. Draft of a parliamentary bill to incorporate Westminster, quoted in Merritt, *Westminster*, p. 225.
26. D. Defoe, *Moll Flanders*, ed. E. Kelly (New York: Norton Critical Edition, 1973), pp. 167–68.
27. *PD* IX, 285: 22 Aug. 1668.

28. *PD* IV, 28: 28 Jan. 1663.
29. *PD* I, 303: 27 Nov. 1660.
30. Quoted in Beattie, *Policing and Punishment*, p. 20.
31. Ibid., p. 21.
32. Quoted in Archer, pp. 208–09.
33. *Original Letters, Illustrative of English History*, ed. H. Ellis (1824; reprinted New York, 1970) II, 295–99, from BL, MS. Lansdowne 44, art. 38.
34. Sir Stephen Soame, quoted in Archer, p. 234.
35. The Ordinary of Newgate's account, quoted in P. Rawlings, "Mary Young," *NDNB*.
36. Quoted in Inwood, pp. 369–70, on which this account of the Mohocks is based.
37. Quoted in A. McKenzie, "Jonathan Wild," *NDNB*, upon which this account of Wild's life is based.
38. *A Narrative of all the Robberies, Escapes, . . . of John Sheppard* (1724), pp. 5–6, quoted in P. Sugden, "Jack Sheppard," *NDNB*, upon which the following account is closely based.
39. Sugden, "Jack Sheppard," *NDNB*.
40. *Select Trials 1735* II, 244–45, quoted in A. McKenzie, "Jonathan Wild," *NDNB*.
41. Quoted in Inwood, p. 378.
42. W. Bullein, *A Dialogue Against Pestilence*, quoted in *LE*, p. 648.
43. de Saussure, *A Foreign View of England*, p. 68.
44. Defoe, *Moll Flanders*, p. 151.
45. Quoted in T. Wales, "Thief-takers and Their Clients in Later Stuart London" in *Londinopolis*, ed. Griffiths and Jenner, p. 70.
46. Defoe, *Moll Flanders*, p. 150.
47. *Post-Boy* No. 2904: 17–19 Dec. 1713.
48. Quoted in D. M. Palliser, *The Age of Elizabeth: England Under the Later Tudors 1547–1603*, 2nd ed. (Harlow, 1992), p. 365.
49. All quotes from *LE*, p. 584, on which the paragraph is based.
50. Old Bailey Proceedings Online: http://www.oldbaileyonline.org.uk/static/The-old-bailey.jsp, on which this account of the building and the following description of a trial are based.
51. Misson, p. 124.
52. de Saussure, *Foreign View*, p. 124.
53. Defoe, *Moll Flanders*, p. 150.

7: Riot and Rebellion

1. Quoted in P. S. Seaver, "Thomas Decker's *The Shoemaker's Holiday*: the Artisanal World" in *The Theatrical City: Culture, Theatre and Politics in London 1547–1642*, ed. D. L. Smith, R. Streier, and D. Bevington (Cambridge, 1995), p. 91; and Rappaport, *Worlds Within Worlds*, p. 11.
2. R. B. Shoemaker, "The London 'Mob' in the Early Eighteenth Century," *Journal of British Studies* XXVI (1987).
3. Quoted in T. Harris, "Perceptions of the Crowd in Later Stuart London" in *Imagining Early Modern London*, ed. Merritt, p. 252.
4. Quoted in Merritt, *Westminster*, p. 203.
5. Shoemaker, "London 'Mob,'" p. 282.
6. Misson, p. 129.

7. *The Weekly Journal or Saturday Post*, 7 May 1720, quoted in Linebaugh, *London Hanged*, p. 20. See also Ward, *Metropolitan Communities*, pp. 125–43.
8. Quoted in Archer, *Pursuit of Stability*, p. 1, which this account follows closely.
9. Archer, *Pursuit of Stability*, p. 257.
10. *PD* VII, 415–16: 19 Dec. 1666.
11. *PD* II, 187–89: 30 Sept. 1661.
12. Quoted in T. Harris, "The Bawdy House Riots of 1668," *Historical Journal* XXIX (1986), p. 539. See also P. S. Seaver, "Apprentice Riots in Early Modern London" in *Violence, Politics and Gender in Early Modern England*, ed. J. P. Ward (New York, 2008), pp. 17–39.
13. Quoted in *The Oxford Book of Royal Anecdotes*, ed. E. Longford (Oxford, 1989), pp. 226–27.
14. *A Letter from Mercurius Civicus to Mercurius Rusticus* (1643), quoted in V. Pearl, *London and the Outbreak of the Puritan Revolution* (Oxford, 1961), p. 1.
15. Quoted in Manley, *Literature and Culture*, p. 534.
16. *ED* III, 246: 29 May 1660.
17. All quotes from Harris, "Bawdy House Riots," pp. 537, 538, 540, 541 on which this account is based.
18. Quoted in J. Scott, *England's Troubles: Seventeenth-Century English Political Instability in European Context* (Cambridge, 2000), p. 192.
19. Quoted in G. S. De Krey, "Sir Thomas Pilkington," *NDNB*.
20. Quoted in De Krey, "Sir Thomas Pilkington," *NDNB*.
21. Quoted in G. S. De Krey, *London and the Restoration, 1659–1683* (Cambridge, 2005), p. 258.
22. *ED* IV, 586–88: 8 June, 15 June 1688.
23. Dr Williams' Library, London, Morrice MS Q, pp. 352, 359; App. 13, quoted in Scott, *England's Troubles*, p. 219.
24. T., Earl of Ailesbury, *The Memoirs of Thomas, Earl of Ailesbury, Written by Himself* (1890), pp. 214–15.
25. *Ailesbury Memoirs*, p. 218.
26. Quoted in Scott, *England's Troubles*, p. 221.
27. Quoted in R. Beddard, *A Kingdom without a King: The Journal of the Provisional Government in the Revolution of 1688* (Oxford, 1988), p. 61.
28. Defoe, *Tour* I, 338.
29. H. Sacheverell, The *Perils of False Brethren in Church and State* (1709).
30. According to *The Oxford Companion to British History*, ed. J. A. Cannon (1997), p. 427.

8: Plague and Fire

1. Quoted in *LE*, p. 344.
2. Quoted in *LE*, p. 344, which this account follows closely.
3. *PD* VI, 120: 7 June 1665.
4. *PD* VI, 130–31: 17 June 1665.
5. Quoted in *LE*, p. 327.
6. W. Boghurst, *Loimographia: An Account of the Great Plague in the Year 1665*, ed. F. F. Payne (1894; repr. 1979), pp. 30–31.
7. Taken from Table 7: Major Epidemics in London, 1563–1665 from P. Slack, "Metropolitan Government in Crisis, the Response to the Plague" in Beier and Finlay,

p. 62. Figures from 1563–1625 cover only the City and liberties; those for 1636 and 1665 include the out-parishes as well.

8. *PD* VI, 175–176: 31 July 1665; ibid., 186: Aug. 8, 1665.
9. *PD* VI, 192: 16 Aug. 1665.
10. *PD* VI, 210: 3 Sept. 1665.
11. *PD* VI, 164: 22 July 1665.
12. *PD* VI, 342: 31 Dec. 1665.
13. *LE*, p. 345.
14. Quoted in Slack, "Metropolitan Government in Crisis," p. 74.
15. Quoted in Slack, "Metropolitan Government in Crisis," p. 73.
16. *LE*, p. 345.
17. *PD* VI, 201: 22 Aug. 1665.
18. *PD* VI, 93: 30 Apr. 1665.
19. *PD* VI, 268: 16 Oct. 1665.
20. *PD* VI, 282: 29 Oct. 1665.
21. *PD* VII, 41: 12 Feb. 1666.
22. *PD* VI, 204–05: 28 Aug.1665.
23. PD VI, 187: 10 Aug. 1665.
24. *PD* VII, 3: 5 Jan. 1666.
25. J. Evelyn, *A Character of England* (1659), p. 9; Defoe, *Tour* I, 324–25.
26. Quoted in Inwood, p. 242.
27. *PD* VII, 267–68: 2 Sept. 1666.
28. Ibid., pp. 268–69.
29. All quoted in N. Hanson, *The Great Fire of London: in That Apocalyptic Year, 1666* (Hoboken, New Jersey, 2001), p. 130.
30. *PD* VII, 271–72: 2 Sept. 1666.
31. Thomas Vincent, quoted in Inwood, p. 243.
32. *ED* III, 451–53: 3 Sept. 1666.
33. *ED* III, 454: 4 Sept. 1665.
34. *PD* VII, 276: 5 Sept. 1666.
35. Quoted in Inwood, p. 244.
36. *PD* VII, 276: 5 Sept. 1666.
37. *ED* III, 457: 5 Sept. 1666.
38. Quoted in W. G. Bell, *The Great Fire of London* (1923; repr. 1994), p. 208.
39. *LE*, p. 559.
40. Defoe, *Tour* I, 330.
41. Ward, *London Spy* III, 7.
42. *Boswell's London Journal*, p. 232.
43. Quoted in *LE*, p. 559.
44. Quoted in *LE*, p. 809.
45. Defoe, *Tour* I, 349.
46. Defoe, *Tour* I, 314.

Conclusion: London in 1750

1. P. J. Grosley, *A Tour to London; or, New Observations on England, and Its Inhabitants* (Dublin, 1772) I, 47–48, 49.
2. *PD* I, 269: 20 Oct. 1660.

<ol start="3">
<li>Quoted in Rudé, Hanoverian London, p. 135.</li>
<li>Swift, "Description of a City Shower" (1710).</li>
<li>Quoted in Linebaugh, London Hanged, p. 135.</li>
<li>Defoe, Tour I, 340.</li>
<li>Kirk, "London in 1689–90," pp. 332–33.</li>
<li>Ward, London Spy III, 1051; Kirk, "London in 1689–90," p. 333; decision to suspend visitation quoted in LE, p. 64, on which this account is largely based.</li>
<li>Quoted in Inwood, p. 243.</li>
<li>Quoted in Hitchcock, Down and Out, p. 36.</li>
<li>Quoted in Inwood, p. 327.</li>
<li>Spectator No. 454: 12 Aug. 1712.</li>
<li>PD VIII, 193: 1 May 1667.</li>
<li>Quoted in LE, p. 78, which this account follows closely.</li>
<li>Quoted in LE, p. 847.</li>
<li>Quoted in LE, p. 847, on which this account is largely based.</li>
<li>Quoted in Thorold, The London Rich, p. 89.</li>
<li>Quoted LE, p. 534, on which this account is largely based.</li>
<li>Spectator No. 403: 12 June 1712.</li>
<li>PD IX, 487: 18 Mar. 1669.</li>
<li>Quoted in LE, p. 116, on which this account is largely based.</li>
<li>Quoted in LE, pp. 764, 770, on which this account is largely based.</li>
<li>Sarah, Duchess of Marlborough, quoted in LE, p. 530.</li>
<li>Quoted in Thorold, p. 214.</li>
<li>Thorold, p. 103.</li>
<li>Contemporary ballad, quoted in LE, p. 969.</li>
<li>All quotations from LE, pp. 681–82, on which this account is closely based.</li>
</ol>

Further Reading

(Place of publication is London unless noted otherwise.)

General Histories of London

Ackroyd, P., *London: the Biography* (2000).
Barker, F. and Jackson, P., *London: 2,000 Years of a City and Its People* (New York, 1974).
Gray, R., *A History of London* (New York, 1979).
Hibbert, C., *London: the Biography of a City* (1969).
Inwood, S., *A History of London* (1998).
Porter, R., *London: A Social History* (1994).
Richardson, J., *The Annals of London: A Year-by-Year Record of a Thousand Years of History* (Berkeley, 2000).
Russell, J., *London* (1997).

General Works on London 1550–1750

Clark, P. and Slack, P., "London" in *English Towns in Transition 1500–1700* (Oxford, 1976).
Earle, P., *A City Full of People: Men and Women of London, 1650–1750* (1994).
Imagining Early Modern London: Perceptions and Portrayals of the City from Stow to Strype, 1598–1720, ed. J. F. Merritt (Cambridge, 2001).
Londinopolis: Essays in the Cultural and Social History of Early Modern London, ed. P. Griffiths and M. S. R. Jenner (Manchester, 2000).
London, 1500–1700: The Making of the Metropolis, ed. A. L. Beier and R. Finlay (Harlow, 1986).
London in the Age of Reform, ed. J. Stevenson (Oxford, 1977).
Marshall, D., *Dr. Johnson's London* (1968).
Material London, ca. 1600, ed. L. C. Orlin (Philadelphia, 2000).

Merritt, J. F., *The Social World of Early Modern Westminster: Abbey, Court and Community 1525–1640* (Manchester, 2005).
Picard, L., *Elizabeth's London* (2003).
———. *Restoration London* (1997).
———. *Dr. Johnson's London* (2000).
Rappaport, S., "Social Structure and Mobility in Sixteenth-Century London," *London Journal* IX (1983), X (1984).
———. *Worlds Within Worlds: Structures of Life in Sixteenth-Century London* (Cambridge, 1989).
Rudé, G., *Hanoverian London 1714–1808* (Berkeley and Los Angeles, 1971).

London Maps

Print

The A to Z of Elizabethan London, comp. A. Prockter and R. Taylor (1979).
The A to Z of Restoration London, comp. J. Fisher and R. Cline (1992).
The A to Z of Georgian London (1982).
Barker, F. and Jackson, P., *The History of London in Maps* (1990).
Whitfield, P., *London: a Life in Maps* (2006).

Online

Agas Map of Elizabethan London: http://mapoflondon.uvic.ca/
http://www.british-history.ac.uk/subject.asp?subject=7&gid=63
http://www.collectbritain.co.uk/collections/crace/
http://www.londonancestor.com/maps/maps.htm
http://mapoflondon.uvic.ca/

Bibliographies

http://www.rhs.ac.uk/bibl/bibwel.asp
Bibliography of Printed Works on London History to 1939, ed. H. J. Creaton (1994).

Encyclopedias

The London Encyclopaedia, ed. B. Weinreb, C. Hibbert, J. Keay, and J. Keay, 3rd ed. (2008).
London Past and Present: Its History, Associations and Traditions, ed. H. B. Wheatley and P. Cunningham, 3 vols. (1891).

Periodicals Dealing Mainly with London

East London Papers (1958–1973).
Guildhall Studies in London History (1973–1981).
London and Middlesex Archaeological Society Transactions (1860+).
London Journal (1975+).
London Topographical Society Publications (1911+).

Primary Sources

Boswell, J., *Boswell's London Journal 1762–1763*, ed. F. A. Pottle (New Haven, 1950).
De Laune, T., *The Present State of London* (1681; rev. ed. 1690).
Evelyn, J., *The Diary of John Evelyn*, ed. E. S. DeBeer, 6 vols. (Oxford, 1955).
Kirk, R., "London in 1689–90," ed. D. Maclean, *Transactions of the London and Middlesex Archaeological Society* ns 6 (1927–1931).
London in Miniature; being a concise and comprehensive description of the cities of London and Westminster, and parts adjacent, for forty miles round (1755).
Manningham, J., *The Diary of John Manningham of the Middle Temple*, ed. J. Bruce (1868).
Pepys, S., *The Diary of Samuel Pepys*, ed. R. Latham and W. Matthews, 11 vols. (Berkeley and Los Angeles, 1970–1983).
Saint, A. and Darley, G., *The Chronicles of London* (New York, 1994).
Seaver, P., *Wallington's World: A Puritan Artisan in Seventeenth-Century London* (Stanford, 1985).
Stow, J., *A Survey of London: Reprinted from the Text of 1603*, 2 vols. (Oxford, 1971).
Stow, W., *Remarks on London* (1722).
Swift, J., *The Journal to Stella 1710–1713*, ed. H. Williams, 2 vols. (Oxford, 1948).

Anthologies of Poetry and Prose about London

The Image of London: Views by Travellers and Emigres, 1500–1920, ed. M. Warner (1987).
London in the Age of Shakespeare: an Anthology, ed. L. Manley (1986).
The Norton Book of London, ed. A. N. Wilson (1995).

Demographics and Topography

Appleby, A. B., "Nutrition & Disease, The Case of London 1550–1750," *Journal of Interdisciplinary History* VI (1975).

Ashton, R., "Samuel Pepys's London," *London Journal* XI (1985).

Boulton, J., *Neighborhood and Society: a London Suburb in the Seventeenth Century* (Cambridge, 1987).

Finlay, R., *Population and Metropolis: The Demography of London, 1580–1650* (Cambridge, 1981).

Glanville, P., "The Topography of Seventeenth-Century London: a Review of Maps," *Urban History Yearbook* VII (1980).

Harding, V., *The Dead and the Living in Paris and London, 1500–1670* (Cambridge, 2002).

——. "The Population of London, 1550–1700: a Review of the Published Evidence," *London Journal* XV (1990).

Landers, J., *Death and the Metropolis: Studies in the Demographic History of London, 1670–1830* (Cambridge, 1993).

Ogborn, M., *Spaces of Modernity: London's Geographies 1680–1780* (New York, 1998).

"The Places and Spaces of Early Modern London," ed. D. Harkness and J. E. Howard, *Huntington Library Quarterly*, LXXI, 1 (2008).

Population of London: http://www.cch.kcl.ac.uk/legacy/teaching/av1000/numerical/problems/london/london-pop-table.html.

Stone, L., "The Residential Development of the West End of London in the Seventeenth Century" in *After the Reformation*, ed. B. C. Malament (Manchester, 1980).

Ward, J. P., "Imagining the Metropolis in Elizabethan and Stuart London" in *The Country and the City Revisited: England and the Politics of Culture, 1550–1850*, ed. G. MacLean, D. Landry, and J. P. Ward (Cambridge, 1999).

Economic London

Beier, A. L., "Engine of Manufacture: The Trades of London" in *London, 1500–1700: The Making of the Metropolis*, ed. A. L. Beier and R. Finlay (1986).

Brenner, R., *Merchants and Revolution: Commercial Change, Political Conflict and London's Overseas Traders, 1550–1653* (Princeton, 1993).

Carswell, J., *The South Sea Bubble* (Stanford, 1960).

Dickson, P. G. M., *The Financial Revolution in England: A Study in the Development of Public Credit, 1688–1756* (1967).

Earle, P., *The Making of the English Middle Class: Business, Society and Family Life in London 1660–1730* (Berkeley and Los Angeles, 1989).

Fisher, F. J., "The Development of London as a Centre of Conspicuous Consumption in the Sixteenth and Seventeenth Centuries," *Transactions of the Royal Historical Society*, 4th series XXX (1948).

——. "The Development of the London Food Market, 1540–1640" in *Essays in Economic History* I, ed. E. M. Carus-Wilson (1954).

_____. "London as an Engine of Economic Growth" in *Britain and the Nether-lands* IV, ed. J. S. Bromley and E. H. Kassmann (The Hague, 1971).

French, C. J., "'Crowded with traders and a great commerce' : London's Domin-ion of English Overseas Trade, 1700–1775," *London Journal* XVII (1992).

Grassby, R., "English Merchant Capitalism in the Late Seventeenth Century: the Composition of Business Fortunes," *Past and Present* no. 46 (1970).

Guilds, Society and Economy in London 1450–1800, ed. I. A. Gadd and P. Wallis (Center for Metropolitan History, 2002).

Horwitz, H., "'The Mess of the Middle Class' Revisited: The Case of the 'Big Bourgeoisie' of Augustan London," *Continuity and Change* II (1987).

Peck, L., *Consuming Splendor: Society and Culture in Seventeenth-Century England* (Cambridge, 2005).

Schwarz, L. D., "Income Distribution and Social Structure in London in the Late Eighteenth Century," *Economic History Review* XXXII (1979).

Thorold, P., *The London Rich: the Creation of a Great City from 1666 to the Present* (1999).

Ward, J. P., *Metropolitan Communities: Trade Guilds, Identity and Change in Early Modern London* (Stanford, 1997).

Wrigley, E. A., "A Simple Model of London's Importance in Changing English Society and Economy 1650–1750," *Past and Present* no. 37 (1967).

Court and Government

Archer, I., *The Pursuit of Stability: Social Relations in Elizabethan London* (Cambridge, 1991).

Ashton, R., *The City and the Court, 1603–1643* (Cambridge, 1979).

Beattie, J. M., *The English Court in the Reign of George I* (Cambridge, 1967).

Bucholz, R. O., *The Augustan Court: Queen Anne and the Decline of Court Culture* (Stanford, 1993).

_____. "Going to Court c. 1700: a Visitor's Guide," *The Court Historian* V (2000).

De Krey, G. S., *A Fractured Society: The Politics of London in the First Age of Party, 1688–1715* (Oxford, 1985).

_____. *London and the Restoration, 1659–1683* (Cambridge, 2005).

The English Court from the Wars of the Roses to the Civil War, ed. D. Starkey (Harlow, 1987).

Henderson, A. J., *London and the National Government, 1721–1742: A Study of City Politics and the Walpole Administration* (Durham, North Carolina, 1945).

Keay, A., *The Magnificent Monarch: Charles II and the Ceremonies of Power* (2008).

Loades, D., *The Tudor Court* (1986; rev. ed. Bangor, Wales, 1992).

Rogers, N., "Resistance to Oligarchy: the City Opposition to Walpole and His Successors, 1725–1747," in *London in the Age of Reform*, ed. J. Stevenson (Oxford, 1977).

Smith, H., *Georgian Monarchy: Politics and Culture, 1714–1760* (Cambridge, 2006).

Smuts, R. M., *Culture and Power in England 1585–1685* (1999).

Thurley, S., *Whitehall Palace: An Architectural History of the Royal Apartments, 1240–1698* (New Haven, 1999).

———. *The Whitehall Palace Plan of 1670* (1998).

High Culture and the Arts

Brewer, J., *The Pleasures of the Imagination: English Culture in the Eighteenth Century* (1997).

Dillon, J., *Theatre, Court and City, 1595–1610: Drama and Social Space in London* (Cambridge, 2000).

Foss, M., *The Age of Patronage: The Arts in England 1660–1750* (Ithaca, New York, 1972).

Gurr, A., *Playgoing in Shakespeare's London*, 2nd ed. (Cambridge, 1996).

Harkness, D. E., *The Jewel House: Elizabethan London and the Scientific Revolution* (New Haven, 2007).

Howard, J., *Theater of a City: The Places of London Comedy 1598–1642* (Philadelphia, 2007).

The London Theatre World 1660–1800, ed. R. D. Hume and A. H. Scouten (Carbondale, Illinois, 1960).

Manley, L., *Literature and Culture in Early Modern London* (Cambridge, 1995).

The Press

Atherton, I., "The Press and Popular Opinion" in *A Companion to Stuart Britain*, ed. B. Coward (Oxford, 2003).

Berry, H., *Gender, Society and Print Culture in Late-Stuart England: the Cultural World of the Athenian Mercury* (Aldershot, 2003).

Black, J., *The English Press in the 18th Century* (1987).

Ewald, W. B., *The Newsmen of Queen Anne* (Oxford, 1956).

Foot, M., *The Pen and the Sword: Jonathan Swift and the Power of the Press* (1957).

Harris, M., *London Newspapers in the Age of Walpole* (1974).

———. "The Management of the London Newspaper Press During the Eighteenth Century," *Publishing History* IV (1978).

Rogers, P., *Grub Street: Studies in a Subculture* (1972).

Inns, Taverns, Coffeehouses, and Clubs

Allen, D., "Political Clubs in Restoration London," *Historical Journal* XIX (1976).

Allen, R. J., *The Clubs of Augustan London* (Cambridge, Massachusetts, 1933).

———. "The Kit-Cat Club and the Theatre," *Review of English Studies* VII (1931).

Aytoun, E., *The Penny Universities: A History of Coffee Houses* (1956).

Berry, G., *Taverns and Tokens of Pepys' London* (1978).

Chartres, J. A., "The Capital's Provincial Eyes: London's Inns in the Early Eighteenth Century," *London Journal* III (1977).

Clark, P., "The Alehouse and the Alternative Society" in *Puritans and Revolutionaries*, ed. D. Pennington and K. Thomas (Oxford, 1978).

Field, O., *The Kit-Cat Club* (New York, 2009).

Key, N., "'High feeding and smart Drinking': Associating Hedge-Lane Lords in Exclusion Crisis London" in *Fear, Exclusion and Revolution: Roger Morrice and Britain in the 1680s*, ed. J. McElligot (Aldershot, 2006).

———. "The Political Culture and Political Rhetoric of County Feasts and Feast Sermons, 1654–1714," *Journal of British Studies* XXXIII (1994).

Lillywhite, B., *London Coffee Houses* (1963).

Pennell, S., "'Great Quantities of Gooseberry Pye and Baked Clod of Beef': Victualling and Eating Out in Early Modern London" in *Londinopolis: Essays in the Cultural and Social History of Early Modern London*, ed. P. Griffiths and M. S. R. Jenner (Manchester, 2000).

Pincus, S. C. A., "'Coffee Politicians Does Create': Coffeehouses and Restoration Political Culture," *Journal of Modern History* LXVII (1995).

Rogers, N., "Clubs and Politics in Eighteenth-Century London," *London Journal* XI (1985).

Popular Culture and Entertainment

Altick, R. D., *The Shows of London* (Cambridge, Massachusetts, 1978).

Ashton, R., "Popular Entertainment and Social Control in Later Elizabethan and Early Stuart London," *London Journal* IX (1983).

Berlin, M., "Civic Ceremony in Early Modern London," *Urban History Yearbook* XIII (1986).

Boulton, W. B., *The Amusements of Old London . . . from the 17th to the Beginning of the 19th Century* (New York and London, 1901; repr. 1969).

Burke, P., "Popular Culture in Seventeenth Century London" in *Popular Culture in Seventeenth Century England*, ed. B. Reay (1985).

Shoemaker, R. B., "The Decline of Public Insult in London 1660–1800," *Past and Present* no. 169 (2000).

The Streets of London: from the Great Fire to the Great Stink, ed. T. Hitchcock and H. Shore (2003).

Warner, J., *Craze: Gin and Debauchery in an Age of Reason* (New York, 2002).

Poverty and Charity

Beier, A. L., "Social Problems in Elizabethan London," *Journal of Interdisciplinary History* IX (1978).

Boulton, J., "The Poor Among the Rich: Paupers and the Parish, in the West End, 1600–1724" in *Londinopolis: Essays in the Cultural and Social History of Early Modern London*, ed. P. Griffiths and M. S. R. Jenner (Manchester, 2000).

Griffiths, P., "Building Bridewell: London's Self-Images, 1550–1640," in *Local Identities in Late Medieval and Early Modern England*, ed. N. L. Jones and D. R. Woolf (Basingstoke, 2007).

———. *Lost Londons: Change, Crime, and Control in the Capital City, 1550–1660* (Cambridge, 2008).

Hitchcock, T., "Begging on the Streets of Eighteenth-Century London," *Journal of British Studies* LXIV (2005).

———. *Down and Out in Eighteenth-century London* (2004).

Jordan, W. K., *The Charities of London, 1480–1660: the Aspirations and Achievements of the Urban Society* (1960).

Macfarlane, S., "Social Policy and the Poor in the Later Seventeenth Century" in *London 1500–1700*, ed. A. L. Beier and R. Finlay (1986).

McClure, R. K., *Coram's Children: The London Foundling Hospital in the Eighteenth Century* (New Haven, 1981).

Porter, R., "The London Foundling Hospital," *History Today* XXXVIII (March, 1988).

Schen, C., *Charity and Lay Piety in Reformation London, 1500–1620* (Aldershot, 2002).

Crime and Punishment

Beattie, J. M., "The Criminality of Women in Eighteenth-Century England," *Journal of Social History* VIII (1975).

———. "London Crime and the Making of the 'Bloody Code' 1689–1718" in *Stilling the Grumbling Hive: the Response to Social and Economic Problems in England, 1689–1750*, ed. L. Davison, T. Hitchcock, T. Keirn, and R. B. Shoemaker (New York, 1992).

———. *Policing and Punishment in London 1660–1750: Urban Crime and the Limits of Terror* (Oxford, 2001).

Burford, E. J., *Wits, Wenchers and Wantons: London's Low Life: Covent Garden in the Eighteenth Century* (1986).

Dabhoiwala, F., "The Pattern of Sexual Immorality in Seventeenth- and Eighteenth-Century London" in *Londinopolis: Essays in the Cultural and Social History of Early Modern London*, ed. P. Griffiths and M. S. R. Jenner (Manchester, 2000).

Griffiths, P., "Overlapping Circles: Imagining Criminal Communities in London, 1545–1645" in *Communities in Early Modern England: Networks, Place, Rhetoric*, ed. A. Shepard and P. Withington (Manchester, 2000).

Linebaugh, P., *The London Hanged: Crime and Civil Society in the Eighteenth Century* (1992).

McMullen, J. L., *The Canting Crew: London's Criminal Underworld 1550–1700* (New Brunswick, New Jersey, 1984).

Rumbelow, D., *The Triple Tree: Newgate, Tyburn and Old Bailey* (1982).

Salgado, G., *The Elizabethan Underworld* (1977).

Shoemaker, R. B., "Reforming the City: the Reformation of Manners Campaign in London, 1690–1738" in L. Davison, T. Hitchcock, T. Keirn, and R. B. Shoemaker, eds., *Stilling the Grumbling Hive: the Response to Social and Economic Problems in England, 1689–1750* (New York, 1992).

———. *Prosecution and Punishment: Petty Crime and the Law in London and Rural Middlesex, c. 1660–1725* (Cambridge, 1991).

Tales from the Hanging Court, ed. T. Hitchcock and R. B. Shoemaker (2006).

Riot and Rebellion

Brenner, R., "The Civil War Politics of London's Merchant Community," *Past and Present* no. 58 (1973).

Harris, T., "The Bawdy House Riots of 1668," *Historical Journal* XXIX (1986).

———. *London Crowds in the Reign of Charles II: Propaganda and Politics from the Restoration Until the Exclusion Crisis* (Cambridge, 1987).

Holmes, G. S., "The Sacheverell Riots: The Crowd and the Church in Early Eighteenth Century London," *Past and Present* no. 72 (1976).

Pearl, V., *London and the Outbreak of the Puritan Revolution: City Government and National Politics 1625–1643* (Oxford, 1961).

Rogers, N., "Aristocratic Clientage, Trade and Independency: Popular Politics in Pre-Radical Westminster," *Past and Present* no. 61 (1973).

———. "Popular Disaffection in London During the Forty-five," *London Journal* I (1975).

———. "Popular Protest in Early Hanoverian London," *Past and Present* no. 79 (1978).

Rudé, G., "The London Mob of the Eighteenth Century," *Historical Journal* II (1959).

_____. "'Mother Gin' and the London Riots of 1736," *The Guildhall Miscellany* X (1959).

_____. *Wilkes and Liberty. A Social Study of 1763 to 1774* (Oxford, 1962).

Sachse, W. L., "The Mob and the Revolution of 1688," *Journal of British Studies* IV (1964).

Shoemaker, R. B., *The London Mob: Violence and Disorder in Eighteenth-century London* (2004).

_____. "The London 'Mob' in the Early Eighteenth Century," *Journal of British Studies* XXVI (1987).

Smith, S. R., "Almost Revolutionaries: The London Apprentices During the Civil War," *Huntington Library Quarterly* XLII (1978–1979).

_____. "The London Apprentices as Seventeenth Century Adolescents," *Past and Present* no. 61 (1973).

Plague and Fire

Appleby, A. B., "The Disappearance of the Plague: a Continuing Puzzle," *Economic History Review* XXXIII (1980).

Bell, W. G., *The Great Fire of London in 1666* (1923; repr. 1994).

_____. *The Great Plague in London in 1665* (1924; repr. 1994).

Hanson, N., *The Great Fire of London: In That Apocalyptic Year, 1666* (Hoboken, New Jersey, 2001).

Milne, G., *The Great Fire of London* (1986).

Moote, A. L. and Moote, D. C., *The Great Plague: the Story of London's Most Deadly Year* (Baltimore, 2004).

Reddaway, T. F., *The Rebuilding of London After the Great Fire* (1940).

Slack, P., "Metropolitan Government in Crisis: The Response to Plague" in *London 1500–1700*, ed. A. L. Beier and R. Finlay (1986).

London's Religion

Brigden, S., *London and the Reformation* (Oxford, 1989).

Liu, T., *Puritan London: A Study of Religion and Society in the City Parishes* (1994).

Seaver, P., The *Puritan Lectureships: the Politics of Religious Dissent 1560–1662* (Stanford, 1970).

London Women

Gowing, L., "'The Freedom of the Streets': Women and Social Space, 1560–1640" in *Londinopolis: Essays in the Cultural and Social History of Early Modern London*, ed. P. Griffiths and M. S. R. Jenner (Manchester, 2000).

Jones, A. R., "Maidservants of London: Sisterhoods of Kinship and Labor" in *Maids and Mistresses, Cousins and Queens: Women's Alliances in Early Modern England*, ed. S. Frye and K. Robertson (Oxford, 1999).

Kent, D. A., "Ubiquitous but Invisible: Female Domestic Servants in Mid-Eighteenth Century London," *History Workshop Journal* no. 28 (1989).

Shoemaker, R. B., "Separate Spheres? Ideology and Practice in London Gender Relations, 1660–1740" in *Protestant Identities: Religion, Society, and Self-fashioning in Post-Reformation England*, ed. M. C. McClendon, J. P. Ward, and M. MacDonald (Stanford, 1999).

———. "Gendered Spaces: Patterns of Mobility and Perceptions of London's Geography, 1660–1750" in *Imagining Early Modern London: Perceptions and Portrayals of the City from Stow to Strype, 1598–1720*, ed. J. F. Merritt (Cambridge, 2001).

Index